CAT
ON THE ROAD TO FINDOUT

CAT
ON THE ROAD TO FINDOUT

YUSUF/CAT STEVENS

CONSTABLE

CONSTABLE

First published in Great Britain in 2025 by Constable

1 3 5 7 9 10 8 6 4 2

Copyright © Yusuf Islam, 2025

The moral right of the author has been asserted.

All rights reserved.
No part of this publication may be reproduced, stored in a retrieval system, or transmitted, in any form, or by any means, without the prior permission in writing of the publisher, nor be otherwise circulated in any form of binding or cover other than that in which it is published and without a similar condition including this condition being imposed on the subsequent purchaser.

A CIP catalogue record for this book
is available from the British Library.

ISBN: 978-1-40872-083-7 (hardback)
ISBN: 978-1-40872-082-0 (trade paperback)

Typeset in Brabo and Canela by Hewer Text UK Ltd., Edinburgh
Printed and bound in Great Britain by Clays Ltd, Elcograf S.p.A.

Papers used by Constable are from well-managed
forests and other responsible sources.

Constable
An imprint of
Little, Brown Book Group
Carmelite House
50 Victoria Embankment
London EC4Y 0DZ

The authorised representative
in the EEA is
Hachette Ireland
8 Castlecourt Centre, Dublin 15,
D15 XTP3, Ireland
(email: info@hbgi.ie)

An Hachette UK Company
www.hachette.co.uk

www.littlebrown.co.uk

www.catstevens.com

Contents

    The Roof   ix

1. Brown-eyed Handsome Baby   1
2. The Old Schoolyard   11
3. Jesus vs. Superman   31
4. The Scene   47
5. A Cat Is Born   65
6. The Decca Daze   75
7. I Got Experienced   89
8. I Think I See   101
9. The Redroom   113
10. As Clouds Parted   129
11. Tillerman Goes to the USA   145
12. The Bodhi Tree   157
13. Bull and the Polar Bear   175

14	Exile	193
15	Wave	211
16	The Gift	221
17	Joseph's Story	237
18	The Golden Dome	249
19	Shahadah	265
20	Back to Earth	279
21	New Cultural Home	291
22	Last Love Song	307
23	Year of the Child	321
24	Where Do the Children Pray?	335
25	Trouble	349
26	Call to Alms	361
27	Hampstead to the Holy	373
28	Satanic Forces	387
29	Paradise Beneath Her Feet	403
30	Peace Camp: Between East and West	415
31	A New Millennium	431
32	Hijacked	441
33	A Guitar Comes Home	453
34	On Stage Again	465
35	Prrr . . . Grrr	475
36	An Other Cup	487
37	Shamsia	499
38	All Aboard!	511
39	Road to Findout	525
	An Unspoken Poem	539
	Notes	541
	Credits and Acknowledgments	553

This book is dedicated to:

The Seeker

The Roof

IT'S A DIM, *starlit night in London. The shadowy silhouettes of two daring young teenage boys clamber over the rooftops next to the Princes Theatre. Music and applause echo up from the walls within. Andy, the bigger and braver of the two daredevils, jumps confidently from a balcony overlooking the lower courtyard to the safety of the other side. His friend looks down at the dark abyss below. After hesitating and shuffling his feet a few times, he finally takes a deep breath and makes his move. He's decided to take a different route.*

Reaching out to grasp a nearby windowsill, the boy grabs the ledge and lets his body go. Clinging on for dear life, his long legs dangle as he painfully edges across, inch by inch. But the combination of eight stone of bone and flesh with the loose gravel under his painfully sore fingers causes the boy to accept an unwelcome fact: he's slipping. Struggling to keep hold, his frantic hands cannot bear the weight any longer: he is now probably headed down to a grizzly end or worse yet – death!

Andy sees the situation and instantly stretches out to grab his friend's arm, and like some mighty guardian angel he manages to wing him up to safety. Wow!

The now white-faced, shaken boy dusts himself off and thanks his big buddy, who dismisses it with a grunt. Then, like victorious knights returning cut and bruised from a battle, they make their way back down to street level and bid each other goodnight.

Yes, the "other boy" in that story was me.

Later, seriously rattled, back in my room above my dad's café, I turned the lights off and lay down on the bed. Staring upwards, I practised being dead, trying to hold my breath and imagine nothingness. I realised that death could have easily claimed me that night and I might not have known anything more.

Blank, void, darkness.

> "Be wise, look ahead,
> Use your eyes," he said.
> "Be straight; think right."
> But I might die tonight![1]

Brown-eyed Handsome Baby
1948–52

I ARRIVED ON the full moon of July 1948. Like most newborns starting out in life, it felt that I had landed somewhere quite close to the centre of the universe. But there were some serious questions to deal with, the first being: "Who was I?" My background and origin were not very clear: Dad (from whom I must have got my black hair and dark-brown eyes) was from Cyprus, Mum was fair-eyed and from Sweden; our dominant culture and language at home were English and, on top of that, we lived above our café, which had a French-sounding name – in London!

Looking enquiringly around at the world into which I had just tumbled, it was clear that life was not without knocks and rather irritating experiences. Quite apart from suffering bumps on the head inflicted by wooden dungeon bars – otherwise known as cots – hunger pangs and poo seemed to haunt most of my operative hours as a babe; that's if I wasn't busy sleeping.

Despite this, there were some tangible upside gains too, like earning tickles and kisses just by smiling at Mummy and other big softies. My elder brother David, however, was definitely not interested in kissing. Dave was probably quite peeved by the recent intrusion into the family of this cheeky-faced baby boy who now stole the whole show along with most of Mum and Dad's love and attention. He was irritated further by the fact that the rascal was born just one day before his very own birthday! Good thing I had a big sister, Anita, who was older than David and could usually wag a finger at him and hold him in check.

A proud red front door with the number "245" was the entrance to our colourful world. Our flat sat on the third floor of a four-storey building, atop our family café, the Moulin Rouge, strategically overlooking the busy red bus routes of New Oxford Street and Shaftesbury Avenue. We were smack-bang in the middle of a cosmopolitan business area, inhabited and run mostly by enterprising cockneys, Italians, Greek Cypriots, and Jews for whom long hours and hard work appeared to be no obstacle.

Our unique monolithic block was oddly located near Holborn and the British Museum. The neighbours were a furriers, a pub, a snooker ball company and a famous ornate umbrella shop. To add to the intrigue of the area, a large, rather bland, brown-bricked Ministry of Defence building – reportedly harbouring a section of MI5 – was situated round the corner on St. Giles High Street, just opposite the Princes Theatre.

We were situated at the northernmost tip of Shaftesbury Avenue; at the southern end stood Piccadilly Circus and the statue of Eros, daintily balancing on one foot and endlessly shooting his "love" arrows at the revolving rows of black taxis, bicycles and bowler-hatted gentlemen, rushing to and from work. At night the scene was transformed into a dazzling whirlpool of life, play, and sinful opportunities.

As I grew, it soon became clear that there were lots of benefits to living where we did in the hub of London's West End. Like a merry-go-round in the heart of the entertainment district, it was a sort of daydreamy tinseltown scattered with theatres, cinemas, temptingly dressed shop windows, pubs, clubs, coffee bars, and red telephone boxes. Everything was seductively close to Soho, with its bright, noisy pinball arcades and sweet-smelling ladies lounging out of doorways, enticing passersby to stop, play, and pay at the blink of every alleyway and corner.

That was basically my world.

There was another dangerous, parallel underworld, too. Criminal mobsters with names like "Jack Spot" ruled the bars and joints of Soho, while their rivals hid in the shadows, ready to pounce and take over. The underbelly of the West End was a veritable hotbed of villains engrossed in crooked activities and deadly fights. The streets at night seemed to exhume thugs, thieves, conmen, drug dealers and pimps. Thank goodness, much of that was operating too deep beneath the surface of West End life for me to even notice at the time.

The Second World War was finally over and everybody, I suppose, just wanted to have fun. Over seventy million people had been brutally killed. The bloody and gruesome images of war were still present in films and TV programmes aired at the time, and it was impossible to ignore the bombed ruins that lay around us. Just fifty yards across the road, on the corner of Gower Street, was a deep, sunken crater filled with bricks and rubble, once belonging to a busy four-storey shop – it could just as easily have been ours.

My dad boasted of his own wartime involvement in a memorable photo of him toting a rifle in uniform, probably from the time he served in the British colonial army in the First World War. He was assigned to one of the flanks in Eastern Europe or Palestine in their battle against his favourite enemy, the Turks. Dad did not want to sit out the Second World War either; a bit too old to join the army, he signed up to the Local Defence Volunteers, working with the St. John's Ambulance organisation, assisting the injured and seeing first-hand the devastation caused during the long bombing blitz of London. Dad had lived through two world wars.

Stavros Georgiou Adams was a smart, handsome, courageous, and hard-working man with a perfectly trimmed black moustache. He was well travelled and had come a long way from his native village, Tala, in the hills overlooking the ancient coastal city of Paphos in southern Cyprus. Growing up in a one-room house where even a pair of shoes was considered a luxury, my father was never ashamed of his humble background. He taught us the value of having enough food on the table and discouraged waste. "Money doesn't grow on trees!" he never tired of reminding us.

Leaving his home in Cyprus for work in Egypt early on as a teenager, Dad followed in the footsteps of his eldest brother,

Adamos, proudly named after their grandfather. He learned to work in restaurants to make a living. In Alexandria, the young Stavros married a Greek girl called Katina, and they had one son, George. The memorable articles Dad kept hidden away in his cupboard from his early life in Egypt included a large crimson-red fez hat. He must have loved the culture, and might have even stayed in Alexandria, but things became tighter. As time went on there were fewer prospects open to Stavros; the whole country was politically heading for greater unrest. So he left his small family in Egypt to look for better opportunities and managed to get a job on a boat headed for the US.

Those were the "Roaring Twenties." Dad's stories about Prohibition, gangsters, and speakeasies were spellbinding. He would often repeat the tale of how he began scraping a living by shining shoes on the sidewalks of New York and Philadelphia. Unfortunately, the Great Depression arrived in the 1930s (so, not the best of timing); there were few jobs and scant likelihood that things would get better anytime soon.

After trying to work his way up, Dad's situation might have improved and he nearly made America his home, but eventually he became *persona non grata* when he was caught while working in one of the speakeasies. We knew very little of the details of what had actually happened, but it seems he was furious with his wife and younger brother, Demetre, who had also followed his elder brothers' route to find work in Alexandria. Apparently, they did not send the funds needed to help bail him out, and Dad was finally deported. A line was drawn, and he broke up with his family and brothers in Egypt.

Now separated from Katina and their young son, Dad travelled home through Cyprus. After a chance meeting with his father, George, walking with his mule along the dusty hillside road to Tala, Dad realised that his old village life would no longer suit him. Mind made up, he decided to try his luck and make his way to the grand capital of the British Empire: London. At that time, Cyprus was a colony, so Dad got the necessary papers together and followed his dream, journeying over by sea.

Once on Britain's shores, via a close network of Greek-Cypriot friends and contacts in the great metropolis, he based himself in the busy heart of the West End. That's where he met my mother, while she was sitting alone having tea one afternoon in a Lyons tearoom, on the corner of Tottenham Court Road.

Ingrid Elizabeth Wickman, my beautiful, azure-blue-eyed mother, was a gentle but adventurous soul. Hailing from the small northern port town of Gävle, Sweden, she had arrived in Britain to work as a young twenty-year-old, with the slightly reluctant acquiescence of her parents, and was employed as a nanny for a wealthy family in Richmond. Good-natured, ash-blonde, and possessing strong, characteristically Swedish looks, Mum sang more than she spoke with a melodious Scandinavian tone, while her cheeks seemed to be continuously blushing.

Beholding Stavros daringly walking over to her in the busy tearoom, she quickly changed tables, indignantly resisting his initial advances. But he was undeniably handsome, bold and difficult to ignore. In the end, she fell for his smart, sharp, Greek romantic demeanour. Although she had only come up to the West End for the afternoon, her brief outing ended up being a pretty extended one!

Stavros and Ingrid got married on 8 June, 1938.

Soon, war had broken out. Within the chaos and smoke of London during those years of battle and destruction they gave birth to Anita and David. Both children had to be frequently woken up at unearthly times of the night, sirens blaring, and rushed to the bomb shelter in Mummy's arms, while Daddy was busy attending to the increasing numbers of killed or injured. It must have been quite an introduction to life on our suffering, war-ridden planet for the unsuspecting siblings.

Thankfully, the horrible hostilities came to an end in 1945. Peace was declared, and a new life of opportunities opened up. The husband of a lady with whom Mum had happened to share labour pangs bumped into my father in the ward and they became friends. He was a wrestling promoter and later assisted Dad in acquiring the lease on a Shaftesbury Avenue building which had ready-let flats. Not long after they moved in, the flower shop on the ground level became vacant. Mum and Dad took over that lease too and started a café. The Moulin Rouge business was on its feet around the time I arrived, playing with my own baby toes, in 1948.

The hugely successful enterprise was the nest of our family life. Lunchtime was always hectic with queues stretching from the café doors round the corner to the umbrella shop. My sister, Anita, was a first-class mother's helper; she would butter the soft-white bread and make heaps of sandwiches before trotting off to school, her two hair plaits flapping under her grey felt beret. All of us at one

1 | *Brown-eyed Handsome Baby*

time or another had to work in the shop. David was the shrewdest at managing to escape that responsibility – much to the utter disgust of Anita.

We all loved our mother so much. Loving and extremely dedicated to a life of service, she was always looking out for us. We cherished being close to her, but she was always kept so busy working long hours in the café; Dad relied heavily on Mum to run it and keep the customers well looked after. For that reason, it felt like we never saw enough of her. She looked a lot like the Mona Lisa and always wore a permanent smile, which seemed directed at anybody she looked at, melting the stone-faced customers who strolled into the café and making them feel right at home. Mum was especially adored for baking the most delicious chocolate éclairs, rock cakes, and macaroons this side of the Thames.

One of my enjoyments as a little lad was to dress up as a cowboy or bus conductor and gallantly march up and down in front of the shop to the simulated applause of grown-up footsteps as rushing workers clattered by. They were obviously amused by my serious frown and commitment to make the part look as convincing as possible. This was probably the first indication of the showman within me. The family soon noticed I had a talent to entertain.

There were certainly indications of my having a rather powerful creative imagination; my mother had noticed that I was able to hold a pencil perfectly at the age of three. I used to love drawing whatever wonders I saw in my head. Mum must have made a kind of genetic connection between her elder brother Hugo and me. Hugo Wickman was one of a handful of skilled abstract painters in Scandinavia known at that time and it seemed that I had picked up similar attributes.

David was rarely seen hanging around the shop, so the inevitable day came when Dad looked over at me and noticed I was old enough to balance a plate without dropping it and promptly assigned me a waiter's job. That is where I learned to earn my pocket money from the customers' tips. It was also because of this work that I was first able to understand – as my father must have done – that serving the public well could often be highly rewarding. Being quite a "handsome-looking young boy" (to quote my loving sister), busily buzzing around the tables or behind the counter of the café in my new, starched, white waiter's jacket, I certainly attracted a lot of valuable gratuities – monetary and otherwise.

Another big incentive for me to work in the shop was so I could spend more time being near to Mum and Dad; for that reason, working late hours didn't feel so bad. Family life naturally carried on, even if it was mostly behind the counter. Sometimes I felt a bit sad that we didn't have a mother who made us all sit down and have tea and toast with jam after school, like other kids; on the other hand, those kids were probably jealous of us – we could have fizzy drinks and Mum's delicious rock cakes all day long if we wanted!

Looking at myself in the mirror in that little white waiter's jacket I noticed a striking resemblance to Antonio, the famous Spanish dancer who was a frequent attraction on stage at the Cambridge Theatre down the road. I loved those hand-clapping Spanish dance performers, fired with the blood-rushing passion of flamenco guitar music, and I soon mastered the art of clicking my heels at great speed, yearning for the day I would possess my very own pair of black Spanish boots from Anello & Davide, the theatrical shoemakers. I definitely broke with catering convention when I forced Mum to dye my white starched jacket bright toreador-red. But hey! Did I look good, or what?

To rid me of my pride and imbue a satisfactory amount of guilt, it was my destiny, along with Anita and David, to attend the local Roman Catholic school round the corner, just off Drury Lane. It was run by a flock of committed Irish nuns headed by a taut-skinned, bony-nosed, fairly elderly but tough-as-nails head teacher: Sister Dominic.

The Old Schoolyard
1952–9

MUM WAS FROM a strict Baptist background but was not confirmed, while my father was Greek Orthodox. My brother and I were circumcised, probably for hygienic rather than religious reasons. Anita, David, and – lastly – I were all enrolled in St. Joseph's Roman Catholic primary school based on the vigorous insistence of Mum's friend Aunty Josephine, a powerful, no-nonsense Catholic lady from Austria, who also happened to be married to a kind-faced, balding Cypriot called Michael Koritsas. They ran a café called the Anchor on St. Giles High Street, next to Denmark Street, otherwise known as "Tin Pan Alley."

There were a lot of similarities and tight bonds between our two tribes, the Georgious and the Koritsases: their son Andy (even though he was a few grudging months older than me) became my best friend at school; Helen, their eldest daughter, was like a sister to Anita; and Aunty Josephine and Mum were kindred companions. Both families ran cafés, and both dads came from the small island of Cyprus – that didn't make the two fathers natural friends, of course. Business is business.

The school we were all forced to attend was buried in a side street behind the famous theatre district, squeezed between some council flats and small, red-brick terraced houses. Most of the playground space for the boys was underground, dimly lit in the lower basement pit below pavement level – boys needed to know their place, I suppose.

Regardless of the physical drawbacks, the school had a very good reputation. As we were brought up in the middle of the West End, it was probably a very good idea to get us all grounded in some moral concepts at an early age. On Sundays, Mum used to take us to the nearby Catholic church, next to the green square of Lincoln's Inn Fields – probably one of the key reasons why the school enrolled us.

Tuesdays we went to midday Mass with the class, shepherded by nuns and teachers from the school. Hymns in church, thankfully, were in English, but I really didn't understand much else listening to the lengthy incantations chanted by the priests dressed in bright red or green-and-gold silk robes, swirling clouds of incense in all directions during those hour-long, Latin-dominated services. Even so, the rituals did help create an atmosphere of sacred "otherness," which resonated with me. There were certain constraints non-Catholics (like me) had to suffer; we were not allowed to take part in rituals like Confession and Holy Communion. On top of all that exclusion, we were also compelled by socio-religious demands to be neatly dressed for the occasion.

Nevertheless, the spirituality of Mass made a strong impact on my young heart and mind. Even though my knees hurt when we had to kneel down on the bare wooden slats for long periods of the service, there was certainly a tangible peace I could feel inside me; a heavenly connection with what I naturally believed was sacred. When I shut my eyes, I sensed the close presence of God in my prayers. To my fellow classmates – unaware of that transcendent experience occurring within me – my non-Catholic status still branded me as an outsider.

Deep down, I possessed an innate faith of some kind, but that's not to say I didn't have plenty of questions. One day, amidst the screams of playtime, I boldly stopped and asked one of the more kindly faced brigade of tall, black-draped nuns, "Sister! When do the angels start writing down your sins?" my neck stretching heavenwards, anxiously awaiting a sympathetic answer. Sister Anthony leaned over and peered down awkwardly towards me from her stiff starched habit; I stared nervously at the huge wooden crucifix dangling from the leather belt tightly strapped around her thin waist. She gave me a friendly Irish smile, perhaps seeing a spark of innocence in this cheeky dark-haired little boy.

"Hmmm? When you'r-r-re eight," she said jovially in her rolling Gaelic accent. Whew! That was reassuring – for the time being at least. Still in short trousers but rapidly approaching that dreaded age of accountability, I obviously had a serious interest in knowing how close the deadline might be.

At school I remember thinking about the choices given to me. Religion constantly made me feel guilty about nice-looking things, warning about the mortal dangers lurking in fleshly life. These threats were represented in clear pictorial terms by the Devil, depicted as a vile snake or beast with two horns; the temptation of Adam and Eve with the tree of forbidden fruit; and Jesus, suffering and bleeding on the Cross, representing the only key to salvation.

But balancing those kinds of fearful images with what was going on outside the doors of the church after school, I felt the pull of the world mighty overpowering. I loved the thrill of skipping school to explore the streets on my own. Sometimes, during the escape, I'd wander through toy departments in large, high-street stores; not having any cash to buy anything, once or twice I actually pocketed some toys (being non-Catholic, of course, I couldn't confess it). The British Museum was my favourite hideout; it was nice and warm in there, especially in winter. I'd expertly tread through thousands of years of human history, in and out, slipping round, past the noseless sphinxes and glass-cased Egyptian mummies, trying to avoid being caught by the sharp-eyed attendants on duty.

It must be said, there were some benefits to attending school, too. A cute little girl called Linda captured my heart; she knew it but was too uninterested to provide any more than a passing glance on the playground.

> *Remember the days (of the old schoolyard)*
> *We used to laugh a lot,*
> *Oh, don't you remember the days (of the old schoolyard)?*

CAT ON THE ROAD TO FINDOUT

When we had imaginings
And we had all kinds of things
And we laughed and needed love,
Yes I do. Oh, and I remember you.[2]

Come Christmastime, I remember always waiting on stand-by, frustrated and longing to be selected to fill the role of Joseph in the school nativity play. It was a chance to get close to "Mary" (more precisely: whichever pretty little girl was playing her at the time). Inevitably, I would be cast as another simple shepherd extra. Once, I believe, I managed to be appointed as one of the Three Kings – no doubt because I looked like a foreigner!

Luckily, I was not entirely alone in that respect; my best friend Andy shared my mixed background, which made me feel less vulnerable and exposed. Andrew Michael Koritsas was burlier, more extrovert, and taller than me, which made me slightly jealous as I was quite a skinny, shy young lad who couldn't kick a ball straight to save my life. But Andy was my twin soulmate and best friend at school. Apart from sport – particularly swimming, where he always outdid me at the local Oasis baths – we both enjoyed our time together and loved the same kind of things.

The desire for adventure as street-loose lads was strong in both of us. Apart from spending hours after school on the swings and roundabouts in the solid cement playgrounds close by, daringly we would creep into the crumbling bombed ruins, delving into dark, damp, smelly rooms, clambering up derelict stairways, through collapsed brick walls and broken window glass. Our parents would probably have had heart attacks if they knew what their two little "bubble and squeaks" (cockney slang for "Greeks") got up to.

Unfortunately, just as I was reaching the age when I could grasp what was happening, my mum and dad started going through real rough times. My father had hired a new blonde waitress from Manchester to help in the café; she was younger, a fast worker, and looked very pretty in an apron. Soon Dorothy had Dad in hand – and that's when the troubles began.

My mother must have known what was going on, but she didn't reveal the deep hurt she must have felt. Business in the café was going on as usual, but arguments were always flaring up. I noticed that when I was in the room, my parents cooled down and didn't say much. Sometimes I would try to act as peacemaker; I wanted them both, and didn't want to have to choose. It appeared to me that grown-ups found it almost impossible to say "Sorry" and make up. But I couldn't fully understand what was going on; it was unimaginable for me to comprehend how broken Mum must have felt at the time.

They moved into separate bedrooms. They both loved me so much, some nights I'd go to sleep in Mummy's bed and wake up with Dad. I was caught in the middle. Blinded by love, I could see nothing wrong with either, but because Dad's passionate Greek temperament made him shout loudest, most of my childish effort was spent just trying to calm him down, which may have looked as if I was taking Mum's side and that made him even angrier. Nothing I did worked.

The war clouds at home grew ominously dark, and it looked like they were not going to lift. It was only the café that kept the lights on and forced Mum and Dad to work together. Dorothy stopped working there – but she didn't go away.

Mum was naturally angelic; she did everything in a dignified way. She'd had enough of Dad and his new Mancunian romance. One summer evening she simply packed our bags and herded us onto a boat from Tilbury to Gothenburg. I thought it was just going to be a kind of holiday. The boat took two nights and a day to cross the North Sea. It was an exciting new experience, but the sea air combined with the rough waves made my tummy turn, so I was glad Sweden wasn't too far away.

We eventually arrived in Gävle, Mum's hometown, and moved in with Gulli, our step-grandmother. She was a kind, but firm, petite lady with curly white-silver hair, whose world was radically turned upside down by our stormy arrival, as we squashed into her cramped, two-room flat in the middle of town. Life must have been quite a test, especially having to deal with David, who was a pretty uncontrollable fourteen-year-old by then!

Who was I to question the wisdom of all this? Anyway, it was a fun time; I loved Sweden and was looking forward to the snow. I had a lot of cousins and relatives there to skate and bicycle around with.

Mum quickly packed me off to the local primary school. There was a big surprise in store for me. I was the only dark-eyed, black-haired lad in town. I'd inherited my Mediterranean, Greek-like features from Dad's side and was treated like a visitor from a not-too-distant planet.

This astronomical attention was a surprise to me. I was a

2 | *The Old Schoolyard*

novelty for most blue-eyed Swedish natives; they crowded round me at playtime as if I were a film star attending his big premiere! Chaotic scenes drove the teachers to extricate me and provide me with an exclusive play area till things settled down. Boy, was I the lucky one? They even allowed me to pick friends to join me in my own private fun zone.

Over the course of five months or so, Dad was on the phone to Mum, emotionally pleading with her to bring us back home again; he missed his children – especially "the little boy." Finally, out of the pure compassion that came so naturally to Mum, she relented and we all boarded a boat back to London.

By the time we returned, Dorothy had moved into Shaftesbury Avenue and I had a new half-sister, Lindsay. Dad had rented us a terraced house round the corner in Holborn, 18a Barter Street, which sat about five hundred yards away. That's where we lived for the next six months. I was happy because Mum was home most of the time. The café became a no-go area for her, but I sneaked in, and Dad would spoil me rotten with rock cakes and Pepsi, whatever I wanted. I went back to St. Joseph's to continue my primary education.

While I didn't really take sides, I knew it wasn't a good idea to tell Mum about my secret excursions with Dad, like the time he took me to Cornwall; a really long drive, but I got to know Dorothy and my little half-sister. Dad had bought a new house in Oakley Square, Euston. Once he and Dorothy moved in, Mum promptly led all of us back to Shaftesbury Avenue. Dad never lived there again, but we saw him every day, downstairs, busily working in the shop. Frankly, that was good enough for me. Mum became the heart and centre of our home, and she and Dad were still both looking after us . . . as well as the customers, of course.

The West End was full of rascally enterprises for cheeky young boys like me and my buddy, Andy. After school we were always tempting trouble; it was like a contest to do something really naughty and get as close to being caught as possible, then smartly dash away from the scene of the crime: ringing doorbells and running off, or dropping stink bombs into crowded restaurants (not ours, obviously) and waiting just long enough to see the foul expression on people's faces – oh, we had so much fun!

One of the capers we attempted ended up being very dark and dangerous. Both Andy and I had mastered the art of bunking into local cinemas, prising open the fire safety bar on the exit doors with a coat hanger, and slipping through unnoticed. On one occasion, Andy wasn't around – I was alone, attempting to break in through the back alley of the Odeon cinema on Tottenham Court Road to see *The Incredible Shrinking Man*. Suddenly, a slightly balding, bespectacled, middle-aged gent in a beige-coloured raincoat walked up behind me and swiftly pried the door open like a skilled professional. As we entered, he grabbed me and forced me to the floor. He unzipped his fly and pinned me down on the cement steps, trying to make me kiss his dick. I firmly resisted, wriggling under the weight of his knee and started to yell as loud as I could. The noise made him give up. He zipped up his trousers and slipped back out through the door onto the busy street, and disappeared.

2 | *The Old Schoolyard*

I was only eight at the time and had never experienced anything as spine-chilling as that before. I felt numb. I just proceeded up the stairs to the cinema and watched the film. Because I had bunked in illegally, I was too scared to tell anyone what had happened. It was an afternoon show, so the cinema was pretty empty. As I sank into the velvet seat, sitting alone and comfortably surrounded by darkness, the film quickly helped me forget for a while.

Later, I saw Dad in the café. An awful feeling was still with me, so I told him what had happened. Bellowing every known curse in Greek, he went totally berserk and picked up a large bread knife and rushed out, scouring the streets for the man. David followed, searching round the whole St. Giles area. That taught me a lesson. I understood that apart from stink bombs and gangsters, there were other nasty goings-on in this city, and bad things happened if you weren't careful.

Elsewhere on the radar, pop music was on the rise and capturing the hearts, shillings, and pence of my generation. The world was on the brink of a brave new musical takeover; Buddy Holly, the Everly Brothers, Little Richard, and Elvis were the trailblazers, leading us out of the monochrome memories and web-draped halls of history. Mario Lanza, Perry Como, Doris Day, and Vera Lynn were all about to be parked in the back garage of music collections. Rock 'n' roll was bulldozing towards us at great speed and ferocity; the highway was opening up!

After collecting enough pocket money of my own, I bought my first 45 rpm single: "Baby Face" by Little Richard, with "Tutti Frutti" on the B-side. His soulful voice was so tight, gutsy, and amazing. Music was exploding in our hearts and on the airwaves. The growing power of radio and TV connected kids all around the world, like us, to this new, chorus-driven revolution.

I was ready to be called up. The world was about to change! Britain came up with its own sprout of imitation would-be Elvises like Tommy Steele and Cliff Richard, but they were not manufactured in America, so we knew they were not authentic – like the tight-fitting Levi's jeans we all wanted to run around in.

My big brother was seven years older and was already quite skilled at running around. He had tasted the world outside and was intent on asserting his manhood early on in life. David got married at seventeen. It was a strange and very untraditional type of wedding, very different from the Greek-Cypriot kind I was used to; big reception parties with lots of tables, guests, and loud Greek music, dancing and wine. But Dave and his bride – Anita Tobias, a Jewish girl from Stepney – tied the knot discreetly in a West End registry office. We had a photo of the family taken in Russell Square. Dad shared a cigar with the father-in-law, and the formalities were complete. David and his wife then moved into a bedsit somewhere in east London.

Back on Shaftesbury Avenue, Mum, Anita, and I adjusted to a home without David. It seemed quieter and more peaceful – but notably emptier.

Things didn't go so kosher over on the east side, however. After a few months, the honeymoon was over and the marriage was at an end. They divorced, and he came home.

2 | *The Old Schoolyard*

Feeling pretty disturbed by the experience, David was referred to Colney Hatch asylum for treatment. Eventually, they kicked him out after he started psychoanalysing the doctors – that was a good sign of his return to normality.

David then got involved in the fashion trade and was much more motivated – probably because of his proximity to a lot of pretty ladies (in that respect, he was a lot like Dad). "Lanky-Lazy-Casa-Dave" was my nickname for him, a six-foot, incurable Casanova. He looked like the film star John Cassavetes, and I had a depressingly long way to go to reach his kind of height or status with the opposite sex.

My talents lay in another department: I was the artistic one, following on from my uncle Hugo in Sweden. Music was not seen as a possible vocation as far as I was concerned; it was just something I enjoyed. By this time, though, my other six-foot-and-a-bit tall, half-brother, George – he was another very handsome piece of work – had reconnected with Dad and migrated to London, and he played bouzouki guitar and violin at Greek weddings and clubs.

It was David who first toyed with the idea of my becoming a singer. Laurie London had just had a massive hit with "He's Got the Whole World in His Hands." That was an impressive message coming from a young boy from east London's Bethnal Green. Soon after Laurie came Emile Ford and the Checkmates, who had a smash hit with "What Do You Want to Make Those Eyes at Me For?" Now, Emile was much closer to home, being someone who David had actually bumped into in the corridors of Kingsway day college, not far down the road from us.

"You could do that, easily," David told me, semi-jokingly.

CAT ON THE ROAD TO FINDOUT

However, I didn't fully believe him at the time. Though I was clearly acknowledged as the "entertainer" of the family, especially when it came to dressing up, everybody admired my illustrative skills and knew that's where my heart was. It even earned me special privileges and elevated my status at school, where the teachers would ask me to draw scenes from the story readings and display them in class. Mum was especially proud of my talents and encouraged me by providing lots of watercolour paints and paper. My ambition was firmly fixed on becoming a "famous" artist like my uncle.

Art was my gateway to freedom; it took me to a place where I could envisage a world of my own choosing and gradually became a means of communicating my thoughts and bright Technicolour dreams to those who stood outside my private walls. It was the gift of looking at things more closely and seeing something not necessarily spotted by others.

Apart from Uncle Hugo's cubist abstract style, my vision swung to the great Impressionists and I soon fell in love with the bold colours and brush strokes of Vincent van Gogh. One evening, Mum read some pages of his biography as we sat round the tiny gas fire in our front living room. During the emotive story I started crying, hearing how he cut off a part of his ear in a moment of manic frustration. For some reason I innately empathised with how difficult it must have been for him to contain such brilliant, bursting visions that caused him to be labelled a mad social outcast.

Being born in the middle of the twentieth century meant I saw that art and the visual media were changing how we perceived things, in a totally new way. Pictures, once silent and imprisoned, were now breaking free of their shackles, yelling loud and coming to life using a technique called animation – and I soon became a huge fan of this new, alternate world of cartoons and characters. Walt Disney was the absolute sovereign master of this cinematic magic, and I became a devoted subject in his kingdom. *Fantasia* introduced us kids to enchanting full-length films, creating incredibly powerful epics like *Snow White*, *Bambi*, *Pinocchio* and *Dumbo*, the flying elephant.

Weekly I would trot off with my sister to the local Tatler cinema on Charing Cross Road, buy an orange popsicle and watch Laurel & Hardy, the Three Stooges, Flash Gordon, and the latest cartoons. Heaven! When back home, I began to invent my own characters and storyboards, and dreamed of seeing them one day bouncing onto the screen. Everybody admired my little doodles and encouraged me to go forward and make a name for myself.

Cartoons became my favourite form of art through which I could create my own band of heroes and villains. The duel between good and evil is a never-ending feature of life – children's cartoons not excluded. No one should doubt that violence played a vital part in the spectacular success story of animation studios like Disney's. At the end of the cartoon, the victim (a cute, timid mouse) would always wreak his bloody revenge on his tormentor (a nasty cat): justice was done. Walt had no qualms at the end of *Snow White* about striking down the wicked Queen with lightning, making her sizzle and fall to her death and die. We loved it!

Today, times and techniques have moved on, yet it's still the same essential old story. Modern action movies, using ultra-powerful digital effects, have created new worlds full of extraordinary saviours, all busy with the job of slaughtering evil mutants and saving our endangered planet. These have gradually replaced the need for the saints of the age-old religious narrative and guided us towards a more visually entertaining and instant version of divine justice – and (commercially speaking) are considerably more lucrative than the customary collection boxes that were passed around the congregation during Mass. Truth was, churches were rapidly emptying, while cinemas were cramming them in.

As a growing lad with fast-developing male tendencies, I naturally gravitated towards any danger-filled subjects of a magnetic, action-driven nature involving as much violence, destruction, and death as possible; images of wars, ghoulish monsters, horror films, and bloody revolutions became frequent favourites of mine.

After seeing a film of Dickens's *A Tale of Two Cities*, my fascination with the French Revolution even drove me to build little guillotines out of balsa wood late into the night – to the visible repulsion of my sister, whose stock of LPs provided the soundtrack to my new, "boyish" pursuit. I soon developed a permanent attachment to her shiny mahogany Philips record player – a gift from Dad on her twenty-first birthday. Dad must have really loved my sister Anita a lot because, previously, on her eighth birthday, he had bought her a little black baby grand piano, which occupied a good quarter of our upstairs living room. It was probably my mother's suggestion, as most proper, high-bred Swedish homes possessed a piano for family members to entertain themselves on. It certainly looked rich!

Anita's new record player was much more practical for me. I could load up a small stack of her LPs, then switch on and watch the automatic stylus arm swing into action as the twelve-inch black discs dropped one by one onto the turntable. It was magic! Background music spurred my creative process. I squeezed my eyes and focused, as I delicately painted uniforms of model toy soldiers in my poorly equipped little army of "desert rats," or carefully assembled the fearful French execution machine, staining the head-hole with red enamel paint to add a touch of bloody realism.

Stirring melodies from a range of classical composers provided a potent means for transportation towards soaring, exciting new aesthetic thresholds. Gershwin's *Porgy and Bess* became one of those LPs I played over and over again. Anita had some truly inspirational black vinyl, and I would spend hours levitating my artistic imagination: Tchaikovsky, Beethoven, Rodgers & Hammerstein, and Gershwin, so masterfully revealing their musical genius – compared to crooners like Frank Sinatra and Nat King Cole, who happened to occupy a romantic "girly" space in my sister's LP library too. But I didn't mind them, either.

Alongside Disney's animation, action comics were also super-sized influences in my young life, until my attention gradually turned to realism and contemporary conflicts that dominated the news, such as the Cold War between the West and the Soviet Union. I became drawn to a new and more serious form of illustrative reporting: political caricatures.

Nikita Khrushchev, Harold Macmillan, and John F. Kennedy were perfectly mutable faces and figures for this purpose. In a drawing of Khrushchev, the communist leader of the USSR exposes his spiky, atom-bomb-shaped teeth, about to devour Cuba with one ravenous bite, while Kennedy threateningly stands on the sidelines. That's how I pictured things at the time, poised – as we were – on the brink of a nuclear war which would probably see the annihilation of the world as we knew it, if no one had the guts to back down.

The Giles cartoons were the only reason I'd pick up a copy of the *Daily Express*; they portrayed a British working-class family commenting on the headline news of the day – I just loved the wild grandma who rode a motorbike and was blissfully oblivious to whatever was upsetting everyone else.

But powerful satirical magazines like *Private Eye* and *Punch* would soon take over and became my favourite sources for dry humour and inspiration. I drew my own cartoon sketches with a new ambition to one day be an illustrator and join the ranks of cartoonists such as Gerald Scarfe, Ronald Searle and Ralph Steadman, whose sharply grotesque and demonic ink characters were now overshadowing Batman, Dennis the Menace, Bambi, and even Grandma Giles. Get back into the trunk, you lot – I'm grown up!

Drawing people's faces and characters was my speciality, so I decided to make a business out of it; Trafalgar Square and the National Portrait Gallery were only down the road and seemed like an ideal spot for me to set up my stall. So one Saturday I strolled down Charing Cross Road and put up my easel and A2 white cartridge pad with a sign, "Portraits 2/-" (two British shillings, that is). In no time I had my first customers, which led to a huge crowd, tightly gathered around me, watching avidly as the portraits gradually materialised. I sketched people's faces, handing them over, neatly rolled, in exchange for hard cash.

It was all going splendidly until a sweet young couple approached to have their portraits done together. I sweated profusely over this particular work of art until it was complete. As I finished I went to peel the page and roll it up for them – ripping it right down the middle! The crowd of spectators gasped . . . and then laughed. I blushed a tomato red, grabbed my tools, and hurried home. That was the end of that brief enterprise.

Andy and I were advancing in age together and shared a relentless fascination for thrills – and heights! Our new escapade was to go out late in the evening and scale the local buildings, climbing dangerously high up onto the rooftops in our area. From those dizzying heights we'd gaze at the noisy city below, undeclared champions of London's skyline. Nothing could beat the full-body tingle we both felt climbing up through escape hatches, overlooking the streets of the city, surveying the open horizon under the black night sky, trying to spot the glowing face of Big Ben between ranks of chimneys. Skilfully defying fear and gravity, we conquered the lofty, inaccessible plateaus of mountainous tiles – like explorers of a highly secret, nocturnal world.

To my utter astonishment and disbelief, this unworldly experience was totally captured in a hit single by the Drifters, called "Up on the Roof." Incredible! When I first heard that song I realised how music could seize my feelings and emotions more powerfully than any other medium – even art – preparing me for what was to come.

Providentially, "what was to come" might never have happened, and events could easily have taken a terrible turn for the worse that night when I nearly fell climbing the roof of the Princes Theatre. I was possibly just an inch or two away from knocking on heaven's door – or something much worse awaiting me down in the scary basement of God's great mansion. Potentially, there was a defining moment where death looked at me – and blinked. Thank God!

Jesus vs. Superman
1959–63

EVEN THOUGH IT was terrific to be born in an age where TV had arrived and comic fiction – even shiny white spaceships – was coming true, it was odd how the human spirit still seemed as deep and mysterious as the vastly uncharted universe itself – equally borderless.

The war to define the soul of man was on. Out on the battlefield we heard the explosions and saw opposing camps, all violently clashing, contesting with each other to make credible sense about the object of human existence and how on earth we all managed to be here in the first place.

The prize fight between Adam and the Apeman was a life-or-death tournament conducted within the vast Colosseum of public opinion, as the robed philosophers and historians gazed down, making bets on the outcome of the homicidal spectacle.

The materialist vision – at least from the predominantly scientific, Western vantage point – seemed to be winning: church and religion were looking fairly antiquated against the massive advances science and technology were making. The idea of self-replicating molecules, living and driven by some innate survival-gene factor, leaping and branching into multifarious species, supported by lifelike images of hairy apes gradually stretching their backs and walking upright into the shape of a clean, white-skinned man, was very convincing. Billions of years certainly provided scope for many things to possibly happen in terms of time and space, didn't it?

Death, in the meantime, was still lurking, awaiting everybody, and science didn't seem qualified or prepared to hypothesise what happened to us after that. One of my earliest childhood awakenings to the mysteries hidden in the boundless depths of the universe took place one night while I was leaning out of my bedroom window gazing up at the starry sky: "Where does the night end?" No answer ever came back. This was probably the genesis of my future probings into metaphysics. Death was the greatest and most frightening frontier facing us.

There were lots of puzzles to life that needed to be solved before my time ran out. But they would all have to wait, as I had an urgent issue pending. Unfortunately, like Andy, I had failed my eleven-plus [exit] exams. That meant I was doomed to attend a common high school, not fit to remain with the saintly intellectual class any longer. I was thus packed off to Northampton secondary modern, just off Old Street in the City, while my best buddy Andy got shunted elsewhere.

Making new friends was virtually impossible. I looked for someone to play with but the clan of pure East End kids dominated the turf, full of cold, hard-faced rockers (Mile End was only round the corner), and I was a West End lad, still hopelessly useless at football. It was a time of fear and isolation.

Having a foreign-sounding name was already bad news: "Steven Demetre Georgiou" was just as unpronounceably damned as it could get. Eventually, I was lucky to make friends with a short but tough Greek boy called Demetre who, as well as sharing my middle name, was easy to get along with. We began to hang around together a lot, especially outside school hours. He introduced me to pornography; I still remember it was an old Victorian erotic picture book and pretty difficult to put down – like the ghastly feeling of guilt that came with it.

The pull of the world continued to get stronger and, by then, the church at Lincoln's Inn seemed a long, long way away. I had gradually stopped attending Sunday Mass, increasingly making decisions for myself as to where I went or what I did with my spare time. My parents were quite open-minded in that way, and I suppose they trusted me not to do anything daft. I had it quite easy; Andy had a much harder time coping with his heavy-handed, strict Catholic mother.

Dad wasn't around much, apart from shop working hours, and Mum, fortunately, was much softer on me. Though she had a strong ethical character from her own Baptist upbringing, she never hit me. If she frowned, that was enough! My sister, however, was another thing. Anita would threaten to lock me in the toilet if I said something naughty or got out of line. One time she actually did it; that was enough to teach me not to expose any of my private sexual thoughts to my big sister. She was pretty off-limits regarding that stuff.

My early days at St. Joseph's also had some effect on calibrating my moral barometer. Though my hands were not red-sore from being caned by nuns anymore, my conscience still hurt whenever I fell into sin; it felt uncomfortable – but not too distressing, I hope, for the "scribbling" angels who had not yet moved into overtime.

As per the rules of nature, the age of my sexual awakening had well and truly begun, and I was on the lookout for girls, desperate to get more acquainted with the opposite sex. My brother had always been a role model for me. Roaming around in his suave, Burton-tailored suits, big Dave's confident charm was in stark contrast to my shy and awkward approach to "birds." In some way, he replaced Dad as a father figure. I looked up to him and sometimes he'd stop and lecture me. "You'll never find a woman better than your mother," was one of his wisdoms I never forgot.

David's age, experience, and victories with the ladies made him an exemplar for Andy and me. He was able enough to do exactly what he wanted. Tall and attractive to girls, already married and divorced, he was even plucky enough to go out with a couple of beautiful South African cast members from a musical running at the Princes Theatre, which made me crazily jealous! His late-night destinations were the Whisky A Go-Go on Wardour Street and the Empire Ballroom in Leicester Square, where the minimum age for entrance was eighteen – I was eleven! It was going to be impossible for me to compete with big brother and his buddies; I was going to have to establish my own personal scene. It was time to create some action of my own.

Lots-O-Fun was my favourite hangout; it was a neon-lit "palace" full of colourful pinball machines, in Cambridge Circus; I'd pour all my hard-earned tips into the cash-hungry monsters, doing my utmost to win another desirable five-pack of Player's Weights cigarettes. After the café, that was where I'd be. The ching-chinging of bells as the shiny chrome pinball shot out, bouncing around the colour-flashing rubber rings and targets as the scores rolled higher and higher, was pure heavenly music to me.

There was always something going on in our groovy part of town: hanging around Soho one day with Andy and another pal – Eddie, who lived round the corner – I got my first part as a film extra. Anthony Newley was making *The Small World of Sammy Lee* on Old Compton Street, and we happened to be standing on the pavement by a lamppost as the film crew with heavy cameras arrived. The scene involved Newley running down the taxi-bustling street. As he passed us, I put on my best cool, nonchalant look, trying not to glance at him. It was over in a flash.[3]

They never paid us a penny, of course. The movie was just another cheap black-and-white British film of the late fifties; extremely grey in nature and nothing like the dazzling drama and excitement found in Hollywood's epic productions. I never even went to see it, probably because it was X-rated with quite a few topless scenes. (Mightily frustrating!)

3 | *Jesus vs. Superman*

Beyond those "underage" teeth-gritting annoyances, I was a fully liberated youngster and had a chance to stay out till late. I'd meet my friends outside school hours at twilight and got familiar with some local girls in the nearby block of flats off Southampton Row in Holborn. That's where I met Anne, a plain, dark-haired English girl who became my first "steady": wow! The first kiss in the lift was really something. In those days, if a girl let you kiss her, that was a pretty strong indication of your "going steady." Not much else required. Just a brief time together after school, sharing sweets or cigarettes – and having to put up with friends and outsiders pointing and making fun of the two lovebirds.

Regrettably, the grounds outside Anne's flats became the scene of a battle with a brassy boy from the area. We picked up splintered wooden bars as a crowd of kids shouted and egged us on. Untrained in the art of wielding a caveman club, I was instantly struck on the head, and the duel was over in seconds. Feeling around in my hair, I could see blood pouring through my hands! Luckily, Great Ormond Street Children's Hospital was only a few hundred yards away. David heard the news and came rushing to the hospital. They fixed me up good. But after this, my interest in Anne faded away. I was probably too embarrassed by the incident and lost contact. But the scar remained.

Looking for new things to connect with, fashion seemed to point the way. These were the days of Cuban-heeled pointed shoes, called winklepickers, and tight, drainpipe trousers. At school I was an outsider who envied the smart local lads. To compete I would spend ages in front of the mirror dipping into a bowl of Dad's Brylcreem, trying to perfect my spiffy hairstyle. My local barber had direct instructions (under the threat of death) regarding the exact length and shape of my hair, so that I could resemble as closely as possible my favourite film idol of that time, Tony Curtis.

Mum was always there, sympathetic and ready to serve my fashionable whims. When I dictated split-end trousers, she would patiently update my wardrobe, running all my favourites under the sewing machine. No one was kinder to me than my mother, always giving me whatever I wanted. She probably didn't realise the pressure I was under at school. Similarly – in some ways – being caught up in my own adolescence, I never spent a great deal of time trying to imagine what my mum's life must have been like. She kept her feelings quite private, always caring for others but never revealing what may have been hurting her inside.

In an effort to fit in with local "hard nuts," I tried to look tough and quickly learned my next art: smoking in the toilets without expelling my guts. The boys' urinals were as foul-smelling as one can imagine. It was all part of the process of needing to appear as cool as possible. A new brand of cigarettes, Salem, had just come onto the market. They were mint-flavoured, which probably made them slightly easier for me to inhale and keep down.

Movies did a prime job of promoting the lifestyle and image of what most youngsters wanted to mimic, and the blockbusters imported from the US almost always displayed handsome stars casually puffing away on the big screen, fearless of censorship (or death). Mystery movies and glorified gangster films absolutely billowed with smoke, as the audiences in the cinema watched on with reverence.

Marlon Brando and his student, James Dean, were probably more responsible than anyone else for iconising the moody, loose-cigarette-toting, introverted, restless, anti-establishment hero. Dean's influence on me as well as on my brother's generation was mighty and immeasurable; it represented the desire to get away from the constraints of a nine-to-five life sentence. He glamourised our dreams of a more beautiful and carefree existence – along with the help of his female counterpart, Marilyn Monroe – making tomorrow's world all ours for the taking.

Dreams did not always take the direction we wanted them to. That hard lesson arrived with the death of James Dean in a car crash in 1955, followed not long after by Buddy Holly's plane going down.

These tragedies rudely reminded us that there is a limit to everything and that fate stood more proud and powerful than any passing jubilance. If only we could understand what it was going to do next.

In 1961, without warning, the latest American hit musical movie, *West Side Story*, suddenly burst onto the world's screens – and imploded into Andy's and my life. We were wild city trippers, and, because of our street background, we instantly fell crazily in love with this urban epic. We were infatuated with all of it: the T-shirts, jeans, and sneakers, juxtaposed against the backstreets of New York and its tribal precincts, with metal fire escapes, criss-crossing tenement buildings, silhouetted against a burning red skyline . . . Leonard Bernstein was a genius!

West Side Story had captured the currents of the time.

Marlon Brando started it with *The Wild One*, James Dean refined it with *Rebel Without a Cause* – but Stephen Sondheim and Bernstein put all of it into words and music.

Andy and I were insane fans. We created our own fictitious gang, "The Belts," and began imitating modern choreography steps, dancing round telephone boxes and pavements near our cafés. The groundbreaking score was so electrifying and just too incredible for words; the music entered our bloodstream. After seeing the film endless times, everything was different. "Somewhere" became our theme song, and I wanted to marry Natalie Wood . . . but reluctantly I began to accept that she was probably never going to even know my name – it was a dream too far. What Andy and I could do, instead, was dance around the streets, clapping and tapping our heels in jagged staccato style, singing, "I like to be in America!"

Because we lived in the centre of theatreland, it was easy to feel the buzz all around us. Musicals brightened our world. Even before *West Side Story*, I'd seen all of the great Technicolour stage-to-film movies like *Carousel* and *South Pacific*, as well as being a fan of music soundtracks like *The Magnificent Seven*, written by Elmer Bernstein, who also happened to write one of the most remarkably catchy theme tunes of all time, "Walk on the Wild Side," from the 1962 movie of the same name.

Across the road from my front door, *King Kong*, an all-black musical from South Africa, had opened. It was full of infectious melodies and African rhythm; Andy and I had seen it a couple of times and we adored it, but couldn't afford to keep on buying tickets. We ended up hanging around at the back entrance of the theatre and listened to the muffled sound of the songs, trying to glimpse the actors and dancers through a gap in the stage doors, night after glorious night.

Music was intoxicating. I'd dance and sing all the choruses I knew at the top of my voice, floating six inches off the pavement, bellowing up and down the street, oblivious to everyone.

Knocked out by the lightning charge of all these adolescent emotions, we were finding it harder and harder to think about the watchful angels who were busy recording our actions. While I wasn't attending church on Sundays much anymore, I still believed in God. However, it seemed the prevalent belief at the time was focused on the capabilities of *Homo sapiens*, a futuristic-minded creature with so much undeveloped potential to imagine, explore, and enjoy. There were so many joys in this world to choose from but, for me, music was the one thing that always made me feel good. It started to dominate most of my life.

Meanwhile, other serious choices were being constructed for me on the compulsory education side of life. I was approaching thirteen, and Northampton secondary was being merged with a couple of other schools in east London. Mum must've got wind about the perils of this particular move, given the notoriety of the Islington area, which had a reputation for sprouting gangs, pregnancy, and seriously not-so-nice behaviour. Plans changed.

I was duly enrolled in a private day school called Hyde Park college on Craven Hill, Bayswater, a boys' school catering to the children of fairly well-off, busy parents whose trades were mostly in central London. The college was distinguished enough to send us horse-riding in Rotten Row. This school was where I hitched up with another two Cypriot lads, Costas and Mozouras.

They say you can take the boy out of the West End, but you can't take the West End out of the boy. This was made evident by the fact that, before long, I had established a business in the college along with my two Greek compatriots. Most of the other students had posh accents, and their pockets were bulging with stipends from Mummy and Daddy's coffers. So the "Greek gang" began a protection racket. Unfortunately, it crumbled one day when a brave and stocky student refused to pay up. We slunk back into the background and gave up on that short stint of racketeering.

The college had some pretty ancient teachers, including Mr. Moorland; he was about two hundred years old – or that's what he looked like. White fluffy hair, stiff mortarboard, and a chalk-infested, black master's gown; he taught Latin.

Being a bit of a prankster, one day I tested the poor man by pretending to be sick; it was a real "West End production." I had prepared a concoction in a bottle, mixing rhubarb juice, corn flakes, peas, and whatever other leftovers I could find in Mum's kitchen. At the appropriate moment in the middle of the lesson, I sucked up a mouthful of this sickly looking guck and spewed it out onto the floor, groaning with pain. As predicted, I was permitted to go home, to the sheer admiration of my classmates. I took my bow and exited the college doors – the only thing missing was the applause.

What you give out comes back. It wasn't very long after that I got my well-earned payback. Another eccentric teacher, of the loathsome subject of algebra, was Mr. Machacek, from

Czechoslovakia, a communist Eastern European country as it was back then. He turned to me in the corridor after lunch one afternoon, probably after hearing somebody muttering "Commie" under his breath as he passed – but it wasn't me! Mr. Machacek decided that it was. He instantly assigned six black marks in his little punishment book, which meant I was certainly headed for a caning on Friday.

I bawled out my innocence, but to no avail. We were summoned to the high court of Mr. Evans, the headmaster. Mr. Machacek told his side of the story, in which he repeatedly and falsely accused me of bad-mouthing him. My blood boiled! I picked up the weighty algebra book in my hands and hurled it with all the power I could at his incredulous face. I was expelled . . . but what a superb way to go!

This taught me that full payment of justice was not easily afforded to the weak in this world. On the other hand, it saved Dad about three thousand pounds a year in school fees.

Following my memorable exit from Hyde Park, I was sent to my third high school, Hugh Myddelton in Finsbury. It was a straight number 22 bus ride from outside my front door. I was enrolled as Steven Adams, to make my accommodation within the hub and chatter of English class kids easier.[4]

Regrettably, and without me knowing, I had picked up a bit of a posh accent from my brief time at the college, so I was labelled "different" again. In some respects, it was not all negative; the girls at school seemed to take a fair bit of notice of me. Uniforms were not compulsory at Hugh Myd, so I even had a chance to show off my smart new mod clothes: swanky hip jackets and bright, luminous green socks. All that was perfectly dandy, but chatting up the girls was a million times harder than just looking "good." So I kept my mystique and avoided talking to them as much as possible; that way, I wouldn't lose my image. It earned me a lot of points, but very few tangible rewards.

Living in the West End meant that challenges and confrontations were inevitable. One threat I had to deal with came in the shape of a tall, Asian lad who adopted me as some kind of tag-along puppy. His name was Meru. He was a few years older and lived just round the corner in Neal Street, Covent Garden. Everywhere he went after school or weekends, I was dragged along and expected to accompany him. What his fascination with me was, I didn't quite get, but because of his height, strength and muscular build, together with his dagger-like eyes, it felt dangerous to say "No."

Week after week, month after month, the torment just got worse; the dread of seeing his face after the school gates closed made my stomach turn. I was like a slave on a chain having to follow my victimiser around everywhere: clubs, pubs, alleyways; he'd expect me to hang about all the time. The gift of freedom had been snatched away from me – something just had to give.

One day I woke up and decided I'd had enough. It had to be victory or servitude – win or lose. Marching over to the front of his house I stood on the pavement.

"Meru! Come down here!" I yelled.

Finally, and quite unsuspectingly, he opened the front door and came out to meet me, at which point I ran at him and began a ferocious volley of punches to his face and body that caught him completely by surprise. After about a minute or so he crumbled and dashed back into the house to take shelter. Whatever superhuman power got into me that day surprised even myself. Perhaps it was the agonising build-up of tension and hatred, being pressured and terrorised over a long period, which suddenly snapped and made me into an unbeatable underdog champion at that moment.

But the battle was not over as far as he was concerned. Meru managed to find me late one evening hanging around my favourite coffee shop in Soho and called me out. As I stepped out of the doors, he and a bunch of his pals pounced on me, kicking and beating me, and leaving me sprawled across the hood of a nearby Volkswagen. Meru and his crew sped away, mocking and laughing. I lay there aching and dizzy from the onslaught, but at last my hell was over. As far as I was concerned it was all quits. At least I had no fear of him ever bullying me again. I had earned my peace, at the cost of a little bruising.

Some years later, I found out he had become a professional wrestler and taken the title "Mohamed Meru Ullah – the Royal Tiger of Bengal." So that's who I'd been dealing with!

While conflicts and violent youth "wars" were going on around me, something inexplicable and quite non-worldly happened. It was a strange, sun-filled afternoon in the schoolyard at Hugh Myddelton. I was all alone at breaktime when a spiritual alter-self within me started to speak. It seemed crazy to imagine – especially after all the rotten things I'd seen and done. The inner voice soundlessly told me there was "Jesus" inside me. "Hey! Who said that?" It was never revealed.

Maybe it was a religious relapse after all the strenuous preaching I had received at St. Joseph's or a pang of conscience stemming from a greater calling. I often thought that if I ever were to reform and restrain my wayward impulses, I might become a priest. But it seemed there was never a break long enough when I could categorically confess to have given up the tendency to sin.

A cataclysmic event was about to occur – fortunately, not yet the Day of Judgment, but an earthquake that would make every youngster twist, shake, and forget everything else they had previously done, seen, or heard. It began to rumble beneath the ominous grey clouds that overshadowed the remote terraced backyards of Liverpool. Near the creaky docks of Merseyside, four lads called the Beatles took to the air like a tornado spinning everything in its wake, all emanating from the sound of a shiny, black vinyl disc with the name Parlophone on it.

The Mersey Beat was born. This was followed by the raunchy R & B sound of groups like the Rolling Stones, the Animals, and the Yardbirds churning out a new twangy rock, borrowed heavily from the rhythm & blues stars originating Stateside. For ideology-starved teenagers like me, it was a calling. The pounding drums and rally for freedom meant that every enemy of change could be overcome by anyone armed with a simple electric guitar, drums, bass, and a catchy song.

The first explosive Beatles single that blew me away was "Love Me Do." It was so sparse and bluesy – and totally Liverpudlian. All those elements formed a volcanic eruption of musical innovation and a genre never heard before, light years away from the prehistoric singers like Frank Ifield, Shirley Bassey, and Andy Williams. The mop-haired group's uninhibited style – together with their competitors in that regard, the Stones – was totally unlike the look and fixed nature of those "aged" music fossils. That was probably one of the things that made us realise it was now possible to do anything, providing it was different from whatever was done before – and sufficiently younger.

Thank Your Lucky Stars, a new British TV show, was launched in 1961. Gathering round the TV set and watching the four powerfully talented lads perform "Twist and Shout" in 1963 was probably the biggest breakthrough: John Lennon's piercing, primal scream launched us into a space and time drastically beyond our previously placid universe. Thereafter, it was impossible to sleep peacefully again.

The Scene
1963–5

DISCOTHEQUES: THAT'S WHERE it was happening, down below in those dark and sweaty hangouts deep in the basements and alleyways of Soho. The Marquee and the 100 Club were a short trip down the road. Manfred Mann, the Yardbirds, the Who, and the Animals – all the great bands used to play those gigs, and occasionally a great American rock artist would drop in, like Chuck Berry.

I soon discovered a cool club in Soho where the top new R & B records were being played at ground-breaking volume: the Scene Club in Ham Yard, just off Piccadilly Circus. Guy Stevens was the boss DJ. It was *the* place to go, particularly for mods, the fashionable mob I most resembled.

Membership was expensive, and so here's where my artistic talents came in useful: I simply forged my own membership card. Being just black and white made it really easy.

Soulful new sounds and rhythms were arriving all the time from Black US artists: Jimmy Reed, Bo Diddley, Booker T. & the MG's, Ray Charles, Tamla Motown's Four Tops, Smokey Robinson, Little Stevie Wonder. It was musical heaven. Oh, how many times we danced to "Louie Louie." None of us bothered to stop and work out the words; you'd have to be a genius anyway to decipher what the Kingsmen singer was croaking about . . . but damn! It sounded so good!

After school, Andy and I would meet to go down to the discos or hang around the local coffee bars, spending whatever coins we had, repeatedly listening to singles played by bright, neon-lit jukeboxes. One of my favourites was Sam Cooke's "Another Saturday Night."

The Lorelei, a pokey Italian café, was my favourite destination. It was squeezed between Greek Street and Frith Street, in the heart of Soho. Frothy coffee was the only thing we drank as we sat for hours, elongating our sips and listening to the riveting stream of hits radiating from the robotic music machine. When a new Beatles or Stones single was released, we'd charge straight down to the Lorelei to hear it spin over and over and over again.

Musical lunacy increased. Andy and I would venture out, like werewolves at night, hunting for more. Darkly, under the dim, ultraviolet lights of the clubs, silhouetted DJs spun records like magical wizards of our souls, charged with a mission to keep us dancing on our feet till the morning hours. They provided the endless soundtrack to our well-past-midnight life.

Soon we got hooked on a new Jamaican rhythm called Bluebeat. Prince Buster was the king of the new offbeat genre. But that's not all we got hooked on; we were easy prey for pushers who peddled discreet, paper-wrapped packages of pick-me-up tablets called "purple hearts." We popped those illegal delicacies at three-hourly intervals to keep our legs and wings flapping.

Strolling dazedly back into school the next morning, I'd have to put on dark glasses to shield myself from the glaring chalk on the blackboard. Not many in the class understood why I looked so depressed and disconnected, particularly the teachers. That was one of the big downers of taking speed – as well as the gigantic hole it made in your pocket.

For me, life began after dark. One rainy night, a bunch of friends I knew from around Gower Street got together for a laugh and we formed an imaginary band. Dancing along the pavement, recklessly stomping over the bonnets of poor people's cars like Peter Pan and his pyjama gang, we sang and imitated the sounds of our instruments. Haji (who looked a lot like Pete Townshend) was on trombone, Andy on trumpet, Jimmy Mitchell on percussion, John Anderson on drums, and me miming guitar. Needless to say, this was not going to satisfy me for long. It had to get real.

The pressure of music swirling around my head was too much. I had occasionally watched my mother settle herself down at the piano and play some of her native Scandinavian childhood melodies. It was a little pastime of hers. Mum wasn't too serious about it, but it sounded so lovely. Following her example, I was inspired to sit down at the piano one day and try to play something of my own, one-finger style. Soon, I had plonked out a verse and chorus, a country and western–style song called "Darling No." The lyrics were totally yucky.

However, testing it on my pals, they all seemed fairly impressed. Problem was, I only had a top line – the rest of the arrangement was in the orchestra pit of my imagination.

Time was up! I just *had* to get myself a guitar and managed to convince Dad to part with eight pounds to purchase my first six-string "box" from Selmer, on Charing Cross Road. It was a cheap acoustic, an Italian make called an Eko. Its action was way too high, but the shape was right and . . . it was all mine!

After buying a *Teach Yourself Guitar* book, I began to practise placing my fingers carefully on the frets, following the dots on the pictures in the book and holding the strings down for as long as I could without buzzing. I wanted to change chords fast, moving from fret to fret, like a Bo Diddley or Kinks riff, but my hands just wouldn't move quick enough.

Playing other people's songs wasn't going to work. I wasn't skilled enough to learn all the keys and lyrics – too much of a job. Instead, I began making up my own ragged repertoire. Mum was patient and listened attentively as I tried to link together my shambolic chords while my untrained voice belted out the chorus. My lyrics were primitive, mostly wailing love songs. "Very nice, darling," Mum would say.

My big brother, however, was not nearly so easily won over. David was always going to be my biggest critic. I tried to catch his attention: "Listen to this, Dave." Reluctantly, he slumped down, tapping his toes impatiently. After not more than about one minute of my loud plonking and vocals, he broke in and snapped, "You sound like a frog! You'll never be a singer. Go back to art." He tramped out the door – leaving me more determined than ever to prove him wrong.

I still adored Bernstein and Rodgers & Hammerstein and dreamed that I might one day become a musical composer. When it came to writing, I didn't perceive any boundaries. I was free to draw on musical influences from all sources – even the ethnic music played at the Greek weddings had an impact. Dad also used to sing his own unique stock of songs, mostly in Greek, but also in Arabic, which he had learned in Egypt. I loved the twiddly things he did with his voice. Growing up in the West End of London, all kinds of genres were floating in and out.

But my lack of ability on the guitar was an impediment. Tired and weakened, I decided to give up playing it for a while, put the box down and just immersed myself in the waves of hit singles flooding over us at the time. My fingers ached too much, anyway.

David had a friend, Gerry Horgan, from Stoke Newington who was a part-time boxer and had many other useful talents. One day he came over, sat us down, and put on an album; as he shut the door he said, "After you've heard this, you'll never be the same."

Of course, he was right. Bob Dylan cracked the walls of our imprisonment in the lyrical hall of murmurs and pointed towards a blaring new era of protest and change. The chimes of freedom were truly flashing. Bob opened our ears – a new, iconic, guitar-wielding, darker, slightly less well-fed version of James Dean, with a cigarette flimsily dangling from his mouth.

During those years, the message Dylan delivered – being so un-poppy, so nakedly raw and nasally – gave birth to another kind of folk music movement. Bob helped us to define our ultimate ideals for global peace and invented a new authentic approach to urban poetry, something that the more melodious "cavern-sound" of the Quarrymen (otherwise known as the Beatles) had not been able to do. These weren't just easy-going, teenage love songs like "She Loves You" (yeah, yeah, yeah). Dylan soon became the high priest of protest; his words demanded a political change at ground level, and his music was defined by anthems like "Blowing in the Wind" and "The Times They Are A-Changin'." We were all prepared for the revolution, and it would have to be massive to meet our expectations.

"House of the Risin' Sun" was one of my favourite tracks on his incredible debut album. It drove me to seek out its origins. Luckily, a specialist jazz and blues record shop stood only a few steps across the road from our café. Collet's overflowed with all the latest obscure LPs from across the pond and played authentically great-sounding records all day. That's where I came upon one of the true grandfathers of the blues, Huddie Ledbetter (Lead Belly) and his Stella twelve-string guitar, including an early version of "House of the Risin' Sun." His songs were so true and gutsy. It was an education for me into the roots of early American Black music.

Leadbelly was also the original source of "Midnight Special" and "Rock Island Line," songs made popular by Lonnie Donegan, a major pioneer who brought American blues and folk music – which ultimately morphed into rock 'n' roll – to a British audience. With his humble skiffle group, Lonnie also inspired almost every young would-be British musician to grab Mum's washboard, bang together those crude "bass" crates, and start making music – even John Lennon, after recruiting Paul McCartney and George Harrison, following Lonnie Donegan's lead, actually began his band that way!

The next time I picked up the guitar, things had miraculously gotten better. The short break had done me good. Chords were sounding stronger – and the rotten buzz had gone! Not long after, I had a breakthrough when I wrote my longest song to date (two choruses and two verses), called "Mighty Peace."

> *How I'd love to be a child*
> *With friends spread all around me*
> *Playing games and running wild,*
> *With nothing more to do,*
> *Than to watch the sun make light*
> *And watch the moon take over*
> *From the day into the night,*
> *What mighty peace I'd find*

David's mind was also willing to change. After hearing Dylan's grating voice, he realised it was not necessary to sound like Bobby Vee anymore. He was beginning to get used to my quirky style; he even liked a couple of the new songs I'd written.

Progress: frogs were in!

So, my big brother became a convincing advocate and, on my persistence, he asked Dad to fork out more cash for a classier guitar. This time, he suggested, it would be more like an investment: eighty pounds' worth. Dad listened and gave me the cash. Ecstatic, I bought myself a new six-string, Swedish-made, Hagström guitar. She was the new love of my life. Songs sounded so much larger and more powerful on it, ideal for playing live – that's if I ever found the guts to actually step out and face an audience. There were psychological barriers I needed to jump over. But my urge was to make it, to earn a place among the new generation of saints in that star-scented heaven. It was a dream I had no wish to wake from.

Living so close to the heartbeat of London's music scene, I was always keenly on the lookout for any gap in the walls of the music business stronghold. So when word reached me about a "do" where Brian Epstein himself might drop in, I was fired up. The idea of such a chance, to actually rub shoulders with the Beatles' very own mentor and manager, was too wild to be true. Grabbing my pal Andy, we headed straight for it.

The address was an elite club in Knightsbridge. It was a hot summer evening, and their windows and doors were all wide open, so we didn't have to sneak in. It seemed pretty trendy, like a darkly lit disco. The rooms were packed with people gaggling and laughing loudly. We squeezed ourselves through the crowd up the stairs to the second floor, where the music seemed to be loudest. After helping ourselves to a few glasses of vodka and lime, things got a bit hazier. Not long after, some smart-suited guy approached and asked if we wanted to make it over to Epstein's flat. What? Bingo!

Hopping into a taxi, we arrived at Lowndes Square, behind Belgravia. As we entered the deluxe-looking flat, mingling with a whole lot of other bodies, we saw Brian

Epstein in a corner, swigging a glass of whisky. He glanced over to us from the other side of the room. There was obviously a lot of posing and subtle seduction games going on – we knew Epstein was gay – but Andy and I felt savvy and tough enough to deal with it.

Brian was eventually introduced to us. I noticed him staring quite a bit at Andy, who was much better-looking than me, in my opinion. In this situation, however, perhaps I didn't mind not getting that much attention. He guided us both across the room to look at Elvis's silver six-shooter, proudly hanging in a leather holster on the wall, a gift from the king of rock 'n' roll himself to the Beatles!

It was like a scene from *A Hard Day's Night* – but I reckon that excessive drinking probably had a lot to do with that particular phantasm. Brian disappeared, and the flat got emptier; the party had lost its glitter. Everybody seemed to have moved off somewhere. I was feeling pretty solitary; Andy had wandered away too. The records were sounding duller and more repetitive.

Withdrawing into my shell, I found a suitable refuge on a luxurious sunken sofa, stubbing out cigarette after cigarette. Thankfully, it wasn't long before Andy came over to me and signalled for us to leave. The anti-climax (remember, there were also no girls around), together with the consumption of too many vodkas, made us both feel headachy and nauseous. I was happy leaving that posh compound of notorious nobility to get back home and feel my feet touch the ground, enjoying the comforts of being an average member of the public again – at least for a while.

*

The baby grand had remained almost unnoticed in our front room for years. While broadening my musical capabilities and improving my home-cooked technique on acoustic guitar, I started transposing the three-part chords I had learned onto the ivory keys. The piano opened a new, fascinating door and helped me branch into a more classical side of my passion as a composer.

As usual, Mum would pass by while I unabashedly plonked out my new ideas; "Very nice, darling," she'd repeat in her Swedish, lilting voice, definitely impressed by my newly found, multi-fingered method. Mum was naturally musical; labouring long hours in the shop, she'd often be humming some pretty tune or other. One time she sat down with me at the piano. Right there and then, we wrote a sweet Swedish lullaby together, Mum helped to choose and translate the words as we went.

> *Kom vill du ta min hand och leda mig bort,*
> *Leda meg, leda meg bort,*
> *Kom vill du ta min hand och leda mig bort,*
> *Vägen till mitt hjärta är så kort*
>
> *Come will you take my hand and lead me away,*
> *Lead me, lead me away*
> *Come will you take my hand and lead me away,*
> *The way to my heart is so short*

Through some Soho connections, and as a way of earning some extra cash, I got a job painting murals in a new basement club called the Rendezvous in St. Anne's Court. It was a great, off-the-grid, virgin venue; I sensed its potential to try out my musical talents on an actual audience. Boldly, I approached the manager and managed to fix a gig, and enlisted my best mates, Andy and Jimmy Mitchell, to form an instant three-man band. Good old Jimmy worked in a bakery; cheery-faced, he was the artful joker, the proper wage-earner, and procurer of illegal substances among us. We used to spend many a purple-heart-filled Saturday night playing our favourite card game, pontoon, in his flat off Mornington Crescent.

During our elongated sessions, we'd listen to records. Jimmy had exquisite taste in music and an enviable collection of jazz LPs, ranging from Nina Simone to organist Jimmy Smith, plus some musicians with obtuse names like Yusef Lateef, an eclectic wind and sax player whose album *Eastern Sounds* I put on over and over again. Truth is, I never got those three notes from "The Plum Blossom" out of my head. The melody sank into my musical sinews (some years later, the tune re-emerged in what was going to become my first hit).

"What should we call ourselves?" Andy asked before the gig.

Taking our initials, we called ourselves the JAS Trime. Heavily R & B influenced, but contrary to a normal line-up, we sported a rather impoverished and sonically curious choice of instrumentation: Jimmy played a single tom-tom, Andy shook a pair of maracas (à la Jerome Green, Bo Diddley's sideman), and I strummed my shiny new jumbo Hagström.

On the opening night at the club, we were all popped up to the eyeballs with purple hearts, experimenting with our peculiar, percussive caveman "sound." Kicking off with one of my new songs, "Pull on the Line," which simulated a Lee Dorsey "Working in the Coalmine" feel, we managed to somehow entertain the packed crowd in the sweat-drenched atmosphere. But the absence of any meaningful PA system meant that I was whacking much too heavily on the strings to combat the dominance of Jimmy's drums, which were so damned loud. There was only one measly microphone available, which had to be dedicated exclusively to my vocals.

As the night wore on, Andy and Jim just got tired and slunk further and further behind, leaving me to carry on with the show. After this nutty first night, it was really becoming obvious to all of us that I was born to go solo. With no real band, no manager and no record contract, it was going to be a tough ask.

Career-wise, I was at a critical juncture and had to make some drastic decisions. Humbly walking out of Hugh Myddelton secondary, aged sixteen, with only one single grade-A General Certificate of Education for art in my pouch, I managed to scrape into the only art school in London that would accept me with such a meagre academic trophy – Hammersmith Art College in Lime Grove, Shepherd's Bush, directly opposite the famous BBC TV Studios.

Art was my chosen path in life, but Hammersmith was not really at the top of my list of preferred destinations – as well as being one heck of a boring bus journey to have to endure five days a week. Whereas the elite St. Martin's School of Art, just round the corner from Dad's café on Charing Cross Road, was much closer, but streets ahead in terms of prestige. Nevertheless, I admit that I was not the greatest student either. Overshadowed at Hammersmith by infinitely more talented artistic prodigies than myself, I began to skip classes and ended up spending more time lounging on the back stairs with the latest copy of Alan Lomax's popular songbook magazine, *Sing Out*, playing blues and folk instead of working on class projects.

My musical abilities were strengthening, but I needed to boost my confidence level. Still too shy to stand alone in front of an audience (apart from my unquestionably loyal family), I discreetly tested my performance skills at a local kebab house on Tottenham Court Road and even managed a one-time appearance at a rather sleazy strip joint owned by the dad of an ex-student friend from Hyde Park college days. These venues allowed me to slink into the background as part of the furniture, not the main, "hot" attraction.

Remaining incognito was obviously not part of my plan. I decided it was time to rise up and be noticed. There was an open acoustic night at the Black Horse pub on Rathbone Place, near Tottenham Court Road. It was as horrible a trial as being thrown to the lions in Rome. Heart in my throat, I nervously walked through the chattering crowd with my guitar and approached the mic. As it happened, the applause ended up being fairly encouraging; the audience was sufficiently unbored to consider it a success.

Being up front on stage was essentially a shortcut to getting my music heard. Long-term, my ultimate ambition was really to become a composer like Bernstein, Beethoven, Gershwin, or Bacharach. Hence, my songs evolved into a hybrid caustic mix of blues, crossed with a catchy dash of pop and West End stage musicals.

The process of songwriting for me was adventurous as much as it was intuitive. Unlike my quite inward-leaning character, my self-penned songs were uninhibited and experimentally brave. Once I had grabbed a melody or a chord sequence that hooked me, I playfully juggled words around till they sounded right, always twisting towards the unexpected – sometimes even surprising myself!

Les Cousins on Greek Street became a new target hangout, a place to hone my more folky style. Run by a young Greek guy named Andy (yes, another Andy), it was just around the corner from the Lorelei café, but a world away in terms of depth and musical credibility. This was the first truly authentic folk scene in London and it positively buzzed with non-commercial legitimacy, sitting right across from the Establishment club newly opened by the comedians Peter Cook and Dudley Moore, where Lenny Bruce was paving the way for a counter-cultural satirical style of politically edgy and obscene humour.

It's very likely that my social conscience sharpened further in that acutely anti-conformist, smoke-filled corner of London, enlisted, as I was, into the acoustic movement that grew out of that beatnik-ridden basement. Songs – modern and traditional – of protest and rebellion against injustice and the dirty business of war fired our desire to create a new world in which we could all meet and live peacefully together. My art as a lyricist began to mature in this highly critical environment. Words needed to mean something.

Regular artists who played at Les Cousins were the true

cream of British folk patriarchs, proper heavyweights like Davey Graham, Bert Jansch, and John Renbourn. I was enamoured of their masterful guitar skill, biting lyrics, and baggy jumpers. The club was a magnet for all kinds of charismatic characters, among them Judith Piepe, a huge-hearted Soho social worker with a fondness for silver jewellery, which she hung extensively around herself. Judith was always present, like a mother hen, guiding and grooming the new talents pecking around in the folk scene at the time; Al Stewart, Jackson C. Frank, and Sandy Denny all found accommodation under her gracious wings.

Judith was undoubtedly responsible for launching Paul Simon's career. There was already a buzz about this American folk singer who had dropped into London, impressing everyone with his New York "village" credentials. Judith allowed him to sing a few bars during a brief BBC radio show she hosted. After that, he landed an album deal with CBS, before returning to the US and linking up again with his buddy Art Garfunkel.

Around this time, I had linked up with another introverted, guitar-swinging chum called Peter Horgan, younger brother of Gerry (who turned us on to Dylan). Our mutual infatuation with the folk circuit became deeply earnest. He had bought a copy of Paul Simon's debut album, *The Paul Simon Songbook*, which we were both deeply into. I loved Paul's velvet voice – somewhat in opposition to Dylan's. "Leaves That Are Green" remains one of my favourite songs of his.

Pete became a very close friend, teaching me some vital fingerpicking styles. He played a great-sounding Epiphone acoustic guitar and was no stranger to the stage at Les Cousins. We hung around the club a lot. One nerve-racking night, Long John Baldry – a friend of Peter's older brother – stood up on the rostrum and invited Pete and me to play. It was the irreversible moment of truth. My shortcomings were glaringly obvious to me: I was a teenager, dressed a little too well, and couldn't even fingerpick (preferring to handle a plain plectrum and strum instead). Peter was way ahead of me and played guitar much better. He got up and sang "Twilight," a thoughtful song he'd written and performed before, which the audience was already familiar with.

Immediately following the applause, picking up my guitar, I stood up and forcefully dragged my heavy feet across the gaping floor (a whole two yards or so). I sat on the hard wooden stool and sang my number-one song to date, "Mighty Peace." Nobody booed (what a relief!) and the applause revealed a genuine appreciation of my lyrical, childlike outlook on life. Yes! The performance certainly furthered my cred.

Even though I enjoyed wallowing around in the underground exclusivity of a folk music crowd, my ambitions were still much higher, and I couldn't shake the desire to write songs that would move vast numbers of hearts and bodies – as well as penetrate the charts – why not? My songwriting skills were improving and my egotistical side was revving up: *How long must I wait to be discovered?* I pondered.

My sister Anita had just married Alec Zolas – part Greek/part Bulgarian. I was his smartly dressed "best man." One valuable outcome of this new expansion of the family was that Alec moved in upstairs in Shaftesbury Avenue – and he owned a brand-new Grundig tape recorder! Being kind and generous to his little brother-in-law, he allowed me to use it anytime at my leisure. So, into the microphone of this smart, modern, tan-leathered, reel-to-reel machine, I recorded my endless meanderings, which magically developed over time and formed themselves into a growing body of songs, complete with lyrics, beginnings, and ends. No longer was it necessary to rely on my memory. At one time I believed if a song or riff wasn't easy to remember, it wasn't worth anything anyway.

Gradually, my composing ability became more eclectic. Many of my words and melodies would easily have found a home in some West End show or other. This genre would later emerge quite distinctly and shape many of my early, poppy compositions, overshadowing my more acoustic-y side. Lyrically, I was always hunting for something interesting yet purposeful, some kind of worthwhile story or narrative to hang my music on. Writing mere hit jingles held no interest for me.

I was beginning to nurture a strong belief in myself and a place beyond the confines of my uncomfortable obscurity. It was the mid-sixties; everything was happening. I was on the lookout for that "Somewhere," which felt closer, but still beyond my reach. Bernstein had written about that elusive zone; others had too, like the Springfields in "Island of Dreams" or Lennon in "There's a Place," which were three of my favourite songs (four, if you added "Somewhere Over the Rainbow"). There had to be a more peaceful abode of nature and love, clear of conflicts and violent competition for survival, far from the concrete prison in which so many of us native human beings were held captive.

> *High, high where the wind blows,*
> *And the sky is as blue as the sea*
> *I look through the window*
> *of the house waiting for me . . .*[5]

A Cat Is Born
1965–6

TRYING TO DECIDE what to do with my rapidly evaporating teenage life, after having been told by the art college's authorities that I must repeat the initial year internment and start all over again, I gave up that idea and decided to go back and work part-time in Dad's café, while searching for a break to get into the music business.

I needed a new name. In 1965 there were some lucky accidents that assisted this. Films like *What's New Pussycat?* and *Cat Ballou* were in circulation, and around the same time I started dating a girl called Christine, from Wandsworth. We met in the 100 Club on Oxford Street. She was one year older than me, which led me to lie about my age, adding an extra year or so to make me feel less vulnerable. One fateful evening, she was looking at me perched on the couch and, squinting, she said, "You know, you look like a cat, sometimes?" That delivered a precious clue.

Christine was a beautiful girl. I was still extremely immature and excessively jealous about her infatuation with Scott Walker of the Walker Brothers. She was my first real love – the girl I wrote the song "The First Cut Is the Deepest" about. We used to go dancing at the 100 Club, which is where the first theme song that bonded our relationship was played. "I Got You Babe" by Sonny & Cher had just been released, and it personified our happy times together. She even looked a bit like Cher, with her extraordinarily perfect, straight, long, river-flowing hair.

But Christine gave me a difficult time. Because of my suspicious mind, I was always upset by her chatting freely with other guys. Parties were the worst, as she would drink too many glasses of Merrydown cider and then lose her inhibitions. Oh, how can I ever forget that initiation into *Rubber Soul*? We had gone to a party in an apartment block in Wandsworth, where the newly purchased Beatles album was blaring out of the windows – similar to every other hip abode in the country. "I'm Looking Through You" stabbed like a dagger, making my heart gush with pain every time the needle fell to replay.

My tormented soul became audible through my music. I now began to pour everything I felt into songwriting.

I definitely needed a better moniker than Steven Georgiou if there was to be any hope of me making it. While searching for it, another hint arrived through the title of a catchy hit spinning high at the time, called "Walkin' My Cat Named Dog" by Norma Tanega. Signals were shouting at me from all sides! All I did was add "Cat" to my first name, shifting Steven from head to tail: Hey-ho! "Cat Stevens" was born. It was only meant to be temporary – depending, of course, on what happened next.

David boasted the smartest business brain in the family. I needed to secure his support to help me out. He had married a fine lady from Sweden, Birgitta, and was always on the lookout for better ways to earn a living. After listening to my new songs, he became more convinced about my potential talent. Unfortunately, the music biz was like a fortress with no evident cracks to slip in. But Dave managed to find a way in a dramatic fashion. A major break happened when he walked into a Tin Pan Alley restaurant at lunchtime one day. Unashamedly standing on a chair, he shouted loudly for help to get his "genius brother" a record deal. David was instantly offered a name and a telephone number. He tracked down Mike Reagan, who worked for EMI and put us in touch with the West One Agency, an associate company, in Manchester Square, off Oxford Street. That was the HQ of the Beatles' record label, Parlophone – so there had to be something good in it.

    I hastily managed to record a demo in Regent Sound, a studio on Denmark Street, for about fifteen pounds – with echo! The song was called "Back to the Good Old Times," together with a B-side entitled "Everything's Pilin' On." That black disc was all that was needed, alongside a glossy photo of me and my new name: "Cat Stevens." David was impressed: I had instinctively understood the tools needed to unlatch the locks of the "industry."

    West One, although it was based in the lower ground floor of Parlophone's influential offices, was a pretty duff stable. Dave took the demo and my pic into the agency, and they signed me up immediately. My glossy black-and-white picture was soon up there on the wall alongside Muriel Young, a very British blonde TV presenter, and a well-known DJ called Jimmy Young. Not quite rock 'n' roll, but it was a start. Through the agency I was given the chance to sing live on Radio Luxembourg a couple of times. They also booked me to do a couple of obscure gigs up north, and that's when David – now my de facto manager – fully saw the light. I was singing "The First Cut Is the Deepest" when, one by one, all the girls left their fellas and crowded round the front of the stage. *There is definitely a future in this*, David thought.

Not all the gigs were as "hetero." One stint was at the 2-Decks Club in Gerrard Street, Soho, which, I was to discover, was a popular gay club. The crowd appeared to get some kick from watching a baby-faced seventeen-year-old serenade them on guitar for an hour or so. That was flattering, but I was paid less than ten pounds a week; it was definitely not the future for me.

My first real venture into the recording studio happened while I was with the agency. A session was arranged with a producer and contender for Britain's answer to Frank Sinatra: Monty Babson. A smooth, crew-necked, multiple gold-ringed nightclub crooner, Monty was painfully out of sync with my ambitions, but we cut two songs in a studio in Holland Park. The songs were a retake of "Everything's Pilin' On" and a new composition, "Baby Take Me Back Home." The session guys were plainly not inspired and the result was duff. Because of that, I didn't sign any paperwork with him, and that ended that.

EMI had a publishing arm called Ardmore & Beechwood, and I was put under their wing as a type of apprentice and in-house composer. The company was run by Harry Lewis, who seemed to spot a blush of talent in me. He paid me a thirty-pound advance per song, which was useful income for me at the time. I managed to get a lot of acetate demos recorded, looking for that hit which was going to catapult me to the next level and make me famous.

Ardmore's offices were on the third floor in Great Portland Street, round the corner from BBC Broadcasting House. That's where I bumped into Kim Fowley. He was a totally weird and zany American artist who – though I didn't know it at the time – was responsible for producing and singing a massive US number-one hit, "Alley Oop." Kim also happened to share my July birthday – very kooky indeed!

Bursting into the publishers' one day in his tan-suede cowboy tassel jacket and steel-heeled boots, almost hitting his head on the ceiling as a result of being so ridiculously tall, Kim handed me some rough scribbled lyrics about "Portobello Road." I took them away to add music. When Kim finally heard it, he loved it. But it didn't go much further.

My publishers weren't working hard enough as far as I was concerned. Demo discs were piling up, and I was getting frustrated; nobody was actually interested in covering my songs. Desperation drove me to drop one of my acetates personally into NEMS, Brian Epstein's office on Great Marlborough Street. The demo had two tracks, including one called "Love Is Like a Bird."

Soon after, whether by coincidence or a stroke of fate, the new Beatles album, *Revolver*, contained a beautiful ballad entitled "For No One." An important two-bar section of it sounded uncannily similar to ". . . Bird." Well, how could I dare imagine . . .! And, even if it was snitched, why should I be upset? They were the most fantastic band in the world. This – one way or the other – confirmed I was at least moving in the right direction.

But I still needed a break.

David was always on the lookout for contacts and happened to locate Donovan's manager, a guy called Peter Eden. Dave strode into his Soho offices one day, hoping to get me signed. But when Mr. Eden saw my picture he said, "He's got no gimmick, he's too plain, too good-looking. Donovan has big ears!" That might have been another factor in sticking to my somewhat curious name.

Finally: a wondrous stroke of luck! My brother bumped into a guy called Bert Challet in the showroom of the Simon Massey fashion house in Cavendish Square, where David worked as head salesman. Bert was a millionaire from Manchester who had made his money through building up an empire of fashion stores. He was also married to the daughter of Nat Cohen, one of England's early iconic film producers.

David got straight to the point: "Excuse me, but do you happen to know anyone in showbusiness?" With all the brash entrepreneurism and blind nerve needed, he continued, "'Cause I have this brother who is a brilliant singer-songwriter."

"My boy, I have just sold my ten stores," Challet replied. "I'm in showbusiness! Send him over."

Bert happened to have an office on Great Portland Street,

a few yards along the same pavement as Ardmore & Beechwood. Dave fixed it for me to visit him. On the appointed day, I walked in with my guitar and played him some songs. He looked like more of a boxing promoter, with a tough-skinned face and prominent, dimpled chin. Gripping his ever-present, half-eaten, foul-smelling cigar between his teeth, Bert listened and seemed suitably taken by my catchy repertoire. Grabbing the phone, he called up Mike Hurst, who was doing some producing for him at the time. Wow! That was more like it. Mike was one of the Springfields. They must have broken up when Dusty went solo. Their hit "Island of Dreams" was among my most revered songs. I was getting closer at last!

Meanwhile, Christine worked at a company called Foster Wheeler, an energy company in Chelsea. It was frustrating not to be able to see her more on weekdays – I always had to wait until very late, after she finally got off work, went home to change, and was ready to meet. Neither city buses nor the tube ran regularly or that late in those days. Her lack of free time became a sore point between the two of us, but it also inspired in me the idea for a song. "Matthew & Son" could never have been written had I not felt a strong social empathy for the common worker, like Christine, nailed down to the lower decks of slave-ship corporations. The song would later make me a household name all over Britain.

That was yet to come. Unfortunately, my excessive suspicion and distrust of Christine's faithfulness whenever she was not physically by my side, coupled with my mad love affair with myself and my music, soon ended our relationship.

In the midnight moonlight I'll
Be walking a long and lonely mile
And every time I do
I keep seeing this picture of you
Here comes my baby
Here she comes now
And it comes as no surprise to me
With another guy . . .

When I met Mike Hurst, it was an instant psychological and physical match. He was experienced, ambitious and large; I was inexperienced, ambitious and skinny. I started with my usual opener, "Back to the Good Old Times," but it was "Here Comes My Baby" that got his full attention. He immediately liked my unconventional, staccato vocal style.

Mike took me over to the Hyde Park Mansions offices of Economides Entertainment. He got me to sit down and play ". . . Baby" again, this time in front of his boss Jimmy Economides, for whom he was working as a producer. But Jimmy, instead of backing a fellow Greek boy – which is what I would have downright expected – passed me up. He was infatuated by another guy he was producing at the time called Marc Bolan. Mike was as mad as I was. But nothing could be said to change Jimmy's mind.

Marc Bolan was a real sweet guy and I got to know him. We went out to the clubs together and I brought him back to Shaftesbury Avenue, where we played records and shared a bit of brandy and puffed weed – that was one particular skill I did pick up at art school.

Bert Challet was still bullish and encouraged Mike to

follow his instincts. He knew Mike liked my music and was still enthusiastic. So Bert agreed to pay for a recording session in Pye Studios, Marble Arch. There we did four tracks: "Here Comes My Baby," "Come On and Dance," "Smash Your Heart," and "I'm Gonna Be King."

Again, as with Monty Babson, the musicians booked were all professional session men, so there was still a bit of instant, open-tin-can flavour to the arrangements. But "Here Comes My Baby," arranged by Georgie Fame's sax player, sounded quite catchy. It had quite an "up" and poppy feel about it. Mike took the master tapes back and played them to Jimmy, but got the same, negative reaction.

"No, he's a boob, Mike! The other guy, Marc Bolan, he's got the talent."

I was disheartened – but not yet sunk.

Mike still had faith in me and my songs, I had no doubt about that. And yet, little did I know that my whole future was spinning precariously like a whirling sixpence about to fall. Apparently, Mike, the guy who I was hoping would launch me into the music business, was preparing to fly up, up, and away to the US, green card and plane tickets in his pocket. Marjory, his wife, was almost packed, preparing for the big family migration.

Unaware of the approach of this imminent disaster, I had just finished writing "I Love My Dog," and I just knew it had hit potential. So I caught a bus and strode up to Mike's door, 11 Priory Road, off Kilburn High Street, and knocked.

After he made me sit down and listen to his latest rage, *Pet Sounds*, an awesome new album by the Beach Boys, Marjory made tea and a healthy slice of bread layered with thick jam (my favourite!). Then I pulled out my guitar and played ". . . Dog." Mike was speechless. Little did he know I had dishonestly lifted the main three-note melody of the catchy chorus from some obscure American jazz guy, Yusef Lateef. All Mike knew was that it was a smash! No matter what, even if he had to delay the trip to the US, Mike would give it a go.

> *I love my dog*
> *As much as I love you*
> *Though you may fade*
> *My dog will always come through*

The Decca Daze
1966–7

MIKE HAD A business friend, Chris Brough, son of the well-known English ventriloquist Peter Brough, of "Archie Andrews" puppet fame. He finally convinced Chris to lay out three hundred pounds to hire some musicians. Mike had cleverly arranged three hours of session time at Decca Studios through the head of A & R for singles at Decca Records, Dick Rowe (stigmatised forever for having turned down the Beatles). Mike drummed up some fictitious story about how he wanted to record one last "goodbye" track before crossing the ocean. Unsuspecting, Dick believed him.

Next step was accompanying Mike to the suburban house of an arranger called Alan Tew, who lived near Epping Forest. I went through the chords of "I Love My Dog" and sang him all the little arrangement parts I had playing in my head. Alan went away to write the score.

A full-blown recording session was booked and set up for me at the Decca Studios in West Hampstead. Brother David was still acting as my de facto "background" manager at the time, but he realised that this was a golden opportunity with Mike, and so he silently stood aside . . . and waited.

Finally, the big day came. Around 9 a.m. I entered the studio in Broadhurst Gardens, petrified on beholding all the experienced "pros" painfully tuning up and exchanging muso jokes. There was John Paul Jones (future member of Led Zeppelin) on bass and Big Jim Sullivan (best all-round competitor to Jimmy Page) on electric guitar. The rest were top-class musicians, all thumbing through the carefully written music sheets.

As they ran through the song for the first time there was a chilling sensation in the room; everybody sensed something special was cooking. Though it was disjointed and there were some clunky notes and a few corrections needed, the sound of "I Love My Dog" was totally unique: timpani coupled with a solo cello and sparse hi-hat and tom-tom drum pattern, together with the muted trumpets – it sounded better and better with each run-through.

Finally, after a couple of hours, Mike, Alan, and I nodded; engineer Vic Coppersmith-Heaven did too.

"Great!"

It was a take.

I recorded the vocals. Then, almost at the last minute, Mike remembered we needed a B-side. I quickly pulled out my Spanish guitar after the musicians had left the studio and recorded "Portobello Road" in one go. Done!

The next step was going to be make or break. Short,

bespectacled Dick Rowe was still on a blood hunt to make up for his misstep with the Beatles (well, he did sign the Stones after that, so things didn't turn out too badly for him after all). Mike walked into Dick's Decca office on the Embankment with my record in his hand, hoping to give him a nice surprise. I hung about outside the monolithic building with Chris in his top-down convertible, a dark-blue Triumph.

Mike now had to come clean about the studio time he'd been given. There was no "farewell" recording; that was a fib. Instead, Dick was now about to hear "I Love My Dog" by an unknown singer called Cat Stevens. It was a very scary moment.

"Oh, how dare you?" Dick apparently shouted, enraged at this act of deception. "I will never do anything for you again."

Mike eventually calmed him down. "Look, I've got it here and you've gotta listen to it," he told him as he waved the black acetate in the air. Dick Rowe huffed as he sat down, grudgingly.

Halfway through, he went over to the player and took the arm off the record. Mike was now feeling rather unnerved. Dick got on the phone to Sir Edward Lewis, the head and founder of Decca. "Sir Edward, can I trouble you? Can you come down here a moment? Thank you, sir."

He did. And Dick put on the record again. Once the song was finished the big chief turned round and looked at Mike and said, "Did you do this?"

"Um, yeah. I did, sir," Mike affirmed.

"You are a genius!" Sir Edward exclaimed. The two executives were clearly excited. It was almost decided on the spot that this would be a first release on a new elite label about to be launched by Decca, called Deram.

Mike finally emerged from the doors of the building and walked straight over to the Triumph where Chris and I were sitting with the car roof still open, biting our fingers to bits nervously. After a minute of excruciating teasing, he finally blurted out the news. It was one of those surreal moments in life when things go absolutely right.

My heart exploded out of my chest and bounced almost as high as Big Ben – which, coincidentally, was staring at us across the Thames from where we were parked. "What?!" I screamed, "He said *what?*"

Mike repeated Sir Edward's words. We all laughed in utter disbelief, hugging and patting each other on the back, before zooming off in a manic daze to celebrate – looking like the three musketeers after a death-defying escape from the swirling swords of a thousand-strong, armour-clanking legion, laughing and hollering as we sped away with the king's gold spoils jangling in our boot.

I rushed home to tell everybody the good news. Mum beamed one of her most radiant, bursting smiles, like sunshine. She was so overjoyed and happy for her baby boy. David and Anita were ecstatic too. Dad got the word delivered to him in the café, but he was not quite so bedazzled, being a bit out of touch with the music business and what this all meant. But he was always proud of his "sonny boy." And I was going to make him even prouder.

Dick James Music and Northern Songs, the Beatles' publishers, had moved to about a hundred yards along from our café on New Oxford Street. They had rented offices above the Midland bank, where Dad deposited his daily cash takings. I went straight up the stairs to Dick and offered him the publishing for the song "I Love My Dog," figuring that maybe – because he was connected to the Beatles – a touch more stardust might rub off on me.

With Dick James as publisher and a Decca recording contract, things were looking very bright. Everything was falling into place. Naturally, I never told Dick or his son, Stephen, that the melody to "I Love My Dog" had been in part lifted from a US jazz record by a widely unknown sax player. That was known only to me and my close friends Andy and Jimmy – and they were perfectly safe with that secret.

Nineteen sixty-six. London was the centre of a talented musical galaxy at that time and had also entered the "swinging" age of fashion. Carnaby Street was buzzing with teenagers popping in and out of boutiques like John Stephen and Take 6, trying on new mod gear. Bell-bottom trousers were in, as well as paisley flower shirts. I was hurriedly sent off by Mike to get spruced up, ready for publicity shots and the launch of the new single.

These were the Jolly Roger–waving days of the pirate radio stations, without which artists like me would never have had a chance of surfacing. The BBC mentality was still locked in the dungeons of a fortress called "Yesteryear," high up on establishment hill. Stations like Radio Caroline and Radio London became our swashbuckling liberators, releasing new beats and genres against the voluminous gun-barrel sounds of freedom now blasting over the musical shores of Britain. Apart from having to suffer through a few jingles and ads, the music was free for all to hear and enjoy.

When it was released in November of that year, I'll never

forget hearing the single for the first time. It was on a little crackly transistor, just outside the Moulin Rouge. Running through the double doors of the shop, I grabbed whoever I could. We crammed together, ears tight to the speaker, standing on the edge of the pavement on Shaftesbury Avenue, moving around to get the best radio reception, listening closely till the single faded, waiting to hear the DJ mention my name. It was obvious that a song about a dog by a singer called "Cat" was going to get attention; Britain loved cats and dogs, and I was going to benefit from this, big time!

One embarrassing problem suddenly occurred to me: I had never even owned a puppy. Journalists were certain to pounce on me with probing questions about my own fluffy, beloved friend. That particular dilemma was magically solved. One evening while strolling through Soho, I caught sight of a long-haired, black dachshund tied to a post next to a fruit seller's stall, just outside Foyles bookshop on Charing Cross Road. "Whose dog is that?" I asked the stallholder.

"Oh, he's just a stray. I tied him up here to wait to see if anyone might have lost him."

The dog clearly had been miraculously deposited there just for me. I couldn't believe my luck. "I'll take him home, I'll look after him," I said.

"OK, he's yours."

Off home we went with a bag of green grapes, which one by one were popped into the salivating mouth of my little dog – buying them was the least I could do for the fruit seller as repayment for my new little furry friend.

I quickly discovered that "he" was a "she." I named her Willemina and introduced her to Mum and Anita. They couldn't resist such a cute, tongue-wagging little creature and she joined the family – and gained instant fame! I could now talk about her in my forthcoming interviews. Whew! Later I renamed the little gal "Pepe"; it was shorter and easier to yell.

Anita was recruited to purchase as many copies of the single as possible from Imhofs, the record store just down the road near Tottenham Court Road, hoping this would somehow help nudge it up into the charts. (I would have done the job myself, but that might have given the game away.) Just staring at the sand-and-white label with my name on it was such a thrill.

Mike was over the moon; the lucky little cat he'd discovered had brought fame to this ex-Springfield, harmony group-singer all over again. He trained me in the art of looking moody and not hanging around too long at reception parties. I had to behave like a proper star.

Roaming round London in black cabs on the orders of my press agent, Keith Goodwin, I was thoroughly grilled by journalists – mostly in Fleet Street pubs – and forced to pose unnaturally for photographs. Not one of my fondest memories; the shyness within me caused me to clam up and look stiff as a brick. In a few weeks, I was being groomed as one of the new pin-up artists, my embarrassing teenage spots being professionally buried under a thick bed of powdered make-up. Soon I was being interviewed by *Melody Maker* in their "Blind Date" column and asked to judge the new single releases; they included the Beach Boys' monumental groundbreaker "Good Vibrations."

"A very big hit!" I commented after hearing it. Well, that

wasn't very difficult – but much harder tasks were yet to come.

My first TV promo appearance was singing live on *Dee Time* with Simon Dee in front of five million viewers! After poky little Les Cousins, this was quite a jump. Needless to say, if I hadn't set my ambition so high, perhaps I would have fled. But I had to go through with it.

During the rehearsals at the BBC Lime Grove Studios (opposite my old Hammersmith Art College) the floor manager told me where I had to stand. No problem, because my two feet felt like sledgehammers anyway. Then the red light was switched on.

"I love my dog, as much as I love you . . .!" While singing I tried my hardest to shuffle my feet a little, like Mike had told me to do, but my body seemed paralysed; only my arms were light enough to make some pathetic, gyrating movements. We did that a couple of times to allow the cameramen to practise their zooms.

Following the rehearsals, I was led off the set and confined to a tiny prison cell of a dressing room. Oh God! It felt like I was on death row. The second hand ticked on incessantly; time was passing. A knock on the door finally came: "Mr. Stevens! On stage." An executioner posing as a studio floor hand escorted me and positioned me behind a screen. My heart was beating nineteen to the dozen. The best I could do was freeze on the spot, waiting for the dreaded red light – or was it a signal for the gallows' trapdoor to drop? Then the floor manager pushed me up on stage, raised his hands, and counted down with his fingers: five–four–three–two–one!

As the soundtrack to "I Love My Dog" began, I thought of Mum and the family watching. I had to survive. I couldn't let them down.

My career was successfully launched. The single only got to number twenty-eight in the UK but it was a massive turntable hit, thanks to the pirates. Cat Stevens had arrived. Thus began my rapid rise to success and fame, followed by my commensurate head enlargement and indulgence in sex, booze and chain smoking; on an unending tour of noisy dancehalls, social drinking clubs, TV and radio gigs, filthy transit vans, and beer-drenched trains.

A new band of musicians was enlisted to back me, called George Bean and the Runners. But, because of Mike Hurst's use of multi-brass and string arrangements, the four-piece band never sounded like the original records – that was heavily degrading for me. Along with the screaming feedback from the PA speakers, it meant I was doomed to perform my songs looking and sounding like someone else completely.

I was in desperate need of more friendly, close company and support, and good ol' Andy became my road manager. It was a relief to have my buddy along. I had just bought my first car – a second-hand grey Fiat – and "smarty-pants" Andy had casually managed to pass his driving test. So we were sent up and down the country on the orders of my newly appointed agent, the Harold Davison Agency.

My life was not mine anymore. Agents, managers, press agents, record chiefs, club owners, all these people had now taken full charge of my image, my music and my persona. They only knew me as "Cat," the latest money-making,

6 | *The Decca Daze*

teeny-bopper sensation. Even my stage clothes were not my taste. I had been shuttled off to some Berwick Street tailors in Soho, who also outfitted Tom Jones, Engelbert Humperdinck, and co. I already had an aversion to rough, scratchy jumpers, yet here I was locked into a prickly black mohair suit. It was a horror that only a pre-show binge of booze could alleviate.

Meantime, Mike Hurst and Chris Brough had opened an office on Kingly Street, next to Carnaby Street. They had now signed me up to their new management entity and had even organised a new publishing company to be formed, Cat Music Ltd. They, as well as Tito Burns from the agency, were the major shareholders and the directors. What did I care? On reflection, I was probably one of the few singer-songwriters who managed to own a chunk of their copyrights, almost from day one.

It was all rolling along, and I was well on my way. Just turning nineteen, a few months into my career, I began to ask myself, *How much money would I need to enjoy a carefree life without fear, to earn my idyllic plot in paradise?* I started to calculate. Finally, I worked out: if I could work towards owning my very own temple, on a Greek island in the sun, and have about ten thousand pounds saved in the bank, I'd be forever secure. I had no conception about the curse of inflation, and in those days twenty pounds could see you through a week, easily, as I would have no rent to pay; that would give me ten years, at least, of a luxurious existence. What after that? Strangely, I never questioned what I might be doing beyond thirty. That was a mysterious deadline. Somehow, I couldn't see myself growing old, so I had to finish whatever I had to do before then.

Mike had discovered another new singer called P. P. Arnold, an ex-Ikette from the backing singers of Ike and Tina Turner. Mike was totally hung up on "The First Cut Is the Deepest" and recorded the song with her. After that, people started to see me as a "hit" songwriter.

My former would-be-but-never-quite-was manager, Bert Challet, had the publishing rights to "Here Comes My Baby" and placed the song with the Tremeloes, who at that time were looking to start up a fresh career without Brian Poole. They recorded it in a rather inapt, party-style arrangement. Yet it worked. The single was to become a massive hit – especially in the States! Little did I know that Bert had reassigned all the rights of that song (apart from PRS, which paid some royalties directly to me) to his own publishing company, Angusa Music.

"The First Cut Is the Deepest" – it certainly was! That song was also privately registered in North America, to an associate publisher of the Harold Davison Agency, by Tito Burns, slicing off 50 percent of the song's total earnings – in apparent perpetuity. Those things I didn't understand until much, much later, when I learned the term for such practice was "double-dipping" (robbery might be a more honest description).[6]

"Matthew & Son" was my next major single release on Deram, inspired by my ex-girlfriend's heavy work schedule. I picked up the name from a sign while passing through the old City of London, seated on the top deck of a red double-decker bus. The name fit the riff I had, perfectly.

This was to become my biggest hit in the UK. Nicky

Hopkins – who was later featured on John Lennon's *Imagine* LP – was the jangle pianist, playing those famous four unforgettable notes, staccatoed throughout "Matthew & Son." It rose to number two in the charts, held back from the top spot only by the ridiculously successful Monkees. They had a TV series and were the new teeny-bopper sensation on both sides of the Atlantic, mimicking the fun-filled group life of the Beatles.

It was very frustrating not to have made number one, and I especially disliked the Monkees' Davy Jones, yet the one saving grace was that the song that held me underfoot was not actually sung by Davy but by Micky Dolenz. It was called "I'm a Believer." Well, there was more to be revealed about that particular theme later on in my life.

Brian Epstein had just purchased the Saville Theatre on Shaftesbury Avenue. I was invited to join the bill alongside Georgie Fame and Julie Felix for a two-week, post-Christmas stint of shows called "Fame in 67." It was highly convenient, situated only five hundred yards or so from my front door.

Nonetheless, the Saville show was a nerve-wracking gig. I was packaged by the agency and my managers in the mould of a young "Tom Jones" pin-up star, suitably primed in a black tuxedo and stiff patent shoes. Not me! I ran out and bought myself some cheap plimsolls from Woolworth's and a sufficient supply of vodka and lime, just to get my feet moving each night. It worked. Being slightly blotto meant I could move uninhibited, without transforming into an icicle on stage. Alas, my vocal tuning abilities diminished, and manoeuvering became an even riskier business if I accidentally hovered too close to the edge of the orchestra pit – that dark abyss into which the screaming young fans were dangerously beckoning me.

Deep inside, I was still scared to face the spotlight. It was totally in opposition to my astrological "Cancer" nature to imitate the performance of a flashy, sociable extrovert. Every night felt torturous, knowing that all eyes would be on me should I tumble and fall. On stage, there's nowhere to hide. The fact that my songs, when played live by the orchestra, never sounded exactly like the record, and that people called me "Cat," when my friends all knew me as "Steve," meant I had to act like someone else. That tells you how uncomfortable I felt.

> *The view from the top*
> *Can be oh so very lonely,*
> *And you can be missing such a lot*
> *That could be yours*
> *Why can't I stop forgetting myself?*
> *Why am I always trying to be*
> *Like somebody else?*[7]

The next UK tour on which I was invited was probably one of the craziest mixes of pop and rock music line-ups ever concocted by those box-office hungry, tonally clueless promoters. The tour was headed by the Walker Brothers, where the main attraction was – yes – none other than my ex-girlfriend's heartthrob, my old nemesis, Scott Walker.

I Got Experienced
1967

THE TOUR BEGAN in London's Finsbury Park Astoria. On the infamous bill – apart from the top-brass headliners being the Walker Brothers – were Engelbert Humperdinck, Jimi Hendrix . . . and me! All of us were having hits at the time and this, presumably, was the promoter's brilliant logic for bundling us together as a fruit 'n' nut package for that limited UK run.

The first night before the curtains were about to open, I got to know Engelbert. He was very approachable, and we shared the same tailors too. His dressing room felt much more relaxed than the hyper-moody barricade surrounding the Walker Brothers. Humperdinck introduced me to a potent concoction of brandy and port, something that would become my main pre-show pep-drink for many unbearable gigs to come.

Humperdinck opened the show followed by Jimi Hendrix. I waited in my dressing room on opening night, fearful of the moment when I would have to face my inevitable judgment before a jury of screaming thousands. Then I heard a cry echoing in the hall outside my door: "There's a fire on stage! Jimi Hendrix is burning his guitar!"

I was pacing around like some agitated, black-jacketed Spanish bullfighter at the time; too nervous about my own set to venture out and take a peep. True enough: Jimi had started with his notorious gimmick. It flunked everybody. This was, in fact, history in the making. Little did people know what impact he was to have on the direction of music from that night on, and the limitless peaks he would reach and "kiss the sky" with his famous left-handed Stratocaster.

After Hendrix's groundbreaking roasted guitar stunt and his amazing set, there was a short break before I was called to the stage to open the second half. A half-crazed army of screaming girls hollered, "Cat! Cat! We love you."

Well, that obviously made me feel quite purry and superior – even though my backing and PA were never quite what they should have been, not that anybody noticed those sonic shortcomings above the din.

During that experience, I got to hang out a fair bit with Jimi. He was a soft-spoken and much quieter soul than the entertainer who appeared in public. Like me, he favoured sitting quietly in corners, just observing and soaking up the ambience as we traversed and conquered the main towns of the UK, sharing a few groupies along the way. Jimi was a really interesting guy, whose every word seemed worth listening to. So I remained quiet around him, just taking in his stories about the Isley Brothers and candy-stealing cockroaches.

Jimi always appeared very cool and in control – maybe he was just "high" on whatever. Not surprisingly, you would often see and smell a thick cloud of smoky substances following him around. "Purple Haze," Jimi's latest single, seemed to describe that phenomenon aptly; it, too, was buzzing quite high in the charts.

While on tour I sometimes knocked about with Jimi's bass player, Noel Redding. That was a fateful affiliation and one that would find me experiencing LSD for the first time. Noel had invited me for an initiation to the hallucinogenic drug at his flat in Clapham Common. We watched TV, puffed a bit of weed and started listening to some music. When we were chilled out enough, he gave me a tiny tablet, which was to set me on an "almost" suicidal trip for the rest of that haunted night – truly among the worst of my life. The ghastly visions I was induced to witness were most likely a pent-up reaction to the suffocating music biz internment I was now shackled in.

Throughout those terrible hours of darkness, demons around and within me came to life. I entered a frightening dance cycle of life and death, watching myself become born and then age to the point of dying . . . but before I could leave the incessant wheel of existence, I would be suddenly born again, with a vague sense that I'd been here before. Oh, how to escape?

All through this, Noel was placidly floating on a cloud in his own little world, smiling gracefully and quite enjoying the trip. I, on the other hand, was going through an eternity

7 | *I Got Experienced*

of nightmares. I tried to stab myself – unsuccessfully, I might say – with a large coal spade by the fireside blazing furiously in his living room. The fire bounced an eerie light upon Noel's irritating, smirky face.

I struggled to my feet to walk out the front door countless times but, somehow, couldn't. It was like a horror movie where my body was no longer under my control. Finally, after several hours, my mind started to regain some sense of space and normality; I stepped over to the front door, reached up to the handle and opened it. Oh, thank God! As I gazed out of the porch onto the world again, I beheld the most beautiful sight: overnight it had snowed! I was now able to leave bottomless hell and walk upon an angelic carpet of pure crystal-white snow, which now lay serenely featherlike upon Clapham Common.

Some kind of Divine assistance arrived in my life at that miraculous moment. The epiphany was to become the inspiration for one of my all-time favourite songs: "Lilywhite."

> *Back upon the mended road – I pause,*
> *Taking time to check the dial,*
> *And the Lilywhite,*
> *I never knew her name,*
> *But she'll be passing my way*
> *Sometime again . . .*

Life teaches you through painful failures that, when things don't go right, there must be something that needs to be fixed. Regardless of the inevitable collision with my own deficiencies, my nature was to forever seek to improve, looking for something more: a perfection beyond myself. Struggling to progress and rise above the incessant whirlpool of this world, through dedication to music and art, was my life's sole mission. While LSD had rudely forced me to face my own mental confines, something quite otherworldly had come to assist and was working its way to set me free. The negativity of that experience ended up serving as a severe warning, which saved me from hurtling down the route of drugs and drink; it propelled me to think more about how to take a firmer grip of my life.

"I'm Gonna Get Me a Gun" was my heavily Bernstein-influenced follow-up to "Matthew & Son." It did well – also reaching the top ten – but the theme was rather aggressive. Some people took it literally – even Hendrix and his bandits had fun squirting water pistols from behind the curtain as I sang on stage. I didn't notice.

The song expressed an important desire in my life: the yearning to escape the posse of pop-chart chasers and return to one of my main ambitions: to write a West End stage musical. ". . . Gun" was based on an idea I had for a musical called *Mexican Flower*, about the life of Billy the Kid. Another song I wrote connected to it was "Northern Wind (the Death of Billy the Kid)," which was essentially a message of non-violence spoken through the character of a gun-swinging sidekick of Billy, who simply wanted to hang up his holster, go back home to join his wife and return to live on the right side of the law again.

Apart from that, there wasn't much more serious effort spent expanding the story. Still, the "musical" gave me some more ammunition to use profitably in those unwelcome press interviews. I hated being interrogated – it was unnerving to be essentially placed in the stocks, questioned, and photographed incessantly: lean this way; look that way; hold your hands high near your chin; aargh! Reading interviews was almost worse; I always felt like the journalists had a preformed image in their minds, describing everything from what I was wearing to what I was drinking, as though any of that was relevant to my art . . . I just hated the whole routine.

Nonetheless, I was attracting a lot of attention within the business. On the night of the Finsbury Park show, two impressive managers, Allen Klein and Andrew Loog Oldham, strode confidently into my dressing room for a chat, obviously scouting for me to switch allegiances. I was impressed, but David's eyebrows frowned; he was deeply suspicious. "Let's go!" He dragged me out. That was it. Dave was worldly-wise and could read people's intentions much quicker than I could. I relied on his instincts and talent for business as much as he trusted my talent for art.

Following the Walker Brothers' tour, I was deployed straight to the front line by my superiors, to attack European audiences. Most concert venues were trench-like, dark, dismal halls, where promoters refused to speak English. Sound system equipment on the Continent was prehistoric, so we usually had to lug our own bulky amps around.

One unforgettable gig was in Sweden, in the open-air funfair grounds of Liseberg, in Gothenburg. Jimi Hendrix was booked on the same bill. Unfortunately, it became a clash of egos. David, acting as my manager, got into a serious argument with Chas Chandler, Jimi's guy, about who should top the bill. The audience were left standing in the cold for nearly an hour while, backstage, the two almost came to blows. David went to chat with Jimi, and Chas came to my dressing room to help make me see reason. The question was: who was the bigger star? (Of course, to me it was quite obvious.) Finally, some bloke reminded us that there were two shows booked that evening. So we tossed a coin to see who would go out first. Problem solved.

Back in the UK, I was averaging three gigs a night, slogging away like a singing jester, performing at noisy working men's clubs and emotionally surviving by clutching a string of port and brandy bottles every night, as had become my habit. Having drunk a dangerous tankful of success, I soon adopted a sense of superiority that needed to be perpetually serviced. The Hendrix experience was just a small demonstration of that.

Life on the road was becoming intolerable – and so was I. My best friend, Andy, had to put up with my increasingly drunk and bloated ego. But it was all part of the show, mainly, I suppose, to distract attention from my true feelings of insecurity and self-doubt. I projected my frustrations outward, towards those closest. Like Garbo, I began acting the snobby star role: doors would have to be opened for me to strut through, the best-positioned tables needed to be reserved at clubs and restaurants, I was never to be woken up before noon if I had a hangover. Failure to obey these rules would lead to an explosion of foul-mouthed curses.

Finally, Andy's patience reached its limit. He boldly stalked out and abandoned me before a show in Stoke-on-Trent. I had become a spoilt, angry young man who felt that the world owed me more than I was due. The record company felt the same way about me; they demanded another hit. The next single after ". . . Gun" heralded my doom. It was a clever multi-tempo arrangement, leaning somewhat on my fascination with psychedelia. Perhaps the LSD experience had something to do with this, but another "Bad Night" it certainly was gonna be . . .

> *A bad night*
> *It's gonna be –*
> *A bad night*
> *I guarantee;*
> *Tonight, I'll have,*
> *A bad night,*
> *I know I shall*

On *Top of the Pops*, I wore an embarrassingly long, light-blue, silk caftan designed by the elite Soho-based couturier, Thea Porter, to complement my original rose-tinted vision of the song. But I looked more pathetic than psychedelic. The bands that were genuinely creating that sort of experimental music were Pink Floyd, the Yardbirds, Hendrix, Cream, Traffic, and the like. The big, brass band sound arranged by Alan Tew, together with Mike's permanent infatuation with the Beach Boys' *Pet Sounds*, just didn't match the genre I was after – it was also, frankly, light years from what I wanted.

My creative relationship with Mike was plummeting. More flops followed, with "Kitty" only reaching number forty-seven in the charts. I talked to Decca, and they let me have a change of style. "Lovely City (When Do You Laugh?)" was produced by Noel Walker and myself. On the recording, I sang and actually played my own twelve-string guitar as well – but it too failed miserably. Like a party balloon, my career was rapidly deflating; I was quickly heading for the trashcan of popped has-beens.

Being a solo singer with no regular group, I was boxed into a cabaret image, my voice submerged by busy orchestra arrangements. The music scene was darkening and looking more and more unfriendly. Even the Beatles were succumbing to ominous days: John had linked up with Yoko and tension was definitely in the air.

One long-to-be-forgotten afternoon, Dick Katz, my personal agent within the Harold Davison organisation, summoned me to his office. This was to be the final kick in the head that told me how badly things were going. He sat me down, blinked at me through his thick glasses, twirled his cigar stub around his mouth with his tongue, and informed me of a "great" new opportunity, which had just landed on his desk. The offer was for me to play the part of Buttons in *Cinderella* for a season of pantomime. This was the agency's way of saving my plummeting showbiz career. The idea spelled "death."

After that I wanted to bury myself.

It didn't help that I was friendless and lonely in my personal life. As is often the case, when isolated souls try to escape themselves, they club together in discos and bars for rampages of drinking and loud music – trying to drown out the increased noise of loneliness and seek out temporary partners. After Andy broke up with me, I hung around with

Peter Horgan and his brother Gerry a bit. I never really mingled or made any new friends until I got acquainted with a couple of real partygoers: Paul and Barry Ryan. This set of girl-crazy twins were the stepsons of Harold Davison, so they had some credible influence.

Paul & Barry had recorded a song of mine, "Keep It Out of Sight," a year earlier. I linked up with Paul and we got on well together and started collaborating and writing some songs. It was a strange and hedonistic fellowship I formed with the Ryan twins. Getting girls and getting stoned were the priorities of our regular nightly excursions – along with the occasional orgy. We hit all the clubs we could. The Speakeasy, the Cromwellian, the Scotch, and the Bag O'Nails. Occasionally we'd go to parties or hold a private 16-mm film screening at their Kensington flat of some ancient horror film or other. Through Barry, I later met a girl called Patti D'Arbanville – more about that later.

This terrible trio was going to get even worse: we hitched up with an intimidatingly large friend of my brother's, Peter Thompson. He was older, a massive, twenty-stone, gangster-sized figure from London's criminal underworld, which was laced with bruisers like Billy Hill, the terrible Kray Twins, and the like. Pete was a hired hand for them and had seen most of it – or some of the bloodiest parts, at least.

Hashish was Pete's regular fragrance for puffing – and we, naturally, shared the habit. We also admired his taste in music, which was heavily jazz-orientated; John Coltrane and Pharoah Sanders were always on his turntable and Ronnie Scott's was his favourite haunt. The late-night drinking, coke, and smoke binges took their toll. Meanwhile, I was getting thinner and paler; the company I kept was more and more hedonistic. These were the Bad Nights I had seen coming.

My savings were rapidly dwindling. In an effort to climb out of the sinking sand into which I had unwittingly slipped, I considered the idea of joining the "other side" and becoming a manager and producer myself. Together with Dave and an associate businessman called Maurice Press, we started up Doric Management Ltd.[8] Our offices were in Bury Street, opposite the British Museum. My long-time friend Peter Horgan was one of the new artists we took under our wings. I produced his first record for CBS, a Paul Simon-ish epic single with strings called "Emperors and Armies." I wanted him to have a hit. We tried our best to boost his chances as a good soul and talented musician, even changing his name to Peter Janes – but, in the end, we all accepted he belonged more to the folk circuit than the top ten.

Also, there was Sasha Caro, a songwriter with a unique-sounding voice from Armenia. I loved his crazy chord sequences and ethnic harmonies, but his Decca single "Grade 3 Section 2" hardly got played; and Bobby Hanna was a Scottish-born Canadian, black-tuxedoed nightclub crooner, for whom I wrote a song called "Beautiful World." A nice, amiable guy, but he was too incredibly ordinary – we couldn't even secure a record deal. Everything flopped along with my increasingly jaded career and account balances.

Doric Management turned out to be an expensive and fruitless exercise. I had also developed a terrible cold and was generally feeling spent. It was a depressing day when I told my brother David I could not afford to pay him a salary anymore. He would have to go back to the rag trade.

7 | *I Got Experienced*

It was back to square one for both of us.

One of the last ominously doomed projects I did before the burial rites of my "pop star" career was an instrumental piece I wrote for a radio play based on Edgar Allan Poe's short story "The Tell-Tale Heart." It was a horror story, perfectly suited to being the epilogue to one of the darkest times of my life.

I was all burned out at the age of nineteen, after only sixteen months: show business had done its worst and had made me well and truly sick to death. My cough never went away and was getting heavier and more viral. Despite feeling unbearably weak and dizzy, I refused to stop burning the midnight oil. While composing the last part of the "Tell-Tale" piece on the baby grand piano in our living room above the café I had another coughing fit.

For the first time, I saw blood on the keys.

I Think I See
1968

THE AMBULANCE ARRIVED and I was rushed directly to the London Clinic hospital. The doctors realised I was not suffering from what had been initially diagnosed as a bad cold. The medical lab now identified my bacterial affliction to be a serious contagion of tuberculous pleurisy – TB – a medieval disease that belonged more to fourteenth-century Europe than the carefree Age of Aquarius and free-lovin' sixties!

There was no time to lose; the doctors had to work fast. Soon I was in bed, bent over a pillow, while they pierced my back with a giant steel syringe and drained the yellowish fluid out of my right lung. As they did so, never will I forget, the DJ on the radio premiered "Lady Madonna," the new single by the Beatles. Thank God! At least it helped me focus on something other than the torture of that needle delving deep between my ribs.

There were no weeping fans outside the hospital, no reporters banging on the door for an "exclusive." My record company and publicist thought it would be bad for my image, so everything was kept hush-hush. The few "get well" cards I received were mostly from family and my inner circle.

Few people knew what had happened; I just disappeared from the scene. Those who knew me closely sent me cards and flowers, which decorated my little private room off Harley Street. Arrangements were made and soon I was transferred to a specialised sanatorium for treatment and convalescence, far out in the countryside – the King Edward VII Hospital in Midhurst, West Sussex. That would be my new solitary address of exile for the next three, long months.

Everyone has a part of them that yearns for that "otherness" of life, that "Somewhere" place where you don't have to suffer irritable neighbours and their unfriendly dogs; where no nasty bosses are telling you what to do; where no unwelcome brown envelopes from His Majesty's tax-collecting services are dropping through your letterbox. It only needs a little push from fate, and suddenly that "otherness" has become your new home. That's what happened to me.

Often, when you're really down and alone without any distractions, you can start to get back in touch with reality again. While I was riding high on the success of my early hits, I felt it necessary to play out the role of a star, and that numbed me to many things. I had lost control of my life. Although I was not seen as the foreigner with the strange-sounding name, an excess of fame and public adoration had led me to become dangerously disconnected.

Changes often happen while you're looking the other way. The compulsions of the music business, the slavish submission to other people's expectations and demands, all had delivered me, neatly packed in my dragon-print pyjamas, to a place I had no idea existed – and where I certainly never dreamed of wanting to be.

The hospital felt more like a prison. Secrets within the medical profession were well kept, like the keys to my ward. Fear of the dark unknown frightened me and I began to contemplate what spooky surprise might come next. Maybe the doctors were keeping back the truth of my inevitable deterioration from me. The thought of death, like my own shadow, was closely following me around. This had really been the case ever since my skinny legs dangled from the rooftop. My morbid imagination ran away with me, and I began to envisage trolleys rolling by my room every day loaded with corpses. My instinct was partly right: I found out some time later that Boris Karloff, the actor who played Herr Frankenstein's "monster," would pass away in the very same hospital – maybe even on the very same mattress! – the following year in 1969.[9]

The daily rounds of injections and temperature readings – along with the clockwork-precision delivery of breakfast, lunch, and dinner – made the days and nights grimly monotonous. Apart from my guitar – and a few pretty nurses – hospitalisation felt more like imprisonment.

My songwriting had more or less come to a halt, and I really didn't want to play my old songs again as they were too closely associated with my downfall. Thank God I had a window out of which I could peer. The search for peace – a place I dreamed of being – became the single most important goal. Fortunately, my friend Paul Ryan, another ardent fan of the Beatles, had become intrigued by the spiritual excursions the mop-head lads were taking, particularly George Harrison. Their whole experience with the Maharishi from India was the subject of much chin-wagging. Donovan was partly responsible for the introduction; he had been floating on a lotus flowerbed for some time.

A natural development out of the "protest" movement was a growing need to do more than shout or complain about the status of the world and the situation we were in. Against the ugliness and background of the Vietnam War, the urge for a state of utopia was mounting within our hearts, and the inward road was looking potentially more promising.

Through a karmic stroke of luck, back in the London Clinic Paul had given me a spiritual book. He knew I was going to have lots of space and time to spare during my hospital jaunt. *The Secret Path* was written by a Buddhist convert, Paul Brunton, and was undoubtedly one of the most important books I had ever been handed. Almost from the first page it talked about the subjects I was most concerned with: Death, the mysterious Self, and the Beyond – the soul's unavoidable journey towards those things hitherto unknown. The pages delved into profound questioning about what the soul actually is, that sense of "I." How often did I ask myself who or what I really was, behind the mask of my external frame and identity? Looking for the truth within my own limited realm and personality and the four walls of my hospital room, I read the following passage:

When man begins to ask himself who he is, then he has taken the first step upon the path which will only end when he has found an answer . . .

"Oh no!" I screamed to myself. How I wished my eyes had never fallen on those words, being as far as any primary journeyer could ever be from answers at that stage on the road to findout. Yet it was precisely that disturbing reaction that was to set me full-throttle on my own secret path.

Buddhism seemed to be a fast track to where I needed to go, spiritually. Though I still had an affinity to God and Jesus, the Bible was too complicated; there were so many rules and ritualistic aspects – although some verses were spiritually clear, others spoke from a perplexing precinct. I had occasionally tried to pick the Bible up since leaving school, but whenever I became inspired and turned the page, it would suddenly change course and reel off detailed numbers or descriptions of family genealogies and other hard-to-memorise names and places. There seemed to be so many diverse angles within it, let alone the fact that it represented two entirely distinct religions: Judaism and Christianity. Science had also made me somewhat sceptical; biblical paradigms appeared to be designed for a more ancient world, less grounded in the "now" I was living.

The Buddhist path seemed much more modern and focused on the improvement of the "self," keeping a check on one's internal thoughts and perceptions. The subject of death was also prominent, as it needed to be to address the whole nature and scope of man's reality – here and beyond.

I began to practise meditation. Breathing consciously,

deeply, more slowly and evenly (which was probably a boon for my decrepit lungs at the same time), I concentrated on the centre of my being, searching the inner space of peaceful detachment from the world.

One ordinary, grey day, while gazing out of my hospital window at the sagging branches of oaks and elms, I spotted a derelict, rusty, brown bus parked on a muddy path in a disused barn area. Sneaking quietly, unnoticed, out of my private hospital room in my nightgown, I made my way down the stairs and outside to the bus to explore. I opened its creaky door and climbed in. Perfectly secluded, sitting on one of the damp-ridden seats, I closed my eyes tight and began to meditate; addressing the question to myself in that mysterious darkness, *Who is this being within my body?*

Somehow, in that strange, un-clinical, centipede-infested, rickety old bus, I slowly lost all sense of bodily attachment, realising my infinite littleness, as if my soul was shrinking fast from this material world. Then, in a timeless space, lasting less than a billionth of a second, I witnessed a bursting bright light shining everywhere at the centre of my focus. The awesomeness of that blinding "big bang" was powerful enough to extinguish my whole personality and take my universe with it. I almost let go . . .

But a silent over-voice stopped me from reaching that far. Almost as quickly as I had lost myself, I was tugged back, sensing it was too soon to leave this world. My questing soul needed to be more certain about where I was going. To the safety of my hospital room I dashed.

Naturally, this experience had opened an amazing new

door. The conscious ascent to a higher state of awareness and spiritual discovery had begun.

> *I think I see the Light,*
> *Coming to me; coming through me*
> *Giving me a second sight*
> *So shine, shine, shine*
> *Shine, shine, shine*
> *Shine, shine, shine* [10]

Following the instructions of my newfound internal voice, I covered all the mirrors in my room with old newspapers in an effort to escape from the gaze of my own ego, to the puzzlement and kindly concern of the nurses who – being discreetly courteous – did not probe me too deeply about it. Soon, after a number of less externally bothered days, I felt the outwardness of the world sinking into the distance . . . and, unintentionally, I had begun to grow a modest beard.

The intensity of my inward journey increased dramatically. It was hard to stop the raging flow of thoughts and ideas from rippling the calm, inner lake of tranquillity I sought. Wherever I found myself, at any moment, I'd try and stop to consider my actions and involvement in the material things around, imagining myself floating ten feet above.

A walk in the rain would suddenly become a lesson in spiritual detachment (very beneficial if you happen to live in the British Isles). On a seemingly ordinary, cloudy English afternoon, I exercised my lungs and took a stroll in the manicured, green leafy grounds of the King Edward VII Hospital. Nearby, there stood some unsterilised, brambly, and more interesting-looking woods. I decided to head towards the shadowy hollows of the thick trees and bushes. No sooner had I reached them than a very large raindrop landed on my face. The clouds grew dark and tense. Drop by drop the rain started, and quickly it became a downpour.

Fearful of becoming drenched, I turned around and made a dash for the safety of the sanatorium. The rain pelted heavily. I was getting breathless from running – then suddenly the thought hit me: *Stop! I am not getting soaked at all!* The conscious "I" within was perfectly dry and not getting the slightest bit wet. Wow, my Zen-pop approach to enlightenment was not going to come by sitting cross-legged and meditating, after all. Who should care? I didn't have a spiritual guru or "master," but it felt like I was getting somewhere.

I strolled back slowly, leisurely, and soaked – to the obvious bewilderment of my fellow patients, who gazed bemusedly as I entered the lounge, my hair and clothes drenched and dripping. It was difficult to communicate to others what was going on inside me. This was my top-secret induction into the art of Zen.

The hospital was quite a drive from London, and I received very few visitors. Mum only managed to come once. So you can imagine my surprise when Andrew Loog Oldham drove up the pebble road in his long, black, shiny Rolls-Royce for a little, respectful visit. I was determined not to lose my presence of mind.

Andrew had wanted to sign me to Immediate Records for some time. He had already expressed admiration for my writing skills, and P. P. Arnold had done very well on his label with my song "The First Cut Is the Deepest." We rode around the country lanes for about an hour, as the discreet chauffeur kept his eyes on the bends, avoiding the bumps and dips as best he could. Andrew offered me a puff of his reefer. I refrained and apologised, explaining that I was on a health trip. We returned and bade farewell at the gates of the hospital, and I went back to bed, slightly dizzied, but not thrown off track.

Maybe the meeting with Andrew was the external stimulation I needed. I now yearned to go back home and get on with my life. After almost three months of confinement, I'd had enough. The doctors tried to insist that I should stay put in bed a further month or so, but I was going to have none of that. I wanted my freedom back – now!

One afternoon, with the resoluteness of a convict, teeth clenched and preparing for the great escape, I opened the cupboard, dressed myself, packed a small bag with a towel, a tin of pineapple I'd purchased at the hospital store, a penknife, and other little necessities, then strolled calmly out of the hospital doors into the thick country forest.

Not knowing where the road would lead, I was happy just to get out of that suffocating, red-brick prison into open nature again. I continued for an hour or so till I came across a stone farmhouse with a wooden barnyard garage. I sneaked in and climbed up a ladder into the loft area where firewood was stored in piles. I used some cardboard to prepare my bed for the night and lay down.

It was slowly getting dark, and the sun was about to set when I heard the sound of a car approaching. I ducked down and tried to stay as quiet as possible. A man in a tweed jacket and hat parked his car, switched off the engine, shut the door, and then went straight into the house.

So far, so good! I thought to myself.

As darkness fell, I drifted off to sleep, content that this little escapade would prove to those "daft" medics that I was fit and able enough to leave.

The next day I woke up at dawn, my whole body aching. One night was enough in that cramped hideaway. When everything looked clear, I climbed down and continued walking through the forest. As I did so, there was a terrifically loud barrage of sirens passing along the road nearby. I rushed over to take a peep from behind the trees and saw a trail of police motorcycles and cars speeding fast along the country road. They were obviously hot on the trail of something or someone – probably me!

When the sirens died down, I realised – as there were no more provisions in my little bag – the time had come to end my rebellious stakeout. Rambling through the hedges and fields, I slowly headed back to the hospital grounds.

Point made.

When entering the lobby of King Edward's just before midday, everything seemed quiet and normal; there were no police around. I headed straight to the registrar's office. Facing the unsuspecting lady behind the desk, I calmly told her, "I'm Mr. Stevens, and I am now ready to leave."

She looked confused. Without saying anything, she put her head down and fumbled with some papers.

"I'm going back to my room; if you need to check me over, you can. Please inform the doctors. I'm ready to go home."

Early the next morning, a couple of doctors arrived in my room and – as Englishmen do so well – acted as if nothing had occurred. They casually checked the medical sheets attached to my bed and informed me that I could leave the following day. They would provide me with the name and address of a hospital in Wandsworth and put me in touch with a specialist doctor in London, Mr. Tear, who would check me regularly and provide any medications I needed.

It was a moment of victory! I had demonstrated my self-determination. That marked the beginning of a new era, one of inner strength and an illuminated sense of independence.

> *Oh I'm on my way I know I am*
> *Somewhere not so far from here*
> *All I know is all I feel right now*
> *I feel the power growing in my hair*[11]

My return to Shaftesbury Avenue was a welcome relief for the family; I felt like the unknown soldier draped in blood-stained bandages, returning home after a loathsome war. In my case it had been a hellish three-month defensive battle for my earthly future, which I was still fighting within the borders of my bony, fragile frame.

The doctors told me to relax and not do any hard work for at least a year. They gave me some horrendously large horse-sized tablets, streptomycin, which I would have to swallow two of daily until everything was clear. Hey, no sweat. The past was fading like a bad dream and I was starting a new adventure, bearded, fully chastened, and inspired by the inner journey that had been initiated in my hospital temple.

Mum was so happy, she spoiled me rotten and I was able to taste her delicious scrambled eggs in bed again! Dad was pleased, his "sonny boy" was back. He now let me have a whole second-floor studio room to myself, overlooking New Oxford Street. I immediately painted it bright red and covered the floor with a seductive wall-to-wall, long-haired white carpet, transforming the space into the grooviest bachelor pad any young guy could dream of. Here was to be the home of my new musical genesis, where I would write some of my most quintessential songs.

The Redroom
1969

THE WORLD WAS in a major phase of upheaval: Sean Connery stopped being James Bond; the Beatles were falling apart; the Cold War was revving up with cosmonauts and astronauts engaged in a race, competing in a countdown to "conquer" the moon.

But back home, in the sanctuary of my little Redroom, I was inspired. My period in the hospital had given me space and the powerful incentive to release myself from the persona that had been diabolically placed on me by the demanding zookeepers of the music industry. It was time to explore a new sense of freedom.

My lyrics were now becoming deeper, and far more meaningful, at least to me. I didn't have any managers or record executives to tell me what to do. I was unchained and master of my own zone, ready to sound off my ideas the way I heard them: raw and straight from the vault of my heart.

There had always been a gap between the music I wanted to make and the sounds produced on record for Deram. My rough demos always seemed to sound closer to home than the end "product." When I next stepped into a studio, the guitar had to be played by me, not a paid session musician.

"Where Are You" was a song I'd written and desperately wanted to record as a single. I was still contractually obligated to Decca and signed to Mike's management company, and decided to give it one more go. I talked it over with Mike and told him the kind of French, melancholy mood it needed.

We booked into Olympic Studios in Barnes to record it. My voice and acoustic six-string, complemented by an arpeggio harpsichord piano, were dominant. The strings remained subtle, beneath the surface, like an unobtrusive canvas displaying the bold colours and curves of the romantic subject. The approach revealed a much more sensitive core within my music. This was a real, uncluttered me. Clouds of layered sounds and the overcrowded instrumentation were gone; it felt like a new day was beginning to break.

The words of "Where Are You" unconsciously seemed to spell out my yearning for a "companion" spirit. My shipwrecked musical dream needed to be rescued by someone who I instinctively knew was out there, "across the raging torrent of the sea," and who was also looking to find me. The loneliness of life as a castaway on the barren island of hallucinations needed to end.

The "comeback" record didn't really do very well. But the new, minimalist approach was a taste of what my future musical identity would eventually evolve into. The single ended up being my last collaboration and recording with

Mike Hurst as producer. I also needed a way out of the management contracts my former shadow was bound to.

"Dave, I'm broke."

"What do you mean?" David asked.

"I'm down to my last few thousand. Can you help?"

My brother was always my shrewd backroom advisor. He had seen first-hand the disintegration of my physical body and shrinking career as a result of hanging around in the wrong company. Maybe he felt a bit guilty for unwittingly contributing in some part to the sorry situation I was in. Agents and management had effectively licked the cream off my dwindling income through their commissions and added expenses, leaving me with the tab for everything, including press agents, travel, hotels, the band, equipment – and my withering Carnaby Street wardrobe.

Truth is, as with most artists, my contract terms were notoriously weighted heavily in the managers' and agents' favour. Even the Beatles were only getting a couple of pennies per record. Decca was giving me about the same; it was obvious this "cat" was being skinned.

Savvy ol' Dave began to help again, as he had done a couple of years before when I needed to get out of the agreement with EMI's West One agency. On that occasion, he had set up a dramatic scene whereby Dad stormed into the Manchester Square offices of Arthur Muxlow and thumped his fist on the table: "My son, Stevie, must-a come back to the shop to work!" Thud!

The contract ended there and then.

My big brother's ingenuity was unparalleled in such cases

of emergency. If he couldn't solve the problem himself, he'd find someone who could. David began searching for a lawyer.

Maurice Press, our old business partner from Doric Management, came to the rescue and recommended a local guy, Oscar Beuselinck. Oscar was a loud, boisterous solicitor, short, bulk-bellied, and a powerful showbiz expert. He operated from offices in Bloomsbury Square, just around the corner from our café. He wore a dark, pinstriped suit that seemed to be always slipping off his shoulder, complete with brown shirt armbands. His thick-rimmed glasses perched halfway down his nose – presumably to read contracts while keeping an eye on his client's expression as his attractive secretary served coffee. Being from the area, Oscar fondly referred to himself, David, and me as the "Holborn Boys." We bonded well.

After reading my contract with Mike Hurst and Chris Brough, which to me was like a life sentence, he crumpled it up and threw it in the bin! "What contract?" he roared.

Mr. Beuselinck was the man to break the shackles of my pop-music internment. His confidence was unmatched by anything my managers could do. Oscar was so hot in court: he argued that my parents were foreign and never understood the contract they had signed on my behalf; that my career was going nowhere (absolutely true); and that I was back working in the café with just a couple of thousand pounds to my name.

"But look at what he was earning before?" pleaded Mike.

"Immaterial," quipped Oscar. A single court appearance and it was over.

From that day I called him "Battling Beuselinck" and I wrote a song for him, which he loved. Oscar was a true showman – and so was his son, Paul Nicholas, who ended up in the lead role of *Hair*, imported direct from Broadway and about to open right across the road from our shop at the Shaftesbury (formerly, Princes) Theatre. What a scoop!

Let the sunshine in! *Hair* was an overwhelming hit. The war in Vietnam was finally taking its toll on the American psyche, and *Hair* was a young American critique of the whole ideology behind the grotesque project. It represented the best of the sixties' philosophy and shattered all taboos of theatrical rules; at one point the whole cast slowly appeared out of the shadows and stood at the front of the stage – fully naked! The audience was invited to feel part of the act and allowed on stage for the "Be-in" finale: everybody was equal, everybody was a "star."

Hair broke the mould and heralded a new zeitgeist in which the youthful revolution stood up in the name of freedom. An end to conscription and wars seemed possible. Fresh ideas were our weapons. For me, it was a powerful reminder of how musicals could encapsulate the radical mood of the time and help define it.

The call for liberation from the well-mown, silent cemeteries of theatrical conformism blasted out in my ears nightly. The fact that the show was playing just a few yards across the road from me meant I couldn't escape its impact; proximity made me feel part of the anti-war movement. I was almost ready to jump up on stage and join right in.

"Ain't Got No, I Got Life," a new single by Nina Simone taken from the musical, carried another powerful message. The lyrics remind us that even if we don't have shoes, clothes or money, sweets, mothers or land, we still have hair, bones,

9 | *The Redroom*

minds, hearts, livers, blood – we have "life" itself. Having just survived TB and feeling acutely conscious of the gift of still being around, I realised there was a beautiful chance for a new beginning. The optimistic sentiment undoubtedly influenced a yet-to-be-song called "Moonshadow."

Feeling much better and rapidly regaining my health, I reconnected with my old partying chums, Paul and Barry Ryan. They were still very much on the prowl. I'd visit them at their stepfather's flat in Grosvenor Square. Their mother, Marion Ryan, was married to Harold Davison, the top agent in Britain, who had the proud distinction of introducing Frank Sinatra to Europe. Personal pictures of Harold with Frank and Sammy Davis Jr. were hanging all over the flat.

One time, while visiting the boys there, I met Juliette, Barry's latest. She was dark-haired, of a Turkish background, and rode a Vespa scooter. Juliette worked part-time evenings as a bunny at Hugh Hefner's Playboy club in Mayfair – one look at her, and you could easily see why she got the job! I was enthralled, and in time managed to woo her away from Barry.

We had a lot of great times together, dancing to the new prince of funk, Sly and the Family Stone, in the Cromwellian club, which became our nightly destination. We were both strong-headed characters, and she always kept an air of independence, diving on her little scooter and whizzing off after we had a tiff. Juliette was ambitious and trying to survive in a very tough environment, and I was becoming more dedicated to my new music.

*

Lots of exciting and inspired things were happening up in my little Redroom. Next to my bed I had a custom-designed side cupboard that housed my record player and vinyl collection. My musical tastebuds were exploding with albums and artists like Walter Carlos's *Switched-On Bach*, the Band's *Music from Big Pink*, the Doors' *Strange Days*, Love, Richie Havens, Nina Simone, the operatic *Misa Criolla*, Muddy Waters, and so on. I would go to sleep at night playing some of those favourite LPs on automatic mode with my ultraviolet wall lights illuminating my white, woolly carpet, turning the room into a snowy, Disneyesque dreamscape.

My music was going through an organic rebirth; my fascination for seeking out the purpose behind my existence meant I was writing lyrics like never before. Where did they come from? Well, there was no time to think about that – I was too busy writing them. I booked myself into a demo studio on Tottenham Court Road and started recording a whole huddle of newly written songs. Some of them were decidedly quirky and left field; I found it hard to stop the urge to dream up theatrical stories and song structures due to the brooding West End composer bottled up within me.

But there was a new strain of songwriting that began to emerge from my self-taught guitar technique, replacing the complicated, jagged compositional style that was formerly my hallmark. I was coming to a point where it became clear that I was poised at a cliff's edge, looking at a new musical horizon in front of me. The clothes I wore also reflected my own folk-style persona. No more velvet suits or frilly shirts. I was now bearded, leaning towards a distinctively hippified wardrobe, totally relaxed in my T-shirts, jeans, and Indian suede boots.

> *Miles from nowhere*
> *Guess I'll take my time*
> *Oh yeah, to reach there*
> *Look up at the mountain,*
> *I have to climb*
> *Oh yeah, to reach there*[12]

Although my hands were still locked in the rigid stocks of an archaic contract with Decca and Mr. Dick (Dickensian) Rowe, I was at last free from my old-school managers and agents, which meant my next step was to find some logistical support for my career. I looked for a higher grade of imaginative management. *Hair* had rejuvenated my love of theatre, and the feeling would not go away. I needed someone who could perhaps help me fulfill my hope of writing a musical; after all, that was my goal before I got sucked into the pop-star juicer. I was even toying with the idea of becoming an actor.

David came to my aid again. After listening to my new ideas, he walked me back to Bloomsbury Square. Old Beuselinck was ready to come to my rescue, "I know just the guy for you!" Barry Krost was a theatrical agent and manager whose roster of actors and playwrights included Peter Finch, Sheila Hancock, and John Osborne.

At our first meeting I was a little overawed by his suave appearance and posh accent. His offices on Albemarle Street off Piccadilly were much classier than Mike's old dive in

Kingly Street; the expensive art canvases on the walls, the pinkish-grey carpet, antique leather couches, and Cartier pens all reeked of panache.

Barry certainly had style and was incredibly entertaining. Although he didn't know much about the record business, the bright, budding impresario could probably hum a few of my songs – quite out of tune, of course. Mr. Krost was intrigued by the prospect of breaking into the music world. We both had very little to lose. And so began a business relationship and friendship that took us both to the pinnacle of our respective careers.

Before going any further, though, I still had a big obstacle with my record company, Decca, who wanted me to stick to recording singles. They were keeping me back while I was radiating ideas and needing to expand my palette and explore more of the musical cosmos. I couldn't do so while still tied down long-term to recording only singles.

It was time now to ditch Decca. The Moody Blues had recently recorded a successful, full-length, conceptual album called *Days of Future Passed* on Deram with the London Festival Orchestra. I don't know who came up with the plot (probably Dave), but Barry was primed to suddenly demand Deram provide the same treatment for me. He rehearsed his lines and set off to meet Dick Rowe at the Decca offices. He sat down and began to explain the "brilliant new idea" of a whole concept album by "Cat," recorded with the chorus and hundred-piece orchestra of the Royal Opera House at Covent Garden. No expense spared. That was enough for Dick to say, "Ta-ta." He signed a letter releasing me from my contract, not wanting any part of this crazily ambitious project. The outlandish trick worked – at last, I was out!

The doors were open for me to go wherever I wanted.

Having written a short children's story with five new songs about a gypsy boy called Dixie, I excitedly presented it to Barry, together with a small watercolour illustration that I had painted. My idea was to write a full scripted musical adventure based on this little, magically gifted character and his travelling companion, a naughty chimpanzee.

The illustration showed Dixie in a bright red beret sitting at the feet of a wise, old, white-bearded Russian peasant, who was handing the young boy a magic medallion; in the background gypsies danced around the campfire. Barry loved the illustration but was smart enough to see I needed some big help with the script. It wasn't long before he convinced me to consider basing it on an already well-known story: Tsar Nicholas II and Alexandra, and the revolution that brought down the Romanovs! Perhaps it was Barry's Jewish, partly Russian, immigrant background coupled with the illustration that led him to the idea, but my imagination lit up.

I was introduced to Nigel Hawthorne, an actor and writer who later became a household name through his British comedy series *Yes Minister*. We hit it off creatively and started meeting in his studio flat on Elgin Crescent and sketching the plot. Following those sessions, I'd return to my "Cat cave" on Shaftesbury Avenue and work on the songs. That's where I dreamed up a name for the musical: *Revolussia*.

Songwriting was often a transcendent experience for me; melodies would come out of a mood I was in and lead me to a secret place that my inner ear longed to hear again; I'd follow wherever it took me. Lyrics would usually flow after that. The technique was mostly freeform, I didn't have any fixed formula. Sometimes I might begin by experimenting with a few different chord sequences on guitar or piano, until a tune stood out and made itself known. Words wise, I would start with an interesting title or a line I'd written; failing that, I would sing a whole bunch of rhyming babble or vowels until a sentence magically formed itself together – enough to make sense – recording it all as I went along. I'd work on the song until it was complete, then lay it down beginning to end on tape. Only rarely would I start with a page of prewritten lyrics.

Following a dramatic storyline forced me to approach writing differently for *Revolussia* – I now had to conform to some rules. I would lean head down at the white, built-in desk in the corner of my Redroom and write down some words to accompany the dialogue of a scene. Then I'd pick up my guitar, play some chords, and see what melody might be secretly lurking inside. One of the key songs I wrote was specifically for an important character in the musical, a young man called Sasha. His dream was to escape the slow-moving drudgery of rural Russian life to join the march of the powerful Red Revolution – quite possibly a mirror of my own soul's state at the beginning of this new, unmapped era. The boy's father, however, was comfortable with exactly the way things were, and wanted his only son to remain with him on the farm, get married and forget about the idea of trying to change the world.

Chords seemed to emerge naturally, following the pattern

of the lyrics I'd written. I settled on one of my favourite keys, moving from G to D major, until I discovered another inversion – G to B minor! I named it "'Father and Son."

> *Father:*
> *It's not time to make a change*
> *Just relax, take it easy*
> *You're still young, that's your fault*
> *There's so much you have to go through*
> *Find a girl, settle down,*
> *If you want you can marry*
> *Look at me, I am old, but I'm happy*

I'd always loved Slavic male choir music, maybe because it was close to my Greek Orthodox memory soundtrack. So, a lot of the ethnic mood of the music felt natural. The national anthem of *Revolussia* really captured that very macho, revolutionary spirit. Tchaikovsky was also a favourite composer of mine – previously I'd stolen a part of his *1812 Overture* as the intro to one of my late, unsuccessful Deram singles, "Here Comes My Wife."

Nigel was busy typing away, getting the script into shape. I'm sure he had other acting demands, but he seemed devoted to our project. We spent long hours bouncing ideas around; my untrained lyrical imagination certainly helped out here and there. In addition to Tsar Nicholas and his weakling son, Alexis, mentored by a darkly wicked Rasputin, we had some real comical caricatures of Lenin, Trotsky, and Stalin. "Him, You and Me" was a baroque song I wrote for them:

TROTSKY: *I will build a mountain.*
STALIN: *I will build three!*
TROTSKY: *Mine will be higher than –*
LENIN (snidely): *. . . another 5-year plan?*
TROTSKY: *All the hats of Samarqand the world has seen.*
STALIN: *Fine!*
TROTSKY: *Fine!*
LENIN: *But my secret weapon will keep you both in line . . . just give me time.*

Nigel and I bawled with laughter as comical scenes with Lenin, Trotsky, and Stalin played out, adding my goonish humour to the mix (evident on the demos I recorded at the time). Everything was going well with the writing, the songs were flowing, but the problem was – and was always going to be – bankrolling! Musicals are notoriously costly and high-risk ventures; we needed serious backing. So Barry arranged for me to meet a man called John Pringle in his town house at Montpelier Square, Knightsbridge.

Pringle was famous for owning a hotel in Montego Bay, where the likes of J. F. K., Alfred Hitchcock, and Ralph Lauren took off for private, undisturbed holidays. Looking around at this guy's luxurious London residence, it was obvious he was pretty endowed, but prudent too. After I played a few of the songs and explained the script, he decided to discreetly pass on the project, but then arranged a meeting with his friend Chris Blackwell – also from Jamaican colonial aristocracy – who was doing exceptionally well in the music business with a company called Island Records.

We set off to meet at Chris's house in Holland Park, a leafy part of London populated by many well-to-do entrepreneurs. I had brought my guitar and plodded through the *Revolussia* story with him. After tea I played some of the songs from the musical. When I got to "Father and Son," I could see his eyes crinkle; he was moved. Chris skilfully wound out of discussing anything too serious about our grand plan to bring the Russian Revolution to the West End stage. He had another idea cooking.

It wasn't long before we met again in his offices at Basing Street, off Portobello Road. This was new ground for me, even though I'd written a song with Kim Fowley about the famous market road. Portobello came to life on weekends when the wooden stalls were rolled out to offer everything from imitation diamond brooches and silver letter openers to remnants of the British Empire – drums and fraying flags – and the occasional old stuffed bull.

Island Records' offices and studios were a hive of authentic music of diverse genres; reggae from Jimmy Cliff and British rock from Mott the Hoople, as well as Chris's longtime association with Steve Winwood and Traffic and folky Fairport Convention. They were all at home on their famously "pink" label. They also distributed Chrysalis Records' Jethro Tull albums, absolutely one of my favourite-sounding groups.

Barry was just coasting; he could see the interest in me growing and so we made a tentative management agreement for 10 percent. Chris had probably alerted him to the fact that, as a recording artist, I had a much better chance of success than flogging the musical idea. Hey, I was up for anything! Even though it wasn't in my plan, I'd never turn down an opportunity like this. Island Records was a hip place to be and it suited my edgy, unbuttoned personality.

A far cry from Decca, Chris gave talented artists full rein over their music and he just stood back, listened, and smiled as records started selling. This was the second time around for me. Wow! Maybe this was going to be the real Island of Dreams I had been waiting for. But whatever the future held, I was not going to be blown away so easily and went into it with my eyes open. While my inner "I" was still groping around for eternal answers about life, for now, this would certainly do.

> *Well I'm gonna be a pop star*
> *Yes I'm gonna be a pop star*
> *Yes I'm gonna be a pop star*
> *Oh Mama! Mama, see me,*
> *Mama, Mama see me I'm a pop star* [13]

As Clouds Parted
1969–70

DURING THIS PERIOD of re-orbitation, I gently descended into the caustic stratosphere of the harsh commercial world TB had forced me out of. My relationship with Juliette had sadly waned and I was lonely. Barry Ryan was still a good contact at such critical moments and he introduced me to Patti D'Arbanville. She was a beautiful American girl with a European background. Patti had just gained a bit of notoriety from being cast by Andy Warhol a couple of years earlier at the tender age of sixteen in his erotic film *Flesh*. I fell in love with her. Fortunately for me, Barry was not worried. He had many other girls in tow. So Patti and I started dating.

Patti lived in Chelsea, just off the King's Road in Draycott Place. She lodged in a ground-floor flat with a Norwegian girl called Kirsten. We would go out to the Bag O'Nails club and dance the nights away with Kirsten and whoever her latest acquaintance might be. Patti loved my delicious Redroom and got to know my family really well. Mum liked her a lot, and she fitted in nicely.

We shared some real special times together. A memorable one was the night I invited Paul and Barry with their girlfriends to join me and Patti in the Redroom to witness the moon landing on TV. It was quite a wondrous night as it also happened to be my twenty-first birthday. What a gift. Midnight had passed on 21 July, 1969; 2.56 a.m. GMT was the moment that man first leaped and hopped around on the moon. We all held our breath as we watched history unfold, then heard the crackly voice of Armstrong uttering those immortal words, ". . . a giant step for mankind!" It added to my mystical attachment to that zodiacal symbol, as my sign was already Cancer, ruled by the moon!

Not long after, Chris Blackwell (another loony Cancerian) arranged a meeting with potential producer Paul Samwell-Smith. I was already impressed because Paul was an icon in his own right, being the original bass player with the Yardbirds. They were one of the most innovative bands of the sixties, with their roots in R & B. Paul had produced some adventurous recordings by the Yardbirds, co-writing avant-garde songs like "Shapes of Things," a hit single in 1966. I'd seen them live and danced to their vibration back then in the 100 Club on Oxford Street.

Paul had recently produced an interesting album with a British progressive group called Renaissance, a sort of space-echoey version of Fairport Convention, but still very original. It had a warm, acoustically natural feel about the production, rather English, which I liked.

When I met with Paul in Dad's café, we seemed to hit it

off. He was a tweedy, tall, skinny chap with a distinct public school accent – totally dissimilar to me with my West End version of a cockney twang. He was probably hesitant and not too sure about what to expect from this one-time teeny-bopper, velvet-suited, pop pin-up has-been. But Paul soon clocked that I had matured beyond recognition from that past demeanour. I'd survived a close scrape with death and delved into metaphysics and spirituality – sporting a "Jesus"-style beard as evidence to prove it.

All that was made clear to him during the formalities of our introduction. But it was the songs that mattered, and he wanted to hear them. So I invited him up to my Redroom. He gingerly tiptoed over my ashtrays, instruments, record sleeves and tapes lying around on the floor, until he found a space to sit. Then I sat and played him my new songs and a few little unfinished riffs and melodies. Paul was truly fascinated, and desired to go further.

Next was an intimate one-on-one at his pad in a block of flats off Regent's Park. He was married to a fine lady called Rosie, who introduced herself and discreetly disappeared after serving tea and biscuits.

I must have had twenty or so songs finished, which I played with passion on my black Everly guitar, eyes shut, cross-legged on the carpet – that's how I felt most comfortable. "Miles from Nowhere," "Trouble," "Father and Son," "Katmandu," and "Maybe You're Right" were on the song list. Paul may have been haemorrhaging with excitement on the inside yet, like a true British gent, even in his most animated and ecstatic moments he still appeared cool, calm, and reserved. "Pass the biscuits."

I strummed the chords of "Lilywhite," re-enacting my rescue from that tormenting inferno by some ethereal snow-like, genderless angel. I sang with the heartfelt sincerity of that scorched and weary vagrant, thankful to have managed to escape from the jaws of those hallucinatory flames. Paul twitched. "Fill My Eyes," with its whimsical lyrics and madrigal melody, conclusively and successfully sealed the audition.

I had won over the ears of an important new fan: a brilliant, sensitive musician-producer, one who could capture the intimacy of my songs in the same pure, organic way I had delivered them on that afternoon. He must've understood – this was no ordinary comeback.

Paul had been a fan of Joni Mitchell and Bob Dylan for some time and was very into the acoustic genre. Famously, it was good ol' Paul Samwell-Smith who was responsible for introducing Bob to the Beatles during the group's Christmas Show at the Hammersmith Odeon back in the early sixties. That jingly night, Paul carted the latest Bob Dylan LP, *Another Side of Bob Dylan*, up to the Beatles' dressing room and played it to John Lennon. That was the first time he had heard it. History.

Samwell-Smith's great knack for picking up musical breakthroughs was still intact. He lifted out a copy of *Astral Weeks* by Van Morrison, his spindly fingers carefully placing the stylus down on the black groove. "Listen to this." He was obviously desirous to follow something of the free-flowing, improvised dynamics and wooden acoustic bass and guitar feel of that milestone album. Listening to "Madame George" through Paul's Tannoy speakers, it sounded so real; you

CAT ON THE ROAD TO FINDOUT

could almost visually walk into the song and meet the lady herself.

Following this, Chris Blackwell must have chatted with Paul and felt satisfied that he was not alone in his gut instinct. After some spasmodic demo experiments in Advision Studios, Fitzrovia, involving only myself and guitar, a contract was drawn up. On the basis of the songs we had tested, Paul pulled together a group of handpicked musicians and booked our first session at Olympic Studios, Barnes, famous for most of the Rolling Stones' early recordings (and, ironically, the studio I'd used for my swansong single recording with Mike Hurst). The studio had since acquired a shiny new sixteen-track Studer machine, with Dolby, a totally revolutionary "hiss"-compressing technology, and that's what Paul desperately wanted to get his hands on.

My time with Patti D'Arbanville was still hot. We were exploring the night scene: clubs, cinema, restaurants, and the occasional wild party. One of our rampant, jaunty moments happened on the Marble Arch roundabout at high speed in my swanky white Mercedes Coupé. Patti and her friend were precariously trying to balance themselves while holding hands on top of my car hood, swigging the dregs of a bottle of wine seized from the club we'd just visited. A police car immediately screeched up and pulled us over. The bobby delivered a stern warning and booked me, which led me to court, apologising for the incident and promising not to do it again. This was the tail end of the sixties, after all.

The problem was that Patti was a model and often had to skip off to photo sessions and appointments, which drove me nuts. Thoughts of her posing provocatively for some half-shaven, randy fashion photographer bloke boiled my blood on those solitary nights she wasn't there. A jealous and tragic Greek side of me soon expressed itself through an intensely felt, mortifying ode to a love lost: "Lady D'Arbanville."

Studio 2 in Olympic was where I first met Alun Davies. He had stark blond hair and stood out like a gentle Welsh giant. Despite his massive, tree-like hands, his acoustic guitar picking was impeccable and so delicate. Where I was painting broad, silk brushstrokes with my guitar chords, Alun filled in the complementary colour and minute detail. The end picture was full of vibrancy, dimension, and depth. "Lady D'Arbanville" became a marvellous exhibit of our unique euphonic friendship.

Harvey Burns was one of the most sensitive, jazz-trained drummers – admittedly he was probably high most of the time, but it gave him an intuitive feel, which made the kit sound like another layer of lyrical punctuation, raising and lowering the levitation of the song, like legendary Merlin waving his magic drumsticks.

Then there was John Ryan, an Australian double-bass player. John was a very timid character whose notes fitted the songs like a glove; you hardly noticed him as he huddled behind his enormous acoustic bass, peeking through the glass partitions for any indication of an emotional change.

Thank God! Gone were the days of printed music sheets and trade-unified, clock-watching musicians. I now had an intimate band of friends to help capture my songs in the most organic, unpretentious, informal way. Paul was behind the desk in the control room watching the chief engineer, Andy Johns, fiddling with the Dolby. The resulting sound was that much more up-close, but without the irritating white noise that low-level acoustic and classical records commonly suffered from.

With only this group of three guys, I swung back and forth from guitar to piano and organ, then tambourine or handclaps, overdubbing where really necessary. The arrangements were bare and frighteningly honest. A lot of the songs were recorded live, the best requiring four or five takes – once everybody had got used to the odd time changes. There were some songs that didn't come off as well as I wanted, like "Wild World." So it was put on the shelf to ripen in some other session. But something magical was happening, and everybody – including the assistant engineer who never stopped making tea except when the red light was on – felt it.

Del Newman was the arranger for the recordings, a soft-spoken and lovable man, Jamaican-Irish in origin, with a genius for understatement. We did the overdubs later at the same studio. The playbacks were sensational, especially "Lilywhite," the strings of which floated into the song like a snowy-white flutter of celestial birds winging their way upwards through the clouds before dissolving into silent nothingness.

The only other musician to play on the album was Peter Gabriel, who came in for a short flute appearance on "Katmandu." He was a very thin, shy guy, almost unnoticeable if he turned sideways. Paul knew him and invited him along for this pensive and lyrically picturesque song.

The album also included "Trouble," a metaphor for TB and that whole dangerous episode that I had endured. It was like a ghost that still languished around in the vicinity of my overly X-rayed lungs. Its Southern swamp-ish melody leaned towards the Band's great . . . *Big Pink* album – still a massive favourite of mine. "Trouble" was also in a strange key, one I hardly used: F sharp. Musical keys can bring about an unexpected timbre and sentiment in the weird magical process of songwriting.

The overall result of those sessions at Olympic was groundbreaking. Chris Blackwell went overboard with excitement, which was only diminished very slightly by the realisation that his favourite song, "Father and Son," hadn't made it onto the master session tapes. Nevertheless, everyone at Island was jumping. But what was to be the name and cover of this album?

For some time I had in my mind "Journey to Jog," a kind of reference to imply that old Cat was not dead, and here was a new album to "jog" people's memories. But hardly anybody got it. Then I had a meeting with Chris to discuss possible cover designs; at that point he simply glanced at me and said, "Why don't you do it? You're good at art." He knew I was a little clever with the brush and thought that this could be a unique addition to the personal feel of the album. I was choked. At last, it was a chance to create the full, first-hand, personal portrait of my music and art for listeners to enter, listen, breathe, touch, and fill their minds with.

I tried out a few black ink and watercolour ideas and finally came up with something nobody would expect. It was a picture of a weeping dustbin! Why? I don't know, but after sketching and detailing the bin with pen line shading and soft water blots, it seemed . . . kinda right. The original title was "The Dustbin Cried the Day the Dustman Died." But that was too long. Then I had the flash of an idea; one of the songs on the album was called "Mona Bone Jakon," a gutsy, echo-sounding blues track. It was a lyrically saucy allusion to a somewhat sexually frustrated guy, similar to Muddy Waters's "Got My Mojo Working," if you like. That idea stuck.

We gave the teary dustbin a powder-blue background, and the job was almost done, apart from the reverse side of the cover, that is. The poppy Deram LPs had photographs, but they were neither Island's nor my style – that was not going to happen. But I did agree to use a shot of me through a reflection on a rain puddle in Bloomsbury Square (upside down).

Patti and I had essentially split up without anything specific being said. The awful, sickly feeling of not knowing if I was being cheated on while she was working abroad left me with little option but to let her drift. The success and satisfaction I found in building my music career gave me enough things to think about, anyway. Ironically, though, everybody at Island was convinced that "Lady D'Arbanville" should be the first single. It was destined to be the postscript to our relationship, which meant her name was never going to disappear, never quite willing to "go gentle into that good night."

When next I happened to speak to her, she was somewhere over in the States; I played her a bit of the song over the phone, not quite attuned to how macabre the lyrics might have sounded. But we didn't need to argue anymore.

My Lady D'Arbanville
Why does it grieve me so, but your heart seems so silent
Why do you breathe so low, why do you breathe so low
I loved you my Lady
Though in your grave you lie
I'll always be with you, this rose will never die

There was a mutual admiration society going on in those days between emerging singer-songwriters. We were all probably listening to one another's records from behind private walls, but not quite publicly owning up to how much we liked them. Neil Young, Joni Mitchell, Stevie Wonder, James Taylor, all rising out of the shadows of a broken hearts fan club following the break-up of the Beatles in 1970. Elton John was playing beautiful songs on piano with Bernie Taupin's lyrics always original and highly poetic. We all admired each other's work and occasionally bumped into each other here and there along the road.

Elton once dropped in to help me with a duet on one of my early demos before he recorded his classic "Your Song." A mutual friend, Lionel Conway, who ran my new publishing company, Freshwater Music Ltd., arranged the session. The song, "Honey Man," was a potential hit for someone, I thought, and Elton was still available for sessions at the time before the success of his second album. The song finally saw the light of day three decades later on a four-CD box set.

Things were revving up for my new album. *Mona Bone Jakon* was reviewed before its release: "If anyone should be intimidated into believing that James Taylor and family are 'where it's at,' let him listen to Cat Stevens, an English singer-composer of Greek descent, whose style and intonations are so strong as to be almost tactile."

There was great excitement. I was now lined up to do interviews. *Melody Maker* was *The Times* of the music business, but it had not said a good word about me for a long time, because of my history and its elitist musical attitude. I was not convinced things would change. Regretfully, my relationship with certain segments of the press had never been a happy one. Reminiscences of the sixties still stalked my memory. Explaining the inner workings of musical inspiration was an impracticable task. There was something of a brick rampart that separated the artist's creative processes and his or her ability to explain or describe what they had just done. That certainly was my problem back then, as the nervous note-scribbling journalist sipped the froth off a freshly poured pint in a smoky Fleet Street pub and probed me for deeper insight: "So . . . what are your ten most favourite and ten worst things?"

You can imagine what one of the not-so-repeatable ones was!

Ever since the days of "Matthew & Son," I always felt insecure lying submissively down on the couch or operating table and submitting myself to fidgety psychologists and surgeons of the printed word; I could almost see blood dripping from the keys of their typewriters as they stabbed out my lame verbal responses.

Maybe deep down I just hated criticism; it dampened my enthusiasm for what I actually believed in – which was me.

10 | *As Clouds Parted*

Usually, when I got to read the final article, it was like reading about someone else – and that meant one of two things: either the journalist didn't understand me, or I was unable to articulate and express my thoughts and feelings coherently. Frustrating. Maybe I had an inferiority complex due to an inadequate, chequered education: my mind went blurry when being confronted with a difficult question – that was the reason I only ever passed one exam, in art! Whatever. I continued to dread interviews.

To add to my resistance to media examination, back in the day, Mike Hurst had encouraged me to appear hard-to-get and elusive; he warned me about being seen around too much, and generally suggested that I try and look cool. He also might have clocked – after reading a few of my initial interviews – that, in my particular case, "Silence Is Golden" (a useful proverb from the Four Seasons and follow-up cover single to the Tremeloes' "Here Comes My Baby" hit).

Being an outsider was never difficult for me, as that had always been my status, which I held alongside my sturdy, qualified, tea-and-jam, unconfused English background. My introverted disposition was already firmly embedded; naturally shy, I didn't need a lecture on being withdrawn – it was already deep in my original, feline DNA.

Some journalists were sceptical about the new "Cat," considering that my past, crass, "poppy" background as an overly commercialised, teenage pin-up was pretty much ingrained. They were not prepared to digest or understand the transformative experience I had been through with TB, nor the true spiritual epiphany that had ignited it.

It was even less possible to speak about spiritual matters to those of a mostly atheist or sceptical bent. The habit of most journalists would be to stay as far away as possible from the subject of religion. Yet it was not "religion" per se that I was into, it was the quest for metaphysical answers that interested and stirred me; the lyrics of my songs reeked of my inner probing:

> *I wish I knew, I wish I knew*
> *What makes me, me*
> *And what makes you, you*
> *It's just another point of view (yes)*
> *A state of mind I'm going through (yes)*
> *So what I see is never true? (no)*[14]

Strange as it may seem, even though I was nervous about climbing on stage and singing in front of a crowded audience of diverse, critical, and dangerous-looking human beings, I learned to deal with it. The scary, exposed feeling would disappear as I closed my eyes and mystically travelled inward towards whatever private world my songs carried me. There I could lock the door behind me and leave whatever outer situation my body found itself in.

Opening my eyes was not easy during those moments of soul-baring exposure. Therefore, you can just imagine my absolute sense of horror during those bright, burning, spotlight experiences called "photo sessions" – they were definitely the closest to hell I ever wished to get!

"Give us a smile, and try to look straight at the camera," would bellow the black-hooded reaper.

Hey! Snap out of it, I told myself. Times had changed. I felt I could be myself now. Island was doing a fairly good job in picking sensitive reporters for me to talk to, and it seemed the lyrics were actually being heard for the first time. My handwritten words had been reproduced on the inner sleeve with some little doodles. So the actual interview experience was not as bad as I feared; a few journos actually enjoyed my new music and asked some interesting questions. The old Cat's short, pop-star history was well known and the new Cat's songs were pretty naked in their meaning, so I had no place to hide, really.

"Go ahead, call me 'Steve,'" I would say.

Alun Davies was always my right-hand man. When it came to performing, it was just him and me; a dark-eyed, Everly guitar–wielding troubadour with his blond-haired, Welsh-warrior-sized shadow. We were sent to Aberdeen to record a TV show and then to Europe for some promotional gigs, as "Lady D'Arbanville" rocketed up the French hit parade. Soon the fever was rising everywhere; back in the UK, *Mona Bone Jakon* was spinning in all the right places. We were now asked to perform the single on *Top of the Pops* as it had entered the charts.

We then prepared to go on the road. The Plumpton Jazz and Blues Festival was one of the first gigs we did together. The moment we walked on stage, "The clouds suddenly cleared – it was as if the stage lighting had been arranged by God," Alun said.

The crowd loved it. And they didn't even mind me not singing "Matthew & Son" – how good was that? Soft-folk was my home again. Somehow, going back to the music nights at Les Cousins on Greek Street, listening to socio-soul-searching lyrics, combined with the pick and strumming of acoustic guitars, was exactly what suited me and fit the moment. That's how I wrote most of my songs, so I truly felt like I was returning to my roots. Dylan had proved that you can be popular and remain underground, so long as you never comb your hair, blow smoke in people's faces, and refuse to pose for too long while the cameraman adjusts his lens.

Tillerman Goes to the USA
1970–71

THE "WHEEL OF change" that I sang about in "Lilywhite" was really turning now. My second career took off in a way we never could have expected. This happened at a time when there was a growing appreciation for more gentle, reflective music. I found myself in the forefront of the blossoming seventies singer-songwriter boom, and the whole melodious field began to re-pollinate with thoughtful songs in tune with themes of love, humanity, and altruism.

Throughout the whole subjective experience, one of the most important aspects – emphasised in my lyrics, particularly – was my hope for, and thirsty anticipation of, rapid change on a global scale. What I wanted to see was a new era for humanity, born out of the sacred wedlock between music and spiritual ecstasy – a slight modification of the drug-induced, mind-expanding sentiments of the sixties.

It was a massive time for me in terms of record sales, as well as chart-wise, and I was committed to hitting the highest mark – but I was also drastically serious about my spiritual ambitions. My train was rolling on "the edge of darkness," and many of my generation were happy to be aboard, bobbing along with me. As the engine driver, I was slightly separated from the rest of the passengers – but we were still astral travelling on a wonderful journey together.

Europe had accepted me as well, particularly France, where "Lady D'Arbanville" became one of the most played and covered seventies anthems of immortal love. There was naturally a sentimental part of me that felt at home in France. The problem was that, apart from pronouncing "D'Arbanville" quite well, I couldn't speak French for the life of me. So I was cast in the romantic role of a dark, silken-haired, and bearded stranger, alongside my trusted rustic blond companion, head down, caressing his intricate guitar. I was the moon, he was the sun. It was a dreamy and beautifully iconic image.

The single also did very well in the UK. I continued doing *Top of the Pops* and other shows, often bumping into Mungo Jerry singing their "In the Summertime" jug-band hit, and Paul Rodgers of the group Free, fellow artists on the pink Island label (soon to be replaced by a pastel "palm tree," a decision that many righteous vinyl lovers rightly regretted), who were rocking high with "All Right Now." We criss-crossed with them many times in Paris, Amsterdam, and Germany, doing a trail of music TV and radio appearances.

All the UK/Euro success was great, but we wanted to see some positive action Stateside. Paul Samwell-Smith flew to

New York to finalise the pressing of the master at Sterling Sound. We didn't have a label in the US yet, so part of his mission was scouting a home label for *Mona Bone Jakon*. After being turned down curtly by Elektra and CBS, he eventually took off to the West Coast with a copy of my freshly pressed record under his arm.

Arriving in Los Angeles, Paul and his wife, Rosie, stayed with their friends Larry and Carol Peters. Larry worked at A&M Records at the time, a successful boutique label founded by band leader Herb Alpert and Jerry Moss (whose last names formed the "A" and "M"'), and very similar to Island in many ways. A&M's offices were in Hollywood, on the famed site of the old Charlie Chaplin studio lot on La Brea. The front entrance proudly displayed a permanent cement footprint of Charlie's famous ol' boots. Walking into the reception, you would have seen the framed photos of the label's major artists, including Herb Alpert himself with his Tijuana Brass, Sergio Mendes & Brasil '66, Burt Bacharach, and the Carpenters.

It was Larry Peters who was given the task of taking the newly pressed acetate of *Mona Bone* to play to the folks in the "lot." Behold: instant history! They loved it. Jerry Moss heard it, recognised the potential of this new soft-rock "genre," and wanted immediately to be involved. On a following trip to London he spoke to Chris Blackwell, and a deal was done.

MBJ was a new direction for A&M, extending into a different musical neighbourhood, quite distant from the label's familiar slick-pop and Latin locale at the time. That "difference" was used to help market the album; the adverts produced by the in-house promotion department presented

MBJ as a highly catchy, underground record, which soon caught the critics' ears.

Back in the UK, Paul had discovered a new studio called Morgan, in Willesden, northwest London. I had been continuously writing new songs, as well as having a handful that were finished or semi-completed. Thankfully, Island never pushed me to come up with another "hit," as poppy old Decca and Deram used to. Chris gave us total freedom – along with a tight budget – to produce the follow-up album to *Mona Bone* (though we always overstretched the budget, ha ha). This was artistic bliss.

With no plan in mind, other than to create an exhibition of my heartfelt poetic etchings and guitar-framed songscapes, we got to work. I had definitely found my new voice and my faithful band of musicians masterfully interpreted my songs' moods and added their own charms and character to their decoration, without ever cluttering them up. None of us knew what the album would be called or how it would end up, but *Tea for the Tillerman* was slowly being brewed.

Sessions at Morgan were going incredibly well. The band would learn the songs early on in the afternoon; I would go through the chords and odd time changes that speckled the bars here and there. We would run through the ideas, slowly watching the arrangement take shape. It was totally earthy and unpredictable. The best takes were usually recorded at night. Sometimes we would take a break and have dinner or a drink, served in the little canteen/pub on the ground floor. If our session wasn't going so well we'd dwell in the canteen for an extra beer or two. Then we'd return and chase a song down until we captured it.

We had already demoed some of the standout songs back at Olympic, but they somehow didn't make the first album because they needed further work on the arrangement or lyric; "Wild World" was still chanted, "Oh darling, darling, it's a wild world . . ." I'm so glad we waited for perfection.

One night in Willesden, during the sessions, we reattempted "Father and Son." Alun suddenly came up with a beautiful echoing reply to my introductory G to C opening chords, which set the song on its acoustically sublime path. The warm, rounded bass notes by John Ryan entered like a friendly guest who had nosed up to the wood-piled hearth, sitting down unobtrusively to join the camp. And Harvey's exceptional, inspired drums just beat out the emotions of the dialogue as the father pleads in vain, hoping to avoid the inevitable. After Alun's tastefully heartfelt solo, the son's frustration builds – until the climax, where (according to the script) he walks out through the door to join his comrades on the front line of the revolution.

As we were laying down the track, something really unexpected happened: for the first time, I heard the unique timbre of my father's own voice – in mine! It was an extraordinary connection with his spirit and persona I had never really noticed before. Strangely, it came out more strongly while singing the son's part. It resembled the same turbulent ferocity Dad would let out, shouting angrily at some poor soul (usually the kitchen porter) in Greek. The Mediterranean blood in my roots burst through my vocal cords. My musical identity had come home; I was now the son and father – combined.

Barry Krost had recently been introduced to a talented

Polish director, Jerzy Skolimowski, who was making a film with Jane Asher called *Deep End*. He got to hear some of the new tracks from *Tea for the Tillerman* and fell in love with "Father and Son" and wanted to use it. I, however, had different ambitions for the song. It was still my wish to see *Revolussia* on stage as a musical one day. So I made him an offer to write something with the same style and emotion for his film, and it turned out to be "But I Might Die Tonight." The song symbolised one young heart's determination not to join the daily workers' treadmill, signing up for a life of bondage, like so many before him, dropping one by one into unmarked graves. It also resonated the same sentiment as "Matthew & Son," while no doubt mirroring my own story of resisting the subjugation I had felt with the educational conveyor belt – the reason I chose art as my career.

Dad continued working in the café with Mum still by his side. They were beginning to benefit from my success. A new breed of customers would inquire if this was "Cat Stevens's café." My father, of course, made the most of this opportunity, particularly with excited young girls. He never stopped flirting. Dad's charming smile and friendly approaches were innocent; he was about seventy at the time.

   I would try to avoid being noticed by fans and sneak upstairs to the second floor on the New Oxford Street side, above the shop and the rumble of buses, to my Redroom: this was my cosy hideaway and creative workshop. Having purchased and set up a Revox two-track tape recorder, I was able to write and develop my songs, many times way into the night, trying at the same time not to wake everybody in the house, particularly my second-floor neighbours – two lovely elderly Welsh tenants, Mr. and Mrs. Thomas.

After hearing the whole album of *Tea for the Tillerman*, Chris Blackwell was breathless. He couldn't believe the flight he'd just been on, as he found himself back on the ground of the studio control room. The sound and the songs combined to lay the foundation for what would be a lofty milestone of historic proportions for Island Records. The title track, the final song on the album, almost blew the top off his new studio in Basing Street, "Happy day!" sang the chorus. Oh, yes it was.

Chris instinctively knew that "Wild World" was a hit, but I didn't want it going out as a single: the song was a little too "verse-and-chorus" in style. So he suggested I give it to Jimmy Cliff, an Island reggae artist who I really liked. He even suggested I produce it. After singing a few lines over the phone for Jimmy, he loved it. We met in his modest flat in Earl's Court to work out the best key for him. Jimmy was a kind and beautiful soul. I was a brother to his peaceful sentiments, strangely, in more than one way. I learned some time later that he was a Muslim, though we never talked about religion or faith – that was his own private matter as far as I was concerned, and Jimmy never brought it up. At this stage of my life, I was only concerned with talking music. My own spiritual search was still undercover, wandering alone through a dense forest of mystical metaphors and books.

The artwork for *Tillerman* was another massive factor in the success of the album. Inspired directly from the lyrics of the song, in my most naive Yugoslavian painter's style, I created a colourful and enchanting watercolour scene, which looked like it hopped straight off the pages of a children's storybook.

The picture shows a kind old red-bearded tillerman sipping a cup of tea while seated at a white-clothed table in the middle of the countryside; a couple of boys mischievously play nearby, climbing the friendly sized tree, as a mystic lady on a hill in the distance invokes the dark clouds to thunder and rain. It all told a part of my life story, like the album itself. *Tillerman* would ultimately be recognised in its generation as one of my most influential evergreens – like the photo of me on the back, sitting in what appears to be a leafy corner of Sherwood Forest, waiting to join Robin Hood's band of men.

The album perfectly captured the dreams of the lonely bedsit-dweller more than many others at the time (apart from Leonard Cohen, perhaps). In a way, it was a perfect simile of me upstairs in my Redroom, where these aching heart-and-gut songs were pouring out. My words of personal searching ignited a spark in many sensitive hearts, who were looking for a way out of our politically polarised, war-bedevilled world. *Tillerman* was going to make me a household name all around the world, especially in the US.

So, next stop: the United States.

Alun and I were fixed up to do our first American tour.

West Side Story, the Empire State Building, Harlem, Broadway, and Hollywood – the birthplace of films and images we'd grown up on – were about to be visited, first-hand and in real life! The short promotional blitz took us through New York, Miami, Chicago, and a couple of other cities. It was exciting, but equally frightening: cops carry guns in the US, don't they? Mummy!

My songs were already making substantial waves on hip US radio stations, but this was the first chance my audience got to hear me really close up and in person. We began as a support for Traffic at the famed Fillmore East in New York and later played a few days booked at the Gaslight club in Greenwich Village. What happened during that first trip took everyone by surprise. Though we were only a two-piece acoustic act sandwiched between Traffic and Hammer (a heavily rock-based US band), we completely conquered New York's critical Fillmore crowd. And we went on to do the same at the humble but artistically righteous Gaslight, where we had to tune up in the kitchen (uh! back to that greasy dump). Contemporaries Joni Mitchell and James Taylor were rumoured to have dropped in to feel me out.

During this short spin, we went to Washington and stayed at the Watergate Hotel. Little could we have known this would be where Nixon would come a cropper and end up as the one and only president of the US to have resigned from the position. There was little love lost about that from the "hairy" generation, due to his part in the exacerbated ongoing conflicts of Vietnam and Cambodia, which led to the cold-blooded Kent State shootings of college student protestors by the National Guard in May 1970.

At the end of the year, our little combo of two had travelled to the West Coast, to Los Angeles, the home ground of A&M. Hollywood was just around the corner, and the sunny weather was delightful. It was December, after all. We were booked to play Doug Weston's renowned Troubadour club on Santa Monica Boulevard.

Word from the East Coast was out about the new "Cat" – and it was good, but I was still lacking confidence on stage. My embarrassing, unprepared mutterings between songs might have revealed my nervousness. Secretly, my inner voice begged me to shut up and just sing. Foolishly, I ignored the advice. Often I'd babble away, sometimes attempting to explain why I wrote a song, like the one occasion where I ended up intimating to the audience that "Sad Lisa" was secretly about me. Horrors! The fact that my mumbles were not scripted must've added some cred, because I was clearly speaking from the heart . . . unless I'd drunk too much to be able to decipher what my heart was saying. Later, I would remember my words and cringe. Ultimately, I hope the songs made evident my sincerity and soul-searching mission. My lyrics said it all:

> Well I hit the rowdy road,
> And many kinds I met there,
> Many stories told me
> Of the way to get there
> So on and on I go,
> The seconds tick the time out,
> There's so much left to know,
> And I'm on the road to findout[15]

Tillerman hit the world like a gentle earthquake. The impact was immense, and my fame spread quickly, particularly among the college generation, away from home, lonely and trying to find their place in the university of high academic expectations. Its songs were a syllabus for the lost and seeking, for those about to enter the "Wild World" and who were becoming more aware of its ability to wreck their innocence. The illustration on the LP cover reinforced the sentiments and transported the listeners to that childhood place where unwelcome adults and their disturbing attitudes (apart from the friendly faced tillerman, peacefully finishing his tea) were nowhere around.

For Island and A&M records, it was a commercial jackpot. *Tillerman* was outdoing even their most fanciful predictions. Barry Krost observed my soaring career take off in the States, surprised by the lightning speed of it all. Things were getting very busy, so he linked up with Nat Weiss, an experienced lawyer and manager who had business connections with Brian Epstein. Nat assisted Brian during the early Beatles era, after he was ripped off in some blundering merchandise deal. He was a hilarious guy with a great sense of humour and an astute ability for counting the cents – not just the big dollars. Nat became a close ally of Barry and helped to organise my touring activities with great success.

Later, Nat went on to establish Nemperor Records and manage acts like Peter Asher, James Taylor, John McLaughlin, and Miles Davis. That stable of artists was very credible, particularly Miles Davis and John McLaughlin, the latter being heavily into Indian mysticism, fusing jazz with rock and classical music in his Mahavishnu Orchestra. They were way ahead.

My one-man spiritual expedition was making headway too, but it was much slower. Guided by my music, my words explained the exact square inch I occupied at each moment on the secret path. "Miles from Nowhere" clearly describes my reluctant acceptance of the fact I still had a long, song-threaded way to go in front of me.

The build-up of work activities and the demands of the success I was enjoying worldwide delayed my progress towards ultimate enlightenment. Although I meditated in the mornings and did my yoga exercises, the sessions were getting shorter and more rushed. The romantic notion of travelling east, however, fascinated me. But how could I fit pilgrimage to India in with my tour schedule? The demands of superstardom were enormous, and I was not ready to give it up and become a Buddhist monk – not yet at least. It was not easy to live in two opposing universes. Furthermore, I was looking for my "Hard-Headed Woman."

The Bodhi Tree
1971

ONE OF MY favourite destinations in Los Angeles was the Bodhi Tree, a spiritual bookshop on Melrose Avenue. It always emanated a soothing smell of exotic incense and had shelves abounding with titillating metaphysical titles sold by friendly hippie and bespectacled assistants, able to take your hand and lead you to the lost gates of enlightenment.

As I was still "nowhere," I didn't have to commit just yet. "Be Here Now" was the mantra I practised, as per the book of the same name, written by Richard Alpert, who now called himself Baba Ram Dass (servant of God), a friend of seasoned traveller Timothy Leary. The book was very inspirational and considered by many to be the countercultural bible. It led towards a yogic path, closer to Hinduism, very much the method of such practitioners as George Harrison, who had originally written a song with the same title as the book.

> *Drop Out – detach yourself from external social drama which is as dehydrated and ersatz as TV. Turn On – find a sacrament which turns you to the temple of God, your own body. Go out of your mind. Get high. Tune In – be reborn. Drop back in to express it. Start a new sequence of behaviour that reflects your vision.*[16]

Leary and Ram Dass's prescription for enlightenment nested nicely in the culture of the time and it worked as a guide for those who desired to escape the imprisonment of "normality"'; those who sought to expand mental limits and (very often) travel "far out" on an LSD trip and – like me – manage to scramble back alive to talk about it. The new "open" doctrine also subtly embodied a vital paradigm, one especially Hindu in nature: the idea of reincarnation.

The world, according to general Hindu, as well as Buddhist, belief, is a place of symbolic existences; it is an eternal transformative workshop where souls can endeavour to rise – through rebirth and quality of actions – to the point of Nirvana (liberation). If you don't get it right in this life, you have another chance in the next.

The central issue of "Divinity," however, was much more divergent; the belief in multiple "gods" or manifestations of the Divine Self within Hinduism was not present in Buddhism. There also seemed to be numerous variations of both religions, making the job of getting past the illusory and finding the centre of certainty rather more difficult. Due to these variables (and many others), my existential mission wasn't nearing anywhere soon. I needed to keep looking further afield.

I was picking up interesting books and began reading the philosophy of Swiss pioneering psychiatrist Carl Jung. His theories of opposites, the collective consciousness, and archetypes were intriguing, but intellectually confusing; it was really too esoteric for me – I had passed only one exam in art, after all.

Jung took dreams seriously; he is reported to have dreamed of visiting Liverpool (yes, the home of the Beatles) and noted, "Liverpool is the pool of life." For that statement, they erected a statue of him in Mathew Street (should have been Strawberry Fields, perhaps?).

The writings of Hermann Hesse (coincidentally, another Swiss philosopher and writer) spoke more clearly to me. His *Siddhartha* made a massive impact: the journey of a prince who left the comfort of his palace and everything else to attain Nirvana really spoke to me. I had written a song called "Katmandu," but had never been there except through musical hallucination.

So I was karma-bound to keep touring and making albums for a while. That was the way it looked to me. I felt it was my duty to keep seeking, and faithfully record my progress in what was gradually evolving into a vinyl logbook for spiritual tourists.

When the long-bearded, hash-puffing, guru film director Hal Ashby walked out of the mist and made his astral entrance into my hermetic realm, it was going to create one of the most stimulating fusions and visionary landmarks of celluloid. It all happened when Barry Krost introduced me to Colin Higgins, the author of *Harold and Maude*, who handed me a copy of his 110-page script. I took it away and read the whole thing almost overnight. I just couldn't put it down. The story was weird and wonderful, and the main character, Harold, and his preoccupation with death struck a resilient chord with the anti-establishment, semi-dark prankster in me. I loved it!

Paramount Pictures got news about my positive reaction and arranged for Barry and myself to fly first-class to San Francisco where the filming was taking place. That was pretty glamorous and a first for me.

Walking into the darkened preview room, I beheld Hal, feet up, smoking a hand-rolled, tar-papered, foul-smelling spliff. He was already using songs from *Mona Bone Jakon* and *Tea for the Tillerman* in the daily rushes. Hal possessed a child-like enthusiasm for my music, jumping with joy at the syncopation of my lyrics with the latest scenes of young Harold (Bud Cort) driving his converted black hearse to the funeral of some anonymous soul. I seriously wondered how on earth this film was ever going to be finished if the director was so kinda casual about it. Anyway, the film was great; I was ready to do whatever the "boss" needed to make it happen.

Hal asked me if I could contribute any new material. I already had some half-finished lyrics and chords to a couple of songs: "If You Want to Sing Out, Sing Out" and "Don't Be Shy." There was also another much less complete idea called "You Can Do."

We booked time in Wally Heider's eight-track studio in the city; I finalised the lyrics and laid down the first two songs. They were only meant to be demos, and I planned to record them properly at a later date. However, Hal loved them enough to immediately burn them into the film. In one scene he wanted Ruth Gordon to perform "Sing Out" on the piano, so I ran through it with her. She sounded dreadfully out of tune, but that was the way Hal wanted. So be it.

The film was edited before the deal had been struck with Paramount. It was clear that, in *Harold and Maude*, Hal had almost created a new Cat Stevens "greatest hits" album, and I was not happy about that; it was too soon to have one of those just yet. So it was agreed with the lawyers that there would be no soundtrack album. I suppose this, in some way, created part of its underground, cult-like enigma – adding to its longevity as a standalone filmic masterpiece.

Landing in London, I was back to reality and realised it was time to move out of my one-room pad above Dad's café. The Redroom had served me very well but, let's face it, my bathroom was still shared with Mr. and Mrs. Thomas. Confronted by a locked door while rushing to the bathroom for immediate relief was no fun – and my lady overnight guests were expecting perhaps a little more élan from their esteemed host.

Barry Krost had moved to Fulham. I was now rich enough to purchase my own house and began looking around the same area in southwest London. I found a nice three-story terraced property in Walham Grove, number 44; it needed hefty renovation. As I was travelling a lot and jumping around country to country, that was going to take some time. But I was willing to wait to build my new dream home. Engaging an architect, I began to design the rooms – Japanese-oriented, mirroring my then Zen state of mind.

12 | *The Bodhi Tree*

Down in the semi-basement I created a recording studio, with bright, leaf-green walls and hessian panels, framed with bamboo. It had an eight-track Studer recording machine fitted with a tailor-made mixing desk, covered in green leather. Just outside the studio, squeezed into a corner, hid a lazy bachelor's kitchen with just enough room for a two-hob, electric, portable cooker and a titchy sink.

The main upper-ground floor was divided into two areas by a circular, light-studded arch: half the space was dedicated to a luxurious disco lounge with a semi-raised soft, brown-carpeted floor containing a deep, round sunken mattress, with a fish tank and sophisticated Tannoy sound system embedded in the surrounding, matching brown felt walls. The room was lit by two multi-coloured, rotating theatrical spotlights; the other half of the floor provided a dining space with a glass table, dominated by a large resin-moulded *Tillerman*-style tree that occupied one-quarter of the room and served as a dumbwaiter connected down to my microscopic kitchen.

On the top floor was to be my open-plan, heavenly "White Room," a place for meditation and peace, completely devoid of furniture except for a light, woolen, edge-to-edge Berber carpet and a solitary, white, upright piano. Some twelve pinewood steps led up to an open bedroom balcony – a highly hazardous design because there was no safety handrail. Once the nightly ascent was conquered, I could lie down to gaze at the starry heavens through a square skylight above my bed.

Lastly, outside, a Japanese-style, bamboo-fenced, fifty-foot garden was designed around a rock and pebblestone feature, emanating a calm sound of streaming water as it flowed into a small pool surrounded by bamboo plants.

That was to be my go-to retreat between touring and hotels.

> *I built my house*
> *From barley rice*
> *Green pepper walls*
> *And water ice*
> *Tables of paper wood*
> *Windows of light*
> *And everything emptying*
> *Into White*[17]

I was getting slightly worried about the size of *Tea for the Tillerman*'s success and how to follow it. Having released two albums in one year, my store of songs had been slightly depleted. I needed to write some more. It was natural for me to always have about ten or so riffs or lyrical ideas floating around in my head at one time, but they needed to be finished as perfectly as possible; not every song wanting to get onto the next album would be automatically admitted. I refused to allow any space for mediocrity.

Two interesting new songs came out of my experimenting with a tuning: I had retuned my guitar to open E and was playing around with a 7/8 timing, and that became a Greek-sounding song called "Rubylove"; and then another followed called "If I Laugh."

My heritage was obviously responsible for influencing a good number of my songs; the passion and modal patterns of

Greek folk music came out in numerous melodies, "Peace Train" and "Lady D'Arbanville" I definitely counted among them. Through my close connections in the Cypriot community I was able to find a highly skilled bouzouki player, Andreas Toumazis, who did a great job recording "Rubylove." The words were translated into Greek by two close friends from Athens, a brother and sister: Jianni and Natasha. Lastly, the name of the song itself was offered unexpectedly by Alun Davies's young daughter, Rebecca. She had heard me singing "Who'll be my love?" around the house one day and misheard it as "Ruby my love." That tip landed me the title.

I found time to take a short holiday trip to Marrakech with a girlfriend from Denmark named Elizabeth. We stayed for about a week in a famous deluxe hotel called La Mamounia, drinking up tons of sun and Coca-Cola in between dips in the pool. She was tantalisingly beautiful, lean with perfect Scandinavian features and a blonde crewcut, but I was still too introverted to express my love and admiration for her openly. Elizabeth was another model, which meant that my weakness – inability to hold on to a relationship – was tested again. Those feelings inspired "How Can I Tell You."

The blurring heat and mystery of Morocco were mesmerising. The fear of being robbed was always lurking in the back of my mind; the perennial image implanted by the media of Arabs and tales of "Ali Baba and the Forty Thieves" was hard to erase. We had a pretty low and ill-informed estimation of Arabs and entertained absolutely no interest in their religion. Yet, during that trip I heard some Muslim incantation music with drums and strange metal castanets, played under the stars at night in the middle of the central market.

"What kind of music is that?" I asked a nearby stallholder.

"It's music for God," came his casual reply.

That was the first time I'd ever encountered that kind of description. I knew about music for entertainment, music for money, or for applause – but music for God? This was extremely different.

Upon our return, the pressure to write more songs for the next album began suffocating me, so one day I took a stroll to Foyles bookshop on Charing Cross Road. Ending up in the religious section of the shop, I fumbled around, looking at different titles and came across a hymn book, which was full of beautifully inspiring lyrics. I paid for the book and took it home; sitting down at the piano, I deciphered the tunes painfully slowly in my one-finger style, note by note. When I turned the page and arrived at "Morning Has Broken," my ears popped. It was too enchanting for words.

And so I recorded my first cover: a Christian hymn, no less. Fortunately, my elemental one-finger piano style was replaced by a swirling cascade of melodic triplets to complement and grace the in-between breaks of the song, provided by the keyboard wizard and virtuoso Rick Wakeman. Sadly, not many people got to know he played that because of the stringent contractual restrictions his group, Yes, had with Atlantic Records. He was not credited on the album. This omission was rectified later – though he still disputes that.

Another unique experience, while grabbing a short holiday in Spain, empowered me to write another celestially important song. I was staying at an English family pub-hotel in Malaga, and one moonlit evening I went out to the rocks to watch and listen to the waves crash against the jagged shoreline. There were only a couple of night lovers sharing this beautiful scene beneath the black canopy of stars, just a stone's throw away from where I stood balancing, while the water splashed on my bare feet. The timeless voice of the sea was enough to send me into a trance as I jumped with the waves. Suddenly, I looked down and saw my own moon shadow dancing on the rocks with me! It was a revelation. As I had grown up most of my life in a bustling city of streetlamps, the moon's shadow had never been visible to me. Basing it on a child-like calypso melody that I already had at hand, the song "Moonshadow" almost wrote itself.

There were also the songs that I had started to record with Paul Samwell-Smith but never made the grade as far as I was concerned, like "Peace Train." We had intended to put it on *Tillerman*, but I was never satisfied with the arrangement; the problem was that live versions were always so much better. Finally, we captured that song in Island Studios. After having found the right bass part (using a plectrum) and percussive additions, provided by new drummer Gerry Conway, the holy roller was then ready to leave the station.

"Peace Train" represented the overall message of my music more powerfully than many other songs. It needed to be perfect – or as damned close as possible. The rousing chorus delivered tidings of peace and hope; it was expected to arrive sometime in the future.

Not just yet, though.

In an interview given to the *New York Times*, I attempted to appear to be a serious subscriber to the intellectually critical broadsheet class. I discouraged the usual journalistic tendency of such publications to brand me as shallow and rather naive. I gabbled on about the polarities between the harsh graphic truths of world conflicts and the instinctive optimism that my song "Peace Train" radiated. To quote my own words, "It's more a mood. I don't really think there's going to be peace in this age; it would take a ridiculous mind to think that, because there are so many different nationalities and attitudes, all struggling against each other."[18]

Hmm . . . on reflection, my sober assessment might have accidentally stumbled on the blunt truth of the matter.

Completing the final mixes of the new album with Paul and the team, I set about finding the right cover. Darting back to my white-walled room in Fulham, I grabbed my drawing pad and speedily returned to my comfortable, childish cartoon-self, without hesitation or self-doubt, and worked on a fairy-tale piece of art. Soon I had drawn a small boy with his fiery orange-coated cat, sitting on a kerbside under the moon; behind him was a broken fence, overlooked by a black, bare, wintry tree. I called the boy Teaser. His face and character were based on my cheeky little nephew Bobby, David's second son.

After completing the watercolour, I was satisfied. We had a respectable follow-up to *Tillerman* that playfully continued the theme of "tea." *Teaser and the Firecat* was born. My spiritual agenda was made plain in "The Wind" at the very pinpoint-start of the album, introduced by Alun Davies's gentle fingerpicking, joined by my acoustic riff:

12 | *The Bodhi Tree*

I listen to the wind
To the wind of my soul
Where I end up?
Well I think, only God really knows

The fact is, I had always maintained a strong belief in God. What God knew – and what I didn't – was the subject of destiny, over which I readily admitted I had very little control. Whatever elbow room was available was in the realm of free will, and I knew it needed to be used carefully.

Knowing what pitfalls to dodge is essentially the message of all religion. The Buddhist Eightfold Path, the Ten Commandments, the Hindu warnings against bad karma or actions resulting in recycling of negative cause and effect: they all pointed to the same moralistic job of self-improvement.

Learning the dos and don'ts of life is what they taught me in my Roman Catholic school, yet that didn't stop me following my own whims and falling headlong into those pre-signposted, mistake-filled crevices. I'd had a fair share of bumps and burns, but those experiences had taught me a lot – at least to try and stop repeating the same blunders again and again. Learning from slip-ups is what kids do naturally; they remember not to touch Mummy's hot stove twice. I had experienced enough nasty surprises to know that too much self-indulgence – like excessive drinking, orgies, or drugs – was highly dangerous for one's health, spiritually and physically. That elementary lesson was intuitively understood and mentioned clearly in the very same opening song of *Teaser*:

I've swam upon the devil's lake,
But never, never, never, never,
I'll never make the same mistake,
No never, never, never.

Whatever the deficit of spiritual medals, my musical success seemed to be enduring and going from strength to strength. *Teaser and the Firecat* was on track to become a major hit album. There was much anticipation about it. Many songs were finished and mixed while I was travelling. My recent tour had helped me better understand the pulse of my audiences.

The Troubadour in LA was triumphant the second time round; a new singer called Carly Simon was booked as a support act. She was an elegant lady, a great songstress, and another member of the crab constellation club. Touring puts you in sensitive, close contact with those journeying with you; it was difficult to keep away from Carly. We got to know each other extremely well and spent a lot of our much-in-demand time together. She was unique and seemed suited to a branch of Elizabethan aristocracy, an era where princes and barons roamed the Earth. I was the dashing, dark, Grecian warrior, riding a silver chariot. I swept her off her feet and . . . well that was the kind of unreal relationship we fully played out, floating around in love together.

We shared the excitement of being two stars, personally and cosmically aligned, and musically inhabiting the same planet. It was great to have a beautiful female songwriter as a companion; I would play her some of my new songs while sitting on the floor of a hotel – naturally careful not to give

12 | *The Bodhi Tree*

too many secrets away (we were competing for the same high summits of the charts, after all). But our relationship was not based on sharing chords; it was a perfect match of two people who loved and enjoyed seeing their own reflection in the other's eyes.

The affair enriched both our repertoires. Her memories are reportedly encapsulated in two songs: "Anticipation" and "A Legend in Your Own Time." I never understood the endless hide-and-seek of finding out who "You're So Vain" was about, bro! Naturally, I knew it was me! We had proverbial star-hopping fun, singing, recording, and jetting around, meeting together in various cities, including New York and London. On my end, the affair with Carly was beatified in a song I wrote called "Sweet Scarlet." But that was still one album away.

Meantime, I was preparing for the big release of *Teaser*.

As a bonus and to further the cartoonish personality of the album cover, I illustrated and wrote a short, colourful children's book, based on a story about the moon accidentally falling to Earth. After a "thump" and a chase-filled adventure, Teaser and the Firecat end up saving the night and spinning the disc-like planetoid back into the sky, with the help of seven, red, hooting owls.

The book was turned into a short promotional cartoon for the song, for which Spike Milligan – one of the original Goons – did the narration. The cartoon mirrored the style of the Beatles' *Yellow Submarine* and exploited various psychedelic dreamscapes and images. Personally, I was not too happy with the execution of the final characterisation of Teaser; his face seemed to change dramatically from the one

I created into a more badly drawn sketch of his second cousin. Anyway, most people loved it, and it became a forerunner in the field of animated music videos.

I had now succumbed to the record company's repeated plea to allow a larger photo of me to be used. A special photo session was arranged with the fashionable star photographer David Bailey in his studio off Primrose Hill, London. This would result in possibly one of the most iconic images ever taken of me; extremely close-up, saint-like and intentionally pin-up-able.

It was at Bailey's studio that I bumped into John Lennon and George Harrison. I was just bowled over. The Beatles had been my heroes and so much change and explosive invention had followed the arrival of the four-man musical empire. But the meeting was one of those gawky moments in life when everything I meant to say was fumbled.

John greeted me warmly while George was a bit more reserved. During the quick chat, I blurted out some stupid comment like, "Whoah! It took a long time to make it." They looked puzzled, as if to say, "What's he on about?" I was talking about my long, lumbering road to success, but had goofed horribly and missed an opportunity to tell them how much I really loved them and what they had done for the world and music, opening the doors to freedom and the possibility of peace for dreamers like me . . . I could have gone on and on. George's exploration towards the "East" had also indirectly set me on my own path for enlightenment. The impact of their combined lives and unquenchable ambition had led our whole generation to higher plateaus, hitherto unimaginable.

The encounter could have been so profound, and they might have even said something about my work too. Instead, it ended after a few embarrassing moments. "See you later," I chirped. I could almost imagine them under their breath, saying, "Yeah, yeah, yeah."

Teaser and the Firecat was a massive hit. It confirmed my status as one of the chiefs among a neo-elite class of singer-songwriters – a term that was born more or less at the same time to describe the new tribe of prolific writers and musicians who sang solo and exposed their thoughts and heartfelt intimacies to the world. Our relevance and popularity would increase dramatically during the era that had become somewhat vacant following the break-up of the Beatles.

Regardless of the inevitable interviews, photo sessions, multiple gigs, and appearances connected with the promotion to "superstar" status, I was still sincerely devoted to my search for answers and the metaphysical challenge I had set myself at the beginning of the self-conscious journey (with George's and *The Secret Path*'s help).

On revisiting the Bodhi Tree bookshop back in Los Angeles again, I discovered a mind-raising new publication entitled *Zen Flesh, Zen Bones*. This illuminated me with many new visions and observances through the use of Koans: questions and statements designed to provoke "great doubt" and test progress on the path to enlightenment, such as: "What is the sound of one hand clapping?"

In addition, there was Kuòān Shīyuǎn's metaphor of the "Ten Bulls." Based on the progression of thresholds a student of the Truth has to pass through, it illustrated – in etched, black ink form as well as poetry – the journey to the Source, then a detached bodily return back to the world in blissful knowledge of its semi-illusion:

1 *The Search for the Bull*
2 *Discovering the Footprints*
3 *Perceiving the Bull*
4 *Catching the Bull*
5 *Taming the Bull*
6 *Riding the Bull Home*
7 *The Bull Transcended*
8 *Both Bull and Self Transcended*
9 *Reaching the Source*
10 *In the World*

Boastfully, at that time, I imagined I'd reached stage four. A rather pretentious overestimation. Sure, I had certainly understood the existence and presence of the "Bull" (a metaphor for Truth and Enlightenment) and had seen the signs and had followed the footprints. If we allow for some artistic exaggeration, perhaps there was some truth to the notion that I had even grabbed a few hairs of its slippery tail. But the Bull was still struggling – stubborn, non-submissive, and beyond my reach. Anyway, it contributed to my progress by becoming the name of my next album.

Originally, I had been playing around with words from a newspaper article, which informed stargazing earthlings of the opportunity to sight Mars – at 5 a.m. The connection of planet Mars with the Bull was basically an astronomical mistake; I got Taurus mixed up with Scorpio. Hey! So what? All that was needed then was to change the number from five to four, my approximate position on the road to Zen enlightenment. Now I had the album title: *Catch Bull at Four*.

Bull and the Polar Bear
1972–3

THE HARDEST PART of success to live with is yourself. When everything goes right, it's time to either create a disaster, or just let it happen anyway.

Apart from the ecstatic musical highs, for which I lived, I found the business of maintaining status and selling records was quite soul destroying. I wanted to keep my feet firmly on the road to enlightenment. Fame was climbing much too high, even over and above my own dizzying head. The cover of *Rolling Stone* was mine; demands for my presence were shouting loud all around and beginning to envelop and entrap me. I wanted to scurry and hide myself far away – but contractual obligations wouldn't allow it.

Barry, whose offices were on Curzon Street, just around the corner from Berkeley Square in London, was anticipating his reward, and it was about to arrive. I had promised him a Rolls-Royce if he managed to get me a number one in the charts.

I'd been – indignantly – beaten to that position by a bunch of Monkees in 1967, when they whooped and jumped over "Matthew & Son," denying it from reaching its rightful place.

The day was coming. There were high stakes riding on my next album, with plenty of people at A&M hoping it would consolidate my (uncomfortable) position in the noble realms of pop royalty. And it did. My fourth Island album, *Catch Bull at Four*, shot to the top of the US Billboard charts and the promise to Barry Krost was fulfilled.

Ah, but that was the problem: Where do I go from there? The songs I had written for *Catch Bull* . . . were getting slightly heavier, soundwise; the whimsical softness of guitars had been replaced by the excessive effect of touring, especially in sports arenas, where everything had to be projected bigger and much louder.

Departing from the colourfully childish illustrations of my previous album covers, *Catch Bull* . . . was a circular, monochrome ink painting of mine, depicting a slightly starved-looking boy, bravely caressing the nose of a bull. The whole image was surrounded by a yellow, ring-thin border – the only other colour I allowed. I placed the image on the stark white brick wall above my upright piano in Walham Grove, then took a photograph of it with my Pentax camera. It graphically described my Zen-like attitude and yearning to move away from repetition and "play-it-again" karma.

"The Boy with a Moon and Star on His Head" was one of the few gentler songs, inspired by a story from a book of Indian fairy tales that I had picked up. Little did I or anyone else know what history was to make of this unlikely title – something of a premonition, perhaps? But at that time, "The

Boy with a Moon and Star . . .," for me, was merely an enchanting tale of love that escaped the confines and boundaries of wedlock and family tradition in an accidental moment of passion and abandon. Marriage, as far as I was personally concerned, was as far away as ever from my mind. There weren't many enviable examples of it in terms of my own background with Mum and Dad, and my brother David's marriage with Birgitta, his second, had come to an abrupt end around that time as well.

Most certainly, one of my most profound songs arrived with this album, released as a single called "Sitting":

> *Sitting on my own not by myself,*
> *Everybody's here with me*
> *I don't need to touch your face to know,*
> *And I don't need to use my eyes to see*
>
> *I keep on wondering if I sleep too long,*
> *Will I always wake up the same (or so)?*
> *And keep on wondering if I sleep too long,*
> *Will I even wake up again – or something?*

The "long sleep" in the lyric was maybe another way of describing my success; how long will it last? Will I wake up or even exist after it? My journey to the daunting pinnacle of truth had been interrupted by my premature synthesis into a glossy billboard of glittering stars and artists on Hollywood's Sunset Boulevard – as well as the prosperity that naturally came with it. I was now in a sticky predicament.

One of the ways I dealt with my growing bank statements

was to start a charity. It was called Hermes, because I liked the Greek connection. But choosing which cause to support was complicated and being a wealthy pop star made me an easy target for shysters. So, I chose to donate directly to UNICEF (the United Nations Children's Fund) because they were well respected for their work as an international organisation, dedicated to helping children all over the world.

The dent in my pocket was not going to hurt me at all. What did pain me, on the other hand, was the extortionate 98 percent top rate of tax grabbed by Harold Wilson's Labour government at the time – and I was now hitting that illogical economic paradox: the more you earn, the less you get. I didn't mind paying my share towards Britain's public services and general social needs, but this was not like donating a pint of blood to the NHS – this was more akin to being chased with an axe!

So, according to my accountants and lawyers, I needed to look more seriously into choosing a residence abroad. How did that fit in with the fantasy of myself as a potential aesthetic Zen musical monk in search of detachment from the illusionary world destroying his carnal desires, sustained only by a begging bowl? That long sentence and riddle would have to be added to the unexplained mysteries I was seeking answers to. Enter: Jerry Moss of A&M Records with a one-million-dollar cheque. Hey! Nirvana can wait – let's just see what I can do with this.

My main financial wizard at the time was a man called Prince Rupert Loewenstein, who looked like a chubby character from a Quentin Blake illustration of a Roald Dahl story, with a pot belly, sharply pointed nose, and dark, pinstripe suit. He was already acting as advisor for the Rolling Stones and had set up certain arrangements from which I could definitely benefit.

The prince's area of expertise seemed to be in alleviating the burden of fortunate, wealthy, young pop stars and introducing a sense of long-term planning and generous pension schemes for our old age. I was convinced by him, and duly assigned the rights of my income from my massively successful records (taxed at well over 70 percent at that time) to a commercial bank, in return for lifelong payments of regular amounts. Sounded like a plan!

Becoming non-resident, however, was quite a stupendous step. I had always nested in London; I knew it like the back of my hand. Leaving my beloved city roost was a hard decision, and I was just beginning to enjoy my pad in Fulham, especially the sweet little black and grey kitten I had acquired and dubbed Kabuki. Unfortunately, being so sweet, she caught the eye of a shifty Siamese whom I had to spend time shooing and chasing out into the garden. So I hovered around southwest London for a while longer to guard my cat and my castle.

Following my celebrated victory march through no end of unmemorable hotel rooms in North America, I was showered with similar petals of adoration at home in the British Isles. Many a sceptical music critic who would have previously been fired up with hostility, eager to boo me, now cheered along. My transformation from teeny-bopping, chintzy pop singer into elusive troubadour and poet took many by surprise. But now I had the legitimate stamp of the mighty US Billboard establishment, so the British music industry simply followed suit.

On a rainy night on 4 December, 1972, fans and followers waded their way through the downpour and puddles towards the grand red, circular building of the Royal Albert Hall in South Kensington. The event was to be a joyous coronation for this cheeky West End lad who made good.

Mike Hodges, who had directed *Get Carter*, starring Michael Caine, oversaw the cameras on that night. Mum, Dad, and the family were in the audience too. They were very proud, having seen their little boy conquer New York, Los Angeles, Paris, and now the capital of the old Empire: London itself.

The prestigious gig was followed by a special after-show party, flamboyantly thrown by Barry in the exclusive White Elephant on the River club and attended by many of his circle of theatrical clients such as Maureen Lipman, Peter Finch, Helen Montagu, producer and general manager of the Royal Court Theatre, and other "somebodies."

All this success meant that I now had enough money to look after Mum and the family without worrying anymore. David had found Mum a semi-detached house in Hampstead Garden Suburb, close to where he was living, in a lovely lush, green, and quaintly "countryside" corner of Barnet. I immediately put down the deposit and bought it. At long last, she didn't have to slave away in the café and could retire amid Hampstead Heath's picturesque, vast, open area of long-grassed woodlands and ponds.

David and Birgitta had three children: Danny, Bobby (the

inspiration for Teaser), and Rebecca, the youngest, who was able to scamper across Hill Rise to drop in and see Nanny anytime. Dad was keeping the Moulin Rouge going; he and Dorothy now had two children, my half-sister Lindsay and new half-brother Mark. Our family base was diversifying. My sister Anita and her husband had moved to Vienna, where Alec had decided to take a new job with the US embassy. He was an extremely clever man, and a multilingual, avid reader. I hoped one day they would both return to London, closer to Mum, so we'd have a better chance of meeting all together again.

Dad may still have been going to work every day in the Moulin Rouge, but its heyday of long queues and crowded lunchtimes was over, especially with the growing trend for different food experiences. Major opposition had arrived some years earlier on our doorstep: the very first Pizza Express restaurant opened its doors just around the corner on Museum Street, taking over the old Express Dairy premises, where Dad used to buy milk, butter, and eggs in the last antique days of real glass milk bottles. Pizza Express's famous art nouveau logo took shape and was boldly imprinted on the large circular window. Pizzas exploded into a craze, and Dad's Greek fury was commensurate; he probably planned to burn down the new enterprise (of course, he didn't). Time marched on and we now know how successful that original Italian joint went on to become.

In an effort to help Dad out and allow him to take on a less hectic, more managerial role, I suggested he turn the café into an authentic Greek restaurant and kebab shop. He agreed. David and I began planning for the renovation and launch of the new venture, renamed "Stavros Restaurant." We sketched ideas for the design. David organised the builders (mostly Greeks, of course), including one compatriot who had worked for Dad's best friend, a successful wrestler-cum-hotelier called Milo Papadopoulos. David oversaw the work, which I was now comfortably able to bankroll.

My brother's job as manager of my career had effectively ended the second Barry Krost took over. He was doing so well, and David didn't want to spoil a "good thing." Dave had set up his own successful property development company, renovating old houses and turning them into flats. All I had to do was stand by his side as guarantor for his bank loans.

My rip-roaring career left less and less time to spend in London with family. I had hardly any opportunity to visit my own house in Fulham and was again seriously considering the idea of becoming non-resident of the UK. Most of my days were spent living out of a suitcase, relying on room service to keep me breathing. Whenever there was a break in my gallivanting, however, I loved to drop in and see Mum and enjoy her delicious Scandinavian-infused cooking and serene company. Though we remained close, Mum had got used to me living away from home after my move to Fulham and her relocation to Hampstead.

Even with all the love and adoration, life on the road was lonely and I needed to connect to something higher than my own self. Occasionally I'd pick up an interesting-looking book and read a few chapters or pages, trying to get the gist of it and perhaps hook into some new inspiration. But before I could grasp the total meaning, my mind was diverted onto some other task that I'd created for myself. Attention deficit hyperactivity disorder (ADHD) is something you could call it – boredom is another.

There would always be a Gideons' Bible in the hotel-room drawer. Sometimes I would delve back into it for guidance, only to become either confused by the Old Testament or frustrated with the New, and the distance I was from the sheer purity of Jesus and his sublime teachings, and ultimate sacrifice. I'd close the book only to find myself in the very same place as before: lost, alone, and back in the dark.

Feeling the heavy pressure of success, I started to undergo a serious period of doubt and self-examination. I needed to shake off some of the spotlight attention. Unsurprisingly, perhaps, I had already stated my determination to keep moving, even considering the preposterous idea, at the time, of leaving the music business as early as 1971 in an interview with the *New York Times,* in which I said: "I can look at my music and think, Yes, that's nice, but it's not exactly what I want, it has to keep evolving. In two years I won't be doing the same things. I promise that much. I may not even be in music."[19]

My songs were fewer and farther between, as it became harder to decide what to write about. After listening to Stevie Wonder's latest album I was quite simply floored. He had made a monumental leap of brilliance with *Music of My Mind*; it was light years ahead of anything else out there. The use of synthesisers combined with funk, Stevie's new songs and his incredibly soulful vocal exploits and musicianship didn't just overwhelm me . . . it made me depressed!

My love of Black music – whether the blues, R & B or soul

– had been embedded in my heart from my early teenage years. Ray Charles, an inspiration for Stevie himself, Motown, and the more recent Sly and the Family Stone, the Spinners, Gladys Knight and the Pips, and the "Philly sound" artists like Harold Melvin & the Blue Notes, rocked my sensitively balanced world.

   I locked myself away and began work on an ambitious idea, composing and blending various soulful melodies and themes on my upright white piano. Various loose words and chords were vortexing in my brain, and it soon occurred to me that they could be linked together. My writing was laboured and complicated; far from the simplicity and elegance of my earlier songs, the piano brought out the more complex composer in me. My words seemed to accept a lesser status in priority and meaning: "There are no words I can use . . ." I declared at the start of my ebony-and-ivory "Foreigner Suite."

   My spirit began to battle with my intellect. Even the choice of reading had become chance-riddled; I read a book called *The Dice Man* by Luke Rhinehart and was now throwing I Ching sticks and consulting the "Oracle." *The Book of Changes*, as it was called, suited my uncertain status, both musically and spiritually. Daily I would wake up and religiously throw the fifty yellow stalk sticks and decipher which hexagrams they symbolised, thus establishing what I should accept to do or not to do that particular day, week, or whatever. A game of fate with a simple six-sided die would have achieved the same result, probably, but this was a thousand-year-old method used by Chinese soothsayers, and certainly more interesting than Snakes and Ladders.

CAT ON THE ROAD TO FINDOUT

It was a strange time. The alienation from my former soft folk-rock self, as a result of Stevie Wonder's musical comet, had caused my ship to lose its orbit. I needed to break away from Cat Stevens's trodden path. Hence the title, as I explained later in an interview with *Circus* magazine: "As black music was happening, I decided to get down to it. Because I was a stranger in the world of black sounds, I called the album *Foreigner*."[20]

After I had written and named "The Foreigner Suite," my next step was to organise its recording. Paul Samwell-Smith was pretty unimpressed with my new direction, including the concept of the suite, which was almost entirely piano-and-keyboard driven. It looked like I had to go it alone. With that decision made, I departed from my usual band of musicians, including Alun, and found myself some talented musical collaborators.

Bernard "Pretty" Purdie, the drummer for James Brown and Aretha Franklin, was my target. He brought in Paul Martinez on bass and Phil Upchurch on electric guitar. Later, I added Patti Austin, Barbara Massey, and Tasha Thomas on vocals with Gerry Conway and Herbie Flowers on drums and bass overdubs.

To complete the stylistic departure, I required an off-the-map studio environment. Recording in foreign surroundings was nothing new to me; *Catch Bull . . .* had been recorded mostly in the Château d'Hérouville in France (painted by Van Gogh, who lay buried nearby). I finally chose Dynamic Sounds Studios in Kingston, Jamaica, hidden in the depths of the jungle thickets on the outskirts of town, surrounded by hazy-eyed Rasta engineers. It seemed about as far away from familiarity as I could possibly get without falling off the Earth entirely.

The album never turned out to sound exactly the way I wanted, but the statement was clear. What would the public and my fans think of it? I recalled Dylan being condemned for going "electric"; maybe I would be similarly lambasted for going "piano." Well, I wasn't going to back down. Fate had brought me to a point of frustration with my self-pitying condition – so I just had to get on with it.

Some of the most durable words of that album were contained in a song called "100 I Dream." It was going to be tough, but I had to get ahold of my life and make the necessary changes:

> *Pick up the pieces, you see before you*
> *Don't let your weaknesses destroy you*
> *You know wherever you go, the world will follow*
> *So let your reasons be true – to you*

Foreigner was a record that unashamedly explained my feelings and fluctuating state of mind and heart. The album tested the loyalty of my fans by turning my musical style around and appearing to be a stranger again, contradicting the familiar persona most of my admirers had grown to feel at home with. Considering that I was already on a search to find my true self and ultimate destination, it suited me perfectly as a statement of my statelessness.

At the height of my popularity as a perceived "superstar," one question troubled me: did people really love me or someone they imagined? I wanted to be honest with myself and them too – how was it possible for someone to truly love another so transient, not quite sure of who he is? That was a hard one to work out and it left me sceptical of people's possible motives in desiring my company. I concluded that most people loved the enigma they wanted me to be; it was that simple. I could have been wearing a Batman mask, who would know the difference? I needed to know who I was, and that was not easy in the environment of that uncertainty.

It was not necessary to guess what the response to *Foreigner* would be; I was doing everything to put off people's automatic, jukebox repeat-play expectation and follow the unbeaten path my life was taking me along. Even the album cover itself was a declaration of the same, a close-up headshot in black and white; my beard was even trimmed differently. I included one of my Japanese ink-styled drawings, a white polar bear, on the back of the lyric sheet, symbolising the puzzling incongruity of such a cold-nosed fellow roaming the sands in the blazing heat of a Jamaican sunny day.

Following its release in July 1973, the result of the *Foreigner* experiment was fairly predictable – particularly from the music business establishment's quarters. Some fans really loved it, maybe because it was so hot and steamy and unself-conscious, like the sunny Jamaican environment in which it was recorded. But the self-appointed guardians of music morality, *Rolling Stone*, slammed it with a loathing only reserved for traitors who have dared to betray the vital tradition of remaining true to the religious ethics of musical genres – well, especially if Cat Stevens dares to try it.

I had not quite prepared myself for the likelihood of such damning reviews. But it exposed my own weakness and the emotional hurt I felt, being so distant from my chosen goal – the Truth – that made *Foreigner* more valid than some predictable repeat of *Tillerman*, who to my mind was better left alone under the tree drinking his lukewarm tea. I needed to be critical of myself, something that can be discerned subtly in the very words I sang on the album.

> *You say you want to seek the Truth,*
> *But it's hard to find*
> *No one to help you*
> *Your friends don't have the time*
> *So you ride around in your car*
> *Switch on the radio*
> *You want to relate to*
> *Something you once read in a book*
> *What kind of a way to try to take a look?*[21]

Criticism is useful, but rarely welcome. And, when it comes to the irresistibly competitive nature of the musicians' world, the idea that Elton John would one day become as big as Elvis haunted me – like the memory of the fateful night we bumped into each other at a studio somewhere in the States. The new video game *Pong* had just surfaced, and Elton instantly challenged me to a tournament. He proceeded to beat me silly, running rings around me while his giggling group watched on – I didn't win even one puny match! I found out later, of course, that he was a keen tennis player. A lesson learned.

Something had to be done quickly to regain my princely ground and reconnect with my fans – not necessarily to please the gatekeepers of the industry, except insomuch as I needed some kind of personal endorsement on my ticket to get past them. A coast-to-coast live national TV concert would certainly do it.

On 9 November, 1973, a national US TV special on ABC, *The Moon and Star Concert*, was recorded and aired from the Aquarius Theater in Los Angeles, which crowned my musical aristocratic role. A historic "first," the whole eighteen-minute long "Foreigner Suite" was performed without advertising interruption and ended in unrehearsed standing ovations. The one-hour special was a major musical triumph, incorporating full-blown string and brass sections along with my usual band with two powerhouse drummers, Bernard Purdie and Gerry Conway. Dr. John and Linda Ronstadt appeared as guests, singing "Pop Star" and "Fill My Eyes" respectively.

Buddha and the Chocolate Box reopened the doors of my familiar melodious soft delivery and sentiments. Although still experimental in compositional terms, it was what most of my fans desperately wanted to hear next. Following the disappointment of *Foreigner*, the *Buddha . . .* album proved – especially to those who had no faith – that the missing Cat had simply wandered away from home for a while. My principle of independence was asserted; as with most cats, don't ever dare think you own them! As far as the critics were concerned, album-wise, it marked my heralded return to "Cat Stevens" form.

The message of *Buddha and the Chocolate Box* was very obvious: stuck in the middle between the material and spiritual worlds, I was still undecided and treading a rice-paper-thin line. The idea for the title came while sitting on an airport transit bus on my way to a plane. I was carrying my favourite little encased statuette of Buddha along with a box of chocolates. It struck me that what I had in my hands represented the perfect epitome of my wavering soul.

The Buddha statue adorned the front of the album, and I illustrated the back cover with a miniature comic-strip story of a little Buddha boy looking for enlightenment. He gets stopped on the path by a flute-playing spider whose mystic melody transports him into a trance, wherein he sees an apparition of what his heart deeply desires: a box of golden foil-wrapped chocolates. As the boy hastily opens the foil, he realises the chocolates are all shaped like a sitting Buddha. His face becomes "enwhitened," and he awakens. After that, he peacefully continues on the path, but the gloom-clouds in the sky have vanished, and the sun is clear and shining.

Paul Samwell-Smith and Alun Davies rejoined me for the making of *Buddha . . .*; we all enjoyed the pleasant experience of getting back together again. Most of the tracks for the album were recorded in Sound Techniques, a studio near the World's End district in Chelsea. It felt like familiar ground.

The songs I had written represented a collection of scattered thoughts and melodies developed in my basement studio in Fulham. One particular song seemed to be a mysterious peep into the future, "Resign Yourself to God." But that was too committal, and I hadn't yet acquired enough conviction to any such path or ideal. It was, however, a clear indication of my readiness to submit to a divine power – if only I could be more certain about who or what it was.

CAT ON THE ROAD TO FINDOUT

Another song and indicator did make it onto the album, hinting again at my willingness to one day let go: "Home in the Sky." The lyrics captured the essence of my longing to ascend from the gravity of earthly things. The track we recorded ends with a beautiful kalimba coda, fading high into the heaven of stars while I sing with Paul in a multi-tracked, slightly sped-up Mickey Mouse chorus:

Bye, bye . . .

Exile
1974

BECOMING NON-RESIDENT WAS the next step, which in practice required very little change to my transitory lifestyle. Seeking a country was not so easy; the places I knew best were mostly in Europe and the US, but they had heavy tax regulations, like the UK.

I purposefully avoided Switzerland or the "Bahamas" crowd. It was part of my methodology to avoid well-trodden paths and go in an alternative direction to where most people were headed; that was because I enjoyed discovering new things for myself. Travelling was a way to explore different sides to life. With my own mixed background, I could slip into the landscape more easily. Somehow I felt drawn to South America and temporarily took up residence in Montevideo, Uruguay – until I discovered what was next door: Brazil!

Rio de Janeiro wooed my adventurous spirit. It was the city in which I finally decided to put down my bags in 1974. Rio had lots of pluses: first and foremost, it was far enough away from the spotlight and all the showbiz hassle. I couldn't be spotted easily, even walking along Copacabana Beach with a guitar – that made it extremely comfortable as a hideaway.

The weather in Brazil is hot and semi-tropical; while it was freezing or snowing in London, it would be summertime in Rio, with fresh coconut juice and delightful ladies posing on the beach in December – who needs pudgy old Father Christmas? To add to this, everybody seemed able to sing in tune; the country is endowed with great jazz-fused music, steeped with its roots in African rhythms, making it so electrifying and danceable. This was like discovering musical utopia.

While checking out villas to rent, I had booked into a room at the Tropicana hotel on Copacabana. Then, something crazy happened, like a chapter from an Ian Fleming novel. It was almost too cloak-and-daggerish to believe. I'd put on my sunglasses to grab a cup of coffee on the beachfront. After an hour, feeling hot and bored with my own company, I decided to head back to my room to try and write a song. As I neared the hotel entrance, my heart stopped. The pavement outside was teeming with police cars, blue lights flashing.

Oh no! I thought to myself, *The British tax authorities have found me.* In fact, the police had tracked down the whereabouts of Ronnie Biggs, the Great Train Robber, who was staying in the very same hotel. The famous detective chief superintendent, Jack Slipper, had apparently used information provided by the *Daily Express*, which led him to Room 909 at the Tropicana in February.

Whew! What an escape for both of us. The officer had made a boob by not informing Interpol about the extradition. So Slipper had to leave empty-handed – and Ron and I were able to get on with our holidays.

With some help and scouting by my record company rep, Maria Creusa, I switched from hotels to a scenic bungalow high in the exclusive hills just past Ipanema in an area called Barra da Tijuca, close to Joatinga Beach. It was hidden among the thick trees of a hill, designed in Brazilian dark wood and glass, with one bedroom and a massive porch bearing a string hammock. That's where I would settle down with an upright piano, guitar, and my four-track TEAC recorder.

When carnival time arrived, things got wild. Everybody sang, danced, and dressed up outrageously, each displaying their alter-identity without an inch of shame. I just mingled in with the raving crowd, singing along as best I could with the popular chorus-driven hits that had won the hearts of the *Cariocas* (the people of Rio) that year. The familiar African beat I'd danced to in West End clubs as a teenager – made famous by Bo Diddley – was right at home here, hammered loudly on snares, supported by the thumping of thirty-inch-wide, deep, shiny metal bass drums. It made me feel instantly connected. A popular drum pattern in Africa, the Diddley rhythm must have been shipped over along with the slaves by the Portuguese colonialists.

Amid the all-night festivities, I soon discovered most of the people were out of their heads on "lança-perfume." They inhaled miniature "poppers" of this ethyl chloride gas-based drug for an extra rush of blood-pumping frenzy. *Why not?* I thought, after being offered a "pop." The hallucinatory effect of the drug was intense as I danced, zigzagging through the crowd-filled streets, propelled into a musical delirium by the earth-trembling surdo drums, which banged like sledgehammers against my chest.

Due to the combination of the "perfume" and hundreds of wild bouncing bodies squeezed tightly around me, my rapid heartbeat suddenly reached exploding point. I was losing control and struggling to hold on to myself – and consciousness. Inexplicably, I called out a name I'd never even heard before, "Nestor!" Nobody around me understood my sudden psychotic outburst, but for me it seemed to work; the name strangely and mysteriously calmed me.

By dawn, the carnival was over. I caught a taxi and headed back to my villa to sleep. A night in Rio never to be forgotten.

Anita and Alec had returned to the UK from Vienna. "Smart" Alec was exceptionally bright and had a fantastic head for numbers; on David's advice, I offered him a job keeping an eye on the financial end of my business in my absence. He accepted and was appointed as my finance manager at the Curzon Street offices. The move was a hark back to Dad in the café, who always made sure he had eyes in the back of his head. Barry Krost was slightly irritated, having his star client's brother-in-law constantly looking over his shoulder at the books. On the other hand, I could now breathe easier.

"Bamboozle" was the next major tour fixed on my calendar. The title reflected my continued fascination with the mysterious spiritualisms of the East. It also coincided with the release of *Buddha and the Chocolate Box*. The tour was going to cover not only the US and Europe, but all the way to Australia and Japan. This was going to be an important boost for my spiritual journey. I was thrillingly anticipating my first visit to a Buddhist temple.

But bad things do happen – especially to a would-be Buddha training to cope with life's unavoidable bruises with karma: my house in Fulham was burgled! The Revox tape machine and my beloved black Gibson 180 guitar, on which I had written so many standout songs, had been stolen. But like all material things, I suppose, they are ultimately removed from us at some point or other; "all things must pass," said Guru George. So I just adopted a Zen take on it.

The "Bamboozle" tour brochure looked like an off-Broadway program; my sumi ink illustration was on the cover, white bamboo stalks on a lilac background. It was not particularly informative, with only a handful of pictures and names of the group and some crew members, plus a record company advert for the *Buddha* album.

Linda Lewis joined us on tour as a support act. I had gone out with Linda some years before, frequenting her pad on Hampstead Way, north London, for evenings of music and puffs of weed with musician friends – a very hippie evening would ensue. She was sweet and flower-child-like, a naturally talented singer with a beautifully unique, high-pitched, nightingale voice.

We did a bunch of select gigs in the UK, then carried on through some major cities in Europe before we headed down under to meet the kangaroos.

Australia was absolutely insane. Audiences had discovered my music and adopted it en masse by the time I first visited in August–September 1972. Almost one in every four homes had my albums. "Cat Mania" struck again as I arrived with my group at Sydney airport. After being provocatively searched and almost fully undressed by immigration officials looking for unlawful "substances," I was released to carry on with my bamboozling. Unfortunately, my tour assistant, Eddie Gold, was held back after they found a little stash of hashish in his rucksack. Outside the airport, I was well and truly mobbed.

Apart from my latest, eye-catching, Honolulu tan, it seemed that my soul-searching message had hit a chord with the Australian psyche. There is something of a "let's go walkabout" philosophy with which my music must have been in tune. It possibly resonated with that unique habit of escapism ingrained in Australia's Aborigine culture.

During this visit down under, I was introduced to two new major clues for the ongoing sojourn of my soul.

The first tip-off came from an earnest and spiritually concerned fan who managed to pass on to me a beautifully bound, green velvet copy of Jalal al-Din Rumi's *Mathnawi*. It was my introduction to all-encompassing, universal, Sufi philosophy. I was enthralled. The poetic nature of Rumi's writings and the symbolism he used were astounding; they reminded me of a more God-centred view of existence, with a subtle touch of Buddhist detachment. His view of the all-embracing religion, being of no particular brand, reverberated strongly with me. One poem about the Reed held my breath:

Hearken to this Reed forlorn
Breathing, ever since 'twas torn From
its rushy bed, a strain Of impassioned
love and pain

The secret of my song, though near,
None can see and none can hear.
Oh for a friend to know the sign, And
mingle all his soul with mine

'Tis the flame of Love that fired me,
'Tis the wine of Love inspired me.
Wouldst thou learn how lovers bleed,
Hearken, hearken to the Reed![22]

This poem tore me apart. It awakened inside me the highest sense of love unleashed; a longing for union that many a solitary heart carries throughout life, in hope of one day uniting body and soul with a spotlessly pure and perfectly adorable companion. Rumi's poem was aimed even higher, towards the supreme attainment of Divine Love, a plea for reattachment on a non-material level; harkening for a return to that which is hidden behind the surrounding seven veils of the unseen and literally inexpressible – the Face of God. This ode of mystic outpouring was something I'd never read, seen or heard before.

The second major metaphysical lead I picked up in Australia was an initiation into numerology. While lounging lazily on my bed in a Sydney hotel one afternoon, I received a call from the receptionist, saying someone in the lobby called Hestia Lovejoy wanted to see me. Fascinated by such a fake-sounding name, I immediately invited her up. When I opened the door, in walked a six-foot-tall, elegant, silver-haired lady old enough to be my grandmother. She sat down and confidently explained to me the symbolic power of numbers and their meaning. *Maybe those clever Greeks got it right*, I thought to myself. *Perhaps the whole universe works on the basis of a mysterious numerical formula.* Possibly.

I already felt quite proud of my father's heritage – it was mine too! I had some vague notion of the Greek connection to this particular science through the oracles of Pythagoras. That was all I needed to spark my interest. It is suggested that Pythagoras was first to have used the word "philosopher" (lover of wisdom), and is credited as having influenced Plato and Aristotle and thus a major chunk of Western philosophy to follow. He was a musician as well as a mathematician, scientist, and mystic, but most information about him was written hundreds of years after his passing. Because his sect was so secretive, myths grew around his personality and teachings.

Thanks to the gracious lady, I began my research. The only problem was that – taken on their own – numbers don't have much spirit and possess very little flexibility. Apart from the symbolic value of numerals, it remains a rather sexless view of the cosmos. No one could sensibly argue against the logic and consistency of numbers: adding one and one together will inevitably produce two; whether in a poky betting shop in Birmingham this end of the universe, or in an elementary college for green, metallic scale-skinned aliens somewhere in the farthest galaxy imaginable, the result would be the same.

So, for the time being, I put the whole theory to one side and went on with my life (although I did look more carefully at the flight numbers of planes I flew on after that).

The trip to Japan was eye-opening. Apart from certain misty mornings in L.A., I'd never seen smog as thick as that we drove through from Tokyo airport to the hotel; though it was a sunny day, you could hardly tell. That didn't really bother me; there were other more important issues to deal with. I was eager to visit a real Buddhist temple, and that was arranged.

Alun accompanied me as we travelled early to Kyoto on the bullet train, trying to balance our shaking teacups at over two hundred miles an hour. The scenery was magical, with mountains resembling the famous etchings of Hokusai and Hiroshige.

On our arrival we went to the "100-Moss Temple."[23] Never have I seen so many hues of mystic green. Alun strolled a few steps reverently behind me as I soaked up the deep meditative atmosphere of the temple grounds. The stone garden was astounding; its sparse boulder rocks were meticulously placed to conjure up a miniature world within an infinite sea of finely raked granite, all set at perfect proportions and distance within the courtyard of the sanctuary.

A tall monk approached in black, stiffly starched attire and invited us to partake of some light refreshment under the eaves of the wooden porch inside a special room for guests and travellers. Alun and I patiently waited as the formalities began, the iron pot of brewing tea ceremoniously centred on a low, blackwood table, hypnotically occupying our attention.

Finally, it was ready, and the man slowly poured a dark green liquid into our cups, which produced a strange swamp-like froth on the surface. We slowly sipped. Nothing was said, but it tasted like a clump of moss from the garden that had been collected and boiled in our honour. No sugar? Of course, I realised this was one of the frugal rules of abstinence and selflessness implicit in a dedicated monk's life. The whole experience left an indelible impression on my mind . . . and woeful tongue.

Not much was said as we left the confines of the temple, but it seemed that I would probably have to remain a spiritual tourist for a bit longer. Conforming to such bare and rigidly strict conventions was the opposite of the life I knew and wanted. Though I respected and envied the monks' commitment, my soul was still on a journey to a more comfortable state of being. I was not necessarily the type to sit passively at the foot of a guru or master and bow my head in reverential humility. I was still a Westerner and needed to feel at home with reason, to understand the clear objective of rules or rituals before accepting them. I couldn't silently submit without knowing a whole lot more. Anyway, I had a show to do.

> *The truth knocks on your door and you say,*
> *"Go away, I'm looking for the truth,"*
> *And so it goes away. Puzzling.*[24]

The shows in Tokyo, Osaka and Kyoto were a great success. We recorded our gig at the Sun Plaza hall in Nakano, Tokyo, which later would become *Saturnight*, a live album released only in Japan, with the income happily donated to UNICEF.

While touring, I recorded a couple of tracks with the band. I'd been playing around with a couple of the most-loved songs from my past: "Another Saturday Night" by Sam Cooke and "Blue Monday" by Fats Domino. Both were from an era of rock 'n' roll that I missed and wanted to revive. Sam Cooke in particular was an inspiration to me. His song brought me back to those melancholy nights roaming London's streets as a young unknown, before fame came. I missed that feeling.

We travelled back to the US and ended "Bamboozle" in New York at Madison Square Garden. It was a magnificent pinnacle to the tour. It felt like the whole city was there, whistling and applauding. Among that night's audience were Joni Mitchell and the Rolling Stones; Mick Jagger apparently couldn't stop laughing and making jibes against my rather oversized keyboard genius, Jean Roussel. It's always tough to sit in front of such contemporaries – especially if they are icons in their own right – and be judged.

To mark the end of the road for our musical "Bamboozle," Nat Weiss and Barry Krost had arranged a celebratory farewell party in our favourite club, JP's. It was invite-only, mainly to maintain the great family atmosphere we had created on the road. Nat, Barry, and my girlfriend from New York, along with the band and main members of the crew and their wives or consorts – all were present and accounted for, getting more and more riotous and inebriated as the night went on.

Nothing could have spoilt it, until . . .

Everything came to a bitter end when I found out that my road manager had turned away John Lennon and Yoko Ono at the front door.

"You did what?!" I screamed.

"But you told us . . ."

"Forget what I said, you piece of unworthy ****!"

I was ashamed that my own guys had snubbed the founder of the Beatles, a luminary genius, without whom the world would have been so totally different – so much musically duller a planet altogether. Frankly, the sin was never forgiven.

The next morning I was ready to escape New York and lose myself.

Back at the ranch in Rio, I inadvertently fell into an elite clique of odd partygoers, led by the film actress and model Florinda Bolkan, and Helmut Berger – the latest prodigy of film director Luchino Visconti. Florinda and her unique posse of film stars, musicians, and artists became my ritzy alter ego companions. Though I kept mostly to myself – writing for much of the time – during my brief stops "home" to Ipanema between tours and recording, whenever I was in a social mood I'd link up with Florinda and her courtiers. We'd go to the beach, eat, go clubbing, or get stoned.

In reality, this was getting to be a dark and extremely estranged period for me. Though I had everything at my fingertips and endless opportunities to stimulate my ego and cash in on my worldwide popularity, life was more or less devoid of true friends – there were very few I could trust – and my family were an ocean away.

I withdrew even further into myself and began writing *Numbers*.

The concept of numerology had affected my thinking quite deeply, and I started working on a story that would explore the subject, while at the same time assist my expedition into a field of art I always wanted to explore more: animation.

Barry connected me with two authors, Allan Scott and Chris Bryant. I explained my idea to them in London and we began writing a script about nine cheeky characters called Polygons, who lived on a little planet (Polygor) in a corner of the universe. They worked from their palace towers on the peak of a high mountain above the pink clouds, producing millions and billions and zillions of numbers, which were then distributed to every world that needed them. The emperor of the operation was Monad; he symbolized everything a selfishly single-minded tyrant could ever represent (me on tour?).

One day on Polygor, a tiny boy appeared and knocked on the great door of the palace. His presence was to shake the confidence of Monad and the rest of the Polygons. The little stranger introduced himself as Jzero. He looked a bit like the Little Prince and had a sweet smiling face with a selfless character, ready to help anybody to do anything without repayment. That was the day everything started to go wrong for Monad.

> POLYGONS: *Well he says he hasn't got nothing*
> *But he seems to possess less,*
> *He walks through the door*
> *Like a tap dance with death,*

What kind of fool is he?
JZERO: *No need to guess, just call me Jzero.*

Pythagoras is said to have believed that there is no crime equal to that of anarchy. The introduction of zero-selfishness to the world of monarchy was the ghastly challenge Monad and his subjects had to now face.

The story had many levels; it contained a liberal mix of the Christian and Buddhist elements embedded within me. Its symbolism and characterisations were heavily based on the arrival of Jesus to the then empirical hierarchy of Rome – certainly the name Jzero was a clue to that. The notion of being disconnected from worldly things, "like a free-walking tree . . ." was very much part of the Buddhist concept of the "non-self" state of emptiness.

Another interesting substratum of the "Pythagorean Theory Tale" was that early Greek philosophers also used the term "Monad" for God – the first being and ultimate source of all that exists.

Simply put, however, Jzero represented the kind of hero I wanted to be: selfless, ready to rush in and save the planet when everything seemed heading towards an inevitable implosion and terminal annihilation – quite an ambitious idea, really.

The music and words of *Numbers* were mostly written in my Rio bungalow at the cost of great pain and personal sacrifice. The Brazilian hills were infested with mosquitoes; at night they would organise themselves and attack! I would have to cover up as much of my body as possible, wrapped up tight in a hoody, with my face and fingers the only parts of my body exposed. Between playing chords and scribbling I would have to stop and whack the nasty aliens who breached my defences, thrusting their daggers into my skin for a taste of my blood. Not nice.

Enough of bloody songwriting! It was time for a break. Shaving off my beard and hair and looking like somebody else, I decided to do some charity work.

UNICEF arranged for me to visit Kenya and Ethiopia, towards the end of 1974. The former emperor of Ethiopia, Haile Selassie, was in custody at the time (as were his pet lions) following a revolution that same year. The country had gone through two years of famine, and many children looked like walking skeletons. This visit helped put me in touch with reality, if only for a short while. I didn't allow too many photographs of the visit but, instead, made a large donation direct through UNICEF, which seemed to me the most neutral and active organisation where children's needs arose.

Winter was coming, and I was confused with the unnatural sight of tanned Santas singing and dancing samba on the beach. Summoning all the family together, I organised a Christmas holiday in Davos, Switzerland, in December 1974. I had hired the chalet of a German opera singer; luckily for me, it included an upright piano so I could continue finalising the new songs for *Numbers*.

Mum, Anita, and Alec came, followed soon after by David. I felt at home again. Living away from London was not easy. It was great to see Mum's smiling face and taste her delicacies again – all my washing was taken care of too!

The snow in Switzerland was stunning; it reminded me of Sweden and the younger days spent in Gävle, but with a lot more mountains. We all built a snowman and did a few Charlie Chaplin skits, comically falling over several times with the skis angled in all directions and almost ending up in our noses.

When David arrived, he was very excited; he had been writing his own songs and wanted me to hear them. I had no idea he had started working on a new musical project; that was quite a surprise. For a while, David had the keys to my house in Fulham and he had apparently been using the studio to record his ideas with a few co-writers and musicians. Though I didn't know it at the time, he had written "No More Riders," the B-side of the Hollies single "The Air That I Breathe," with Terry Sylvester, his "Hollie" neighbour who lived round the corner from him in Hampstead Garden Suburb.

I could see in his eyes that he was bursting with sincerity about his message for the world and his own ambition as a musical composer. The onerous hassle of getting up on stage every night and singing himself was not a role he fancied nor suited; David was always ready to admit that. I listened as he passionately plonked and sang his compositions on the slightly out-of-tune piano. After he finished playing me his new song, "Superman," I actually thought it was quite good, but in a rather selfish, unkindly, but brotherly way, I said, "Why are you doing this, Dave? Haven't I always fulfilled your dreams for you?"

David, who had already gone through a hell of a lot more hardships in life than I ever did – being a war child born during air-raids and rations; beaten heavily by Dad; ran away from home; married twice with children; referred to an asylum; written endless reams of thoughts and wisdoms since his teens – patiently put up with his little brother's brazen remark. Although he knew there might be an element of truth in my statement, David was deep into his own creative voyage. All he wanted was a bit of support and encouragement from me.

Was that so hard? I knew what it felt like to have a song inside that you believe the world should hear. In reality, it was David who originally inspired me to think more deeply about life and express myself. Though he never taught me how to draw, he introduced me to perspective. He never taught me to play guitar or write, either, but he was ready to stand on a chair in the middle of a crowd and declare his kid brother a "genius." Now he just wanted his own passionate message of peace to get out. I was not going to get in the way of that. We both dreamed of making a better world. Despite my initial remark, I was ready to help him whichever way he wanted.

After David and the family left Davos, I was feeling much better and more grounded. Alun Davies dropped in for a week and we played around with the new songs, in preparation for recording. Paul Samwell-Smith had organised a great new studio near the snow-topped mountains of Quebec close to Montreal, Canada: Le Studio.

Wave
1975

WINTER HAD COMFORTABLY settled by the time the band and I arrived at Le Studio, Morin-Heights, in the Laurentian Mountains. The view was a delicate piece of art, serene and perfectly idyllic. Situated on a small hill next to a frozen lake, the studio had large windows stretching from ceiling to floor so you could take in the entire, snow-white panoramic landscape. Owned and run by an eccentric engineer, André Perry, and his wife, Yael, the complex provided everything you could wish for in terms of technical equipment, accommodation, and delicious helpings of French food. The only problem was making it through the two-metre snow wall to the studio after a flurry – a brutal and bone-freezing task.

Perhaps Paul was just feeling the cold. For whatever reason, he couldn't get into *Numbers* and ended up abandoning the project, leaving me to continue with the band and get through my emotional storm.

During the sessions, I invited Art Garfunkel to add his impeccable voice to a couple of tracks. He was quite interested in how I shifted time patterns and constructed the arrangements. I loved Simon and Garfunkel's songs and always felt that Paul played guitar much better than I ever could. We all admire each other for different things.

To capture the odd fairy-tale sound for the album we located a children's choir in Ottawa to sing on "Monad's Anthem" and "Home." We also hired a professional actor to read some lyrics in a freakishly deep voice, like a giant booming down at us from a pulpit in the galaxy. *Numbers* was progressively sounding less and less commercial (Paul Samwell-Smith had probably seen that coming). The album's theme was offbeat and myopic. Without a book or a full-length animation film to explain the story, it was going to be a struggle.

Wrapping up the recordings in Morin-Heights, I travelled for a short time to Paris where I could sketch and develop the characters and drawings that had been shaping in my head. After a week or so locked up in my private little world off the Champs-Élysées, the task was beginning to look and feel pretty monumental; my hands and my imagination were sore and needed to rest. I had greatly underestimated the amount of time the drawings would require. After about twenty illustrations the idea of a full-length animation started shifting to the rear storage shelf of my garage.

Returning to base in Los Angeles, I checked in at the Chateau Marmont hotel on the Strip and locked myself away to design the twelve-inch vinyl cover. Innumerable concepts and veggie burgers later, the artwork ended up dark and rather black-heavy, totally the reverse of the pristine white, light ambience in which it was recorded.

Hit-wise there were very few grabbers. The only one that sounded slightly single-ish was "Banapple Gas," a remnant of my breathing lança-perfume during those crazy carnival nights in Rio. There was not much for the unsuspecting public to relate to: they were probably thrown further off track by one of the most bizarre and zany music videos I ever made. Filmed exclusively in Hollywood, it starred me as a "Gas" pusher in yellow waistcoat, dark glasses, and yellow cheesecutter, squirting intoxicating puffs of "Banapple" smoke in people's faces and smelly underarms, sinisterly turning them into clueless zombies.

That same year – adding to my darkened state of mind – I had a kind of crisis that demonstrated my insecurity and mistrust of the world in which I had buried myself. It was my twenty-seventh birthday, and Barry Krost threw a party in my honour at some Hollywood hotel restaurant. There were a few surprises in store for me: the candles on the birthday cake were trick ones – the moment you blew them out, they ignited and relit again. Great fun. As the evening went on, people gave me presents. One surprise "gift" brought a truly explosive halt to the event: it was a parcel given to me by Jackie Krost, Barry's younger brother. Eagerly ripping open the wrapping paper, I looked and gasped – there in front of me was a straitjacket! My size. Everybody laughed, of course . . . not me.

My blood boiled. I quickly sobered up, blasted some verbal obscenities and ran as fast as I could out of the restaurant, leaving the guests bewildered. That night I

15 | *Wave*

walked and walked the lonely streets of Los Angeles; I wasn't in the right place and needed to get away – but knowing sweet nothing about where in heaven's name I should go next. Back to square one:

> In the blackness of the night
> I seem to wander endlessly
> With a hope burning out, deep inside
> I'm a fugitive, community has driven me out
> For this bad, bad world, I'm beginning to doubt
> I'm alone and there is no one by my side[25]

It felt like I had reached the end of the paved world – and it really nearly was. Something massive was about to occur, which brought me that much closer to it.

After a respectable space of time, having patched things up a bit between me and my friends, I abjectly accepted my subjectively enviable position. Driving in an open convertible, I was on my way to visit Jerry Moss and his wife, Sandra, for lunch at their beach house in Malibu by the Pacific Ocean, with my manager, Barry Krost.

It was another one of those L.A. afternoons and, at some point as the food was being prepared, I decided to take a dip. It was getting pretty dull and cloudy, and not as warm as I would have liked, but the ocean looked so tempting. Unknown to me, it was not a particularly good time of the day to go for a swim; it never occurred to me, as I stared out at the uncommonly empty beach, that there was hardly anyone else paddling around in the sea that day. Nevertheless, that was part of my style – characteristic, even in my music – to do something unexpected, which no one else was commonly doing. Dashing to put on my trunks, I ran out for a swim.

The temperature was bitingly cold. Having swum out some distance and passing about a quarter of an hour in energetic splashing around in the icy ocean, my hands began turning anaemically yellow – a familiar sign, telling me my body had endured enough. I turned to swim back to shore. After a dozen or so weary strokes, I realised something was wrong; my muscles were slow and tired. The powerful Pacific Ocean's undercurrent was too mighty and compelling, steadily drawing my body out and away from the shore! My heart froze.

Strenuously, I struggled to stay afloat, but my legs and arms were now badly aching and were too weak and limp to get me back to land. Barry's solitary figure was still visible on the beachfront just by the house. He appeared minuscule, and far too far away from where I was now frantically flapping. He was totally unaware of the danger I was in and could not have heard me nor done anything to help, anyway.

Death filled the horizon and stared directly into my fragile soul again, catching it half-naked and totally unprepared in the sparse vastness of the ocean. Bolts of fear shot through me. The battle to stay alive was on.

In a split second of the rapidly dwindling moments that remained of my life, I looked up to the sky and prayed, "O God, if You save me, I'll work for You!" No sooner had those words flown from my heart, than a gentle wave rose behind me and nudged me forward.

God was right there.

My life energy suddenly returned, and I was on my way back to shore with all the power needed; the tide had changed and was now rolling in my favour. Within a few world-changing minutes, I was out of the water, shaking and shaken, and safely back on land.

Within my subconscious, I had always been aware that some ever-present power behind life was close, watching and overseeing. That monumental day, far from any church or temple, I sincerely renewed my faith and commitment to the omnipresent will of the universe in the form of a verbal agreement, confirmed by the only other witnesses there at the time: the ocean itself – and my songs.

> *Yesterday I was on the edge*
> *Hoping everything was going to work itself out*
> *A good honest man doing the work of God*
> *Trying to make things better for him*[26]

The thinnest of barriers fluctuates between life and death, yet we act as if we are going to bundle on forever. What normally happens with human weaklings, after being saved from the jaws of a deadly unremitting storm, is that, as soon as the weather settles down again, we quickly forget what we promised and then go about our everyday business.

At the beach house, I kept the spiritual epiphany to myself and never told Barry, Jerry, or anyone else what had actually happened. But life had somehow altered. Regardless of my engagements with a continuous flow of worldly diversions, a promise was made out at sea, and a time would come when it had to be fulfilled.

My ethereal boat was apparently approaching its destination.

The statue of Christ high on the peak of Corcovado mountain looked down as I turned the shiny silver key and entered the door of my new, seventh-floor flat in the exclusive lagoon area of Rio. The luxury block on Rua Baronesa de Poconé had just been completed and was totally bare and painted chalk-white. I had little interest in furnishing the flat; there was no incentive without family or a permanent companion to turn this place into a home. A king-sized bed, a table, and some chairs were all I had, and that's all I needed.

Opposite me, on a sharp mountain slope across the lagoon, I could see the overcrowded, corrugated tin huts of the favela, the slum housing thousands of impoverished nomadic city dwellers. In some strange way, I was homeless too; it was part of my guilt complex not to take advantage of my privileged wealth and position. I didn't bother to lavish myself with overtly palatial bric-a-brac or flashy wardrobes. Rio would just remain a temporary transit stop. I kept my jeans on and hardly bothered to unpack.

This was going to be the year of the "Majikat Earth Tour," one of my most ambitious world tours yet. Designed by a Los Angeles graphic artist friend, Jeremy Railton, it included the construction of a complete transportable stage set with a semi-circular, white sail backdrop, incorporating a video screen, lights, PA system, a robotically driven, sparkly red-top piano and automatic pop-up stool.

As a support act, we hired a magic troupe to keep everybody smack-eyed and entertained with a display of stunning tricks (including sawing a luscious blonde lady in half) during intervals and musical breaks. At the start of the show, I would jump out of four coloured boxes, placed one on top of the other. *Presto! Look, it's Cat!* Los Angeles was extra-special because we were able to hire a real tiger that dramatically appeared from an empty, cloth-covered cage. It was going to be a show unlike any other.

Rehearsals for the world tour began in Frankfurt, Germany. During one of the breaks I took a stroll and picked up a strange, crooked walking stick from the nearby forest. I christened it Amberthwiddle; it was added to my collection of good-luck charms and travelled with me everywhere.

The tour kicked off in Gothenburg, Sweden, in November 1975. It coincided with the release of *Numbers*, which was getting mixed reviews. I half expected that.

My mission in life was not to go on producing commercial albums; it was to continue my search while inviting my audience to share my latest philosophical obsession. I'd try to make some musical sense of the various combatant views of existence that hit me along the way . . . while, admittedly, making a respectable living at the same time.

"Majikat" was a great success, wowing audiences in the UK, Europe, the US, and Canada. It was to last for eight months with a short break for Christmas before returning to Europe and culminating in what was expected to be a triumphant conquest of Athens, Greece, the following summer.

Just as the tour got off the ground, David was getting married again. He had been going steady with Yael, a Jewish girl from Tel Aviv, for some time following his break-up and subsequent divorce from Birgitta. David had met Yael through a friend while she was visiting London on a European sightseeing tour. My brother had worked most of his life in Jewish business circles and felt at home in their tight-knit community. Because of our Mediterranean background and David's characteristically Levantine looks, he fitted in easily and had even adopted the surname Gordon; doubtless, it suited his persona and was much more convenient. The powerful energy field of this youthful Israeli girl certainly made David feel charged and reconnected.

At the end of 1975, after journeying to pay a dutiful visit to Yael's parents, the couple honeymooned in Eilat, the Red Sea resort in southern Israel. But David had somewhere else he dreamed of going: Jerusalem. Like me and our elder sister, Anita, David was brought up as a Christian on a healthy diet of biblical stories, schooled in the heavily religious environment at St. Joseph's. He had a strong feeling of respect and love for sacred places and roads in the Holy Land, where Jesus and so many prophets had walked, preached and performed miracles. David had been given a prophet's name, after our highly religious maternal grandfather.

The couple went on to visit Jerusalem. One day, witnessing some angry priests of different clerical orders indignantly shouting at each other near a church, David's peace was disturbed. He gazed across towards a golden-domed mosque that stood at the centre of the Holy City and apparently thought to himself, *What is that religion?*

Islam was relatively unknown in the West, and David, like me, had grown up hearing only negative stories about Turks and those dark and dangerous "Muslims" who had inhabited "Constantinople," proudly waving blood-red flags, stamped with sabre-like crescents and a star.

Yet, being a bold, self-taught, relentless seeker of universal wisdom, big brother Dave decided to take a chance and have a closer look inside the mosque, perched high on the square compound of Masjid al-Aqsa.

That was a turning point. After taking off his shoes and stepping inside he sensed an air of peace. Walking around the ornately carpeted sanctum and watching the way that Muslims worshipped – devoid of statues, icons, or figurative paintings, purely engaged in serene bowing and prayer – moved David immensely. He stood quietly behind some worshippers as they humbly prostrated themselves. Moved in the spirit of the moment, he made an attempt to mimic them – not very successfully, obviously. A large, well-built man soon walked towards him and inquired, "Are you Muslim?"

"No."

"What are you doing, then?"

He was asked to leave. What David did not know was that, just one year earlier, a fanatical Jewish tourist from Australia had set fire to al-Aqsa mosque in the sacred precinct. Security since that time had been strengthened.

The incident didn't dampen David's interest in the religion. When he finally got back to Britain, he went and bought a translation of the Qur'an and began to read, soon realising there was a lot more to this religion than we had previously been told.

The Gift
1975–6

IT WAS JULY, and I was visiting David's flat in Golders Green, London, where he had settled with his wife, Yael, and their new baby daughter, Naomi.

One of the basic ground rules I had agreed with my brother was that I would not buy him presents and he wouldn't buy me any, either. Our birthdays are only one day apart, and it seemed an economically satisfactory arrangement for both of us to maintain. Strange it was, then, when he decided to break with the tradition this particular year and offer me a gift, wrapped and nicely ribboned.

As I slowly opened the decorative paper, I beheld a beautiful, vermillion-red, glossy book bearing the words "The Qur'an." What an unusual surprise! He had been intending to give it to me since his trip to Jerusalem but wanted to wait for an appropriate moment to do so. He had apparently purchased it from Foyles, exactly where – years earlier – I had picked up a hymn book containing "Morning Has Broken."

The cover carried the title *The Message of the Qur'an – Presented in Perspective by Hashim Ameer Ali*, in an English translation published in Japan by Charles Tuttle. It looked and felt very heavy and handsome. This was obviously something special, as David had already told me what had happened to him in Jerusalem and how peacefully moved he felt in the mosque. Passing the book on to me, he said, prophetically: "Maybe there's something in here people have overlooked."

I hugged and thanked him.

Still on tour, I packed the Qur'an with my other possessions in preparation for my travels, intending to read it whenever I had the chance. Interestingly, I had visited the Bodhi Tree bookshop in Los Angeles many times, but always walked right past the Islamic section. There was a natural aversion I had to things connected with my father's longtime enemies, the Turks. Also, the image of Arabs was really not much better; *Lawrence of Arabia*, starring Peter O'Toole, left a recent imprint from a slice of Arab history that only reaffirmed the superiority of Western military intelligence and tactics over the tribal desert dwellers and fractured Arab nations.

Holding a copy of the Muslim "Bible" in my hands, I wondered what the Qur'an was going to tell me. It would certainly need to be pretty powerful if it was to overcome my Western viewpoint and the inherent animosity built up in the crusading collective Christian subconsciousness, acquired since Richard the Lionheart. Going back even further, since the early days of European antiquity, Greeks and Romans regarded only themselves as "civilised," while everything foreign – including Britain, and all that lay to the east of the Mediterranean Sea – bore the unflattering label: "barbarian."[27]

But, hey! I considered myself modern and aloof from historical ties, and resisted the tendency to bolt myself to anything that belonged to the chains of the "past."

We had kicked off the second North American leg of the "Majikat" tour, starting in Lakeland, Florida, and were on the road to notch up twenty-eight shows over the next three months. Seven band members, three female singers, a crew of almost thirty, three magicians, and countless doves and rabbits were my supportive entourage.

As a self-confessed universalist, who ardently believed in the concept of one world, I tried to join together musicians of different colours from all parts of the globe: I was half-Greek Cypriot, half-Swedish; Alun Davies was originally Welsh; Jean Roussel was Mauritian; Bruce Lynch a New Zealander; Mark Warner an American; Larry Steele from Jamaica; Gerry Conway was a British Jew; and Chico Batera was Brazilian. The female singers were Black, Blonde, and Brunette. Ha, ha . . . excuse that sneaky, misogynistic gag: their names were actually Suzanne Lynch, a New Zealander, and Angela Howell and Kim Carlson, both American.

Aside from me boasting about my broad and embracing view of humanity, I was a strict taskmaster as far as touring and rehearsals were concerned. So, being the perfect "star,"

I was aloof and maintained my enigmatic control over the troupe.

Although my concentration was sharply focused on the "Majikat" tour, while checking into hotel rooms with my suitcases and guitar I now held tightly onto the Qur'an. Not wanting the cover to get stained or spoiled, I carefully wrapped it in a dark-blue, bamboo-imprinted piece of cloth – a cherished memento from my earlier visit to Japan. I valued the gift from my brother; it became a highly privileged item next to my faithful walking stick, Amberthwiddle, which I also kept close. Whenever I found some free time, I would open the pages and take a peek.

Initially, I had a job to break through general negative attitudes, built up over years of absorbing reporting on Muslims: photographs of the Munich Olympic Games massacre, the violent Black Panther movement (which I somehow mistakenly linked to Muhammad Ali and the Nation of Islam) and the recent military invasion of Cyprus by Turkey; all were pretty damning indictments. My instinctive tendency was to look for something to confirm my doubts about Muslims. But, then again, here was a book written before such militant political events and images. So I actively tried to put such impressions aside, following the spirit of my lyrics:

> Well, the answer lies within
> So why not take a look now?
> Kick out the devil's sin
> And pick up a good book now . . .[28]

The first expectation was to find some foreign descriptions of Muslim history and exploits. I had heard the names "Muhammad" and "Allah," but knew little more than ideas about mountains, harems, and turbaned heroes; images (courtesy, once again, of Hollywood) came to mind of good-looking American princes being chased through bustling Arab market places by a horde of ugly, angry, unkempt-bearded brigands, being thwarted by an intersecting herd of slouched, slow-moving camels. What else could I expect?

The inferior picture and generic prejudice I had been exposed to needed to be swept to the side. I didn't have to be told that the West was superior – that was already accepted: de facto! My position was to remain a free thinker; I should not be captive to stored-up, unfriendly concepts – no paper book could hurt me. So I entered cautiously into this new literary work, not knowing quite what to expect.

It was about to surprise me, big time.

> **In the name of God – the Most**
> **Compassionate, Most Merciful**
> **All praise is for God – Lord of all worlds,**
> **The Most Compassionate, Most Merciful,**
> **Master of the Day of Judgement.**
> **You alone we worship and You**
> **alone we ask for help.**
> **Guide us along the Straight Path,**
> **The Path of those You have blessed – not those**
> **You are displeased with,**
> **or those who are astray.**[29]

16 | *The Gift*

Never in my wildest imaginary excursions did I ever suspect that I would find the name of God in the Qur'an. That was the first big lesson and quite the opposite of what I expected. I had heard the name "Allah" being pronounced and referred to as some kind of Arab deity. Never did anybody tell me that, for thousands of years, it was the same generic name for God among Aramaic-speaking Jews and Christians, still used today in the print of every Arabic Bible. Wow!

What next? I kept turning.

I might have predicted seeing the name of Muhammad extolled and glorified like an Arabic version of Christ, as some kind of immortal or avatar to be worshipped and adored along with mystic stars and moons. After all, Muslims for many years had been called "Mohammedans" by orientalists, and the crescent and star were their symbol. I was on the verge of finding out something very different.

Fortunately, the unique translation I had been given by brother David presented the original chapters according to their chronological sequence, based on the order in which they were revealed. Therefore, the shorter and older revelations were at the beginning, and the longer, more legally complex ones at the end. That was particularly useful for a beginner like me. The first chapter opened with a call to learn:

> **Read! In the name of your Lord Who Created –
> created humans from a clinging clot.
> Read! And your Lord is most Generous,
> Who taught by the pen –
> taught humanity that which they knew not.**[30]

There was no sign of an author on the cover of the Qur'an, the only allusion being that each chapter began, "In the name of God (Allah) Most Gracious, Most Merciful." The notes in the translation made it clearer, and I soon realised that the Qur'an was understood to be the words of God speaking directly to Muhammad and giving him messages for the guidance of humankind. Similar in nature and tone to the Bible, but with less historical data and fewer stories with beginnings and ends, and closer to the Psalms in many respects, it had a powerful air of certitude and authority.

I was now in a face-to-face encounter with the core message of Islam. One of the very early and shortest chapters was so straightforward, it stunned me in its simplicity and myth-shattering implications:

> **Say, "He is God – One and Indivisible;**
> **God – the Sustainer needed by all.**
> **He has never had offspring, nor was He born.**
> **And there is none comparable to Him."**[31]

For the first time, I read the description of God in terms of supreme and eternal Oneness. Just that notion of undivided unity somehow began to make me feel more comfortable and, in some sense, secure. It pointed to the single source of determination and power behind the universe. This seemed to link everything together, from my past delving into the mystical meanings behind the Pythagorean and Eastern metaphysics, to the *Bhagavad Gita*, the Buddhist Middle way, through the Holy Bible's first commandment – and even present-day science.

16 | The Gift

This singular view of the cosmos made me less jittery about the latest, mind-bending scientific exploration of physics, from the smallest subatomic particles to the largest structures in the universe, its numberless worlds, stars and galaxies, light years, dark matter, or black holes – regardless. It was all one entity!

Just by reading this short chapter, the elimination of birthly attributes from the Godhead, silenced all those endless thoughts and nagging images that reduced the belief in an all-knowing, glorious divine being down to our own human, blood-level requirement of sexual dependence and bodily representation.

My fascination increased.

The "Majikat" tour rolled on. The book would accompany me everywhere as we travelled through the various cities of North America and Europe.

A gig was booked at the Oakland Coliseum, near San Francisco, a city famed for its hippie history. During a gap in the afternoon before the show, I strolled into town and walked into a misty, incense-laden, free-spirit bookshop. Looking around at the shelves choked with perplexingly titled books, lava lamps, and oriental knick-knacks, a brightly coloured object caught my eye: an oriental-ish carpet. Even though it was a synthetic, imitation "something-or-other" and probably manufactured in Taiwan, it soon became another of my closely treasured travel attachments. I exchanged some crinkly paper dollars for it and carted it away awkwardly under my arm to the hotel.

My daily routine, after crawling out of bed, was to lay the

carpet down and do some yoga exercises. If there was time, I remained sitting on it with the Qur'an and read through its pages slowly, line by line, like a mountain climber, each step elevating me to a new view of Earth below and the skies above, where I would peg my bookmark and ponder.

Life went on like that for a while.

It was a conflicted time: I would walk off stage after a show in front of ten thousand fans, hearing the sound of voluminous applause gradually ebb into the background as I headed back to my hotel room, all alone, and locked the door.

More aware than anyone else that I was not perfect, by that time I had accumulated a lot of ugly smudge marks in the exercise book of life and was seriously interested in knowing how to erase the burdensome guilt and start earning some stars. I wanted to give the angels something to smile about as they started noting my new endeavours. They could stop writing down my sins and begin a new page. There, by myself in the privacy of my hotel room, I continued on my internal quest, and quietly read on.

One powerful subject I encountered in the early verses of the Qur'an was that of the afterlife. Yes! That topic was something I certainly wanted to know more about: death and the beyond. I was confronted head-on by the inevitable reality that this great executioner, annihilator of human ambitions and worldly loves, usurper of all property and the accumulated treasures of a life, was silently awaiting everyone – me included! An uncomfortable fact.

Thankfully, these early revelations in the Qur'an were accompanied by lots more information. There were elaborate descriptions, loaded with hope of eternal joys of exquisite

16 | *The Gift*

fruits and beautiful angelic companions, relaxing within heavenly palatial gardens of infinite pleasure, all awaiting the most fortunate souls in *Jannah* (the Arabic name for paradise). But wait! These delightful glimpses of Paradise would – almost always – be coupled with extremely disquieting threats of the opposite abode: the blazing, flesh-eating flames and boiling-hot drinking waters of hellfire: *Jahannam*! Too frightening for words. I wondered: Could those bits about Hell possibly be skipped?

Not surprisingly, my Catholic upbringing had prepared me for the terminology and warnings of the Qur'an, the stories of burning flesh, morbid images of screaming skulls, demons, and eternal damnation for those who strayed from the moral path. They were brought back to vivid life here in true depth and full colour, hi-def. I was already familiar with the satanic picture – even in my own song lyrics, Beelzebub had been clearly mentioned: "the devil's lake," "the bad ol' debil," and "Old Satan's tree," to mention a few.[32]

But, in contrast with the message of Christianity, the solution to avoiding such doom and perdition was not achieved by belief in a "Saviour" as a guarantor for one's sins.

> **By the passage of time!**
> **Surely humanity is in grave loss.**
> **Except those who have faith, do good,**
> **and urge each other to the truth,**
> **and urge each other to perseverance.**[33]

Every time an important question arose in my mind, an answer would not be far behind. This short chapter called

"Time" provided the basic principles of salvation. It was all beginning to look fairly reasonable. The ultimate responsibility for the state in which we find ourselves, according to the way I understood the Qur'an, rested with each of us, individually. The prerequisites for human success on an eternal measure were reduced to only two major factors: belief and good actions. There was no particular "hand" to hold here . . . or was there?

The more I read the Qur'an, the more I found it emphasizing the highest principle of faith, being the unshakable bond and attachment to God – and to Him alone. In terms of Christianity and Judaism, that already sounded familiar; after all, I remembered reading somewhere in the Bible that when Jesus was asked what the greatest commandment was, he replied, "Thou shalt love the Lord thy God with all thy heart, and with all thy soul and with all thy mind."[34]

The Qur'an went even further by describing the opposite to this love and affection for God: the most prohibited deed a soul can commit is the sin of shirk – to worshipfully adore or associate anything, any partner or being, with God:

> **Indeed, God does not forgive associating others with Him in worship, but forgives anything else of whoever He wills. And whoever associates others with God has indeed committed a grave sin.**[35]

This was clearly an elaboration and confirmation of the first law given to Moses, "You shall have no other gods beside Me." Thankfully, the verse in the Qur'an also, compactly, included

16 | *The Gift*

the opportunity to receive God's all-embracing forgiveness, provided we remain true to that first principle.

I was also pleased to find that true monotheistic faith, according to the Qur'an, did not start with Muhammad. In fact, biblical prophets and messengers – including Abraham, Moses, Solomon, Jacob, Jesus, and so many others – were mentioned too, their lives and missions relayed in amazing detail and reverence throughout many chapters. According to the Qur'an, these were all chosen apostles of God, but were still human. There was an element of empathy and connection with a real person you could spiritually and literally "hold" on to and follow.

Although history proves that Christopher Columbus was not the first to set foot in North America (another subtle distortion of imperial European bias), I was roughly beginning to know what it psychologically might have felt like.

The Qur'an was the single most important discovery in redrafting my map of religion and the rapid expansion of my spiritual coordinates. I kept on gradually assimilating all this exciting information, reading slowly to absorb and understand the meaning within these sentences without surfing in the way I had become used to with so many other books. The key to success, as I had just learned from that valuable short chapter about the value of time, was to patiently keep going: word by word, sentence by sentence. I ventured down to the hotel bar less and less and had fewer nights out clubbing with the band. Whenever I did so, I would usually feel bad about it the next morning.

*

Looking after my health was important; I had seen too many talented musicians fall foul in that particular discipline: Jimi Hendrix, Brian Jones, Jim Morrison, Janis Joplin, too many to mention.

Slowly, I began to cut down on cigarettes, particularly because they affected my voice; it was impossible to sing show after show if I just puffed away when I felt like it, which was my habit. My new method was to restrict ciggies to only one every hour. Also, I had developed a particular method for loosening up before the curtain rose: after swigging a bottle of beer, to make me less self-conscious (healthier than my previous brandy and port combo), I would breathe in a few large gulps of pure O_2 from a 75kg portable tank of oxygen. My army of roadies were condemned to ritually heave those heavy metal containers around hall to hall, city to city. The combination worked marvellously; it helped me to regain my balance, while feeling pretty "zesty."

Apart from that cumbersome device, I also started practising vegetarianism, carrying a transportable kitchen in a tailor-made flight case full of compartments containing various natural vitamins as well as space for my snazzy fruit blender.

Willpower was vital if I wanted to survive the fatigue and hangover of heavy concert touring. Apart from the pre-show beer with the oxygen trick, I had drastically reduced my alcohol intake. Whether that was as a result of what I was reading in the Qur'an or not, I am not quite sure, but it seemed like a good idea. All I really needed was an alternative to replace it with. While sitting in a bar somewhere in the southern States, I asked the barman for something that tasted nice but without alcohol. He mixed me up a pink, fruity concoction of pineapple and orange juice, with a little helping of cream and a drop of grenadine.

"That's it!"

I sincerely thanked him and from that day on started drinking it wherever and whenever I could, naming it a "Pickaxe," but changing that later to a "Picasso" because, with lots of square ice, it looked so Pablo-pink and cubist.

Keeping a private, personal space, away from unwelcome disturbances, was necessary, especially during tours. I tried to remain incognito and avoid the exhausting intrusion of press or fans. My agents would book me in under the name Mr. Ivon Toby Allon. It was a great insider joke; when a call came through via the reception, the announcer would call my name over the loudspeaker in the lobby.

"Attention! Mr. 'I-von-to-be-alone,' please come to the front desk, there is a call waiting for you."

The result was hilarious: we would all yelp with laughter.

While in the States, we managed to film one of the shows in Williamsburg, Virginia. Malcolm Leo, who also directed the L.A. production of my "Banapple Gas" music video, was brought in again.

I had a psychotic aversion to cameras on stage, and that made it difficult for the production team to get all the shots they desired. During one show, a cameraman came too close to me as I played "Sitting" on the piano. I stopped the song midway and swore ****ing blind at the poor bloke. It was clearly audible to the audience, who must have been quite shocked to hear their pure-hearted purry Cat suddenly shouting such vulgarities. The cameraman crumbled into dust and disappeared, looking like a naughty boy told off in front of a seven-thousand-strong, seated class.

That was the kind of offensive, tyrannical character I demonstrated on occasion. But I felt guilty afterwards, and it weighed on me to the point where I remember it to this day. So the Qur'an was beginning to influence the deliberations within my conscience (the note-taking angels were no doubt disappointed, wagging their red pens ponderously). Needless to say, following that nasty moment on stage, I wasn't interested in seeing the film finished. Footage remained packed in the vaults for another twenty-eight years.

After the States, we moved on to Europe: Stockholm, Berlin, Rotterdam, Vienna, we swept through cities like a circus with our international troupe of musicians, magicians, fluffy creatures, velvet curtains, floating piano, and twinkle-lit Hollywood Bowl tent set.

It was close to the end of the tour in Barcelona where the fun stopped abruptly, delivering me a big lesson: how to succeed in invoking that long-lost schoolboy-ish sense of sheer pain again. Frolicking around with a couple of the band members in the hotel a day before the gig, I took a wild, giant jump down a whole flight of steps in one of those "look at me – I'm unbreakable" demonstrations of childlike imbecility. I never got up. My right heel had suffered a fracture, and the pain resembled nothing I'd ever had to bear before.

A doctor arrived, and my leg was quickly bound in plaster. Death would almost have been welcomed. That was my night of "Spanish hell." I was quite prepared to pass away if that was God's will. Unable to sleep or escape the pain, I morbidly screamed through the wee hours right up until dawn for some merciful relief.

Like a true hero, I insisted on doing the show the next day. Against the doctor's orders, I took to the stage and played most of the evening with the white-plastered leg awkwardly propped up on a soft, polystyrene-filled beanbag. The Spanish welcomed the show of bravado, and my elevated toes certainly attracted a lot of sympathetic applause that night.

Joseph's Story
1976

FEAR OF DRYING up is every songwriter's greatest nightmare; though I refused to face up to it, my creative well was sapped, and it was becoming noticeable on my albums. Making records took so much longer and was turning out to be a more frustrating, time-consuming job. When songs didn't come, that upset me: I would try writing words, then put a melody and chords to them, going round and round a phrase repetitively, until I reached a break point. To outside ears it must have sounded close to madness – a stylus agonisingly jumping on a cracked record, playing that wretched part over and over again.

Thankfully, I now had an escape from my moments of artistic uncertainty and unrest: I would put the guitar down and open the Qur'an to refresh my spirit.

*

It was like the wheels of our "majik-bus" fell off. The end of the "Majikat Earth Tour" was approaching, and I was exhausted. Athens was to be the grand finale, but the seats were only half sold; the promoter had not considered the impact of June exams and a major football match between Iraklis and Olympiakos in the Greek Cup taking place on the same day. My ego was injured; my fellow Hellenes obviously considered their own future careers and football over and above me! Even with everything I was picking up through my Qur'an reading, it was hard to restrain my baser instinct. "What a bloody insult!" Athens was cancelled. Instead of being my crowning moment of iconic immortality, it ended like just another rotten Greek tragedy. The Cat slipped away, tail down, into the shadows.

To add to the general gloom, *Numbers* had not done that well: predictably – as a Pythagorean mathematician might say – my excursion into numerology had nosedived along with my latest chart position. Like Monad watching the castle walls of Polygor crumbling to dust before his eyes, there was nothing much left to hope for. Depressed and needing to get away from it all, I flew back to Rio where I could be alone again. There, in the empty shell of my flat, I could reflect, and hear myself think.

While my perspectives were widening from reading the Qur'an, my personal "pop star" ambitions were shrinking. Everything a composer writes is usually a reflection of the experiences he or she encounters, even in their dreams or imagination, but mine were appearing less and less significant compared to the spectacle of life – seen and unseen – the Qur'an was revealing to me.

After the exhausting "Majikat Earth Tour," I had enough, and didn't want to think about gigging again. I wrote a slightly tongue-in-cheek song expressing my weariness with the whole business. It posed a serious question, however, about my veiled intentions:

> *I was seventeen*
> *You were working for Matthew & Son*
> *The Beatles met the Queen*
> *And I wrote, I'm Gonna Get Me a Gun*
> *It was like a dream in the star machine*
> *Iz-it-so? Iz-it-so?*
> *I never wanted to be a star*
> *I never wanted to travel far*
> *I only wanted a little bit of love*
> *So I could put a little love in my heart*[36]

Not entirely true. I did at one time desperately want to be a star, yet I had been there and done all that long ago, at the boyish age of eighteen. Keeping up a "star" position with sustained vigour was a much more complicated challenge. But, deep down, what I really wanted was out of my reach.

According to my contract with A&M, it was time to record a new album. I had heard very favourable whispers about a studio in Copenhagen, Denmark, called Sweet Silence. We booked it out for a month with my core band made up of Jean Roussel on keyboards, Bruce Lynch on bass, and Carly Simon's guy, Andy Newmark, on drums. By the time we got there I had finally managed to compose enough new songs.

There was no special concept in mind; it would be just a mixed collection of music, reflecting my Brazilian influences and oddities I had written here and there and everywhere along the way.

In the autumn of 1976 I checked into the hotel near the centre of Copenhagen. I put a DO NOT DISTURB sign on my door, unpacked my vegetarian trunk of goodies, unfolded my travelling carpet, and placed the Qur'an by my bed. There was something reassuring just to know it was nearby, even when I didn't have the time to read it. Studio work was always crazily intense, and the job fully consumed me. The time to lock down, get focused, and go to work on my next album had begun.

The excitement provided by new technology, with a leap from sixteen- to twenty-four-track machines, was going to be fun. My semi-nomadic voyages to different cities of the world, hopping around from studio to studio, were undertaken specifically to experiment and create some fresh element of musical or technical novelty into my recordings.

Sweet Silence had a great new spaceship control room, but the hours of labour it took fiddling with knobs to achieve the right sounds on the desk actually made the recording process much less musically spontaneous. Overdubbing drums and other fundamental instruments became the norm. At that stage, I was heavily into using electronic sounds and synthesisers, which meant the songs and performances became less important. But I didn't see that as a problem at the time. I was looking for a brand-new "sound," so Alun Davies was not invited as the songs were not written for a six-string, folksy acoustic accompaniment.

CAT ON THE ROAD TO FINDOUT

The sessions in Denmark began in a spirit of optimism. I experimented with new chords; a soft jazz approach met my folk-pop style, and a new half-breed was born. Words and lyrics were now flowing less profusely compared to my traumatic, post-TB song era. But they still meant something to me. The riddle contained in the song "I Never Wanted to Be a Star" eventually delivered me the idea for the title of the album, *Izitso*.

A deeper look at some of the lyrics in songs like "Life" shows that I was still struggling schizophrenically, trapped between two worlds: one enticing me to keep playing in a love-filled fairground; the other convincing me that I'd really had enough and needed to get off the carousel. This conflict was emphasised by the battle between 4/4 and 3/4 rhythms between verse and chorus.

> *[4/4] Life, you make it what it is*
> *Love, can change it with a kiss*
> *Love, can take you by the hand*
> *Love, can drop you where you stand*
>
> *[3/4] But still you want to have it all*
> *You like to live it up*
> *But still you want to have it all*
> *I thought you had enough . . .*

It wasn't long into the making of *Izitso* that I discovered Ringo Starr was in town and staying in the very same hotel, so I invited him to the studio. It was a nervous moment for me, as the Beatles had been such a monster influence on my life and ambitions. The solution was to get suitably drunk – enough to be able to feel uninhibited but still remain in tune.

After having a few goes at "(Remember the Days of the) Old Schoolyard," it seemed the odd timings of the song were cramping Ringo's style. I didn't want him to feel let down, so we forgot about the album and simply jammed. The result was a hugely freeform musical party. Ringo was the star guest. I would introduce some natty riff on my red 335 Gibson electric guitar and he would just sit tight and groove while the band filled in.

The tapes of that evening eventually got leaked on a bootleg of some Beatles oddities, *Sink in the Can*. Listening to those recordings, people can get an idea of how I wrote some of my songs. Words would be mumbled and jumbled together, repeating a chorus structure or riff, then later I'd return with my glasses on to try and make sense of them. One particular on-the-spot number that deserved to be revisited was "Waiting for the Sailor." What the title meant was yet to be worked out, but it was a hot, catchy song in the bendy-Fender vein of Steve Miller, whom I respected greatly.

Ringo seemed to enjoy the loose abandonment of the explosive creative occasion. As I ad-libbed and developed one of the lyrics he asked, "Did you just make that up?"

I answered affirmatively, nodding.

"Hey! You're goooood . . ." came the endorsement of one of the world's best drummers, who played in the greatest group, the one that would never be eclipsed by any other – in my opinion at least, and that of most others who were lucky enough to live through the Beatles era.

Perhaps we were all a bit too awash with Danish beer and

whatnot; for whatever reason – including my lust for perfection and hatred of uncontrollably drunken moments when I lampooned and sounded like a "Goon" – none of the jam tracks we did ended up on *Izitso* (some being nine uncommercial minutes long). It was just one "fab" night all round. After that I went back to work on the intended album with my band.

I was already carrying a couple of raw tracks, "Killin' Time" and "Child for a Day," from the great Muscle Shoals Sound Studio in Alabama, where I had previously dropped in for some sessions. Roger Hawkins, Tim Henson, and Barry Beckett were the renowned in-house rhythm section there. They had produced the backing for amazing R & B artists like Wilson Pickett, Aretha Franklin, and the Staple Singers. I wanted to capture some of that classic southern Alabama sound.[37]

After more dubbing in New York with Chick Corea, a phenomenal keyboard player who expertly swung into superb Latin jazz-styled performance on a couple of songs, all the tracks I'd accumulated had become saturated with numberless overdubs and retakes, and were unfinished. They desperately needed honing.

As Paul Samwell-Smith was not involved, I needed a producer to help me polish off the album. Dave Kershenbaum, who had worked with A&M on Joan Baez's 1975 album *Diamonds & Rust*, was suggested. Dave took over the arrangements to mix down the album and booked us into Sound 80 studios in Minneapolis, one of the most unmemorable metropolises in the US (except, perhaps, for being the incidental birthplace of Prince). Unbothered, I was basically in "auto" mode with regard to the album. There was something more important going on underneath the surface.

Deeply into my Qur'an reading, the words were beginning to really affect me. There were so many verses about prayer; I started bowing more regularly and asking God for help. Whether by coincidence or the fact that I'd seen Muslims wearing them, I bought myself a red woolly hat, as seen in the photos taken by Moshe Brakha for the cover of *Izitso*.

When I returned to Rio during the last stages of making the album, it was coming up to the New Year celebrations. The tradition for natives of Rio was to make their way to the beach shore at midnight dressed in white, light candles, and cast flowers into the ocean as offerings to the goddess Lamanjá. These gifts were supposed to appease the sea deity to make the waters calm. Some ardent devotees would enter the waters and energetically jump over the waves to increase their portion of luck.

Though not being at all Brazilian, nor interested in any sea goddess or drowning flowers, I decided to join in the collective gala and made my way down to Ipanema before the clock struck twelve. Because of the usual tendency to make resolutions, here was a chance to do something symbolic. In my hand was my dearly beloved walking stick, Amberthwiddle, who had become a close and handy friend, a token of good luck and support on my travels.

Gazing out towards the deep, black expansive ocean, suddenly an urge rose within me to grab the moment and make a personal sacrifice. I also needed to let go of long-held concepts, not wanting to be crippled any longer by irrational or unreliable superstitions. Somewhere out there I believed was the answer to my searching questions. After a long moment of hesitation, I picked up my faithful woody companion and, half remembering some words of the Qur'an, I threw it into the distant waves and called out, "Guide me closer to the truth than this!"

Amberthwiddle was gone – forever.

My prayer was not in any "name" other than the ultimate power behind all things in this universe. There were still competing belief-notions in my mind; I still had major doubts as to the direction in which my life should go. This emotional gesture – ridding myself of a material prop and tightly held possessions – was my way of loosening those chains, as well as freeing me from the burdensome bond of indecisiveness. Climbing up the steep streets towards my flat, I felt lighter and liberated. Sacrifice seemed necessary to achieve some spiritual gain. I had to take a step closer, and was waiting and hoping for the unseen power above to do the same.

Back in the echoing space of my isolated living room, overlooked by the statue of Christ, I continued my reading. I had become a student again, but this time a very willing one. The Qur'an was my highly engaging new teacher, and I didn't want to miss a single lesson. My thirst for knowledge was quenchless.

It was still a sticky challenge for me to accept the notion of a new prophet, Muhammad. The stockpiled effect of years of poorly lit and sketchy information about him and his place in history, drilled in from primary school onward, made it very hard to give up my negative suspicions. A marred view of Arabs and my natural loyalty to Judeo-Christian homelands and culture remained strongly rooted, regardless of my spiritual cruises into Zen Buddhism, Taoism, yoga, and other belief systems; the Arabian waters still looked dark and dangerously rocky.

Then I came across chapter twelve in the Qur'an, the story of Prophet Joseph and his jealous brothers. It was similar to the narrative in the Bible, but there was something very different about it.

As the plot unfolded, so many unbearable disasters befell Joseph, the eleventh son of Israel (Jacob), beginning with the day his brothers threw him down the well. He survived. Subsequently, he was found and sold as a young slave and worked devotedly for an Egyptian nobleman, enduring many years of bondage. On reaching manhood, Joseph's character was unexpectedly and ethically tested by the seductive advances of his master's beautiful wife, who deeply loved and desired him. He resisted, but his shirt was torn in the tussle. Finally, Joseph was cast into jail, through no fault of his own.

Languishing in the dark and criminal-infested dungeons, he continued to bear the injustice gracefully, until the day he was asked to interpret the king of Egypt's strange dream. Explaining the dream, Joseph predicted a seven-year period of abundant harvest, followed by a similar period of drought in the kingdom. On learning this, at last Joseph was exonerated by the king and set free. At which point he was chosen to be the Wazir, the honoured keeper of the entire country's food and wealth storehouses.

While I was reading Joseph's story, a monumental change erupted within me, especially towards the end of the chapter. The time came when his brothers, who had previously thrown him down the well, came face to face with Joseph, humbly seeking food and rations. But they didn't recognise him. While he played host to them, generously offering the brothers refreshments, the king's cup went missing, and the small clan found themselves directly accused. The allegation was focused on Benjamin, Joseph's younger, full-blood brother, in whose saddle bag the cup was discovered.

Trying to absolve themselves from guilt, the brothers started to scorn and talk nastily about Benjamin, claiming that the boy was obviously following the in steps of his elder sibling, Joseph, "who had stolen before him."[38]

This was the worst and cruellest cut of all for Prophet Joseph. His pure heart was deeply wounded. Listening to their blatant lies, he silently wept inside, still hurting from the separation and loneliness of the long years he had spent away from home and his beloved father, a love he had kept hidden within his breast. Patiently, he remained quiet.

Oh God! Something tore open inside of me. "All the times that I've cried, keeping all the things I knew inside."[39] My true identity had been concealed from myself, as well as the external world around me. For nearly thirty years I had been wandering, lost. At last, all the phases of my life seemed to meet together in the extraordinary story of Joseph. My tears began to drop onto the pages.

Though far, far beneath the unsurpassable level of Prophet Joseph's patience and character, I could see certain similarities to my life: I too had been separated from my family and sold in the marketplace; had gone through radical stages in status, lonely and imprisoned, with an ocean of love trapped inside me; been raised to a highly honoured position in society, but felt lost and exiled from home. Reading the life and the journey of Joseph was like looking into a mirror. The final face-to-face meeting with Joseph and his unsuspecting brothers, made me feel – just like him in one heart-wrenching moment – that I too had been viewed and treated as other than myself for most of my life.

After so many years of wandering in the shadows of self-oblivion, the dust of my soul felt wiped clean through my love and connection to Prophet Joseph. This book just couldn't be another humanly written work: it was truly a message from my maker.

> **My Lord! You have surely granted me authority**
> **and taught me the interpretation of dreams.**
> **O Originator of the heavens and the Earth!**
> **You are my Guardian in this world and**
> **the Hereafter. Allow me to die as one who**
> **submits and join me with the righteous.**[40]

I shivered inside, realising how much would have to change.

The Golden Dome
1976–7

THE WORD "ISLAM" is directly linked to *salam* in Arabic, which means entering into a state of peace and security. Oh, of course! Didn't I write a song called "Peace Train"? The picture before me was getting less blurred. That unexpected gift from my brother was a sign that the "holy roller," which had once only existed as a metaphor, was now emerging out of the edge of darkness and heading full speed straight my way. It would accelerate my journey towards that final station and help me to keep that promise made to God in the ocean.

Reading the Qur'an had opened my heart; now my mind was rushing to follow. Even with all the questions that arose after that monumental moment (and there were still plenty of them), I knew for sure one thing: I was on the right track. After exploring various religious provinces and delving through the pages, between the covers of some amazingly interesting books of diverse creeds and philosophies, my mind and my spirit were now approaching a place of unity; I was now becoming aware of the presence of a singular, omniscient intelligence, the Universal Lord of all things, alone, who is without any associate partner, or man-made, concept image. His was the only voice I needed to hear.

After that breakthrough, there was nothing left for me to do but to surrender . . . but I wasn't quite ready, so I decided to put it off for a bit longer.

> *Hark, O drop, give thyself up without repenting,*
> *That in recompense for the drop,*
> *Thou mayst gain the ocean.*[41]

Following the powerful instinct of love and maternal gravity, whenever possible I would drop into London to visit Mum. Unfortunately, my days spent in the UK were limited because of my non-resident status. I could usually only stay for a week or so. Still, my mother was always happy having me around. Enjoying Mum's company, her neat, petite suburban garden and her irresistible cooking, I realised how much I missed a simple family life.

She had brought us up well and sacrificed most of her living breath in doing so. Mum was a perfect example to us all: forgiving and kind, with a gracious air of independence; she never asked anybody for anything. It was a joy to watch her delightful expression when I brought home gifts.

When my dog Pepe died, unknown to me Mum was personally relieved. Some years later, after she moved to Hampstead, I decided to buy a little shih-tzu dog to join the family. Mum smiled and welcomed it as if it was exactly what she wanted. We called it Shugo. Mum had kept her real feelings secretly inside, not wanting to hurt mine, but she really disliked those doggy smells. I only found this out later, being totally oblivious at the time.

A major breakthrough in helping me communicate to my mother what I was learning about Islam came with the release of the film *The Message* in 1976. We both went to see it at a cinema on Old Compton Street, Soho. It depicted the life and times of the Prophet Muhammad and his early struggle with the Makkan idol worshippers in bringing them to believe and worship the one true God of their forefathers, Abraham and Ishmael. Anthony Quinn played Hamza, the Prophet's uncle.

The film was a landmark for me as well as my mother. She began to understand the link I had already made between Islam and Christianity; the trials, torture and persecution that the first Muslims had to bear while professing their faith were closely paralleled by the examinations faced by the early Christian believers and followers of Jesus.

Watching the film had a major impact, for more reasons than one: it was also the night I decided to give up smoking. Turning around and noticing the look of disgust on the face of the elderly lady sitting next to me, as a cloud of my puffing floated past her crinkled-up nose, was enough to convince me it was time to quit. I already knew from my flare-up with TB that cigarettes were bad for me, but that lady's ghastly frown finally made me understand how selfish and antisocial the habit was. On reflection, that little blip of illumination may have contributed to a few more smoke-free years for me on this Earth!

18 | *The Golden Dome*

While making the rounds back in London, I popped in to see my old big buddy Peter Thompson and his wife, Christine (and their dog, Minnie), in their flat on Sussex Gardens, Paddington. Peter was a thinker, like my brother, a self-taught, streetwise philosopher and graduate from the London school of hard knocks. Although he was a heavyweight-sized man, there was something squashily soft and vulnerable about him. Peter's main weakness (apart from women) lay in not being able to give up the weed. I was already withdrawing from those kind of intoxicating addictions; my interests were aimed towards a different kind of "high."

Though I'd glanced at Pete's bookshelf many times, for the first time I noticed that he had a large, maroon-bound copy of the Qur'an. It was a thick translation by A. Yusuf Ali with a lot of interesting commentary. Seeing my interest, he gave it to me to read. I shook his hand firmly and thanked him. Bidding Peter farewell that day with his Qur'an in my hands, I was thrilled to have my first detailed commentary in English. At last, here was my chance to find out what some of those more difficult verses meant.

Izitso was released in April 1977. It was quite well appreciated by the critics, who understood that I was a difficult artist to box into a corner, and some even raved about it. The up-tempo single "(Remember the Days of the) Old Schoolyard" made a respectable mark in the charts.

One of the album's instrumental tracks looked also set to create a few historic ripples. It was entitled "Was Dog a Doughnut." As well as utilising sample loops and odd sound effects, I sourced and incorporated a barking dog (which later famously became a feature of synthesiser presets) into the fracas. It turned into something of a template for future electro-techno pop music (so "they" say).

The idea for the song's title came from a preposterous article I had seen in a Sunday newspaper: WAS GOD AN ASTRONAUT? Although I might have been somewhat sympathetic to such sci-fi theories in the past, the comic-like headline now energised me. To imagine the omnipotent creator of heaven and earth, every atom and galaxy and form of life in existence, squeezing into the clumpy shoes of an extra-terrestrial, space-suited being from a distant planet, landing on Earth, then commencing to seed a crop of human embryos – aaaargh! This just drove me to a furious mode of creative malfunction. Hence, the most utterly dopey title I could hit back with became . . . "Was Dog a Doughnut?"

OK. Now I have got that out.

Moving on, I had to admit there was, in fact, a certain amount of potential regarding the subject of alien beings, which was certainly not outside of the realms of God's purposeful design. The notion of such creatures sharing our common universe was indeed Qur'anically possible. In fact, the premise of alien beings residing somewhere in our shared universe is alluded to in certain chapters of the Qur'an. The frequent description of *jinn* (or "genies") clearly indicates the presence of another category of species who dwell in the "space between the heavens and the Earth." They were certainly not fiction. In the Bible these are mentioned as mazzikim, elemental spirits or demons, and according to traditional religious understanding, are not necessarily

18 | *The Golden Dome*

visible to the human eye. *Jinn* apparently inhabited the universe and were created by God before humankind.

To my mind (and that's why I can freely say it), this could easily explain the vast phenomena of supernatural encounters with the "other" that people have experienced or described throughout the epochs and ages of man in the pages of time: trolls, fairies, gnomes, ghosts, spirits, mythical deities, muses, hobbits, and so on, all the way through to Carl Jung's archetypal tendencies that dwell within the collective, unconscious dimension of human thought. Strange, but true? This even suggested how one person could possess (or be possessed by) that elusive characteristic we term "genius," a highly sensitive state where brilliant ideas seem to suddenly jump into your mind out of nowhere. Very creepy. Indeed, Einstein may not have worked alone.

Comparing more objective theories – beyond modern man's fascination with the search for elusive lifeforms in the universe – when it came to verifiable scientific matters, the Qur'an seemed to be unnervingly in concurrence with certified, deductive realities. It mentioned the actual movement of the sun, moon, and planets as orbital,[42] and a yet-to-be-discovered cryptic secret about the stratospheric sky, describing it as a "protective roof" – protecting us from all sorts of unpleasant cosmic weather such as meteors and harmful ultraviolet light, let alone freezing cold space itself, approximately minus 455°F![43]

**So I do swear by the positions of the stars –
And this, if only you knew, is indeed a great oath.**[44]

The Qur'an also provided grounds for what scientists term the "big bang," the birth of the expanding universe itself. In a chapter called "The Prophets," it describes the initial split of elements from a mass or "primordial mist," and then continues in the very same verse to state the universal principle that all living things are evolved from water (not dissimilar, but more specific than the equivalent message contained at the beginning of Genesis in the Old Testament).[45] It also details the staged development of the human from a sperm drop advancing to a fetus and finally forming bones, limbs, and organs within the concealed darkness of the womb, way before microscopes, X-rays, and scanners were available to examine and confirm the intimate process.[46]

Wow! This was written over fourteen hundred years ago.

I kept a conscious window open, looking for mistakes. Nevertheless, there seemed to be much less incongruity between science and faith in this modern addition to the genealogical family of sacred books. It seemed the more I read, the more it became uncomfortably clear that most faults I discovered were not with the Qur'an, but with me.

The view of the universe from our Earth was at one time substantially more mysterious and incomprehensible than human scales could measure ("Twinkle, twinkle little star, how I wonder what you are?"). Along with many of my generation, I ardently hoped that science would one day help to rationally explain all the mysteries of life. However, it looked to me as if God, in the Qur'an, was not really bothered about us finding out about the function of quasars, supernovas or the DNA of invisible beings, He was more concerned about the imperative for us to wake up to total

18 | *The Golden Dome*

reality itself. "Nothing comes from nothing, Nothing ever could." Those were the wise words sung by Julie Andrews in Rodgers & Hammerstein's *The Sound of Music*, and had always seemed prophetically incisive. As the Qur'an says:

> **Indeed, in the creation of the heavens and the Earth and the alternation of the day and night there are signs for people of reason.**[47]

My own private starship itself was dangerously out of range of human warmth. Fame and distance had dislocated me too far from being able to stay close to my family. The Qur'an had awakened me to the sacred duty of looking after my parents – also a biblical principle, which, sadly, has become almost mummified in the rapidly expanding museum of present-day life, where everything is more about gratifying one's self in one's own private grazing field.

Love of Mum and Dad was subliminally behind everything I tried to achieve and was always a strong motivational reason for me to go forward in life. I had always been extremely attached to them, especially my mother, and I wanted to see her and Dad become closer again. I was always best situated to be the peacemaker, so I decided to work harder to make it happen.

My parents had a lot more spare time on their hands now the restaurant was being run by Lambros, an older cousin. My dream of one day buying a Hellenic temple and living like a demigod on a Greek island was not my idyllic dream anymore. The idea now was to find a reasonably picturesque place in the sun where Mum and Dad could share each other's company. I wanted to find a neutral ground where we could all gather under bright blue skies, some natural, scenic place for the family to enjoy some more quality times together.

With that intention, I started searching.

My focus shifted to Cyprus. It was Dad's place of birth, after all. As far back as 1973, my father and I had journeyed to the dusty old homeland together for a visit. It was nice to see Dad in his birthplace surroundings. He enjoyed my company, proud to show off a little with his "famous" son. We booked into the most expensive and luxurious, top-floor presidential suite of a swanky hotel in the centre of Famagusta. The only problem (I found out then) was when I coaxed Dad out onto the balcony to get a better view of the city and seascape, immediately his face dropped and his knees started physically shaking.

"Take me down, Stevie! I do'ni-like it!"

Naturally, I was going to have to take this acrophobia into consideration if I was ever to get Dad to feel at home – wherever that place ended up being.

In 1974, not long after that trip, came the Greek military junta's unsuccessful union (*enosis*) with Cyprus, which was followed immediately by the Turkish invasion that violently split the island into two. The war didn't last long, but the bitterness did.

It had been three years since that shocking military offensive; things had settled somewhat, and the southern section, including my father's original birthplace near Paphos, was pretty secure; the British still had a presence, and the people spoke more English than they did on the Greek mainland. I thought it would make a suitable location for our family base. Mum adored Cyprus as it had such a sandy, romantic Mediterranean atmosphere.

I was in love with the country too. One of the new tracks on *Izitso* was dedicated to this unique little, golden, sun-drenched island. Entitled "Kypros," it was an instrumental and exposed my roots, showing how Greek music was part of the genetic streaks of my sonic influences. There weren't that many international artists around with links to Cyprus that you could name, apart from yours truly (and a boy named George Michael whose dad also happened to run a restaurant, in Edgware, north London, and who was a mere lad of fourteen at the time I recorded that track).

Looking across the sea, only one hundred and fifty miles from the shores of Cyprus lay the neighbouring Holy Land. After my moving encounter – reading the story of Joseph in the Qur'an and recalling my brother's inspiring recollections about his brief experience there – it became my goal to visit Jerusalem: I needed a connection. The German co-promoter of the "Majikat" tour, Marcel Avram, was Jewish, and I had spoken to him at the time about my wish. He kindly arranged to organise it and accompany me.

I booked a flight from London and met Marcel at Tel Aviv airport. Soon I was whisked away in his white Mercedes towards the Holy City. After about an hour we approached Jerusalem and saw the skyline of interlocking sandstone walls and buildings rising in front of us. We continued driving through the cobbled streets to the old quarter, where I checked into a hotel near David's Gate.

The ancient city was breathtakingly beautiful. I could feel

the presence of something very special, spiritually. The bricks of the houses, new and old, were all built from a similar stone – a warm, dry, sandy colour that calmed the eyes. Another thing struck me while we were travelling on the road: I noticed the paint used by Palestinians for many windows and doors was actually my favourite colour! A light, aqua-turquoise blue, the same hue I had fallen in love with and used predominantly in my *Buddha and the Chocolate Box* back-cover illustrations.

I had arranged to be picked up at the hotel by Marcel later in the afternoon and driven to the sacred sanctuary of the Masjid al-Aqsa. It would be my first visit to any mosque. There was a strong fear factor that preceded me, probably due to my years of absorbing white European complexes and suspicions attached to anything Arabalistic. True, Palestinians were dark and culturally unfamiliar; they seemed to have heavy, frowning eyebrows. But listening to them speak Arabic was extremely sweet. I loved the tone of the language. It seemed to be from the "Middle Earth" of human tongues; not flamboyant or affected like French; not busily tongue-rolled like Spanish or Portuguese; not too harsh and guttural like German or Dutch – just naturally soothing. My dad spoke and sang a bit of Arabic, and I always loved the sound. In fact, looking at Palestinian faces close-up, they didn't look much different from my Greek-Cypriot cousins – probably because, to begin with, many were Phoenicians.

Marcel turned the wheel and the car tugged around one more corner. There I saw it, right smack in front of me: the Golden Dome. There it was, majestically sitting opposite the silver dome of its sister mosque, Masjid al-Aqsa, shining

18 | *The Golden Dome*

like massive crowns high above the historic passageways and streets of the blessed city. My heart pumped hard.

Marcel was naturally worried – he was about to leave a wealthy, world-famous Western icon at the steps of a dangerous forbidden zone. He glanced upwards and prayed that the Almighty would somehow look after me. Seeing the confident look on my face, Marcel probably understood that I knew what I was doing. We arranged to meet at the same place an hour later.

I stepped through the large stone arch.

It was like entering a new world, a world which my heart had dreamed of for so long, but my eyes could hardly believe they were glimpsing. It was like walking upon the face of the moon, so firm and familiar and yet unreal. There, inside the ancient walled compound, stretched the expansive open square and paved quarters of the mosque grounds. As I began to walk slowly around, a loud voice sang out from the speakers of the minaret – it was the call to prayer.

"Allahu Akbar, Allahu Akbar . . ."

This was the first time I had ever heard these words so clearly. I remembered that in Marrakech I heard something similar, but it was always muffled, smothered by the noisy market sounds and other goings-on. The words soared out like an echoing chorus around the city, everywhere. I didn't know exactly what they meant, but it seemed that my arrival was right on time; people were headed towards the entrance of the silver-domed mosque of al-Aqsa. I noticed there was a special place for shoes just in front of the door, so I took mine off and entered.

Sitting down quietly, I first observed the tranquillity and

aesthetics of the space, with light entering through the geometrically designed, coloured glass windows. An expansive array of vibrant carpets covered the floor from end to end. As my eyes further surveyed the surroundings, I noticed there was some construction going on; scaffolding had been erected at the front-facing wall of the mosque, around the central niche beneath the large window. It seemed they were still slowly repairing the damage inflicted by an arson attack three years earlier.

Rapidly spoken Arabic suddenly came over the loudspeaker and the crowd broke up, hurriedly made its way to the front, and formed a line behind the "priest" (this was the imam, but I didn't yet know that religious title). I timidly followed. Standing in line with the other worshippers, I felt a bit conspicuous, but just tried to copy what they were all doing: bending, bowing, and placing my head to the floor.

Ah, so that's how it is supposed to be done, I thought.

After the prayer I hung around the rear of the prayer hall. Some men noticed me and slowly approached. I stood up. They started talking to me in Arabic; I told them with accompanying hand signals that I only spoke English. Then one of them asked in a thick accent, "What your name?"

"Steven."

They looked a bit dubiously at me, not quite sure what to make of this questionable figure with a foreign name. I quickly interjected to calm their doubts, jabbing my finger at myself: "Me . . . I am Muslim." Immediately they exhaled, smiled broadly, and hugged me tight. It was the first time I had ever said it aloud or told anybody. Although an internal decision had already been made, it was simply time to let

18 | *The Golden Dome*

people know. There was something so liberating about mouthing something out loud that I had previously kept hidden deep within myself. I felt immense relief at that moment by identifying openly with what I believe – not bothered by what people would think or how some might react to my choice.

That prayer was actually the mid-afternoon congregational worship, *salat al 'Asr*. I knew there were different hours of worship, but it was all a bit vague to me. The Qur'an was not specific about the exact times and only spoke in generalities about the hours and requirements of prayer.

As everyone started leaving the mosque one of them said, "As-salamu alaykum" ("Peace be upon you"). I tried to reply, but didn't manage very well. "Goodbye," I sort of answered. By the time I emerged out of the mosque into the warm glow of the sun, my future was sealed. There was nothing in the world left for me to do but seek out some English-savvy Muslims who could teach me what I needed to do next. This would have to wait until I got back to London.

Marcel met me by the outer gate as promised. He looked relieved to see me arrive back all in one piece. I was on heavenly cloud nine and thanked him with all my heart for arranging the visit. During the drive back, my mind reflected on what had just happened; so many questions were spinning around in my head; I just couldn't wait to get the answers. But there were some other things I had to take care of first.

That same year, on 8 December, 1977, I had received the Sun Peace Award by the Symphony for the United Nations in New York. Along with legendary comedian Danny Kaye, for some time I had acted as a peace ambassador for UNICEF and donated quite a lot of my charity funds to the organisation. My music and message had made a mark with many of the peace workers of the sixties who, like me, sought a harmonious, less violent and less troubled world. The UN seemed a perfect platform for mending the political fractures of the world; that's how I saw it.

Having visited Jerusalem, I was not involved with the political or military issues facing the Holy Land, which now resembled a quilted map, part Israel and part Palestine. Although I wanted peace ultimately to win, there were other pressing issues facing me regarding my own future. The spiritual momentum I had gained from my visit to that resplendent, prophetic city was the most powerful force that impelled me onward and upwards.

On my return to the UK, I began to develop and consolidate my connection with Islam. Peter Thompson became an important intermediary. Nafeesa, a friendly Muslim, lived in the basement below his flat, and she worked for the Sri Lankan embassy. He promised to introduce me to her.

It was evening when we met, and Nafeesa was just back from work. Dressed in a maroon-coloured sari, she smiled and seemed to have already been informed about the purpose of my visit. She invited me in and sat me down; I wasted no time in asking her how I could go about learning to practise the faith.

She surprised me by first asking "why" I wanted to become a Muslim, doing so almost humourously, as if she was looking at someone archaically out of step with modern times. Was there something she knew that I didn't? That blew my flame

18 | *The Golden Dome*

sideways for a second; I had to adjust myself. It was hard for me to understand how a Muslim, who knew Islam and its potential to lead a soul to eternal peace and happiness, could ask such a weird question.

I could see that Nafeesa didn't have much to offer in terms of concrete advice; after chatting a bit about the morals her good mother taught her ("Always choose to do the thing you don't want to do"), she informed me that a brand new mosque had just been built in Regent's Park; perhaps I should go there to ask for further information. That's exactly what I needed! I thanked her for the advice, and we said goodbye.

How strange life is. Since baby days, I had known Regent's Park – I had been pushed in a pram, taken to the zoo in shorts, played, run around, climbed its trees, fallen, bruised myself, explored its broad spaces, and fed the ducks. I never expected to see anything other than mothers and strollers, playgrounds, birds, trees, and mown grass. The pieces were coming together – my past and future merged, neatly laying out my entrance to the Muslim world.

Friday 23 December, I plucked up enough courage, dressed up warmly, and took that decisive step towards Regent's Park. The Qur'an had already informed me that Friday was an important day for Muslims to go to the mosque. As I approached, rising up above the bare, leafless treetops, I saw a new golden dome, which had not been there before. That was the symbol of everything that I was discovering about Islam: suddenly it was there – where it wasn't before.

Shahadah
1977

ON A COLD, wintry day in 1977, I arrived at the London Central Mosque in Regent's Park to officially declare my belief. There were large throngs of Muslims bustling down the stairs to the basement hall where the midday congregational prayer was taking place. A lot of them looked quite serious and I felt too self-conscious to stop anyone and ask for help. Meekly, I shuffled my feet and hovered in the bitter cold for about an hour, until the service was over and spilling out onto the street. The hall looked almost empty, then I hesitantly made my way down.

The large floor was covered in a beige and orange-brown wide-strip carpet, a few worshippers scattered here and there still doing individual prayers. I focused on a shortish figure at the front talking to some people – he had a white turban and long, dark-blue coat on, so I presumed he was the right guy to approach.

Dr. Sayed Mutawalli ad-Darsh was a cheerful, red-faced man and the chief imam at the Central Mosque. He gave me a kindly smile, which instantly made me feel relaxed. I told him of my wish to become Muslim. He probably thought me an interesting oddity, with my white silk scarf, long, black Yves Saint Laurent overcoat and matching black hat. I must have looked a bit like a prosperous young, slightly lost rabbi. He spoke clearly and temperately with a strong Egyptian accent, telling me to hold on for a while as he concluded with another man who had also been waiting to speak with him.

Quite some time had passed since the congregational prayer ended. Being winter, daylight hours were shorter, and it was now getting close to the afternoon prayer. The call began over the loudspeaker. Unexpectedly, Dr. Darsh invited me to join the line. Having taken part in the similar service in Jerusalem, I knew what to do, lined up, and followed suit.

After the bowing and prostrations had ended, he led me upstairs to a small white Portakabin standing just in front of the main building. The new mosque was still undergoing final decoration work in the main ground-floor hall, and the cabin was the temporary office of the imam. He offered me a seat and then introduced me to a tall, Indian-looking gentleman in a charcoal, curly lamb-hair hat and three-quarter-length coat. He had a strikingly long black beard. This was Dr. Azam Baig. After a short introduction he was asked to witness my conversion. He sat down next to me and asked, "Do you believe in one God, Allah?"

"Yes," I confidently replied.

"Do you believe in the messenger and servant of God, the Last Prophet, Muhammad?"

CAT ON THE ROAD TO FINDOUT

"Yes."

Dr. Baig then asked me to repeat those two statements in Arabic. He spoke them to me slowly and I repeated with a little difficulty, but as best as I could:

Ash-hadu an la ilāha illa-Allāh
Wa ash-hadu anna Muhammadan
'abduhu wa rasûluh

After I finished speaking those words, he got up, put his arms around me and warmly embraced me, as did the imam and another worshipper who happened to be there at the time. Everybody looked radiantly pleased – not to mention how relieved and ecstatically happy I felt. A small, light-green booklet about the prayers and how to perform them was handed to me, along with Dr. Baig's telephone number. That was it. I was now a Muslim!

As I walked out of the cabin into the softening glow of the afternoon, I felt the world had changed. My feet no longer touched the pavement; I was floating on an invisible cloud, carrying me softly forward towards the brilliance of a divinely lit field that was opening up before me, far from the past darkness of worldly entanglements, walls and bondage. Free from wandering! My soul had found its home, at last.

Of course, I was very conscious about the weight of this decision. I knew it would have a big impact on my family, on my friends, let alone my fans and the public. I could imagine what people would say: "Cat Stevens, the reclusive hippie poet, has converted and become a Muslim? Ha, ha . . . you must be kidding." But the most important thing at that moment was not what others thought – God Most High was now my guide and companion; He had saved me out there in the ocean and slowly shown me my destiny. There was no one else and nothing outside of that reality I needed to worry about – oh, what mighty peace!

Over the next few months I concentrated on my prayers and practised reading the first chapter of the Qur'an in Arabic, seven short verses which are repeated in every daily prayer. My musical training was obviously very useful at this point; I had no difficulty in making the right sounds and intonation. What was going to be more problematic was how to inform the world that I was now a Muslim.

The first to know was my mother. She had been observing me read the Qur'an studiously and had seen the changes it was making to my character and behaviour. Mum smiled understandingly when I told her and accepted my decision without question. Good ol' Ma. She had always supported me through every inch of my growth and never held me back from doing anything I wanted to. Now, Islam was the only thing I wanted.

From that day on, Mum faithfully stood by me, present at every dangerous, rocky learning curve. Although she believed deeply in God and Jesus, she had never gone through confirmation in the Baptist faith and maintained her own private spiritual space. Without making a fuss about it, Mum used to kneel quietly at her bedside and pray every night. Always being kind, doing good, and keeping away from hurting anyone; patience was her major attribute – it was certainly going to be required more than ever.

Dad was not quite so easy to approach. He used to go down to the restaurant in Shaftesbury Avenue regularly and look over Lambros's shoulder at how the cash in the till was doing. The chance came one day when I was able to sit down with him and give him the news. Dad didn't smile – but he didn't frown either. He obviously had some first-hand knowledge about Islam from his time in Egypt. Many times in the past we would hear him decorating his sentences with "Allah Karîm," meaning, "God is most Kind." I suppose Dad was more concerned with the way the rest of the Greek-Cypriot community would take the news. After all, I was embracing the religion of the Turks. It would doubtlessly be perceived as an open act of treachery by many Greek hardliners, especially following the recent military partitioning of Cyprus.

Thank God Dad had understood more about the closer, friendlier side of Muslims from his years in Egypt. He accepted my decision, gallantly.

Anita and Alec appeared shocked. My sister's rooted uprightness and Christian character were thrown off balance. She respected and loved me but couldn't come to grips with it – not right away, at least. Rationalising such a drastic, life-altering move within her own frame of understanding, Anita probably came to realise that I needed a more peaceful, regular life; entering the entertainment industry as a jaunty seventeen-year-old, my life had been wildly hyper, swayed by the erratic currents of the music business and full of impulsive extremes. Perhaps for Anita, this was part of my "normalisation" and re-entry into my role of being a younger brother again. She duly accepted my conversion.

19 | *Shahadah*

Out of the entire family, bizarrely, it was David – who had given me the Qur'an in the first place – who became most "anti" of all. Here was his little brother, standing up independently and choosing a path that he himself had by chance stumbled across. It just wasn't really part of his plan. But it was part of God's. From that moment, in David's mind, it was going to be an unpredictable future.

"What do you mean you're a Muslim?"

"Dave, there's only one God. Don't you believe that?"

"Look, I've thought more about God than you and – "

"It's not just thinking or talking, Dave. You've got to follow a path, that's what Moses and all the other prophets did – "

"Don't you lecture me about the Bible!"

David's response was unexpected. He was as quick-tempered as I was, even more so. Our conversation soon descended into a quarrel, and he quickly became my biggest headache. *Maybe it's just a phase*, Dave probably thought to himself, hoping he had not unintentionally blown a hole in our family boat.

One by one, I informed friends and fellow musicians about my conversion. Most realised that this spelled the end of my career. I was no longer hooked to the music world; our points of interest were heading further apart – for them, this new development would alter everything.

Alun Davies, like most non-busybodies of British upbringing, understood that religion was a personal thing; he would never dare encroach on that area. He was deeply respectful and knew it was wiser to keep a safe distance, rather than directly engage me on the subject. Even in the studio, he'd listen to my songs and take on board my views, then interpret them his way. I suppose he also might have wondered how far this Muslim thing would go, or if it was just my "latest fad."

Alun aside, it was coming to the point where I felt something unsavoury might happen – and it did. The crunch arrived one evening as I was sitting together with my buddy twins, Paul and Barry Ryan, along with Peter and Christine Thompson, in an Italian restaurant in Soho. I had stopped drinking by that time, but they were emptying a bottle of red wine, getting more and more unsteady as the night went on. Soon they became a bit too lubricated and began exchanging silly jokes. Then Peter lifted up his glass, shouting: "Hey! Blood of Jesus."

I was upset. Smack-talking the name of one of God's most beloved messengers for a laugh was too much for me. "Look! He is my Prophet, you shouldn't . . ." Seeing he was too inebriated to listen, I began to walk out of the restaurant. Before I could jump in a cab, Peter rushed out and threw a heavy right hook to my face. My lower lip was cut and bleeding. That certainly made it much easier for my heart to recognise who my friends now were.

Meanwhile, across the pond, UNICEF in New York had been calling and asking me to visit some of their projects in the struggling regions of the "Third World." I had been to Ethiopia and Kenya with them some years earlier, but there was a desire on my part to see how those in poor Muslim countries were living. I suddenly felt connected to this huge family of people out there who I had previously not noticed before. It was early in 1978; they arranged for me to travel to

Egypt and Bangladesh. George Harrison had once famously put on a major concert for Bangladesh, which highlighted the hardships suffered by refugees escaping persecution; I will never forget that, mainly because it seemed an amazingly conscious and un-poppy thing to do. Alun was invited to come along with me. He was happy and very willing to do a bit of charity work.

Our first stop was Cairo. We were greeted by UNICEF's official representative, a very tall, broadly built gentleman with a recognizably Egyptian nose, dressed in a dark blue-striped suit. His name was Mohammed Islam, and he was deputed to guide us around while we visited various orphanages, schools, and playgrounds. I asked to see a few mosques, too, one being the famous great Muhammad Ali Pasha Mosque, picturesquely perched on top of the ancient city's hilltop citadel.

Still learning how to memorize my prayers, I spotted a market stall selling cassettes of the Qur'an. Egypt is known to have produced some of the most sublime Qur'anic reciters in the world; their voices are so extraordinary and the closest one can get to true "soul" music. I fell in love with Abdul Basit's recitation more than anyone else's. While collecting these recordings, I also picked up a few additional Arabic music cassettes, mainly of the Egyptian diva, Umm Kalthoum. She was the most adulated and renowned singer in the Arab-speaking world, her voice at one time heard on every transistor radio in the Middle East. These became part of my treasured mementoes from the trip.

Next stop was Bangladesh. Dhaka, the capital, was much less historical or developed than Cairo; most houses and huts in the country villages were built from bamboo and clay, with straw-thatched roofs. Again, we visited orphanages and shook hands with lots of poor but very smiley kids. We were quite a novel attraction for them. At one point, in Chittagong, I got up on a modest, six-foot-wide, creaky old stage in the middle of the bazaar with Alun and surprised everybody by spontaneously performing a couple of songs. It seemed like they didn't quite understand the strange major scale of "Moonshadow"; it must have sounded odd in comparison to their own quarter-tone modal music melodies, but they listened and stared appreciatively, probably fascinated more by my continuous head-wobbling than anything else. When we finished, they offered some mild but grateful applause.

During my time in Dhaka, I asked my guide to drive me to the famous Star Mosque. It was a beautiful, but fairly small, white building with pretty star shapes speckled all over the dome. Before going in I made my ablution at the fountain in the courtyard. Appearing a little shy, perhaps – not quite having mastered balancing on one foot while bathing the other – I must have looked like a lobster out of water among the casually composed worshippers in their skull caps, loose shirts, and lungis. That remained one of my biggest challenges: to master the act of worship without sticking out from the congregation or being told I was doing something wrong. Luckily, I managed to perform my prayers with no one bothering me. I suspect many would have been unaware that there was a so-called "superstar" in the prayer line that day – and that was just how I wanted it.

I began wondering whether I was in the right job. Still

under contract to go on making records, I knew how much of music business culture – basically trading in egotism, endless groupies, bodyguards, hotels, bars, nightlife rampages – rubbed rather uncomfortably against Islam's ideal version of a humble God-conscious life. I had naturally distanced myself from being identified with the excessively raw-meaty, deafening-rock breed of artists, and was closer to what could be described as an eccentric acoustic vegetarian. But was that enough? The Qur'an didn't specifically mention "music" or say it was forbidden. So I simply continued fulfilling my obligations and went about preparing for my next record. I had written some songs that subtly referenced my new perceptions and conscious attitude. The intention was not to stand up and shout out that I was now a Muslim. I would allow it to dawn more gently through my words and music.

> *In the daytime*
> *Time for celebration.*
> *No use looking down,*
> *If it's over here . . .*
> *It's a world*
> *A new creation*[48]

For many years, music had been my religion, and the rules I had made up for it were simple: write interesting songs, look good, sing in tune, don't give too many interviews, try to employ good accountants, and try not to make enemies. The black vinyl disc had been the epicentre of my life and culture for over half my lifetime. The importance of riding high in the charts, chased, applauded, and adored by millions, these achievements were highly prized by successful stars and wannabes alike – as were the wildly decadent amounts of dough associated with "the trade." But for me, the spell was rapidly wearing off.

I now sought to become the antithesis of what I had represented before and shrink back to human size. There was definitely a conflict brewing as I stood between the external and internal walls of my persona, trying to work out who I was really supposed to be.

As for the media, I had never felt comfortable with the manufacturing of my glossy public image; critics had never been comfortable with it, either. I used to hide away as much as possible, so, for all intents and purposes, we were running around in circles and viewing each other's backs. Truth is, I sincerely did want to see the back of them, especially when word finally got out that I'd embraced Islam. One of the first comments I read was: "Good news for music lovers, maybe, but it's the blues for Allah . . . Cat Stevens has retired from the wondering world of rock 'n' roll to devote himself to his recently assumed faith, Islam . . ."[49]

Of course, it was partly my fault, and I take the blame for not being able to come out and explain myself coherently for much of my interviewed life. That's not what fans or the journalists expected, anyway. I couldn't be crystal clear and transparent while remaining dark, mysterious, and enigmatic, as untouchable stars were required to be (according to the sanctimonious code of rock 'n' roll). In any case, I gave out most – if not all – of what I had to say in my lyrics. Miles from nowhere, belonging to an unfixed abode, I was always looking towards something more interesting than the square metre of space I occupied at any given moment. Mortified by fears of creative stagnation, the moment my albums were released and on the shelves, I would be off, chasing some other new, elusory idea.

Giving interviews was now going to be even more unstable, not least because I was frantically trying to learn to balance on my own two feet, as an infant Muslim. A major problem I faced was that there were no British cultural prototypes for me to follow; the vast majority of Muslims had moved to the UK from a luscious array of foreign countries with their own customs. Like an unexpected guest at a large banquet, I needed to find a place for me to sit. Also, Muslim converts – apart from being rare even if you did bump into one – usually had a scholastic or unglamorously normal background. The role for a high-profile ex-sex symbol in normative Muslim tradition was really as out of place as a dodo in Times Square. Life left little room for such odd species.

As I flew back to Rio, a new chapter of my life was beginning. I decided it might be appropriate to take a Muslim name. It wasn't absolutely necessary, but I remembered how the Palestinians in Jerusalem found it awkward to deal with "Steven." So I set about thinking about what I would like to be called.

One name quickly stood out: Joseph. It was the name of the first school I ever went to, the name of the revered husband of blessed Mary (who I always wanted to snug up to in the school nativity play); Yusuf (the Arabic version of the name) was also the name of the musician whose melody I dishonestly lifted for my first hit; it was the middle name of the amazing commentator of the translation that expanded my Qur'anic horizon of knowledge as well – and, to top it off, Joseph was the name of that specific chapter of the Qur'an that had broken open the locks on the well of faith in my heart.

I thought about choosing Salaam ("peace") as my surname, but had also liked the name "Islam" itself, a derivative of "peace." Islam was my goal; it epitomised my aim to achieve a state of true submission and peace with God. I wanted to make it a reminder of that objective, so I wouldn't easily forget. Of course, I could have adopted my father's first name, as was the norm in Mediterranean, Arabic, and traditional cultures, but Stavros meant "crucifix" in Greek. It would be a bit weird to be known as Joseph, son of "the Cross"!

And so my new name was decided: Joseph Islam. That would be easy for my family and English-speaking friends to pronounce, something that needed to be considered. *Yes!* I thought: *problem solved*.

When I returned to London, I was invited for dinner at Dr. Baig's house in Whetstone. A few unexpected things cropped up. I was still a practising vegetarian at the time. Because I had not informed my host of that beforehand, his wife had gone ahead and prepared dinner as usual. There was delicious curried lamb and red chicken tandoori, with only a humble scattering of tiny lettuce leaves and a few slithers of sliced tomatoes for company. Then I remembered a verse of the Qur'an, which indicated that most meat – apart from

19 | *Shahadah*

pork – was lawful and when eating anything, one should begin with God's name: OK, "Bismillah." That was the first time I'd tasted a meat dish for years.

Boy, was it delicious!

Following this came another unexpected revision. When I told Dr. Baig that "Joseph Islam" was my new name, he looked up thoughtfully, rolled his eyes and pondered. After a long moment, in a very gentle way, he suggested, "Why don't you choose the Arabic pronunciation: 'Yusuf'?"

The thought had crossed my mind already. "Yusuf" was still an easy name for Western tongues, and Muslims would find it easier. Coincidentally, my late maternal uncle's name from Sweden had also been "Josef" (pronounced, "Yosef").

Yusuf covered all bases. I accepted the idea.

Although it wasn't necessary to change your name to become Muslim, it felt like the right thing to do. Similar to Cassius Clay becoming Muhammad Ali, I wanted to draw a line of distinction between the past and the present. Anyway, "Cat Stevens" wasn't my real name, and it could still remain a stage name for the record. It was generally understood by those "in the know" that if anyone addressed me as "Cat," they were considered outsiders; not part of my close circle of family or friends. To intimates, "Steve" was my name.

I contacted my lawyer in London and requested the preparation of whatever steps were necessary for an official name change. We arranged to meet after a couple of days, while I was staying at the Montcalm hotel, off Marble Arch.

It was fated that the deed poll was signed and sealed on 4 July, 1978: US Independence Day.[50]

Back to Earth
1978

NOBODY KNOWS HOW long we have to dance on this earthly ball.

Dad was looking weaker and not feeling very well. Born just on the cusp of the new century, and having bundled through an amazing punch-packed life with relatively few sicknesses – apart from the average British cold – my father had developed a problem with his kidneys. He changed his diet and was drinking lots of water. Dad hardly drank or smoked, apart from on social or festive times like Christmas or New Year's, when he would puff on a cigar and blow it out aristocratically – without inhaling. He was now cutting out fat-heavy meals and eating lots of onions – whole – with yoghurt and rice, probably on the advice of some close Greek friend (or *koumpáros*).

It was strange to see Dad looking that fragile, just sitting and watching customers come and go. He had always been such an active and charismatic figure, busily going round the tables and chatting to the customers. My elder cousin, Lambros, who was running the kebab restaurant together with his wife Joan (under Dad's keen and watchful eye), had been brought over from Cyprus many years before to work in the shop – he was reliable and faithfully loyal to his beloved uncle Stavros.

This worrying situation, compounded by those persistent thick grey clouds over London, deepened my sense of urgency. I resumed the hunt for that place in the sun, homing in on Cyprus. Lambros knew a lot about the island, so we arranged to travel there together and explore the southern coast for a villa or a piece of land to build on.

Limassol is a scenic port town on the southern coast, close enough to the British military base in Akrotiri, but far enough away from Dad's original village in Tala to deter a queue of relatives knocking on the door anytime they fancied a small loan to replace their clanky old car or buy a swish new washing machine.

As Lambros and I drove down towards the main street of the town, we glimpsed a brand-new luxury block of flats being built right close to the seafront. The name on the attractive-looking development sign caught my attention: "Economides" – that hurled me back to the pre-Decca days of Mike Hurst and his big boss man, Jimmy Economides, who refused to sign me all those years earlier.

We arranged a quick inspection of the half-built construction. I instantly fell in love with it. Choosing the first floor in order to ease my dad's fear of heights, I picked two adjoining flats with a beautiful southern view of the sea.

The plan was to open up and link the flats together: the north end of it would contain a room and en suite for Dad, and the south end would be set up similarly for Mum. All the floors and cupboards were crafted from beautiful Russian redwood. Mum was enthusiastic about the prospect of a Mediterranean home with an extended balcony overlooking palm trees and a sunny beach. She couldn't wait until it was finished.

My first year as a Muslim was 1978, and I had decided to step down off my high throne and help my brother with his peace project. David had written *Alpha Omega: A Musical Revelation*, an ambitious pop opera. He was working non-stop with a keyboard player friend, Richard Sharpey. The songs had come a long way since Davos and revealed his highly classical and mature musical talents; the melodies and structure of David's new music had flourished; his songs were really moving. I bankrolled and produced the album for him.

The sessions were recorded and mixed in CBS Studios on Whitfield Street, London. A host of different artists sang the leads, including David Essex, Maxine Nightingale, Arthur Brown and Gloria Jones (the wife of Marc Bolan, she had been driving their car the year before when they crashed and he died). Most songs demanded a hefty orchestra, and the arrangers, Derek Wadsworth and Richard Niles, were both brilliantly gifted. Each had strong filmic leanings, which suited David's magisterial compositions.

The time had also arrived for a new album of my own. I'd written a handful of songs and had some basic tracks like

"New York Times" laid down from past sessions in Copenhagen. The plan was to bring in Alun Davies and Gerry Conway to record with me again on guitar and drums, along with Bruce Lynch on bass, guys who had played with me over the years. I invited Paul Samwell-Smith to jump on board and co-produce the album with me. Paul and I had hit it off so well in the past, and his talents in the studio were stellar. He was a master architect and producer, always able to produce a spark. Paul knew how to coax – sometimes even chide – me into giving my best.

The old musical gang was happy to be together again. We chose a variety of locations, including Long View Farm in Massachusetts, London's Advision, and CBS in New York City. The album was completed at Le Studio in Quebec, back at good old Morin-Heights (minus the freezing snow this time round).

Everyone in the band, as well as Paul, knew that I was a Muslim. I had given up alcohol, and during the recording sessions I would occasionally stop for a break to pray. It was quite tough, especially if something was really cooking, musically.

Friday came round while we were laying down tracks in Le Studio; as usual I made an effort to find the nearest mosque. Scanning the telephone directory, I came upon one in Saint-Laurent, on the outskirts of Montreal. I hired a car and made my way.

It was a very small, plain structure; there was no dome or minaret, just a refurbished one-storey building turned into a masjid (a congregational place of prayer). It was there that day I fatefully bumped into a group called Tablighi Jamaat

(Society of Preachers). After the main midday prayer had finished, a man from among them stood up and gave a short talk. He looked like an Arab traveller who had just ridden out of the dust sands of time, dressed in a spotless but unironed white jalabiyyah, which ended above the ankles, and flaunting a long, disheveled beard and a white, whirly turban. I was mesmerised.

The lecture he delivered was about the oneness of God and the importance of prayer and other inspiring words connected to kindness and the treatment of others. It ended with an invitation to the "path of Allah." This was the closest image I had ever seen in relation to the historical description of the companions of the Prophet, peace be upon him. A prime goal for me then was to learn more about the Sunnah (ways and habits) of the Messenger of God. I was deeply impressed by this saintly man's dress and uncomplicated manner.

Afterwards, one man from the group approached, sat down next to me and convincingly sold me the idea of doing "forty days" of travelling and *tabligh* (calling to Islam). I agreed, at which point he wrote down for me an address of a mosque in east London. I had never done anything like that before, but I wanted to learn as much as I could about how to do my prayers and become more grounded, mixing with these souls from diverse Muslim countries, as far away as possible from the spotlight. It was part of my process of evolution. Getting back into the car, I returned to Le Studio, slightly apprehensive about having pledged myself to such a commitment.

Alun Davies keenly observed the changes taking place in

his old friend. Regardless of my radical fluctuations, he continued to be a faithful partner in music, always there and solid as a Welsh rock. It is fair to say that the most prolific contributions to my legacy of musical recordings have been made with Alun close by. For the first time in our long relationship, I invited him into my private compositional parlour, and we sat and wrote a couple of songs – "Bad Brakes" and "Daytime" – for the album together.

Once the recording sessions were complete, my attention turned to the album cover. It needed an intelligently inspired title that would denote my new state of being.

Back to Earth.

Subtly, it pronounced my growing disdain for solitary star status and my orbital descent to a more modest plateau of humankind. What better idea for the cover than simply to show a picture of this stunningly beautiful planet which we call home? Trying to avoid over-inflating my own ego-balloon, averse to putting my picture on the artwork, I was inspired by a gorgeous photograph in *National Geographic* of a lucent waterfall gently gliding over ageless rocks, surrounded by greenery – it was perfect.

I designed the title font in a long, sweeping oriental style and on the back credits added "Bismi-llahir-Rahmanir-Rahim" ("In the name of Allah, the Most Gracious, Most Merciful"), written in decorative gold Arabic calligraphy. This was the boldest public statement yet of my newfound path.

Back to Earth was destined to be my final "Cat Stevens" album and was scheduled to be released in early December 1978.

Charging ahead into my new life and identity as Yusuf Islam, it was getting harder to maintain a full-time career in music, and I had growing doubts about the medium. These were rapidly escalated by a complaint from the Malaysian government; they were outraged by my calligraphic use of the name of "Allah" on the album cover and demanded that it be removed at once. Oh no! It was scary to think I might have overstepped some sacred bounds. Yet what I did was done with good intentions, having been told early on that whatever action or major work we undertake must begin by the mention of God's holy name. I immediately contacted the record companies; they placed a sticker over existing copies and removed the writing from future printings.

Another colossal earthquake was about to shake the ground beneath me. Dad's condition had taken a serious downturn. The doctors had little optimism about his prognosis. There was a possibility he might not make it through.

I rushed back to London and went straight to his home in Muswell Hill. As I entered the room he smiled, happy to see me. My father had never been this ill before. His eyes appeared weak and weary as he lay immobilised on his bed in his smartly ironed pyjamas, next to a slightly open window; the soft-blowing lace curtain floated from side to side. My respect for him was deep and binding; I would never deliberately upset his feelings. He was my father. I had always looked up to him, rarely asking him questions about what he thought or felt about simple, ordinary things. Strangely, to this day, I don't know if he ever possessed a single copy of any of my records. I was too shy to ask.

20 | *Back to Earth*

Anyway, that kind of thing wasn't important, because I had known since childhood how much he loved me.

We avoided talking about his condition. Instead, I surprised him by pulling out a portable cassette player and some of the tapes from my trip to Egypt. I guessed he might like listening to something while stuck in bed. Soon, the enchanting sound of Umm Kalthoum's voice began to circulate around the room. He stared fixedly out at the sky as tears began to well up in his eyes. I could see that the songs were transporting him back to his years as a young man in Alexandria. Early life in Egypt had a massive influence on Dad's character. He would warmly greet the occasional Arab customers walking into the café with "Salamu 'alaykum," and at times of gratitude he would repeat "Allah Karîm."

I dearly wanted my father to share the happiness I had found with Islam, but was hesitant to talk openly about it. There was also the pressure of surrounding family; they would not appreciate any attempt to make him Muslim – especially David, who was now getting extremely agitated by my unshakable certainty.

Dad's health soon got worse, and he was moved to University College Hospital, on Gower Street. The family gathered around and stayed close, visiting his bedside daily. We all took turns sitting by his side, but there was nothing more we could do except hold his frail hand and share a secret hope that some miracle might happen.

George, my half-brother, flew in from Greece; he was the eldest and still held an important role as Dad's first son. George could speak Greek, of course, and he and Dad laughed and joked a bit about the bad food service in the hospital and a fictitious "Spanish lady" who seemed to be forever occupying the bathroom, not allowing anyone else in.

The first clear sign of Dad's total acceptance of my being a Muslim happened one afternoon while he was lying in bed. Mum told me about it later. She was sitting next to him, when he whispered to her. She couldn't make out what it was at first because of the frailty of his whispering voice. He kept on repeating the question. Mum probably didn't understand because she had only ever heard him call me "Stevie" from the day I was born. Then Mum finally realised what he was saying: "Where's Yusuf?"

"Oh, yes. Yusuf? He's in the mosque."

On hearing that, Mum said, Dad sat back and relaxed. He was pleased.

During those last few precious days, I received one of the most lasting gifts of my life: it was the beautiful smile that came across his face when I entered his hospital room. A loving look I will never forget.

No one could really predict how long Dad could last or how things would end. Considering the possibility of his closeness to the afterlife as I was sitting at his bedside, I finally gathered up enough courage to directly ask whether he believed in the one God. I knew that his declaration, at this stage of his life, would be a guarantee of a place in heaven according to the saying of the Prophet.[51] To my amazement, Dad had no hesitation. He nodded and quietly said, "Yes." I asked him to say the words, "La ilaha illallah" – "There is no god except God" – which he repeated in perfect Arabic. I was euphoric; it was hard to believe how quickly and willingly he said it.

20 | *Back to Earth*

Two days later, on 3 December, 1978, my father left this world.

The last stage of my father's journey to his place of earthly rest was challenging. I needed to know how to deal with his body correctly, according to Islam. It was early in my own path of learning, but I did my best. There were books that explained the steps following death. It was first necessary to wash him, which I did personally, making sure as I wiped and rinsed his body that it was not exposed at any time by keeping a loose sheet over him. The nurses watched as I did that and then carefully wrapped him in three pieces of white cloth, which I speckled with some drops of perfume.

Things take on a great significance when a loved one dies, and they certainly did for me. An uncanny but reassuring thing happened the following day. I had gone to check on the state of Dad's body at the hospital morgue, somehow slipping in unnoticed into the private area where they had placed his body. Lifting the sheet from his face, I saw the corners of his lips ever so lightly upturned; a blissful smile had appeared overnight! It seemed to me a sure sign. I knew that Dad was in a good place.

The tranquillity I felt was wonderful. But that was soon disturbed. Arranging for the burial, I had to make sure that no cross was put over his grave. My brother David was still the biggest obstacle in my early days as a Muslim. He was adamant there should not be any indication of Islam on the headstone. In the end, after Mum intervened, everyone agreed on a simple, natural, rock-shaped piece of white marble with an inscription, a passage that I had read one evening during a family gathering, bringing comfort to us all:

> **Surely to God we belong and to
> Him we will all return.**[52]

I wanted a funeral service for my father in the Central Mosque, but the pressure of thousands of critical Cypriot eyes bore down heavily and it would not have been good to start a dispute at an already emotionally sensitive time. We held a service in the Greek church in Kentish Town, and Dad was finally buried in Southgate, close to Muswell Hill, where he had spent the last period of his long, adventurous life. Dad died on the same day my final Cat Stevens album, *Back to Earth*, was released.

> *Father, oh, father!*
> *Hear me if you can*
> *Is it true what they say*
> *That life is a dream?*
> *I don't understand*
> *The things that make rain in my eyes:*
> *Are they real, or are they lies?*[53]

New Cultural Home
1978–9

TIMING IS EVERYTHING. The new London Central Mosque and Islamic Cultural Centre became my gateway into the world community of Muslim organisations and movements. It had been built and opened, miraculously on schedule, in the same year I embraced Islam. Designed by a renowned English architect, Frederick Gibberd,[54] the new, starkly modern Islamic centre, with its towering minaret peering over Regent's Park, would become a magnet for Muslims from all over the world (as well as a few stubborn pigeons).

Although it was mostly paid for and financed by a donation from King Faisal of Saudi Arabia, its trustees hailed from almost every Muslim country: Egypt, Libya, Algeria, Indonesia, Malaysia, Sudan, Pakistan, and more. Most were ambassadors and diplomats belonging to embassies or consulates based in London. That political flower arrangement seemed a good thing to me at the time as the mosque represented a great image of Muslim unity; lots of lovely, colourful flags all waving together in a line. Being new to Islam and political history – little did I know!

The story of how it came to be built was not quite clear, like a lot of diplomatic deals done behind thick doors. According to one version of events, the plan was said to have been begun in the early twentieth century by Sir Winston Churchill who, as a young man, was on the fringe of accepting Islam – until he was convinced by his family to throw ice water on that idea. This did not stop Churchill's influential war cabinet from allocating funds for a prime location for a mosque next to Regent's Park in 1940, in recognition of the sizeable Muslim population within the Empire and its support during the war.[55]

The background to the mosque landing like a flying saucer in the middle of my childhood playground didn't concern me. I was too interested in my habilitation into a new Muslim life. On Fridays I would attend the Jumu'ah (congregational) prayer, and each week I made more and more friends. If there was a need for explanations, I would approach Imam Darsh and he would gently nudge me in the right direction.

I was overwhelmed by a feeling of brotherhood and belonging. Whenever I met a Muslim, I felt at home. Seeing that I was a convert (or "revert," as some like to call it), many brothers loved listening to my story and how I came to Islam. Most had no interest in music, and the name Cat Stevens meant nothing to them. But occasionally, some were taken by surprise: "Did you say … Cat Stevens?!" Their embarrassing exclamation would loudly echo around the mosque. I could see that some Muslims were naturally drawn towards the magnetic allure of music, charts, and pop culture, my former stomping ground. But, oh, what a relief it gave me to be totally unrecognised for the most part; just another ordinary worshipper in the mosque.

Some Arab Muslims seemed quite baffled as to how it was possible for me to understand the message of Islam by reading an English translation of the Qur'an, believing that knowing Arabic was the only way one could grasp it. Frankly, their attitude baffled me more; I couldn't comprehend how distant some had become from the bold clarity of the Qur'an's message for humanity. It seems they had become isolated through years of cultural inbreeding; like a commune of people who had lived on the high peaks of the Earth so long, they'd become quite oblivious to the view they saw daily around them – until the day a climber arrived, stumbling through the misty clouds, and informed them of the fact that they all lived on a mountain!

Stranger to me was the fact that I had lived, worked, and travelled for almost thirty years in pursuit of enlightenment, and had not been told anything about Islam by any Muslim. The faith of one-fifth of humanity was so well hidden in the West, it was impossible to even notice. Islam had been sometimes confused in my mind with Hinduism and Sikhism (certainly in the UK, from an outsider's point of view, many Asians seemed to look, eat and dress the same). When I was growing up, curry houses were on the rise; back then, multi-culturalism in Britain was simply confined to experimenting with various exotic menus. Our education system did not feel it necessary to provide too much information about the lands and peoples Britain had colonized for hundreds of

21 | *New Cultural Home*

years, choosing rather to sweep past rich and vastly important periods of Asian history and focus endlessly on how many wives our previous kings had.

Beyond this, there was a general level of racism when people encountered others who didn't look "white." There were no big news stories and front-page images of Muslim protests and marches – that came later, remember, no Islamic revolutions had yet taken place – and people were generally ignorant about Islam and other "imported" religions.

Most academics viewed Islam, at best, as a cultural novelty, with very few admirers, apart from some curious fellows, like the nineteenth-century explorer Richard Francis Burton (who had at one time daringly ventured to Makkah – disguised as an Arab!); before him there was Emperor Napoleon Bonaparte, and later the writer and philosopher George Bernard Shaw; as well as politicians like Thomas Jefferson, Churchill, and a few others, who had all looked beyond the pastiche Western imagery of Muslims, to read up on and glimpse the invigorating spirit of the last major religion to make its appearance on Earth.

Generally, if Islam wasn't categorised by occidental religionists as a heretic or barbaric cult, it simply lodged under the reductionist heading of "orientalism," which made it look like an out-of-date brand of a defunct culture, belonging to the desert sands, sabres, carpets, and harems overflowing with dozens of beautiful, veiled concubines (which was by far the most popular part of the assumed picture).

At the turn of 1979, the media was still quiet on the topic of Islam, only to be interrupted, perhaps, by a few belittling reports regarding my recent conversion. Islam's status as unnewsworthy suited me perfectly. I was happy to be left alone to get on with my new life, beginning with such basics as trying to find a *halal* meat shop.

Fame had not altogether forgotten me, however. I received a new invitation from the United Nations in New York, which was organising the music for a UNICEF benefit concert to launch the Year of the Child in January 1979. Having supported their work with children for many years and being a UNICEF ambassador, I was probably recognised as one of its first royal pop celebrities, so it seemed only right to attend.

Still very uncertain about my musical future, I explained my hesitancy about performing live – I didn't have a band, and getting it together would be too much of a job – but I would attend the concert. My only condition for accepting the invitation was that they clearly mentioned my new name, Yusuf Islam, along with "Cat Stevens" when introducing me. They seemed cool with that and added my name to the historic event.

The Bee Gees and ABBA were headliners with journalist and comedian David Frost and special guest Henry Fonda as hosts. The whole show was being filmed for broadcast around the world by the US network NBC. The prestigious event took place in the General Assembly Hall of the United Nations itself. It was so nice to be sitting in the audience instead of up on stage for a change. When the time came and they announced my presence, the crowd spontaneously rose up and gave me a thunderous standing ovation. I felt really honoured and was taken aback at such a reaction.

Some weeks later I was back in London, sitting with my

21 | *New Cultural Home*

mother in front of the TV, watching a broadcast of the show. "Here it comes, Mum," I said as the moment arrived for my entrance, announced by David Frost. The moment came and went, like a blip. Hey! I had been dematerialised. They had completely edited out my beautiful, love-filled moment with the audience. It was disturbingly clear that I was now deemed *persona non grata* as far as the gatekeepers of mainstream media were concerned. My heart hurt; I was unaccustomed to such a sting of rejection. They didn't like the name "Islam," I presumed. What other reason could there have been? Meantime, the Bee Gees falsettoed away, explaining that the higher world was pretty hard to access, and even they had to wait in line.

> *Nobody gets too much heaven no more*
> *It's much harder to come by*
> *I'm waiting in line . . .*[56]

The disappearance of Cat Stevens and my evolution into Yusuf Islam were happening plainly before people's eyes. I suppose they were not ready for it, but I was. Furthermore, my songwriting exploits had almost reached a cul-de-sac; the inspiration just wasn't there, and I wasn't going to chase it. I was too engrossed in learning Islam to pick up the guitar or manufacture any artificial lyrics.

My collection of books on Islam was steadily increasing, as I strove to absorb as much as I could wherever available. I was aware that there are five pillars of Islam and, in addition to the testimony of faith, prayer, charity and fasting, there was also an obligation to make a pilgrimage (Hajj).[57] My overriding wish was to pay a visit to the House of God in Makkah. However, it was not yet the month of pilgrimage. But then I learned it was still possible to make a "lesser" pilgrimage ('Umrah), which was available to perform during any other month of the year.

Early in 1979, I headed straight for the Saudi Arabian embassy, in Belgrave Square, to find what I can only describe as a shambling mass of Bangladeshis, Indonesians, Egyptians, and Pakistanis – not the kind of organised line I was used to – all pushing past each other feverishly to get to the reception desk. After an hour or so, I finally walked out holding my very own 'Umrah pilgrimage visa, proudly embedded in my British passport. I swiftly returned home to read up as much as possible and memorize all the rituals I'd have to perform.

The smoke-filled flight on Egyptair to Makkah enabled me to get the benefit of another short stopover in Cairo. I booked myself into the dusty old El Hussain hotel in the Islamic heart of the city, opposite the Hussein Mosque, a bustling area with markets and the irresistible smell of barbecue issuing from fuming restaurants all around. The square was being decorated with colourful drapes and pillared tents, in preparation for the birthday of the Prophet Muhammad, peace be upon him, which was soon approaching.

The atmosphere was quite magical. The calling of busy stallholders in the market, coupled with birds, squeaky cart wheels, and cars hooting, and the fragrance of spices and freshly baked bread filled the air until everything was eclipsed and brought to ground by the loud blaring sound from the mosque amplifier: "Allahu Akbar, Allahu Akbar . . ."

21 | *New Cultural Home*

It was so pleasing to see cats purring and entering the mosque during prayers. What I couldn't understand was why so many Egyptians were not doing the same. Many seemed deaf to the prayer call and continued getting on with their business – joking, laughing, and chatting, instead of going in to bow before their creator for a few humble minutes. As is usually the case with new converts, I was naturally zealous and now had to get used to a global community that had largely lost touch with the sublime spirit of Islam they were so fortunate – by birth – to have inherited.

What a sensation it was to cross over the Red Sea and finally set foot on the ancient sands of the Arabian Peninsula, pursuing the route of the great ancestor of the prophets, Abraham, and following his footsteps in the monotheistic, unchanging land of Ishmael.

The atmosphere was startlingly different. Unlike my experience in the streets of Cairo, here, everybody's day seemed to rotate around the prayers; stall keepers left their goods covered with only a light cotton sheet while they went off to the mosque. There was a strong sense of monotheistic immaculateness; I noticed that the authorities enforced a miniature curfew at prayer times, and the police themselves joined the prayer lines (many, including sergeants, boasted some very long beards).

Another major difference with Egypt was that there were no special decorations in preparation for the blessed Prophet's birthday. Everything was much more austere and bare. It was also unbelievably hot. I had never been to this part of the world before and the desert climate was totally new; the closest I'd come to this climatic experience was entering a Swedish sauna.

I had already removed my usual clothes and covered myself with two simple, unsewn pieces of white cloth, which symbolised my entry into a state of peace and sanctity (Ihram), free from the material finery and luxuries of the world, ready to perform the rites of lesser pilgrimage and go around the holy House of God – Al Ka'bah – following the tradition established by Abraham almost four thousand years earlier.

The teachers and nuns at St. Joseph's primary school had delivered sermons on the history of Abraham from the Old Testament, which describes the heart-rending incident when he took Hagar and their son Ishmael away from Canaan. It was right where I stood, in the once desolate valley – the Desert of Paran – between harsh rocky mountains, where the patriarchal prophet's biblical journey led him.

The Qur'an repeats the narrative but provides valuable new information about what happened next. What the teachers didn't tell me – and likely didn't know – was how this place, where the patriarch left his firstborn, and where my sandals had carried me, became known as Makkah. While the Bible leaves large gaps in the story, the Qur'an establishes the importance of this city and what transpired. Abraham actually visited Ishmael and his mother many more times than are mentioned in the Bible. During one of those visits, as the Qur'an clearly describes, the actual House of God itself was built by the hands of father and son.

Since then, Makkah has been a monotheistic compass point for the believers in God. Countless pilgrims have faithfully gathered here year after year, retracing the footsteps of Prophet Abraham. The pilgrimage traditionally culminates with the sacrificial offering of a sheep or other animal,[58] in remembrance of the moment when a ram was provided by God to Abraham, after he had proved his total submission and willingness to sacrifice his only son. This probably raises a serious question for some as to who may have been offered for sacrifice originally: Ishmael or Isaac? That age-old dispute may not be easily resolved – neither was it really of much interest to me as I stood there.

My heart was simply humbled as I pondered what a privilege it was for me to be chosen out of billions of people to visit the holy house and pray in the very place where Muhammad, who descended from Abraham and was his monotheistic heir, had personally bowed and prostrated. The feeling was indescribable. No matter in what direction I faced, a sense of holiness was present; there was no material distance between me and God. My whole life seemed to have been a travelling shadow, which had begun at dawn and had now reached midday.

"*Labaik!* [I am here at your service], oh, my Lord, I am here!"

After completing the rounds in Makkah, I continued on to visit Madinah, where the blessed Prophet had migrated, lived, and was finally buried. It was like walking into an old, biblical film, the place looking exactly as it must have done over a thousand years ago: people dressed in cotton cloaks and turbans, carrying staffs; elders with white, graceful beards and dark, sun-baked skin. The worshippers all appeared so handsome, models of devotion and Muslim character, from all corners of the world; everyone seemed to be in a state of radiance. I paid my respects at the front of the ornate shiny brass doors shielding the Prophet's mausoleum, "As-salamu 'alaykum ya Rasulullah" – "Peace be upon you, oh messenger of Allah."

Coming out of the mosque after mid-afternoon prayers, I unexpectedly bumped into a Black fellow convert from Canada. He could probably see that I was a new Muslim. It was nice to meet someone from a Western background who spoke English. His name was Abu Ameena Bilal Phillips. We got chatting, and at some point he asked me what work I did for a living. I told him I was a musician and singer.

"Oh! You'll have to give that up," he replied. "Musical instruments are *haram* [forbidden]."

His bold confidence seemed indisputable, even though, having scanned the Qur'an end to end, I could find no clear statement that music was prohibited. Only in the deep crevices of some commentaries and notes were there anecdotal inferences of its possible dangers.[59] Well, that was no surprise to me. But actually branding *all* music as forbidden – now that was something totally new.

Passing through Jeddah on my way back to London, I visited a small local mosque for the afternoon prayers. There I met a kind, elderly, white-robed shaikh, who invited me into his home for tea and dates. We chatted a little, and I told him that I'd recently embraced Islam and desperately wanted to learn how to pray exactly the way the Prophet did. He left the room, then returned with a large box containing twelve volumes of al-Bukhari's collection of the Prophet's sayings.

21 | *New Cultural Home*

"Here is the second-most authentic[60] and reliable book after the Qur'an."

Carting that weighty library-load away, little did I know that – thanks to these publications and Bilal Phillips's emphatic comment – I had been nudged inadvertently onto a Salafi path. Most books in Saudi Arabia were heavily imbued with those of the Prophet's sayings that supported an exclusive school of Islamic thought based on the teachings of the reformer Muhammad Ibn Abd al-Wahhab, the influential scholar who had historically laid the foundations and handed a sturdy religious legitimacy to the early founders of the Saudi kingdom.[61]

Having moved back with my mother in Hampstead Garden Suburb, I was well tended to. Mum was happy to have her youngest son back, albeit with a rather more disciplined lifestyle than before. She was always so accommodating and considerate; when I asked her to empty the bottles of alcohol from the lounge cupboard, she happily agreed, probably as a result of her quite strict Baptist upbringing. Mum hardly ever drank anyway – it was a thing that usually went along with the festivities only when Christmas came around.

That being done, I moved on to the issue of images and pictures. There was a section in Bukhari's sayings of the Prophet that indicated a prohibition of creating statues, images, or any other resemblance of human or animate figures. Mum's heart must have been broken as I asked her to help me while I tore up and burned a bunch of my drawings and cartoons. I didn't notice at the time, but she had secretly tucked away as many as she could while I lit the bonfire in the garden, trying to salvage whatever she could before it all went up in smoke.

I suppose Mum took an objective view of the whole spectacle. Certainly, as the youngest and formerly most unhinged kid of the family, I was reformed and becoming much better behaved. Prayers made me punctual and less lazy. *OK*, she might have said to herself, *if the price of having my little boy back home is to chuck out a few old bottles of liquor and some sketches – it's worth it.*

At the Central Mosque one Saturday afternoon, it was a surprise to bump into a group of real, homegrown English Muslims, a very quiet, genteel bunch of guys. I became very friendly with Razi Abdullah Kane, a soft-spoken Geordie with a very long beard – we were almost in competition with each other in that particular department. The tea-saturated group used to meet the first Saturday of every month and study the Qur'an and the teachings of Imam Al Ghazali in English with commentary.

A couple of them proposed that we form an association for British Muslims, to make it easier for Brits to consider Islam as something that could be for them rather than just for "foreigners." I wasn't interested in that concept, believing it could inadvertently turn into an exclusively "white Muslim" club, whereas I saw Islam as completely neutral and colourless and resisted any idea of standing behind a banner of ethnicity (my background had never actually provided me with a clearly defined sense of that, anyway). I was still "dreaming about the world as one." So I didn't sign up.

My broad non-partisan approach would soon be challenged. One day I was confronted by a fellow in the mosque who, after observing my prayer, tapped me on the shoulder and said, "Brother! What madhhab do you follow?" Hey! I'd never heard of that before. Up to then, I had believed that there was only one Islam.

Gradually, I became aware of four major divisions, or schools of thought, in Sunni Islam[62] . . . And then there was Shia. Crumbs! As well as the carving up of Muslims into passport-waving nationalities, another domestic religious division was revealing itself to me. The madhhab approach represented the accumulation of various juristic interpretations passed down by Muslim thinkers, judges, and scholars over many hundreds of years.[63] I found this quite unnerving, knowing that unity of belief is one of the most unshakable foundations in the Qur'an, as it says:

> **O prophets! Indeed, this religion of yours is only one, and I am your Lord, so worship Me alone.**[64]

My divinely guided space-pod had obviously landed in Islam a long way down the historic Muslim timeline. Though these Islamic fractures were basically academic, nothing like the denominational battles and wars that other religions had suffered, I was not ready to follow suit. Setting up barriers between "us" and "them" – even though "us" and "them" both claimed to follow the same book – no, thank you. As far as I was concerned, the Qur'an was the greatest tool for unity, based on the pure and original Adamic foundation, where humankind began. Yes, it appeared to me, from a Qur'anic perspective, even Christians and Jews were invited to join back together and heal their differences.

Chugging on through the thick mist of my ignorant bliss, I decided to walk a non-aligned path. I didn't feel compelled to adopt a single school of thought. I also had a sufficiently large and growing collection of commentaries on the Qur'an and books of hadith, the sayings and actions of the Prophet, to help me. This was the nature of my studies, since the days of "Majikat," sitting cross-legged, alone in a hotel, inspired, reading words straight from the book of God Himself.

Although I was still in shorts as far as age and experience in Islam were concerned, I did feel I had a unique standpoint to share based on this discovery of unity and all the wonderful things I was learning, unfiltered, through the Qur'an. In order to expand my knowledge further, I set about forming a study circle in the Central Mosque. Open to everyone wanting to deepen their understanding of Islam, I began it on the Saturdays that were not utilised by the Association of British Muslims. The meetings were held in the downstairs lower halls of the centre.

A lot of people descended the steps and joined the circle. We studied the translation of Yusuf Ali and his Qur'anic commentary. The topics soon widened as Muslim speakers were invited to give talks on interesting subjects: Doubt, Love and Friendship, Perfection, The Family, and "What's best?" This oasis of learning became a major source for my advanced research into the Qur'an and hadith, causing me to work late into the night sometimes, preparing for a lecture on whatever theme excited my interest.

Unsurprisingly, when some fans got word that "Cat

Stevens" was giving regular talks in the Central Mosque, they made a beeline to hear him. Many came, listened, and some eventually entered Islam through this humble, open-door approach – others were sadly disappointed. You could almost hear them mumbling on the way out: "He didn't even sing 'Moonshadow'!"

Last Love Song
1979

THE GROWING GAP between my attachment to Islam and my previous religion, Musicism, was fast becoming untenable. I had spoken to Jerry Moss of A&M and Chris Blackwell of Island personally to explain that I needed space and time to do my "thing" for a while, asking them to allow me to take a break from the devotions and rituals of making records. They kindly agreed.

Occasionally I would look at the charts to see whether my album was still floating around. The single "Last Love Song" was my farewell to the music industry; it stated my position quite perfectly, firstly addressing those who were content to see the back of me:

> *If you don't love me*
> *Stop fooling yourself*
> *No more acting*

I know your show too well
Did you think that you could just shake my hand
With a "How d'y'do?"
Cause if you don't want me
Maybe I don't want you

The final words of the song addressed those who still held on to the hope that I might change my mind and (if we all lived long enough) see me return near the end to patch things up:

Oh and as you go through life
It's the little things that come back again
If you came back again
You know I'd give my loving to you[65]

Maintaining a star status and producing hits were not major motors in my life anymore. There were more important things to get on with. Apart from my connection with God and my newly found family of friends and worshippers at the mosque, my world was distinctly different; I was growing a bit lonely. My girlfriends were all spoken to, one by one. There was no more room for "Freelove & Goodbye" relationships, that sort of idea was not allowed in Islam – "Last Love Song" implied that, too. My attention turned to the inevitable: it was time to marry and start a family.

A spirited romance from my partying days rang up my manager's office while I happened to be visiting Los Angeles, wanting to meet again. Juliette came from Turkey, and we had gone steady for quite a few months back in the wild ol'

Paul and Barry days. I had never bothered to ask her about her faith or religious background at the time; that wasn't the kind of thing that seemed important, but was now highly relevant: and she was a Muslim! I wondered if this might be a hint from God.

We met, and I saw she was as strikingly beautiful as before. This felt like an opportunity to see if this reconnection could lead to marriage – like the closing of a circle. The few days we spent walking around, dining, and chatting were lovely. She'd matured and had maintained her strong sense of self-belief, which ticked the hard-headed-woman box immediately. I could live with that, I thought.

This went on for a while. She saw me praying but was always at a distance and never asked to join; maybe she didn't know how to. Those were slightly awkward moments, and I was too shy to ask her up front. After letting her know where I was heading, heart-wise and spiritually, it became clear that we were at cross angles – looking for different prospectives. We mutually agreed that there was no point getting back together and parted ways once more. Times had changed; it was a bright new morning, and faith was now the light of my life.

Practising Muslim girls were hard to bump into. There was no real opportunity to mix at the mosque, and I didn't know many families with eligible daughters. My former, reclusive-star habits, combined with my natural shyness, meant that I did not socialize very much. But one brother from the Tablighi group suggested that I make a special prayer to Allah from the Qur'an:

22 | *Last Love Song*

> **They are those who pray, "Our Lord!
> Bless us with pious spouses
> and offspring who will be the joy of our hearts,
> and make us models for the righteous."**[66]

It worked! Soon afterwards, it all began to happen. My Muslim Geordie friend Razi Kane was engaged to a girl from a family in Kingston, Surrey. He wanted to invite them for lunch and asked if he could use my Curzon Street pad. It was arranged.

The head of the family, Mr. Mubarak Ali, was a solidly built, giant figure of a man, bearing an uncanny resemblance to my own father. His black, trimmed moustache and oiled, flat-combed hair matched my dad's look exactly. The family had migrated from Nairobi in the sixties, after the upheavals brought about by the new independent Kenyan republic.

The family's background was interesting: Mr. and Mrs. Ali had been born in Kenya to parents who had immigrated there during the Ottoman era, a remarkable time when there were hardly any borders between Muslim lands; people travelled, mixed, breathed, and worked freely. For that reason, I initially thought they were Turkish. Later, I would discover the family were in fact a mixture of Kashmiri, Dagestani, and Afghan origin – an Asian cocktail that was just a touch more exotic than mine.

Those borderless days of the Islamic Empire were gone; times had moved on. But Mr. Ali seemed to really enjoy retelling his memories and talking of all the adventurous journeys he had made during his younger years; he was a great storyteller. We listened to him throughout lunch, talking about "old" Makkah and voyages through Egypt and across the Red Sea. We got on really well and the father took a straight liking to me.

Around the same time, a pretty young girl from the US, Lucy Johnson, had made her way to find me at the Islamic circle. We previously had a brief fling and got to know each other during my last tour in the US. She seemed sincere. I easily warmed up to her and even handed her my treasured, red-covered copy of the Qur'an, the one David had gifted me, asking her to read it with an open heart.

Not long after, Lucy returned to the circle and said that she wanted to embrace Islam. I was kind of taken by surprise at how quickly it happened. Those present witnessed her saying the Shahadah (testimony of her faith) and happily welcomed her into Islam. Highly energised, she took the name 'Aisha and immediately wore a scarf to cover her golden hair. I could see a real prospective wife in her.

There were lots of things to think about, not least because a major problem was flaring up in the vicinity of my north-and-south (that's English rhyming slang for "mouth"). The premolar teeth on the left-hand side of my jaw were rapidly decomposing; blame those reckless years of consuming endless cakes and swigging Cokes in Dad's shop. Now dentists – like wives – are important to get right. My brother-in-law, Alec, told me he had heard great praise from his sister about some orthodontic whiz, a professor who lectured and operated from Georgetown University, Washington, D.C., where her husband worked. Because he was a Greek, for some reason I trusted him and flew straight over there to sort it out. The surgery was bloody, long, and torturous.

Perhaps the 3,500-mile trip could appear a little extravagant on my part, but in the end the pain was worth it – and there were other good reasons. I felt it was necessary, if 'Aisha was to be my wife, to know a bit more about her background. So during that journey to the East Coast, I visited her mother in Boston.

She lived in an extremely classic, American home, a cozy, off-white house with a decent patch of mown lawn out front. The mother was kind and respectable, and seemed totally relaxed about her daughter becoming Muslim. There was no father in sight, and I decided it was best not to enquire about him; it might appear a bit pushy. I relied on my heart to guide me on the matter.

On my return to London, before making any big decision about marriage, I waited for a sign from God. It was still very early days, and I didn't want to rush things. Dating was not on the agenda as I was careful to keep things respectfully "Islamic," and I wanted my mother to meet her, so I invited 'Aisha home for dinner in Hampstead. Mum cooked us all a delicious meal; she was always so good at serving others. 'Aisha looked totally relaxed; she seemed to be quite a natural fit (apart from her thick American accent), blonde as well, just like Mum in terms of looks. They got on nicely.

Then came an unexpected invitation for afternoon tea in Mr. Mubarak Ali's house. I knew he had five unmarried daughters, the eldest of whom was betrothed to Razi. This was certainly going to be interesting! After being welcomed into their home in New Malden near Surbiton and enjoying the wonderful taste of their freshly cooked samosas, biscuits, and tea, I knew pretty soon which of the daughters I was drawn to: Fawziah, the third eldest. There was a bashful yet confident air to her that I found compelling. My eyes kept slipping from my plate to gaze at her. She looked a bit Grecian, with dark hair and eyes that made her feel like family.

Still not sure, I asked Fawziah home for dinner to meet my mother. It was the evening before my thirty-first birthday. She came chaperoned by her younger brother Muhammad and sister Kawthar. Razi was invited too. It was a lovely evening; Mum cooked one of her fine roast chicken and vegetable specialities with Swedish lingonberry jam on the side. After they all left, I asked Mum's opinion about the two prospective young ladies. She diplomatically hinted at Fawziah – that was the same way my heart was leaning too. Yes!

Prayer answered – minus lightning bolt.

There were other things engaging my mind. It was now fast approaching my second Ramadan. The days of fasting were very long in the UK in 1979, the month being August, when the sun set at around 8.30 p.m.[67] Boy! Did I welcome hearing the *adhan* (the call to prayer), signalling the chance to eat again – after fifteen hours without food or drink, you can kind of imagine how delicious everything tasted! The first few days were the hardest, but then you just got used to it.

Fawziah's father had asked me home to break the fast with them. Her mother had cooked the most sumptuous Asian meal of spiced chicken, meat curry, and rice, with a sweet dessert that knocked my head off. Wasting no time – as I'd been advised – I unhesitatingly proposed in her parents' presence. It was part of the tradition to have their blessing before asking her. They presented her with the prospect. Fawziah shyly asked for time to pray to God for guidance.

The next time I visited, the father gave me the news: affirmative! But I was told that we still had to wait for Ramadan to come to an end. It took a whole three weeks to arrange everything.

Fawziah and I got married. Ours was the thousandth marriage at the London Central Mosque and Islamic Cultural Centre, performed by the chief imam, Dr. Darsh. It was a full moon on Friday 7 September 1979, corresponding to 14 *Shawwal* 1399.

The press was all there, ready to capture the historic moment, which, for Fawziah, was an unnerving induction into the rock 'n' roll hall of famous wives. The initial burst of rapidly clicking, flashing cameras gradually subsided and the journalists respectfully retreated and lingered outside while both families filed in.

The afternoon prayers had just finished, and everybody sat on the floor of the main hall around the turbaned, long-coated figure of Dr. Darsh. Fawziah was definitely more heavily veiled than most Western brides, so it was hard to see her face. I sat opposite her with Dr. Darsh between us. Mum had put on a headscarf, as had Anita, both highly sensitive to the new cultural environment. David and his children were also there, some wearing skull caps, manoeuvering to be comfortable while sitting with crossed legs. Even my excessively curly- and long-haired personal road manager, Carlos Braganza Jones, looked respectable with a colourful Turkistan cap he'd picked up for the occasion.

The ceremony was short and simple; the imam asked the bride, through her father, if she accepted the proposal of marriage with the dowry agreed, according to the book of God and the *Sunnah* of the Prophet, peace be upon him. She whispered her consent. I was asked the same, responding, "Yes," just as the clock struck four. At that moment, I felt a strange sensation in my stomach – it might have had something to do with that male gut instinct to escape and remain free and unattached for as long as possible. But it was now done: I was committed.

I soon shook off the unwelcome feeling, knowing I was in the company of the best of humanity, becoming a branch of the honoured family tree of humankind, beginning with Adam and Eve – without whose wedlock none of us would have had a nano-atom-sized chance of ever seeing the glorious light of day.

After the ceremony was complete and everybody had warmly congratulated us, hugging endlessly with broad smiles all around, we left the mosque. As we were making our way to the waiting cars, one of the brazen journalists barged up to my mother and intrusively asked what Fawziah was like and what she thought about the wedding, presumably having found out that we had never dated or had close relations before the marriage.

"Oh, she's very beautiful. And love? That will come later."

It was hard to explain the engagement process, and the press made a big thing about the fact we hadn't been in bed together before the wedding. But that didn't bother me; the relationship was pure and based on faith and trust – and that was the way I wanted it.

It wasn't long before I learned, through reading a magazine interview with 'Aisha, that she had another name, "Princess Cheyenne." The *Boston Herald* called her "perhaps the most famous exotic dancer ever in this town."[68] Her quotes regarding me were not very flattering, and the press obviously amplified the worst of them. I held no grudges against her, however. I was thankful that I had been given the wise benefit of my mother's advice.

Fawziah and I moved into 27 Curzon Street, which she immediately named "Taxi-land." As is the case for most newly married couples, the first nest is usually cramped and somewhat awkward; Mayfair was not the ideal place to start a home. The treeless compound was an uncomfortably busy and hectic location, right next door to the noisy White Elephant Club, overlooking the offices of MI5 (again! Just like my childhood home) and only a few steps away from Hugh Hefner's famous Playboy nightclub on Park Lane. It was not quite the ideal environment for a Muslim couple – particularly considering the reputation of Mayfair itself and the red-light history of Shepherd's Market just around the corner. Furthermore, finding a place to park became a recurring nightmare.

My staff also had to adjust to some new rules: nobody was allowed to walk upstairs into the flat; they had to knock and wait for gracious permission. Fawziah was extremely shy and automatically put on a scarf in the presence of any non-related male. My previous problems in terms of jealousy and Greek macho pride were all accommodated by the modest traditions of Islam. What a relief!

Despite her modesty, however, Fawziah was no pushover. She was an extremely talented designer and understood the need for creative space; in many ways, we were perfect for each other. Not to mention that she had five brothers, and so she was used to handling male egos with ease.

To her dismay, the kitchen was titchy, designed mainly to make coffee or tea. Most of the counter space was taken up by a burstingly bright orange Gaggia espresso machine. Fawziah's cooking style was severely cramped. She happened to enjoy making meals and was a marvel when it came to experimenting with different dishes inspired by cuisines from all over the world. Nothing was beyond her capabilities, and she instinctively knew, when tasting a new dish, what it contained and how it was made.

She needed more space, and I was spurred on to look for a new place for us to live. I had already purchased a luxurious flat on Highgate Hill, but decided it was way too pompous and would have too many empty rooms. We decided to look for something smaller and friendly, with a garden.

David moved into the second-floor office of Curzon Street, where we had rehoused the old black family piano. He began work on another ambitious project, based on an enchanting book by Bernard Benson, called *Peace Child*. By this time, *Alpha Omega* had been released on United Artists Records, but it hadn't flown. Perhaps it was the heavy nature of the theme, epically telling the story of humanity from its birth in the universe through to the modern industrial age, global war, and its predictably apocalyptic end. *Peace Child* would adopt most of the songs from *Alpha Omega* and would launch David into the world peace movement. Soon he got involved with activists in the UN. That helped promote his oratorio, which travelled across the US and the USSR, part of the groundswell of diplomacy trying to melt the Cold War iceberg of the time.

My brother had many sides to him and usually never did anything without spiritual or philosophical motivation – he truly wanted to make the world a better place and dreamed of peace. Born at a time of a world war and dragged in and out of bomb shelters with Anita, Mum, and Dad had left a psychological bruise. David had once run away from home to escape Dad's temper. He later joined the merchant navy but was promptly discharged for lack of discipline and went on to be married and divorced – all by the age of nineteen!

I'd watched David closely. Though I envied him in many ways, and while he had a massive influence on me, I also learned how not to fall into some of the same holes he did. I loved him, and it was he who gave me the Qur'an, but I couldn't understand why he was running away from Islam.

David's musical was a brave effort to link people of different faiths and political ideologies, addressing the major threats to our world. *Peace Child* had a strong spiritual connotation. But Dave himself was still hovering between Judaism, Christianity and Islam. His unfortunate experience of ejection from the mosque in Jerusalem was now far enough behind him, and, in an effort to bring him closer, I invited him to visit the mosque in east London where some of my new Tablighi friends were based.

An extraordinary and unexpected alignment with my hopes took place on that lucid, star-filled winter's night. After evening prayers, I left David alone to chat with Khalid, a Kuwaiti guy in a clean white jalabiyyah. No sooner did I turn my back than Khalid came running over to me excitedly,

"Your brother's going to take Shahadah!"

I flew over, and there he was, repeating the words of Testimony: "There is no God but Allah; Muhammad is the servant and messenger of Allah."

My heart bounced ten miles high. God! This was something I'd sort of wished for but never imagined would come to be – certainly, not so soon. We hugged. David took a full shower there and then. After the process was complete, his face seemed to glow like the moon – as bright and shining as the one hovering above our heads that exceptionally unreal night.

Soon we were on our way, driving home together. It was such a mega-moment, I wondered if it would turn his life around as much as it did for me. Dave was dedicated to his wife, Yael, with whom he had a daughter, Naomi. Would this cause a fracture? He didn't want to alienate his daughter or wife and asked me not to tell anyone about his conversion. He just needed time.

Unfortunately – as I would soon find out – David didn't fully embrace the faith. It became obvious that he was taking it all in his stride; like many casual Muslims, he was just concerned with getting on with life without making Islam a priority or the Prophet his personal guide. Although prayer times came and went, David would only join if I directly invited him. Not wanting to push him too hard, I eased up. How he would accommodate himself beyond that east London mosque epiphany was now between him and his conscience.

Later, he tried to rationalise the event, explaining to me that he wasn't fully aware of what he was doing when asked by Khalid to repeat the Shahadah. True or not, I was just comforted by the fact that he had taken that spiritual leap, as the Prophet had said, "Whoever died truly knowing that there is no God but Allah will enter Paradise."[69]

Year of the Child
1979–80

IT WAS 1979. What happened that particular year also may have influenced my brother's decision and his hesitation to appear too close to Islam.

Enter: the Iranian Revolution.

A new Islamic political order had arrived, and the world trembled... big time! The whole Middle East shook violently from the tectonic reverberations of this new, unforeseen uprising. From where I was standing, in the West, any previous placid image of Islam was shattered. Forget about my wish to spread peace and understanding. My dislike of making enemies also became irrelevant; they were forcibly made for me. An insurmountable wall was being built around reasonable, everyday Muslims, and we were sinking into the shadows of a long, dark night.

Journalists, naturally, had quite a time. It was dismaying to see the image of Islam portrayed like a horror movie, with angry-looking Muslims on display every night on the BBC *Nine O'Clock News*, chanting curses at the West. My situation altered drastically; from being one of the white(-ish) majority, I was now one of an increasingly identifiable minority. "Turned Turk" was a common phrase coined by the British forces whenever anyone from their regiment or company converted to Islam. I was shoved further into the realm of outcasts, quite a change from the previous privileged position I had occupied among the most brightly spotlighted, socially acceptable species.

I had peacefully entered Islam just eighteen months earlier. But from the moment that revolution began, there would be no safe space left: either you applauded the downfall of the world's most powerful shah, the ruler of Iran and a staunch ally of the US, or you derided the new breed of theological autocrats – the ayatollahs. But hold on! I was not a Shia, but I was a Muslim, so where was I supposed to stand?

Racial profiling governed most Westerners' view of Muslims. But to be honest, many Muslims – I was now finding out – held their own, equally negative image of the "other"; each was eyeballing the opposition with suspicion. Tempers were rising. I was still a pretty impressionable, young Muslim soul and – considering my sixties upbringing – it wasn't difficult to be moved by the intense power of Iran's Islamic rhetoric against the "System."

No wonder David didn't feel comfortable.

The problem wasn't only Iran, which was actively trying to export its revolution to other countries in the region. The Soviets also wanted more influence and the US needed their Western, capitalist model to win. The superpowers began a replay of the Great Game – the nineteenth-century struggle between Britain and Russia for influence in the region. With the loss of the shah, the Cold War heated up and Afghanistan became the next territorial victim, with both superpowers vying for the prize. Saudi Arabia provided most of the funding for the US-backed resistance of mujahideen (Islamic guerrillas), which included direct CIA support for one notorious figure yet to come, by the name of Osama bin Laden.

The central Asian region became embroiled in ideological and military conflicts. As the countries were mostly Muslim, the use of Islam as a motivating factor was an obvious tool for the Americans to use against the communist generals of the USSR. It was impossible to avoid being stirred by the growing gatherings and voices in the mosques, calling all Muslims to wake up against the injustice, and join the struggle of Islam vs. Atheism. (And to add to the disturbing mood of the era, let's not forget the IRA were still bombing the UK, Margaret Thatcher was elected prime minister, and Roger Moore was still cast as James Bond.)

Next came the ill-fated seizure of the House of God in Makkah in Saudi Arabia. This was one of the most surreal episodes to rock the Muslim world, already reeling from the revolution across the Gulf. A group of about five hundred armed Saudi combatants entered the holy precinct of the Ka'bah and sought to overthrow the king and his government. Madness ensued. Fifty thousand worshippers who had gathered for morning prayers were held hostage. The ideologically fired-up rebels demanded the strict adherence to the sharia and called for allegiance from all Muslims.

Violence had been prohibited in the holy sanctuary since the time of Abraham, so a ruling was sought by King Khalid: How to respond? Finally, French commandos (superficially converted to Islam for the mission) were enlisted. After two weeks of bloody confrontation and hundreds of killings and casualties, the siege came to an end and the last remaining culprits were beheaded.

I just wanted to get on calmly with perfecting my prayers and family duties. The world, alas, was looking decisively wilder than it had in those days when I could place the guitar down beside me and quietly study the Qur'an in peace. Now, my front door and the walls of my home were shaking from events happening outside it.

Above the increasing noise of gunfire and visions of war raging in Muslim countries, I knew that people had little or no information to help them look objectively and access the true meaning of Islam from a spiritual perspective, rather than the militant image occupying the media's frontal lobe in the wake of the revolution. It seemed like the right time to start explaining what I knew, to clarify the essential aspects of the faith, as distinct from the twisted political altercations bloodying the front pages week after week.

My days of music were now numbered. After the disappointment of the UN concert, I had a bad taste in my mouth for the whole nasty "business." There was hardly any motivation for me to go out and sing or do anything except, perhaps, for charity.

Then, unexpectedly, right out of the (UN) blue, I was contacted by the UNICEF office in London, begging me to headline a forthcoming event at Wembley, another show in aid of the Year of the Child. Top billing . . . hmm? I forgave the debacle of the previous UN gig and accepted. One good reason to do so (though UNICEF and most others didn't know it) was that Fawziah was pregnant. Yes, it was really, really going to be the year of the child!

> *In the daytime,*
> *Time for celebration*
> *No use looking down*
> *Children open your eyes*
> *It's a world; a whole nation*
> *Now the white boats have landed*
> *And the innocent are here*
> *So dream for the child*
> *'Cause it's the time of the year*[70]

This was to be my last concert billed simply as "Cat Stevens." I kept it bare: Alun was on acoustic guitar and Richard Sharpey on keyboards. That night I also invited David Essex and Richard Thompson on stage. Unknown to many, Richard, one of the founding fathers of progressive British folk rock, no less, was already a Muslim.

It was a great gig, but my heart simply wasn't in it. Nothing of the bright stage life attracted me anymore. That peak had been reached; I was now happily accommodating myself back into humanity and my new family. My interest lay more at ground level, where I could safely place my head in peaceful prostration.

*

At last, we found a small house for sale just a few doors from my mother's in Hampstead Garden Suburb, close to where David and his family lived, too. The area was quiet and idyllic; every spring the roads would be full of pink blossoms. The cozy three-bedroom, semi-detached property was almost like a doll's house – much more child-friendly and more like a real home for Fawziah and myself than Curzon Street, with enough kitchen space to cook and tons of places to park.

Things happened fast, and it wasn't long before our first daughter entered the world. We named her Hasanah, which means "something good and beautiful." Born one day before Ramadan on Friday, early in July 1980, she was a true gift from God. Following her birth, I rushed straight to the mosque and joined the congregational prayer. Afterwards, I ran back to the clinic, which was only a few hundred yards round the corner in Avenue Road, St. John's Wood, to begin my new role as a father.

Becoming a dad was one of the most pleasing feelings of my life. I took the job very seriously and wanted everything to be absolutely perfect for this pretty little soul. With three of us, our family bond became even stronger: my very own tribe! Everybody was so jubilant about the new member of the "Islam" family, particularly my mother, who adored the hazel-green-eyed, cherub-faced little girl.

I had never actually believed I would one day be called "Daddy." There was a time when the thought horrified me, for a simple reason: I knew that kids ask blunt questions. What would I say if my child were to ask me about the meaning of life? As Steve or Cat, I would have had nothing much to tell them, apart from showing them a bookshelf chock-full of conflicting philosophical and religious views, a semi-vegetarian diet, and a few thoughtful songs and nice, colourfully illustrated album covers. I would have then been responsible for bringing a pure soul into an earthly battleground of chaos, psychosis, bloodshed, and death . . . with no explanation for any of it! No thanks.

Regardless of my altruistic leanings or my attempts to envision a better world through my thoughts and music, I had something infinitely more valuable to offer now. It was possible for me to point the way to a permanently accessible source of understanding – the Qur'an's lessons about the Prophets and Messengers; the highest ranks of humanity, chosen to act as teachers and model specimens of what it means to be fully and consciously in tune with life's awesome reality. In the Qur'an, it says:

> **They are those who remember God while standing, sitting, and lying on their sides, and reflect on the creation of the heavens and the Earth and pray, "Our Lord! You have not created all of this without purpose . . ."**[71]

The secular assumption of a "Godless universe" was infinitely harder for me to believe in than a divinely centred one. With my discovery of Islam, at last I could beget children with a clear heart and a book of wisdom to face every seemingly intractable problem that might confound them on this knobbly road of life – and death. Oh yes! Now I remember, that lurking threat to all those wish-filled tomorrows that we two-legged creatures have to eventually face up to.

How to explain death to a child is not easy for those faint of faith – for believers, leaving this Earth is not the end of the story. The Qur'an, like the Bible, describes it simply as the departure point from this planetary classroom, past the grave to the invisible world of immortality, waiting beyond.

Blessed is the One in Whose Hands rests all authority. And He is Most Capable of everything. He is the One Who created death and life in order to test which of you is best in deeds. And He is the Almighty, All-Forgiving.[72]

OK. Now that was clear (and especially reassuring that God stated He is "Forgiving"). But my question now was: What school will I send my little daughter to? Most schools in the UK – apart from strictly Christian and Jewish ones – upheld a strong secular bias. If education were to have any value, it had to contain the necessary component of moral know-how and advice to deal with the primary function of our internal conscience, to sufficiently prepare children for passing the fatal test of life. Choosing a school for Hasanah was a challenge Fawziah and I would sometime soon need to face.

Knowledge of both material as well as spiritual dimensions was essential for our child to be properly prepared for this world and the next. Sitting exams, which only equip children for a consumerist, grab-it-quick-while-it-lasts, Darwinian, survivalist's view of life, was not going to cut it.

To my mind, the biggest responsibility a government assumes is the compulsory education it provides for its new, unsuspecting crop of citizens. Due to the ever-increasing encroachment of the atheistic view of life, colonialising every inch of the curriculum, we needed to find a spiritually robust alternative.

Having been brought up in a highly religiously infused school from a very young age – even though Catholicism was not the church I personally chose or followed – made me a natural advocate for faith schools. It probably affected my approach to discipline and caused me to be quite strict with my own children (as well as those insubordinate musicians, back in my touring days). All things considered, my primary school hadn't done too bad: it had placed me firmly on the path of morality and made me pretty conscientious, working hard along the way to make a better future for myself, my family, and maybe even a small slice of humanity.

Human beings need large doses of the truth at the outset of life's journey to have a better chance to develop the potential for discernment and personal responsibility. I know how many – including me – would prefer to skip the "hard bits" and the threat of eternal punishment, but justice would have no meaning in the long term without that. According to a proverb from Prophet Solomon: "Fear is the beginning of Wisdom and knowledge of the Holy One is understanding."[73]

Children grasp the miracle of life much more easily than worn-out, grumpy adults do, perhaps because they are closer to the reality of non-existence and appreciate this awesome world, with its wondrous package of unexpected gifts, such as the first breath of life, your very own body, and a gorgeous woman to look after you.

In our new role as parents, Fawziah and I had to go through the normal process of emotional learning: understanding what Hasanah's boo-hooing was supposed to communicate: "Change my nappy," "Give me milk, for God's sake," or "Cuddle me, I just had a nightmare, and a monster's coming to take my mummy away." Whatever our baby needed, we tried to provide.

Something I could offer very easily was a song to help guide Hasanah's early thoughts towards God. It had been some time since I had written, but my skills had not entirely disappeared. I just needed something stimulating to awaken the creative cells. Reflecting on what kind of song I could sing to my child, an idea suddenly struck me. I began to compose "A is for Allah," a journey through the twenty-eight Arabic letters to teach a similar number of beliefs and concepts. The main object was as obvious as the title: changing the emphasis from apples to the creator of apples – presto!

It was coming up to my third year as a Muslim, and another important issue was on my mind. As well as the Shahadah and daily prayers, I had now satisfactorily carried out another two of the five pillars of Islam: I'd managed to fast over the month of Ramadan (Siyam) and had paid my 2.5 percent charity dues (Zakat). There was one pillar remaining: I had not yet performed the Hajj. Every Muslim, as long as they are physically and financially able to do so, should journey to Makkah during the twelfth month of the Islamic calendar, at least once in his or her lifetime.

I began to make preparations.

My father-in-law, Hajj Mubarak Ali (whom I now called Baba), had already made dozens of pilgrimages. I arranged to go with him and other members of the family, including my mother-in-law and the family's youngest brother and sister, Haroon and Tara. My fellow British Muslim and brother-in-law, Razi Kane, also planned to go. Fawziah had agreed to stay home and take care of Hasanah. Baba would perform this pilgrimage on behalf of my father. It was just another of God's gifts for Dad.

The year was 1400 AH in the Islamic calendar, October 1980. We left London and said our salams, making sure that we left behind no debt, no outstanding obligation or unsaid apology in respect of anyone we might have hurt or abused – this in order to start the journey with a clean mind and heart.

The Hajj teaches you how to prepare for leaving this Earth. One thing that really upset me, however, was abandoning Mum. There was no one dearer to me and I couldn't bear to think about what would happen if I left this world a Muslim and she didn't join the highest plateaus of faith. My beautiful mother was first in line; she unquestioningly deserved the best of all heavenly palaces for her selfless kindness and gentle character. So, a day or two before my departure, we sat down and talked.

Having already spent quite some time over the years listening to me explain what I'd been reading in the Qur'an, it was very clear to Mum that Christ's spiritual teachings were not displaced by Islam. The Qur'an even boasts a whole chapter dedicated to the blessed Virgin Mary, which retells the miraculous birth of Jesus; in other chapters, it includes his miracles and healings and his ascension to heaven, as

23 | *Year of the Child*

well as the promise of his return before the end of time – all emphatically stated without any ambiguity or apology.[74]

In many respects, Islam preserves the Messiah's teachings: from the way he prayed – placing his face down on the Earth – and his manner of greeting, by saying "Peace be unto you," to the way he dressed in long, white, humble clothes, and even down to washing his feet during ablution. Mum realised that I hadn't lost Jesus at all, but instead had gained Muhammad and, through him, a much broader understanding of the Son of Man's original nature and message for humankind.[75]

Mum had benefitted from a solid Christian upbringing; her father, David, had been a Baptist lay preacher, and her uncle Josef a pastor who had travelled as a missionary to South America. But she herself was never confirmed – a basic requirement in the Baptist church. Mum knew the difference Islam had made to my life and, by extension, to hers. Though she already had a strong connection with God, I had brought back home the teachings of Abraham, which clarified so many oblique and mysterious compounds within Christian theology.

She didn't need much convincing. I asked her if she believed there was only one God: she affirmed. Then I asked if she accepted Muhammad as His last messenger: she again accepted. A dream of mine had now been accomplished. That meant that I could leave everything under the watch of the Almighty, and continue on to the Hajj.

That first pilgrimage was like no other. The extraordinary feeling of proximity to God; no place felt unfamiliar because everywhere I felt a tangible sense of divine presence. It was as if my life had been an evolution of pre-planned windings and turns, leading to that place at that very moment, in unison with millions of souls, drawn together from the furthest reaches of this world to this centre ground of faith. We had come as pilgrims, following the footsteps of God's close friend, Abraham, everyone an equal, the family of humankind reuniting in submission, adoringly bowing before the Lord of the Universe.

I was clearly experiencing the same wondrous feelings that Malcolm X had felt and articulated some years earlier, during the final period of his life: "Never have I witnessed such sincere hospitality and the overwhelming spirit of true brotherhood as is practised by people of all colours and all races here in this ancient Holy Land, the home of Abraham, Muhammad, and all the other prophets of the Holy scriptures."[76]

Returning to London with my head shaved, I found things hadn't changed much. It was business as usual for the bleak-faced black-cab and double-decker-bus drivers, inching bumper-to-bumper along Finchley Road on another slippery, cold and grey rainy day. My wife and mother – in contrast – were as happy as sunflowers, radiant and smiling, pleased to see me safe and home again.

Hugging my little baby Hasanah in my arms, I knew that London was nothing like the world of faith and unity from which I had returned. What would a future in Britain be like for her? I wondered.

23 | *Year of the Child*

Where Do the Children Pray?
1981–3

LONDON WAS A melting pot for Muslims from all over the world; many were refugees or migrants seeking a better life and an escape from tyranny or poverty. On Fridays, voices outside the mosque were raised, crying against the injustices heaped on oppressed Muslim populations. The Qur'an continually emphasises the need for Muslims to be concerned about the poor and to give generously in charity, so Zakat collection boxes were always being filled for one country or another.

One Friday during the sermon, Dr. Badawi – the recently appointed director of the Islamic Cultural Centre – delivered a powerful speech and presented a case for Muslim schools. The message moved me tremendously. I thought again about Hasanah's future education. At the end of the prayer, I visited him in his office and thanked him for the inspired speech, later sending him a generous cheque towards the cause.

That probably drove him to find out who I was (and quite possibly even to listen to my old records).

The media had more or less forgotten about me. Apart from a few snide headlines, trying to link "Cat" to Ayatollah Khomeini, I was generally left alone to get on with building my family and devoting myself to personal studies of Islam. My task was to get closer to the preserved words of God's book and the sayings of His prophet without relying on English translations, so I took a basic course in Arabic.

Education was top of my agenda. In 1981, with the birth of my second daughter, Asmaa, the question of schools became more urgent. I now had two lovely, innocent girls to look after. While the backdrop of sectarian battles and divisions in the Muslim world dominated the front pages, I wanted to find a place of safe and bias-free learning for my children.

The Muslim schools project launched in Dr. Badawi's speech was nowhere on the horizon. He seemed to have other pressing things to deal with, becoming entangled in a dispute with our much-loved imam, Dr. Darsh, giving him his marching orders to immediately return to Egypt. This was about as good as being exiled to the City of the Dead, Egypt's necropolis, as far as the imam was concerned.

Dr. Sayed Mutawalli ad-Darsh was the kind of man who had a constant beam across his permanently red-cheeked face. Educated in the historical cloisters of the Al-Azhar University, Cairo, he wore a traditional long blue coat and the familiar white turban, wound around a red fez-like hat, under which he packed a great deal of valuable knowledge. Dr. Darsh understood the deep cultural problems facing Muslims in the West, and was very popular with the community he served. Worshippers relied heavily on him for his religious opinion. We certainly didn't want to see him go, so I helped organise a petition in the mosque.

When I first revealed to him that I was a musician, he smiled, without needing to reflect too much on the matter, and encouraged me to continue writing and recording. The shaikh did not balk or criticise me but recommended that I stay away from showy stage performances, especially as they might invite a little too much female attention. He understood that the subject of music was a matter of *fiqh* (contextual reasoning), not a hard and fast principle of faith. His opinion was that music was allowed within certain moral guidelines and conditions.

But Dr. Darsh was not the only scholar I consulted during my formative years; I was eager to seek as many opinions as possible and met various scholars and theologians, like Shaikh Abdul Aziz bin Baz in Saudi Arabia, a blind cleric highly respected among the royal family of Al Saud, who was extremely influential throughout the Muslim world. Most students and preachers who had been educated in the kingdom – and that included the Black Canadian fellow convert I'd met in Madinah – followed his emphatic rulings and took a strict stand against music and singing, declaring that they were *haram* (forbidden) – unless the singer was male and unaccompanied by musical instruments.

While I was busily getting on with life, servicing my fast-growing family and circle activities in the Central Mosque, I saw a bold headline on a newspaper stand: JOHN LENNON SHOT DEAD.

24 | *Where Do the Children Pray?*

To me, this was worse than the assassination of John F. Kennedy. The life-light of one of my biggest musical heroes was blown out over nothing more than a deranged music fanatic's perverse wish to be famous. With soul-destroying news like that, I stopped being interested in what was going on in the music world. What or who happened to dominate the top of the charts was at the bottom of my metaphysical list of interests: Madonna, the Police, Michael Jackson, David Bowie, Kool and the Gang, all were welcome to the howls and hoots of the wild crowds – I was happy to be out.

As time went on, I felt increasingly uneasy about picking up a guitar, even more so after a small vermillion-red booklet about music and instruments in Islam found its way into my weary finger-picking hands. I'd collected lots of booklets on interesting, useful subjects, but this one was extremely on point. Printed in South Africa, it scared the absolute hell out of me. The book repeated various sayings attributed to the Prophet, peace be upon him, which made all musical activities out to be un-Islamic and downright sinful.

I was at the crossroads. The answer, which way to tread, arrived when reading one of the authentic wisdoms of the Prophet:

> *The permitted things (halal) are clear and the prohibited things (haram) are clear and between them are ambiguous matters that most people do not know about. So whoever is cautious of these unclear matters has cleared himself in regard to his religion and honour.*[77]

Following this advice and unless and until such things became more clear, I made a dramatic choice and prepared to get rid of all of my musical instruments. Either I could destroy my guitars (the vermillion-red book's preferred solution) or give them away to charity – I chose the latter.

Carlos Braganza Jones, my faithful Indian roadie from Goa, had been guarding my musical possessions for many years. He was now asked to load up all the flight cases with my guitars, organs, foot pedals, and piles of gold records and drive them to the auction, which was held at Bonhams in Knightsbridge, London. He carried out the request diligently and without question – while keeping one of his beady eyes on the white piano from Walham Grove.

The auction took place, and a lot of people were well and truly shocked. It was like watching a virtual musical suicide, as I set light to the symbolic articles and calmly disappeared across the bridge, past the smouldering flames, into the bleak expanse of pop insignificance. The press made little fuss about it, while the charities Help the Aged and Help a London Child got the benefit of the humble forty thousand pounds-plus the auction helped raise . . . and Carlos got his coveted white piano.

Those who observed both me and Islam from the outside were mystified: how could their iconic, long-haired, half-hippie, half-pop-pin-up, who embodied their most ambitious fantasies, end up being lured by such a violent, dark, foreign-looking creed, stuck in a time-warp filled with dictators, oilfields, and strange-looking prayer caps and rituals?

Obviously, a massive earthquake of spiritual change had taken place in my life, but most of it had happened beneath

24 | *Where Do the Children Pray?*

the surface. For many of my fans it was a complete surprise. There was certainly a lot of clarifying required. So I set to work and wrote a sixteen-page A4 booklet called *Joseph's Surrender*, which included an ink drawing of the old palm-tree corner of the Prophet's mosque in Madinah. The words were as gentle and non-preachy as I could manage: "The truth is this: I have found at last the perfect path which unites together all of my thoughts and beliefs into an entire religion I'd never previously dreamed existed. Man must follow whatever path he/or she wishes to follow, the truth doesn't change, but I believe if more people knew the truth about Islam, there would not be so much misunderstanding in the world."

The cover was designed by my sister, Anita. She had been taking art classes and was heavily into sharp graphic shapes, meticulously producing a beautiful eight-pointed star set in a sky of vibrant royal blue. Alec, her husband, had also taken a few nice photographs of pathways in London parks, which I included, together with a picture of a supernova courtesy of NASA.

I had the final print sent to all my faithful Fantasy Ring fan-club members as a parting gift, hoping it would help soften the impact of my departure from their spinning turntables. I knew, however, there was a lot more work to be done to help people understand.

Requests to speak at universities and gatherings all round the world soon bombarded my secretary's desk. I had lots of time on my hands and felt it my duty to accept as many invitations as possible: from Gloucester, Bournemouth, and

Glasgow to Turkey, Saudi Arabia, Malaysia, and Algeria – all eager to hear me speak. Each audience gave me a warm, enthusiastic reception, plainly inspired by hearing the first-hand twist to this modern-day Joseph's "rags-to-riches-to-giving-it-all-away" tale.

My appearances were mostly arranged and attended by Muslim organisations or students' groups. Not realising it at the time, I had now begun "performing" in my new role as a rare, unrehearsed, celebrity convert of the Muslim world. It sometimes felt as if I were being paraded with pride in front of crowds of admirers, a bit like a mascot with a jet-black, extended beard and strange attire – which was not altogether different from the old days of pop fans' adoration, in a way.

It seemed impossible to forget my fame and track record in music. Often, at the end of my talk, I would be asked to sing a couple of lines a cappella (voice only) on a boomy, bass-heavy microphone. Uncomfortably, I would stand in my characteristic dress, a long, loose-fitted white jalabiyyah, and chug out the only "Islamic" song I knew well: "A is for Allah."

The jalabiyyah had been designed and sewn professionally by my enormously talented wife. Fawziah was a qualified fashion designer and teacher before our marriage, and now not only embraced motherhood with that remarkable intuitive skill women seem to have but, like most women, was a high-functioning multi-tasker. She seemed to relish tailoring my dashing new "Islamic" wardrobe. Because of my desire to fit into mosque culture seamlessly, where styles of the Middle East dominated, the clothes usually ended up being ankle-length white robes.

I was also eager to follow the custom of the early companions of the Prophet and grow my beard as long as possible. Without my being conscious of it – and quite contrary to the description of the friendly, smiling disposition of the Prophet himself – my facial expression at public events turned rather sombre and I began to frown. Oh dear!

My austere exterior was no reflection of the happiness I felt within, but rather was an attempt to remain serious in my new mantle as a representative of a community that was oppressed or despised, and whose God-given choice of faith and identity was being ridiculed. I was beginning to absorb the sense of victimization that Muslims – as well as other excluded and under-represented minority communities – are forced to endure when dealing with the pressure of prejudice. There wasn't much to smile about, anyway.

As the antagonism increased between the West and Muslim countries (mainly the US vs. Iran), the atmosphere, particularly in the media, became more and more toxic. There was also the ancient split between the Sunni and Shia branches of Islam, which had plagued the Middle East. The Sunni world was feeling challenged by Shia-dominated Iran following its revolution, particularly neighbouring Iraq, which was heavily supported by Saudi Arabia and a bunch of major Western allies. Hence, a full-scale invasion of Iran was launched by Iraq to prevent Khomeini from exporting the Iranian revolutionary movement. The world watched as Muslims from both sides lined up for battle, waving their nation's flags, prepared to fight and slaughter one another. It didn't look like we had much universal peace or flower power to offer anybody.

On the home front, pressure was building in the Central Mosque. An uprising against the mosque establishment was underway; it was about as close to joining a real revolution as I ever got. The Companions of the Mosque organisation was formed. Petitions were collected, leaflets were distributed, and membership was made open to all worshippers. A broad constitution was haphazardly adopted and they voted me in as their chairman – no doubt because of my fame (and a healthy bank account, I suppose), I couldn't easily be ignored.

Anger and animosity grew until finally the trustees of the mosque – well trained and groomed in the finest paddocks of diplomacy – settled upon a solution. The compromise would allow Dr. Darsh to remain in London with the full support of his sponsor, Egypt's Al-Azhar University. Even though he didn't win back his role as imam of the mosque, the arrangement enabled him to remain in the UK and continue to serve the British community.

Hooray!

Following this moderate victory for the Companions of the Mosque, I saw the opportunity of turning the organisation into a vehicle to begin the Muslim schools project. Using my privileged position as chairman, I enlisted parents within the group who would be interested in enrolling their children in the first kindergarten class of a would-be Muslim school.

It wasn't long before we opened a playgroup for toddlers. Mothers took turns hosting the tiny tots at their homes for a few hours each week. Most families lived in north London and Fawziah entertained quite a few gatherings in our small house in Hampstead Garden Suburb, preparing tea, cakes, sandwiches, and samosas. The playgroup was a great success: kids loved it, especially Hasanah, now three years old. She made a lot of friends, and the project gained speed.

Being less politically scorched than the Companions of the Mosque, the Islamic Circle was constituted and formally established as a registered charity with educational objectives. A white-haired, well-spoken, elderly British gentleman, Rashid Amin Farah, who had embraced Islam many years before me in Morocco, was a familiar face at the weekly circle and joined me as co-trustee. I engaged a legal firm and committed to supporting the project fully out of my own funds.

Tempers calmed down in the mosque. Dr. Badawi had moved on and, in a charitable gesture, the nice new Saudi director of the centre, Dr. Al Ghamidi, agreed to return the money that I had originally donated for the Muslim schools cause. Starting with that – and with my fully loaded chequebook – I set out in search of a suitable building.

Islam in Britain was already "bad news" as far as the media was concerned, therefore the general public and authorities were obviously going to resist the idea of Muslim schools. So we had to prepare the ground in order to make a stand. For that we needed a property.

The northwest London borough of Brent was quite close to where we lived, and it had a large population of Muslims, so I zeroed in on that catchment area. Driving through Brondesbury Park one day, I saw a "for sale" sign on a large,

Tudor-style house in this nice leafy area of London. The size looked just right. I purchased it, almost immediately.

Thatcherism was being riveted to Britain's cultural foundations, and the Iron Lady from Barnet (the same borough in which we lived) had made her intentions clear: cuts were coming! These would particularly affect funding for education. Obtaining government support for projects like non-Christian faith schools was going to be a colossal struggle. The battle for faith-based Muslim schools was on.

There were already thousands of Church of England government-funded schools, as well as schools for the Catholic and Jewish communities, so why not us? My bagful of tax contributions – 60 percent at the time – as well as those of many fellow-Muslim taxpayers were being utilized in the service of those faiths and others; it was only fair that we saw some of that redistributed to benefit the disenfranchised Muslim children. It so happened that our third daughter, Maymanah, was also born in 1983: I seriously had to get cracking.

The name "Islamia" came about through quite a wacky accident as we prepared leaflets for promotion. The Letraset transfers I used for the text in my artwork only had a limited number of black letters; there was only one "c" left on the page and I needed that to spell "school." I decided to use an extra "a," creating "Islamia" instead of "Islamic" school. It had a softer, more child-friendly ring to it anyway.

Surprisingly, there was absolutely no information or requirement regarding the curriculum in the UK at that time, apart from an obligation to deliver religious education.

Great! Well, that was certainly not going to be a problem. But what about the other subjects? What would we teach and how?[78]

I called together all available Muslim educationalists in the city to attend brainstorming sessions in my Curzon Street office. The task was to define the objectives of each major subject based on the principles of the Qur'an and traditions of the prophets. That meant placing God's existence above all, respectfully back at the centre of the syllabus. History would include reference to the prophets and the civilisations of humankind to which they were assigned.

The aims for every subject were drafted. After the process was complete, it was an electrifying "Eureka!" moment. I felt like Indiana Jones falling accidentally into a sinkhole, only to stumble upon a secret mountain valley of Solomon's lost treasures, hidden deep beneath the sand dunes of the ancient alcazars! It was not shiny jewels, but wisdom that I uncovered. Below the crust of hustling life on Earth as I knew it lay a construct of paradigms and axioms that supported the entire structure of all human aspiration and ambitions, labelled "Education." I realised how this was the ultimate key to the shaping of society, from the playground upwards. What a flipped-out moment.

The word "education" itself comes from the Latin, *educatus*; it means to rear or to bring up. Reading as much as possible on the subject, from the Islamic viewpoint I learned that the pen itself was said to be the first tool that God Himself created to define the shape and destiny of all things in the universe; according to a saying of the Prophet,

> *There was Allah and nothing else before Him and His Throne was over the water, and then He created the Heavens and the Earth and wrote everything in the Book.*[79]

Trying to explain that concept to a dedicated and committed religious sceptic working in the council planning or education department was going to be one sizzling hell of a test, but one I had to dedicate myself to for the future of my adorable children.

Islam was already pretty off the table as far as the average white, Anglo-Saxon citizen was concerned, and religion was not even mentioned on the menu. Many had been denied the opportunity to investigate their own spirituality, let alone explore the realms of others. The exercise of their own God-gifted nature had been paralysed by years of secular anaesthesia injected slowly through the mainstream channels of the media, education, and politics. There were a lot of well-entrenched hurdles we would have to overcome.

Regretfully, a large number of the "educated class" in Britain were indoctrinated by mournful images of their own dark ages and the bloody, religious conflicts that plagued Europe's kingdoms for centuries: Christian army against Christian army, all in the name of God and country. "Religion caused wars! We're civilised now," sang the old secular boys' school chorus. It was also too easy to look back and condemn the fierce duel that took place between faith and science in that same dark period and the hostility that was aggressively unleashed by the church against new scientific notions.

It was a shame that only a few had been taught about the

light and impetus the Qur'an had given to science and the development of public education that came with it: a thousand years of Islamic civilisation, scientific and moral tradition had been surreptitiously erased from the annals of Western history, mainly because it took place in Islamic lands; "You mean those pagans had universities?"

In a huge area stretching from Spain through to the boundaries of China, Muslims advanced, often drawing on the forgotten intellectual and philosophical wealth of previous civilisations; they mined the legacies of ancient Greece, India, and Persia to construct their own distinctive contribution to the canon of human knowledge. This produced scientists of medicine, social studies, mathematics, philosophy, astronomy, history, architecture, law, and so many other disciplines, the benefits of which gradually filtered back through Europe, fuelling the Renaissance and speeding it towards the Age of Enlightenment.

Islamia Primary School bravely opened its doors on Friday 21 October 1983.[80] Through the doors waddled thirteen little children, forming the initial kindergarten playgroup in Brondesbury Park. Two of the pioneering little first-year pupils were Fawziah's and mine: Hasanah and Asmaa.

Trouble
1983–4

WITHOUT KNOWING IT, my bold exit from the world of show business would inadvertently lay the groundwork for a showdown with the press. Some wanted to make an example of me and tried to insinuate that my becoming Muslim was based on some form of unhinged mental defect, the result of a common pop star's LSD-induced brain malfunction. The peaceful overtones of my songs were blanked out beneath the deafening bellow of beastly news provided by wars and conflicts stretching across the Muslim heartlands.

Ignoring the storm that was brewing overhead, I remained enthusiastic. I was trying my best to do things right and follow the Prophet's life and example, peace be upon him. Every day I would try to catch morning prayers in the Central Mosque. Even though our home in Hampstead was a good five miles away and prayers would begin as early as 3.30 a.m. in the summer, I tried not to miss them. But my yearning for a pure and simple spiritual life was not going to be easily attained in an increasingly volatile world. Challenges increased. Most troubling, to me, was the growing chasm between the West and the chanting crowds in Iran swaying to the rousing rhetoric provided by Ayatollah Khomeini.

The reactionary influence of the Salafi movement emanating from Saudi was also growing stronger, particularly in London. They were totally at war with the idea of music and any form of frivolity or entertainment, considering it and its proceeds *haram*. Their persuasive arguments and front-of-the-line presence at prayer times led me to be even more puritanically cautious.

Though I'd stopped making music and had offloaded my instruments, I was now bothered by the thought that I might be enjoying something "forbidden" with the money I was still earning from the sale of records. To be on the safe side, I dissected my music catalogue into three categories: *halal* (allowed), *makruh* (disliked), and *haram* (forbidden). The *makruh* and *haram* songs primarily involved those lyrics containing the slightest hint of sex-and-love-minus-marriage; I signed those over to a newly registered charity called Salafa Ltd.,[81] which was intended to support my non-profit educational projects. The *halal* bunch, which embodied social, spiritual, or ecological messages, were placed with my publishing company, Cat Music, providing the income on which my growing family essentially survived.

Another irksome issue I faced was connected to the income I was receiving from the deal with a bank initiated in the seventies; it dawned on me that most of it was based on interest, which was also banned in Islam. I wanted out, but my solicitors insisted that the arrangement with the bank was cast in stone. I was stuck – or that's how it seemed.

By this time my brother-in-law, Alec, had made up his mind to leave his longtime role as my personal accountant. Perhaps I was getting too "salafistic" and finicky about pigeonholing my earnings. Whatever the reason, Alec took a new job and relocated fifty miles away from Hampstead Garden Suburb to a new house in Reading. Luckily, David was on hand to help manage my music catalogue and the ongoing financial residue of my songwriting legacy. I knew he'd look after my interest (as well as his own, naturally).

Barry Krost was now living full-time five thousand miles away in L.A., and there was hardly anything for him to do anymore as my manager. Considering the distance separating him from my new life, it seemed logical to wrap up our business relationship. David was well able to take over the effective running of things, for a "brotherly" percentage of the royalties.

Big Dave was back. Almost immediately he began sniffing into the deal with Island Records. Soon he noticed we were receiving only a pitiful fraction of the record income from Europe (and the US and UK weren't much better). They were also "double-dipping." My brother was furious and determined to reset the royalty rates to the rightful level. He dusted his halo and, fully charged with all the moral ferocity needed, sped over to Chris Blackwell's offices to sort him out.

Chris turned out a real Jamaican gent and – against the advice of his legal minders – offered us a handsome rise in royalties, right across the board, together with the return of the publishing rights to my early albums, many of which had become classics in the archives of Island Records' pop history. We'd won, without a fight.

Running schools was a costly business, so the uplift in royalties was very welcome, especially as I'd been bankrolling the whole project and underwriting subsidies for most parents. They elected me as the school's chairman and spokesman – a role I was getting used to. In turn, I did my best to include parents in the decision-making process and we formed a board of governors. Kids do grow fast, as most parents know. Soon the pupils of our first kindergarten class reached the age of five, the compulsory school age. Now, Islamia's waiting list sky-rocketed into the hundreds.

Feeling quite brave, with the full support of the community and many mums and dads behind me, I began the long, drawn-out battle for equality for Muslim children. The neighbours and local councillors were up in arms. Our team of teachers were fully registered and trained professionals; there could be no serious objection about that aspect of our educational venture. There was a whole niggly list of complaints about cars and noise – even though there was already a large two-form primary school right next door, whose hullabalooing playground bumped up directly next to ours.

The main problem arose from the council's officious planning officers. We organised a small group to present a petition at the town hall when they met to discuss our plans. The local press tried to appear neutral and approached our parents for comments – but that was only a thin camouflage; they ended up amplifying the local residents' chorus line in essentially reprising their theme about . . . cars!

On top of all that, the local fire department scurried up to add their voice of disapproval. Their argument was based, technically, on a lack of access for their fire engines – even though (if only they looked closely enough) they would see a perfectly convenient, wide, and overgrown access way, council-owned, which led directly to the back of our garden playground. Infuriating!

Forced to clamber through the thick, thorny hedge of objections, one by one, the Muslim parents' brigade slowly edged forward. As the protests became larger, the national media became interested. The BBC, the mouthpiece of British cultural normality, did a short TV piece about the school and interviewed the parents as well as me, casting a decidedly quirky light on us all. Being the only ex-pop singer of any note around, I was made to appear slightly ridiculous.

My dress code in 1984 probably didn't help; it certainly wouldn't endear me to the glossy pages of *Hello!* magazine. If anybody had doubted it before, it was clearly shown in the interview that Cat Stevens no longer existed. In fact, I looked pretty battered, with my extra-long beard, ankle-length robe, and rather untidy turban (nobody had ever taught me how to tie it properly). But, regardless of how I may have appeared, I was blissfully happy not to be a slave to fashion, looking more like later iterations of Jim Morrison or John Lennon, who both sported extremely long scraggly beards at one anti-establishment moment in time. Apart from an absent smile, I arguably embodied the description of the seeker's transcendence beyond the need for a bull at the tenth and last stage of Zen Buddhist enlightenment:

Entering into the marketplace and unadorned
Blissfully smiling, though covered with dust
and ragged of clothes
Using no supernatural power,
you bring the withered trees
spontaneously into bloom[82]

The trees were not necessarily blooming in response to my presence – but press headlines certainly were. Next thing I read was an article in an American tabloid from Miami, displaying the startling headline: CAT STEVENS JOINS THE EVIL AYATOLLAH.

The article's subheading went on to announce that I had turned my back on a life of jet-set luxury, devoted myself to Iran's "Wild-eyed Ayatollah Khomeini" and – among other things – claimed I had shaved my head, taken a vow of chastity, given all my money away to mosques, and was living with a begging bowl in hand and travelling between Qom and Tehran in Iran.

That was it!

The media disinformation showdown had begun. I got in touch with a lawyer in the US and initiated a lawsuit against the paper, suing them for five million dollars (an appropriately Hollywood-sized figure). I couldn't believe how blatantly fabricated the article was and how surreal the picture they presented of me and my faith. I couldn't allow them to get away with this.

During the legal process, I was forced to fly over and attend a deposition in Miami conducted by the lawyer acting on behalf of the Florida publication. Whatever confessions they were expecting, they were very soon disillusioned. Here is an example of the kind of crazy questions I had to respond to, hand on heart:

> LAWYER: "Devoted himself to Iran's Wild-eyed Ayatollah Khomeini." Is that statement true or false?
> YUSUF: False.
> LAWYER: In what regard is it false?
> YUSUF: I have not devoted myself to any human being. As a Muslim I have devoted myself to God, the one and only God, creator of the heavens and the Earth.
> LAWYER: Have you any opinion about the Ayatollah Khomeini as a religious leader?
> YUSUF: He is a very, what you might say, dynamic religious leader, no doubt; that can be testified by the amount of press that he gets today.
> LAWYER: The statement "Stevens, thirty-seven, now lives near his mentor in Iran," is that true or false?
> YUSUF: False. I've never been to Iran.
> LAWYER: Do you view that statement as being injurious to your reputation?
> YUSUF: In as much as it is connected to Imam Khomeini and in as much as he is perceived as "evil," yes, it is – and it also makes a mockery of my marriage.
> LAWYER: How do you draw that ["evil"] implication?
> YUSUF: In the title itself, "Cat Stevens Joins the Evil Ayatollah."

The lawyer obviously understood the gravity of his client's goof and must have informed the publishers that they didn't have a snowball's chance in hell of surviving in court; almost every accusation in the article was a myth except for the spelling of my name. We settled on amicable terms, and they were even kind enough to reprint two articles about the somewhat more rational personality they had now met, face to face.

Returning to my wife and family in London, I was justifiably upset by the distasteful experience I had to endure with the media. Unable to avoid being unfairly linked with the deteriorating turmoil, wars, and chaos erupting in Muslim lands, I saw no way out of being brush-stroked into a distorted portrait of my faith.

The truly liberating and sublimely inspiring aspects of my loving submission to God were being obliterated by the force of the ugly political and militant images of Muslims who – more often than not – were trying to break free of oppressive conditions and the colonial grip they had been held in for decades. The "international community," regretfully, had turned a blind eye to the suffering of populations trying to survive under the feet of harsh dictators and corrupt, self-serving Muslim leaders. Social, political, and economic motivation went unnoticed and under-reported, and was concealed by a press-imposed burqa of darkly distorted images; angry mobs brandishing anti-Western messages on banners scrawled in indecipherable Arabic writing were made to look synonymous with the fundamental message of Islam.

Muslim rulers had little to offer; in most cases they surfed blissfully over the wave of popular resentment (and, often, on billions of gallons of oil). The elimination of poverty, and the social upliftment and protection for the elderly and penniless, were not of material concern to them. The Western media, and particularly "First World" politicians, found it infinitely more convenient to divert attention away from the trillion-dollar contracts the West had with these rulers, than towards the poorly educated lower class of Muslims – especially those calling for change. There was nothing about Muslims' love of God, apart from showing them emotionally waving a copy of the holy Qur'an high above their heads.

Yet, when I stopped and looked back at the life and times of the Prophet, it presented a completely different picture of leadership. Muhammad, from the very beginning, devoted his efforts and limited resources primarily to caring for the poor, sharing whatever wealth Muslims had, and making charity a fundamental and immutable pillar of faith, saying:

> *A man is not a believer who fills his*
> *stomach while his neighbour is hungry.*[83]

The sharing of the public treasury (*Bait al Mal*) through distribution of Zakat and making people's lives easier, opening the doors as wide as possible for people to survive in peace and security with God, was the Prophet's manifesto. He said:

> *Make things easy, don't make them difficult;*
> *give good news, don't make people run away.*[84]

But people were fearful of Muslims and running away in droves. The call of Islam was drowned out by the clatter of war and internal strife; the words "Allahu Akbar" ("God is the greatest"), recited before and during each prayer to humble the heart of the worshipper, were now mostly screamed by a crowd of Muslims angrily shaking their fists while denouncing the West as they burned the American flag, or by mothers or mourners of the dead in destroyed towns and villages during marches and rallies. Obviously, this was not much of an invitation to Islam for onlookers – particularly those brought up on a healthy dose of white superiority and Western "liberal values" – to be drawn to.

But for me, it was impossible not to be moved by the plight of many poor and bereaved Muslim families, whose losses were never acknowledged. I watched with frustration the onset of a new storm of derogatory propaganda, aimed at associating *Al-Islam* (the Islam) with terrorism, lawlessness, and brutality. The impact of increasing tensions in the Muslim world and the deliberate – possibly even coordinated – attempt to construct an influential stereotype of "fundamentalist" Islam as the norm went on successfully to enforce this view. The rabid consumption of news required fresh fuel every day; unfortunately, a new, well-equipped army of deviant shadows, claiming to work "for the cause of Islam," had risen to the occasion to assist them.

Apart from all this, the world was heaving under the weight of natural disasters. A drought in Ethiopia had claimed hundreds of thousands of lives and was spreading to neighbouring Sudan. Through a Sudanese friend, a founding member from the Companions of the Mosque, I was invited to travel to Khartoum and various areas to see the situation and offer direct financial assistance.

Visas were also arranged for Fawziah and my three daughters, Hasanah, Asmaa and Maymanah; I thought it would be good for the children to see how hard life was for some people on this planet of ours. That trip also took us to Kenya, Malawi, Malaysia, and finally Oz; I had been invited by the Islamic community of Australia to deliver some lectures.

Arriving in Khartoum was a true eye-opener. It was 1984. Hundreds of thousands of starving people had been forced out of their drought-stricken homelands into overcrowded camps, flooding the streets of the capital; skinny children with hardly any hope of drinking their mother's milk were barely hanging on to life. The government was struggling and, as usual, unable to cope. They welcomed us and other aid agencies with open arms.

The trip served as a wake-up call, instilling within me the wish to see more relief organisations coming from the Muslim community in the UK. There were hundreds of Christian and other humanitarian organisations working to provide help. I couldn't see why the community in Britain could not do something similar. The idea had already been raised by a fellow convert, Abdul Ghaffar, a dynamic, smart, and determined character of good British stock. We spoke after prayers one day at the Muslim World League offices in Goodge Street. He handed me a well-written proposal for the establishment of a relief charity, to be called Muslim Aid.

Call to Alms
1984–6

CHARITY IS GOOD, full stop. One of the problems we face is how to fulfill our responsibility to give help to those less fortunate than ourselves in this rapidly shrinking world. The sight of bloodied faces in war, the pictures of fatherless children, roofless homes, wars, and global tragedies were appearing with riveting punctuality, like a gripping Netflix series with no end to its episodes in sight.

Back in 1984, the famine in Africa grabbed the world's attention and became the focus for a global blitz campaign by charities. I wanted to help, urgently. Already having visited those areas and seen for myself the parched desert lands and cramped, overcrowded camps, thronging with masses of displaced, sick and starving people, I had channelled my donations through active organisations on the ground. But the demands were immense; much more humanitarian help was needed. The time had come to look more seriously at Abdul Ghaffar's proposal for an international Muslim relief organisation.

Bob Geldof and Harvey Goldsmith, one of my former promoters, announced the launch of Live Aid. Following Bob's successful charity single by Band Aid, "Do They Know It's Christmas?," it seemed the winds of human kindness were in full throttle. The only problem was that many of the famine's victims were, of course, Muslim – Christmas was not what they needed to be reminded of. However, no one could deny the need for such global attention, igniting the hope for massive relief for millions struggling to survive.

Naturally, when Harvey asked me to join the Live Aid concert, planned for July 1985, I accepted, although I really wasn't sure what contribution I could make, having given all my instruments away. I wasn't like a busker who could sing and perform a little tap dance. So, I decided to wait for God to guide me.

Since childhood, I'd had an unexplainable feeling that there was always an unseen hand guiding me through the dangerous, monster-ridden woods of life. It was a sense I had carried within me through my darkest nightmares. Most people are familiar with the phenomenon, but few are able to put a divine name to that force of destiny that saves them from insurmountable and perilous-looking deadly ends. This time – like many before – I would leave it to the power hidden behind the invisible wheel of life to steer me as to what to perform at the concert; as Jesus said: "the Holy Spirit will teach you in that very hour what you should say."[85]

Fawziah was now expecting our fourth child. Because our

first three were girls, I was not particularly vexed, having read a saying of the Prophet, peace be upon him, that whoever raises two girls until they reach adulthood will enter Paradise.[86] Allah is most Generous; I had three! Still, it was kind of a relief when Fawziah gave birth to a baby boy on 1 April, 1985, the evening before my mother's birthday (whose teasing response was, "Couldn't he have waited just a few more hours?").

Everyone in the family was celebrating. Fawziah and I had both made a secret promise that if we were given a boy, we would call him Muhammad. God made it so.

Life was hectic; aside from charging around, driving the kids to school, shopping for the wife, managing the business of the trust, and turning up for various lectures and talks, the job of launching a Muslim aid agency was becoming top priority. I began discussions with leaders from various organisations, trying to enlist their interest.

An Egyptian doctor from Birmingham, Dr. Hany El Banna, had already formed an organisation called Islamic Relief. He was not interested in enlarging the number of trustees, but made it clear that he had no objection to my idea of a sister charity being formed with a broader body of representation from Muslim movements – the more organisations, the better. So, based on Abdul Ghaffar's original brainchild, a proposal was circulated for the birth of a new charitable trust to be called "Muslim Aid." Initially, the invitation to form the new humanitarian project was fielded by my Islamic Circle Organisation. Dr. Darsh was a magnet and encouraged a lot of influential Muslim chiefs to come to the

26 | *Call to Alms*

table. Many quickly warmed to the idea and helped to draft the constitution.

We prepared for the launch.

Excitement around the country was building as Live Aid was securing some of the biggest names in the world of music. It was going to be a historic event, including such names as Queen, the Who, Elton John, U2, Paul McCartney, David Bowie, and so on. Across the pond in the US, a parallel event was being planned with the Four Tops, Bob Dylan, Crosby, Stills and Nash, the Beach Boys, and Madonna – there was nobody who was somebody in the music industry that didn't want to be a part of it.

As the day arrived, the scene in Wembley was chaotic: TV cameras, frantic engineers, and superstars and their minders darting in and out, music blaring from all directions. There was I, Cat Stevens, now a humble Yusuf – minus a band, plus a longer beard. I was scared witless. Trying not to reveal my nervousness, I strolled into the crowded green room, guitarless. So there was a definite air of mystification on the face of Harvey: "What's this Cat up to?" Nobody could have known that I had prepared a song called "In the End," something I'd written on the night of my last concert for UNICEF. I had decided to sing it a cappella, without instruments, like traditional folk singers of old. But Harvey and Bob were nervous – things were going well, and they didn't want any hiccups.

The excitement of the show was absolutely electrifying; it seemed the whole universe – including aliens, if there were any – was watching. As it came closer to my turn, time appeared to drag on forever. Elton's set overran and Harvey kept on coming over to apologise, "Sorry for the delay." After about forty-five minutes of feeling on a knife's edge, waiting to be called, at last I was told that the show had gone well over the deadline. The live TV coverage was coming to an end, there was no more time left for me to go on stage.

My heart sank like a rock. Though my ego had been bruised, my spirit was not dented; deep down I thought that maybe it was someone above saying, *Don't bother with these things anymore. We have other important work for you.* The stage was not where I needed to be; humbleness and charitable work were better than singing songs.

Because of the time delay in the TV broadcast, I was able to make it home in time to watch the end of the show. Would you believe it? They even had my name tagged on the long list of credits. My fans were probably bewildered, still hanging on to a thread of hope for my appearance. I had rehearsed my song many times over, but unfortunately, no one got to hear it.

> *You can't bargain with the truth*
> *'Cause whether you're rich or you're poor*
> *You're gonna meet at the same door*
> *You're gonna know the real score in the end*
> *And if you want to help your fellow man*
> *You better start with what is in your hand.*[87]

Finally, I moved offices from Curzon Street to a new property in Highbury, Islington. We were expanding, and we now even had our very own parking space area! The building was

26 | *Call to Alms*

an old, rundown, ex-leather factory that was soon turned into a spacious, open-plan, Habitat-styled, whitewash-walled HQ for Muslim Aid, as well as a home for my other businesses and charities. The design was influenced by my fond memory of Blackwell's original Island Records offices, converted from an old seventeenth-century brick church building just off Portobello Road.

My old recording equipment (which never went for auction) was usefully refitted into an audio-visual studio in my centre, where I planned to produce audiobooks and video interviews for the Islamic Circle Organisation. The aim was to produce recordings for children and people generally interested in Islam. My nephew Daniel, David's son, was coopted in to oversee the construction and set-up of the studio. Danny had also embraced the faith of Islam, and he was handy with a camera and microphone; I trusted him.

By this time, David had moved to Tel Aviv, Israel, with his wife, Yael, and their daughter, Naomi. The move was quite complicated for me, considering the persecution and suffering Palestinians were facing. My hope was that, one day, peace could return to the Holy Land. But with the expansive nature of the aggression and the occupation bulldozing into more and more of the Palestinian countryside, that looked a long, long way off. There was little I could do except send charity whenever possible to the orphans and displaced victims of the conflict.

Muslim Aid was finally launched. It was a good day. The event took place in November 1985 at one of those cigarette-ash-peppered, red-carpet clubs off Pall Mall, courtesy of the

Foreign Press Association. Journalists juggled their cameras and crowded their microphones as the trustees assembled at the long, white-clothed table, set against a big banner displaying our new, impressive, emerald-green-and-white logo. I felt a great sense of satisfaction, having brought together various leaders and Islamic organisations under one umbrella for the principal sake of charity and humanitarian causes. Dr. Darsh sat in the centre and chaired the meeting. I stood up, having been selected (basically, being the only one who didn't have a foreign accent) to read the press release and manifesto of our fledgling Muslim agency.

As a non-aligned figure without membership or loyalty to any one group or movement, the trustees elected me as their first chairman. The high profile of my name gave us an instant boost and was also doubtlessly useful for raising funds too. The Muslim community trusted us; Muslim Aid became a channel through which people could direct their obligatory Zakat donations.

I continued to push for broader representation on the board, but like Hany El Banna, there was a general resistance in opening the kitchen door any further. That was incredibly disappointing, as I knew it could have helped to heal some of the scars caused by various differences between the many imported ethno-based communities and organisations. But those barriers were not going to shrivel away anytime soon.

The powerful storm of mainstream news, awash with live footage of natural disasters and increasing outbreaks of war, drove the agency to quickly expand its work. The community responded generously. Afghanistan was now the hotspot. Three million refugees had taken shelter in Pakistan's

North-West Frontier Province, and the resistance to the Soviet invasion was a natural cause for Muslims to stand behind. Muslim Aid was soon able to deliver blankets, food, and medical supplies through some of the trustees' associated connections. I was sent to review the work and report on the conditions of the refugees and displaced.

It was my first visit to Pakistan. The camps in Peshawar were crammed, packed full of families and children, all of them dusty and worn out after their tumultuous upheaval, having left their villages and homes across the border for a temporary, makeshift, tent life. Agencies from all around the world were busy doing their best in providing medical assistance and essential food and clothes, with the Red Crescent and Saudi Arabia being at the forefront.

A meeting with Pakistan's president, General Zia-ul-Haq, was arranged at the presidential palace in Islamabad. Although he had a tough public persona, with his starched, pressed military uniform, he was soft-spoken and the mark on his forehead showed he was a regular at prayers. Pakistani politics did not interest me much; I was on a mission simply to help deliver aid. The general appreciated our genuine concern; his country was hosting millions of Afghan refugees on its border and they needed colossal support. Charities like ours were welcome.

My first impression of the Afghan people living in the camps was how devoted they were to the thousand-year-old life and culture of Islam. Steeped in the religious norms of tribal life, they had preserved many customs of dress, language, valiance, and respect for guests and obedience to elders; it had been this way down through the centuries. I was amazed by the way the men tied their turbans; almost every man wore one, while most women were concealed behind their burqas and veils. This was their way of life for as long as anyone could remember. Western values and modernity seemed a million miles away. But now Afghanistan was in everybody's focus, under fierce attack from the powerful, well-armed, atheist Soviet war machine, driven by an ideology that had no place for bothersome concepts like religion or faith.

The US and its allies, particularly Saudi Arabia, were openly supportive of the Afghan armies (*mujahideen*) and were pumping billions of dollars into arms, equipment, and intelligence in a proxy war against the "red" enemy, the USSR. This encouraged the normally fragmented Afghan tribes to bury their differences and unite the principal rebel organisations as the Seven Party Mujahideen Alliance.

Those were the days when the West was happily holding hands with ideological Muslim jihadis, funding and equipping Islamic movements with the object of delivering a fatal blow to its communist arch-adversary. It was a sort of "unholy" alliance both sides were prepared to be part of for a bigger objective.

The war was a magnet for all sorts of Muslim activists. One particularly enigmatic figure was Osama bin Laden, who was head of a foreign mujahideen contingent dominated by Saudi Arabian volunteers. I remember seeing him as he dropped by a busy international relief office I happened to be visiting one day in Peshawar. People's heads all turned and they gazed at this towering figure as he swiftly entered through the door. Many were obviously enamoured of the tall, wealthy Arab Muslim leader with four wives. He held himself aloof, speeding through the room, not raising his eyelids.

The main commander of the Arab volunteer force was Abdullah Azzam, a Palestinian scholar and a highly charged activist whom many later considered to be the "godfather" of the Islamic jihad movement. Commander Azzam didn't look very fierce at all, and he talked somewhat fondly about my past, probably from his student days at university, where he obviously must have got to hear (and even like) some of my music.

Perhaps it was on Azzam's orders that, while doing an interview with a guy from his media team in the afternoon, I was cajoled into recording my voice onto a clunky, portable tape recorder. I finally submitted and sang "A is for Allah." That tape was immediately pirated and distributed freely, firstly through the North-West Frontier, then the rest of Pakistan, followed by India, Malaysia, and into almost every other country in the Muslim world, including households in the UK and the US, ironically making me something of a "million-seller" again.

During that visit, I was invited to give a talk, telling my story in a couple of makeshift schools that were providing basic education to orphans and the children of displaced families. It was heartbreaking to see so many war-battered young faces. Where children grow up observing nothing but destruction, bloodshed, and aggression, there are no alternative models of life for them to follow or aspire to. These students were *talibeen*, which literally means, "seekers of knowledge." Looking back, I realise now that these schools and madrassas became fertile ground for an increasingly radicalised ideological movement – later known to the world as the Taliban.

As if things were not already wacky enough, something was about to happen that proved to me how much of a "Wild World" it really was. While travelling around the Middle East seeking support for the work of Muslim Aid, I had been officially invited back to Makkah to perform the Hajj, compliments of the new monarch of Saudi Arabia, King Fahd. The Muslim World League arranged everything: travel, accommodation, food, even the two white pieces of unsewn cloth necessary to perform the rituals in. It was a chance I just couldn't refuse, an opportunity to feel the peace of the holy city and answer the call of God and touch the walls of His sacred house again.

Having completed three days of pilgrimage, following the climactic day of repentance and prayers on the plains of 'Arafat, I attended a feast organised by the director of the Islamic university, given in our honour as the "guests of the Most Merciful" (a title reserved for those making pilgrimage). Suddenly, I spotted a familiar face across the heavily crowded room . . . no! I couldn't believe it. There, standing humbly alone in two unstitched, white, draping garments, was none other than Jimmy Cliff!

We hugged each other tightly and laughed in amazement about this surreal reunion. What kind of a miracle was it that destined us to be brought together again, now as Abrahamic pilgrims? As well as both having been guided to Islam and delivered here, to this very same spot in time and space,

26 | *Call to Alms*

circling the House of God, we were also both incredulously spinning on the same famous pink record label!

Going back in time to the late sixties and seventies, I remember Jimmy's songs always had a strong strain of hope and love of peace: "Wonderful World, Beautiful People," "Many Rivers to Cross," and "Vietnam," all had spoken about his harmonious dreams for this world. His Muslim name, I found out then, was Na'im Bashir, which means "Happiness Good News." As we parted, we bade each other farewell with the usual parting salutation:

"Peace be with you, brother."

"And peace be with you, too."

Hampstead to the Holy
1987–8

MY MOTHER HAD fallen in love with the flat in Cyprus, even though Dad, sadly, wasn't alive long enough to enjoy it. The flat became a happy retreat for the family, Mum in particular. She loved sitting on the balcony, staring out at the blue Mediterranean Sea, listening to the Greek-chattering children and families splashing and laughing on the beach, not too far away. There was even a purple jacaranda tree, blossoming right next to us, in the small garden below.

Mum liked her independence and never worried about being alone. She'd spend her time the way she wanted, sometimes picking up a canvas and painting – a boat resting on a shore, or a Greek vase guarding a traditional bowl of untouched fruit. Mum had a lot of the artist in her and looked a bit bohemian-like in her blotchy, paint-stained apron.

Especially now, age seventy-three, she had no need to worry about anyone else's opinions.

It was early 1987. David was not that far away in Tel Aviv, so, during Mum's winter getaway in Limassol, he booked a ticket on a boat for her to pop over and visit. The crossing was 220 miles, only a day's journey. David was excited to show Mum the archaeological sites, the homeland of Jesus and the prophets. He guided her around the sacred places and ancient footpaths, visiting the Holy Sepulchre as well as the Wailing Wall. But the climax was her visit to the Dome of the Rock.

Mum was never immoderate about her faith. It was enough to soak up the spiritual air and enjoy the experience of being in the sacred city of Jerusalem, embodying the extraordinary history of all three branches of Abraham's monotheistic message. David took one of the most precious photographs we have of her, looking out on the steps of the golden dome – a symbolic image of her ascent towards that which is holy.

Not too long after, Mum returned to London and decided to move from Hampstead to Caversham, near Reading, to be closer to my sister. Anita had always been a true mother's helper, and Mum wanted a bit more of her loyal companionship again. Almost overnight, Mum sold the house in the suburb and purchased a modern terraced home, just two doors away from Anita and Alec, boasting a large window that overlooked the slow-flowing River Thames, with swans and ducks sailing by.

My sister had been reared in the same strict religious chambers as David and me, but she preferred to keep her faith private. Anita's respect for me and my choice of Islam was unshakable. She was as rock-solid in support for me now as she always had been when I was still a little budding Van Gogh in short pants. Whenever Fawziah and I journeyed with the kids by train from Paddington station to her house, she'd go to long lengths to provide an absolutely 100 percent *halal* meal. Her ability to cook was obviously inherited directly from Mum, and she baked the dreamiest chocolate cake, an old recipe Mum had picked up from Swedish relations who had immigrated to Boston late in the nineteenth century.

Anita never had children, so for Mum, Caversham was a much quieter, more tranquil environment than Hampstead, where Fawziah and I were now expecting our fifth child. Maybe the combination of my religious energy and so many grandchildren scrambling for her attention just asked too much of her.

Fawziah skilfully dealt with the job of cooking, feeding, cleaning, ironing, tidying, and dressing our kids. Dealing with four lively youngsters – and the growing weight of another on the way – was more than any full-time profession. Meanwhile, I got on with my work in the educational battlefield, commanding over the safeguarding and running of Islamia, and financing and maintaining the teachers and staff, while simultaneously running a national campaign for legal recognition and funding for Muslim schools.

The subject of faith education for Muslims was becoming a hot national debate. Our application for voluntary aided status for Islamia primary school was already placed on the desk of Kenneth Baker, the secretary of state for education in

Thatcher's government. Most politicians were against us, and we were also under attack from a barrage of academics and a loud secular lobby. The 1944 Education Act was clear, however: as long as there were Christian and Jewish schools teaching the basic requirements in the three Rs of education (reading, 'riting, and 'rithmetic), it was the right of every parent to choose which school suited their religious affinity. The statute had simply never been pursued by the Muslim community . . . or even dreamed of, until now.

A monumental tragedy disrupted the ongoing academic inter-faith debate. In the Holy Land, four young Palestinians had been brazenly killed in December 1987 by an Israeli Defence Force truck. This was followed by the shooting of four more Palestinian youths at a Gaza checkpoint. The news spread swiftly, followed by massive and spontaneous protests throughout the occupied territories. The intifada had begun. Young children courageously confronted mighty military forces, throwing stones at tanks and automatic-gun-wielding soldiers. The ancient image of David and Goliath vividly sprang to life again; the strength of the resistance must have shaken the Israeli government, and the command was given to put down the rebellion with their much publicised "iron fist."

A sense of urgency was felt by the whole of the Muslim community in Britain, and Muslim Aid and Islamic Relief immediately launched campaigns. Some highly motivated Palestinian and Malaysian students called for more media attention to be given to the tragedy and suffering of people on the ground. So an idea was raised within the Federation of Student Islamic Societies (FOSIS) to travel and report back, first hand, about what was happening. It was suggested that a delegation of mostly "white" British Muslim converts should visit the area – this would help shed light on the suffering of the Palestinians, who obviously had substantially fewer influential allies in the media than the Israelis, in whose favour the news was always weighted. Those under the military occupation were portrayed as violently overreacting, and a sympathetic presentation of the Muslim point of view was hard to find; cameras would inevitably focus on enraged Muslims, at an appropriate distance, marching through the streets, shaking fists and brandishing badly painted banners, boldly written in incomprehensible Arabic.

In the tumult and confusion, the spirit of godliness was buried. The message on the ground was one of pure racial intolerance; there was no front-page editorial space to remind anybody of the heavenly legacy and universal model of the revered prophets who were born and raised in these hill-lands. Palestinians and Israelis were simply made to look like two aggressive, politically opposed entities – so what has Jesus got to do with it? The link with the divine nature of the realm and the purpose of revelation was broken; anything that did not look violent or bloody enough was not newsworthy and was relegated to the level of religious insignificance.

Muslims like myself, being converts to Islam from Christian backgrounds, appreciated the importance of reviving the religious narrative. The Qur'an is packed with stories celebrating the lives and missions of the prophets of the Children of Israel, who along with Christians are termed "Family of the Book." Muslims are repeatedly exhorted to strengthen their love for all the messengers without favouritism:

> Say, "We believe in God and what has been revealed to us; and what was revealed to Abraham, Ishmael, Isaac, Jacob, and his descendants; and what was given to Moses, Jesus, and other prophets from their Lord. We make no distinction between any of them. And to God we all submit."[88]

That harmonious, prophetic message had little chance of being heard above the nationalistic, Zionist battle cry and the deafening roar blaring from Palestinian megaphones. What was so unnerving to me, as well as many other religiously minded onlookers, was that these incredibly gifted people, the Children of Israel, and those Europeans who had become Judaized after them, who had inherited so much knowledge and guidance from the Almighty, were now delivering such an uncompromisingly racist and unrighteous message to the world. The fact that they had suffered themselves so terribly at the hands of Babylonians and Romans, Egyptians, Europeans, Russians, and the Nazis, knowing the meaning of persecution better than any other people, made the ongoing maltreatment of Palestinians impossible to fathom.

Unknown to many, the Qur'an does, in fact, refer to the provision by God of a land for the Children of Israel to dwell in. But wherever that blessed ground was situated (without getting entangled on the thorny issue of its precise borders), it came attached with strict conditions to abide by the Torah and laws handed down to Moses.[89]

It's also worthwhile mentioning that, for at least half a millennium, Jews had been totally banished from Jerusalem by its Byzantine Christian rulers. It was only under the Treaty of Umar, a companion and second caliph after the Prophet, peace be upon him, following his peaceful and bloodless entry to Jerusalem, that Jews were allowed to return. Later on, during their expulsion from many parts of Christian Europe, it was in the Islamic Caliphate in Spain – in a time referred to as the Golden Age – where almost half the entire Jewish population of the world lived and were accommodated, and where Jewish religious, philosophical, cultural, and economic life was allowed freely to flourish. This religiously safe environment actually gave rise to Maimonides, a Sephardic Jewish philosopher who became one of the most prolific and influential Torah scholars of the Middle Ages. All this was possible under the magnanimous protection of the Islamic Caliphate in Spain.

Through contacts with FOSIS, nine British Muslims, including myself, and one German, volunteered to make the trip to the Holy Land. The group consisted entirely of converts: five of us bearing names of the prophets: Abraham (Ibrahim), Joseph (Yusuf), Solomon (Sulayman), Moses (Musa), and Jesus (Isa). Ibrahim Hewitt was chosen to be the spokesman. Prior to departure, letters detailing the planned visit of the delegation were sent to the Foreign Office and various international organisations, including Amnesty International and UNRWA (United Nations Relief and Works Agency for Palestine Refugees in the Near East),

27 | *Hampstead to the Holy*

as a safeguard for whatever might happen and to make sure the British authorities kept a watchful eye on the trip.

Just after the birth of my fifth child, Aminah, with hardly time to celebrate or become familiar with her tiny hands and joyful baby habits, I set off with the group to Jerusalem.

We arrived in the second week of March 1988. The program had been arranged by our FOSIS contacts through the mufti of Jerusalem, the senior Islamic official in the city, and his Islamic Cultural and Science Society, which booked our stay at the Pilgrims Inn. We were introduced to a range of Palestinian professionals and relief workers who had volunteered their services to accompany our delegation. Although the Palestine Liberation Organisation – the PLO – was officially the most dominant body representing the Palestinians at the time, it had very little say over what was happening on the ground. Yasser Arafat, the chairman of the organisation, had been forced into exile and was distantly observing events from his offices in Tunisia.

After greeting the mufti and performing prayers in Masjid al-Aqsa (my second visit to the sacred mosque), we immediately began by visiting hospitals and speaking to the injured who had directly suffered from the fierce military crackdown. The stories were chilling, and the sense of tyranny and cold-blooded brutality was inescapable. I kept a little green diary and wrote down some of the testimonies of casualties, many of whom were young men whose well over two-thousand-year-old historical national identity, whether Christian or Muslim, had still not been sanctimoniously consecrated by the "international community."

As the chairman of Muslim Aid, it was my responsibility to identify projects that would deliver relief to those victims most in need and report back to the trustees. The weight fell heavily on me. I had a few thousand pounds of my own Zakat funds, which I personally handed to individual families, hospitals, and institutions caring for the orphans, injured and elderly. The smiles and gratitude we received made us feel less guilty about being able to simply walk away, back to our own lives, after hearing the harrowing tales of harassment and physical abuse these people were enduring. It is worthwhile noting that the name "Hamas" was never even mentioned during this time; the organisation was probably still in an embryonic stage and hadn't publicly surfaced yet.

We travelled through the West Bank, to Nablus and various villages, as well as to Gaza. Everywhere we went, there were scowling, well-armed Israeli soldiers on patrol, ready to pounce on any slight sign of unrest. We were keenly cautious and tried not to cause a scene, but the more we travelled and saw, it was difficult to hold down our frustration.

On our way back from Galilee, some of the more hot-headed members of our party couldn't help shouting out "Allahu Akbar," as a jeep full of youthful, gun-toting Israeli conscripts passed us. The vehicle screeched to a halt, and they came running up. After realising we were British citizens travelling with Her Majesty's authorisation, they still abused us verbally and, following a brief frisking, barbarically trampled on some "Islamic" tapes and books that a couple of us had been carrying, before they drove off . . . Imagine if we had not been blue-passport-carrying limeys?

*

At the end of our highly disturbing tour of Palestinian towns and villages, the delegation grouped together and started drafting a statement to be read out at a press conference and sent to various media outlets. This task was completed with the help of our enormously tall, blond-haired brother Sahib Bleher, from Germany, who seemed to have some useful political experience.

There was wrangling within the group as to the kind of language we should use. In the end – largely on my insistence – we agreed that it should convey the facts, and stick as closely as possible to the broad Qur'anic paradigm, avoiding involvement in base political rhetoric. Our narrative naturally included stories and vivid descriptions of those injured and bereaved people we had visited during the Intifada. The report ended with a clear condemnation of gross human rights abuses. After hurriedly typing it on hotel headed paper, we squeezed into the hot and impatient press crowd seated tightly, wall to wall, in the lounge of the Pilgrims Inn.

Our spokesman, Ibrahim Hewitt, stood up and took the mic and read the statement. After quoting the Qur'anic verse that directly addresses the Children of Israel, exhorting them to be good to the needy and follow the noble commandments revealed to them,[90] he proceeded to present the findings of our delegation. Jaws dropped to the ground as he got deeper into the descriptive picture of brutality we had witnessed.

The response was probably to be expected: instead of acknowledging our testimony or expressing any sympathy for the inhumane treatment of Palestinian protesters, those journalists present reacted to our report with utter disgust and fury. They were on the lookout for headlines, particularly as their once favourite singer, Cat Stevens – who wrote and sang such sweet songs as "Moonshadow" and "Peace Train" – was standing right in front of them, this time dressed in a tweed jacket and a white turban! Flash cameras lit up like aerial bombardments in the dingy, smoke-filled room as reporters bawled out, battling to ask questions:

> PRESS: *What organisation do you belong to?*
> DELEGATION: *We are not an official organisation; we formed this group from various parts of the UK, most of us embraced Islam in the last ten years and have known each other for some time.*
> PRESS: *Do you support the peace movement?*
> DELEGATION: *Islam means peace so our support for peace is obvious. But any peace proposal which does not restore and protect individual rights of life and property will offer no solution.*
> PRESS: *Do you support the PLO?*
> DELEGATION: *We're not Palestinians; it's not for us to decide who represents them.*

Before the press conference, we had all agreed basic answers to some possibly contentious questions. But sticking to the rules was not possible for some of the impassioned members of the group. When asked what the "solution" to the conflict might be, before Ibrahim could repeat our collective, well-rehearsed lines – namely, for all parties to return peacefully to a just and humane resolution, grounded on the Godly behaviour expected from all parties involved – our young

"Moses" from Brixton sprang up and yelled his personal opinion: "An Islamic state!"

That was it! A machine-gun barrage of questions zipped in all directions; it was a free-for-all. Another journalist shouted, "What would happen to the Jews who live inside Israel?"

"They would have to reapply for visas," came the reply from another unbridled member of our delegation. The protocol of the conference crumbled in the aftermath.

Later that day, I met my brother David, who had driven over from Tel Aviv to see me. He was still optimistic even against what looked like impossible political odds. David had been busy working with his organisation, Peace Child Israel, bringing together Palestinians and Jews in a village called Fureidis, on the Haifa Road. There was no chance that it could have ever happened without the Palestinians being convinced of his good intentions; but once he mentioned that he was Yusuf Islam's brother, everything changed; that opened the door of hope, and they jumped at the idea.

We met near the Damascus Gate. Unfortunately, it was not a very brotherly meeting. As we sat there in his car, I handed him a crumpled copy of the press statement. Dave's eyebrows narrowed – then he exploded! We almost came to blows. He had been expecting a compromising message to pave over the painful issues and open a pathway for peace. On the other hand, I reminded him that the statement was meant to sum up the feelings of the whole delegation and I didn't author it myself; as a group we had all witnessed things behind the mud-stone walls, in the overcrowded sanitation-less camps and alleys, that he never got to see.

Coverage of the conference by news outlets the following day was notably absent. Of the few articles there were, most carried unsurprising epithets, branding us all as "religious bigots" or "Khomeini followers."

Thankfully, the rift between David and myself was not going to cause long-term damage. Our bond as brothers was unbreakable, regardless of differences. He had not really embraced Islam, but would regularly stand up to defend me against those who criticised my choice of religion. Using the everyday power of logic, Dave's answer to them was short and simple: "You only have to look at history to see that, after Muhammad's claim to be the last of the prophets, clearly there hasn't been anyone else to unseat him, has there?"

David had unexpectedly discovered the last missing brick of God's religion in the very streets of the sacred city where we now parked. Without my brother's gift of the Qur'an, I may never have been able to appreciate another side of the story. From each of our viewpoints, we both knew enough to appreciate a much wider picture.

> *It's so quiet in the ruins,*
> *Walking through the old town*
> *Stones crumbling under my feet,*
> *I see smoke for miles around*[91]

27 | *Hampstead to the Holy*

Satanic Forces
1989

AT THE BEGINNING of my Islamic life, I had enjoyed perhaps twelve months of absolute bliss as a newly born Muslim, learning how to pray, visiting the House of God in Makkah, peacefully breathing the air of freedom, far away from the trappings of record business managers and agents. My heart had never been more at peace.

Times had certainly changed. Returning from the trip to the Holy Land, I heard that many of the friendly volunteers who guided our small delegation through the first trip in 1988 had actually been arrested after our departure, accused of belonging to an "illegal" organisation. Before too long there were leaked reports that accused me of supporting something called "Hamas"! I sensed that another nasty picture was being created. Fact is, throughout the entire hostile press conference and during the whole visit, no entity other than the PLO was ever mentioned; no one mentioned that name, and I certainly had never even heard of it.

Only after my initial visit to the region did it become known that the Israeli government had been subtly nurturing some kind of oppositional weight to Yasser Arafat in Gaza. But that piece of intel was still way off the public radar.[92]

Looking further back, to the time when I was a twenty-one-year-old poet of song, I had written a lyric lamenting how hard it was to "get by just upon a smile."[93] Wasn't it just?

> **Do people think once they say, "We believe," that they will be left without being put to the test?**[94]

I was to personally appreciate the wisdom of that Qur'anic verse in much more depth very soon. The next test was going to hit like a blistering asteroid; its reverberations would cause tremors for umpteen years to come; the chasm between Muslims and the non-Muslim world opened even wider, and it was going to be harder to find any safe ground in the ensuing fallout.

Before it struck, there were frantic alerts: I had been contacted by Dr. Manazir Ahsan, a scholar from the Islamic Foundation in Leicester, who forwarded sections of a book published in 1988 by Salman Rushdie, *The Satanic Verses*. The extracts were unbelievably rude and offensive, raining down hard on the sacred and beloved personality of the Prophet Muhammad, peace be upon him; inferring, through a complex weave of dreams and fiction, stories and incidents that made a cruel mockery of Islam, even including a section where whores and prostitutes, who dwelled in a Makkan brothel, took the names of the Prophet's wives. It would doubtlessly cause a deep spiritual wound in the already severely injured and haemorrhaging Muslim world.

Immediately, I sent a personal letter, ardently petitioning the publisher, Viking, a subsidiary of Penguin Books, to reconsider and withdraw the publication of the controversial book.[95] But the editorial director, Tony Lacey, dismissed these concerns, quoting the *Sunday Times* review which had described it as "a masterpiece" and repeating the opinion of the Booker Prize judges who considered it a "deeply serious novel."

"Serious" – indeed it was.

The timing couldn't be worse for Ayatollah Khomeini in Iran. He was already extremely aggrieved, having just been forced to accept a ceasefire with Iraq, with over a million dead from both sides in the futile, eight-year war. It wasn't long before the ayatollah was made aware of the book. Then came his volcanic fatwah, condemning all those connected with it, and calling for the execution of the author as well as its publishers.

Soon, angry protests from hardliners (both Shia and Sunni) were being heard from all quarters of the Muslim world: from Indonesia to Morocco, from Saudi Arabia to Iran. The book raised the emotional temperature of Muslims throughout the world, stoked up by ear-splitting religious leaders reciting verses from the Holy Qur'an that seemed to leave no room for doubt about the issue.[96] The smoke of Muslim fury began to swell and spread in the streets. The book rapidly assumed much wider proportions than the publication itself. The ayatollah's fatwah was one of the greatest signs that the days of romanticised "orientalism" were truly over.

I was a young, comparative minor in terms of knowledge of Islam, standing at the crossroads, my head swivelling between two opposing forces preparing for battle: the powerful Western, secular, journalistic infantry, lined up behind a flag and beating the drum for freedom of speech; opposite them, a large gathering of non-uniformed protesters holding tightly to the Qur'an and shouting, "Death to blasphemers!"

What to do?

Like "music," there was no word such as "blasphemy" in the Qur'an. Throughout my readings, I had never seen any specific verse mentioning the subject – certainly not as plainly as it was being presented by the ayatollah. I approached Dr. Darsh and other well-known muftis in the UK and abroad for an explanation. The replies and research papers I received all focused on the issue of slandering the Prophet, declaring it a capital offence founded on a Qur'anic verse quoted by Ayatollah Khomeini in his fatwah:

> **Those who hurt God's messenger have incurred a painful retribution.**[97]

As far as I could see from my reading of that verse, the word "retribution" (also translated as "punishment") could easily be referring to the Day of Judgment, but most of the responses I received from the scholars seemed to uphold applying the punishment in this world – as well as the next. This view was based on the consensus of the majority of commentaries and interpretations of scholars down through the ages.

There was very little said about the validity of the actual fatwah itself, its context and relevance to me and every other Muslim living outside of Iran. However, the advice offered by Dr. Darsh clarified that for me. He pointed out that there was absolutely no allowance for any Muslim to take the law into his own hands. Even if the generally accepted view of capital punishment for the crime of insulting the Prophet was absolutely valid, vigilantism was inimical and outlawed by the teachings of Islam. Cases like this could only ever be judged and applied in a place where Islamic law was upheld by governmental courts and judges. Otherwise, Muslims were obliged to abide by the common law of the country in which they had chosen to live, particularly if the law did not restrict or interfere with their personal faith and freedom to worship God[98] and perform essential duties, i.e. the five pillars.

As disturbing as this whole controversy was, and against the worsening scenes, like the fatalities during protests in Pakistan and the firebombing of UK bookshops, I just tried my best to get on with my work with family, schools, charity, and the Islamic Circle. But the task of educating people about Islam was getting harder with jumbo-sized controversies like this roaring overhead.

While the controversy continued, onto my office desk landed an invitation from Kingston Polytechnic Islamic

Society, requesting me to deliver a talk about my journey to Islam. I accepted. As it happened, my loyal musician friend Alun Davies and his wife, Valerie, lived quite close to the poly, so I invited them along. Never having sat down to explain Islam to Alun in much detail, I hoped the talk might help him to unpack why I became drawn to it.

The speech went well, as usual. There were lots of Muslim students in attendance, listening closely to the intriguing drama of my pop-star escapades and leading up to my famous walkout. Then the moderator opened up the floor to questions. Suddenly, and completely outside the range of my life story, a young lady raised her hand and crudely asked whether or not Rushdie should die for writing his book.

Uh, oh!

Not knowing who this lady actually was, I addressed the question as openly as possible, repeating the textbook judgement I had been given by Dr. Darsh and the overwhelming opinion of scholars – similar, you could say, to the historic view of blasphemy practised for thousands of years in Judaism and Christianity.[99] But in the rush of the moment I forgot to mention the questionability of the dreaded fatwah.

That omission was probably one of the biggest mistakes of my early Muslim life. Frankly, I doubt it would have made any difference anyway if I had done it any other way. The questioner had been an undercover journalist from the *Today* tabloid on a specific mission. The following day, I woke up to face a bold, shattering headline on its front page: "KILL RUSHDIE," SAYS CAT.

Bloody hell – excuse my French. What kind of dystopian

novel was I living in? Then again, it was a tabloid. This was more about selling papers with violently loaded headlines. The grave had been dug, and I had stumbled into it. "Cat" was well and truly framed. I was getting used to being an easy target for ridicule, but now came the linking of my image to the infamous fatwah of Ayatollah Khomeini. The contest had begun, leaving me with the nigh-impossible job of trying to squeeze out of a macabre, press-nailed coffin to explain myself.

Now I was facing an onslaught of misunderstanding and hatred like nothing I'd ever experienced – before or since that day. My induction into the shark-tooth politics of spin had well and truly begun, with a vengeance. Yes, morning had truly broken, one might say – and I was facing the oncoming heat.

Arriving at my office the next day, I immediately set about writing a detailed press statement to clarify my position:

> *On 21 February, while speaking to a group of students at the Kingston polytechnic, in response to a question, I simply stated the Islamic ruling on the Rushdie affair. Suddenly my picture was splashed on the front page of newspapers all over the world next to the headline: 'Kill Rushdie,' Says Cat. It is very sad to see such irresponsibility from the 'free press' and I am totally abhorred. My only crime was, I suppose, in being honest. I stood up and expressed my belief and I am in no way apologising for it. I expressed the Islamic view based on the Qur'an and the Prophet's sayings and the rulings of the caliphs and renowned schools of Islamic jurisprudence.*
>
> *However, that is not to say I am encouraging people to break the law or take it into their own hands; far from it.*

> *Under the Islamic law, Muslims are bound to keep within the limits of the law of the country in which they live, providing that it does not restrict the freedom to worship and serve God and fulfil their basic religious duties (<u>Fard 'Ayn</u>) . . . If we can't get satisfaction within the present limits of the law, like a ban on this blasphemous book, <u>Satanic Verses</u>, which insults God and his prophets – including those prophets honoured by Christians, Jews as well as Muslims – this does not mean that we should step outside of the law to find redress. No. If Mrs Thatcher and her government are unwilling to listen to our pleas, if our demonstrations and peaceful lobbying does not work, then perhaps the only alternative is for Muslims to get more involved in the political process of this country. It seems to be the only way left for us.*

The press statement was a (not so) "sorry" attempt to sidestep my way out of the mess and to make up for what I didn't say in Kingston, reaffirming my commitment, not to any ayatollah, but to the overriding institution of law itself. Freedom of speech, however, wasn't giving much space to me. Hardly anyone ever got to read what I actually said, or the context in which I said it. Inevitably, whenever journalists interviewed me on the issue, they completely avoided asking me about my own personal statements, and focused instead on things that had been printed or said by someone else "about" me.

Shame. An unbiased eye might see that the only real "threat" contained in the press release was that Muslims might eventually be forced to get more deeply involved in the political landscape of Britain. My little democratic flag of peace, too, was wilfully disregarded by the press – it just wasn't bloodcurdling enough.

But because I didn't apologize, criticise, or attempt to dismiss or turn off the light on thousands of years of religious history, it gave the media establishment enough grumpy grounds to go ahead and publish what the hell they wanted anyway: namely, the myth that I was an unrepentant supporter of the ayatollah and his fatwah.

The mud stuck. My communiqué was conveniently ignored.

The word on the streets about Cat Stevens was going from bad to worse. Stories spread from news desk to news desk. Hating Cat Stevens and his music was now fair game. Soon I heard about an irate DJ in Los Angeles (part Greek, wouldn't you have guessed?) who encouraged his listeners to send in their old Cat Stevens records, which he then proceeded to publicly and gleefully ride an industrial steamroller over – presumably as a sign of support for the principle of "free speech." Strange. In all the years of my songwriting and recording career, I had never sung a song that set out to hurt or insult anybody – let alone a whole world faith and religion.

This seemed to be a replay of the John Lennon controversy. He had faced a storm of protest after a casual comment he made, suggesting the Beatles, at that precise, manic musical moment in time, were more adored than Jesus himself. John had a similar uphill task trying to explain the context of his words. Given his well-known tendency for straight talk, coupled with his dry and witty sense of humour – not to mention his amazing history and catalogue of Liverpudlian love songs – most editors were happy to forget all that in the rush for a damning headline.

Now, I too was on the media's blacklist, and my music was to be shunned.

Chronologically speaking, I was still naive and pretty pubescent, having to deal with the press in my capacity as a twelve-year-old Muslim "representative" of a one-billion-strong religion at the time. Whatever growing pains I had to endure, however, were to be accepted as part of my deal and my promise to serve God; I could not turn back time, and I couldn't change the Ten Commandments either. Respect for the sacred had been firmly planted in me as far back as my early Roman Catholic education. As Thomas More is famously quoted in *A Man for All Seasons*: "When a man takes an oath . . . he's holding his own self in his own hands, like water, and if he opens his fingers then, he needn't hope to find himself again."

"Wise men say only fools rush in . . ." and I was no Thomas More. A call came from Granada Television. They were producing a program called *Hypotheticals*, in which various scenarios were put to a panel, who were awkwardly forced to imagine these peculiar situations in order to evoke a hypothetical response. The host was barrister Geoffrey Robertson – a professional QC, no less – and I was asked to be one of the participants, along with other members of the Muslim community. Blind to the dubious intent of this invitation at the time, little did I know that the venerable QC was cozy chums with Rushdie, and had fed and housed him in the attic of his house in Highbury during the storm over the book.

I was in for a definite toasting.[100]

The stage was set. It wasn't long before I became the focus of Mr. Robertson's attention. At one point, he asked me a question in the negative, which I answered in the affirmative, making my response negative.

"You don't think that this man deserves to die?" said Robertson.

"Who? Salman Rushdie?"

"Yes," he replied.

I answered, "Yes."

That question might well have been one of those Platonic riddles, because my answer was a positive negative; it could actually be understood to mean that I went along with the QC's premise (i.e. "I don't think this man should die").

Confused? Well . . . so the heck was I.

The theatrical impression I got, watching the QC as he strode up and down, holding his chin, spinning around the panel of guests and firing questions, seemed to me quite – well, very Perry Mason-ish. I took that as a stage opportunity to try to cover up my inarticulacy, by spinning my answers into a more comical direction. Not many knew about my particular love of British humour; it was certainly not grasped by those present in the TV-constructed courthouse. Also, for those born outside of the Isles, sarcasm is – like Lennon's gaffe – very difficult to identify if taken out of context (minus canned laughter). The result can appear very sinister indeed. "Satire is traditionally the weapon of the powerless against the powerful,"[101] but in this case, it clearly backfired on me.

Criticise me for my bad taste; I agree. But, try to remember, I was feeling extremely bruised by the impact of that ghastly

Today headline, having become desensitised by the ferocious attacks unleashed on Muslims by the powerful media and politicians. My lampooning became distasteful – I simply got carried away.

The final edit of the *Hypotheticals* program was made to look extremely dark and serious. Much was savagely cut from the three-hour debate, including balanced arguments, and only the most sensational quotes and dotty stuff were left in. "Let that bit be heard," commanded the great editor in the clouds. Other comments were laid to rest on the editing floor.[102]

One pertinent answer did remain, however, right at the close of the program. Mr. Robertson turned and asked me to imagine if Salman Rushdie were taken to court in the UK and the jury found him "not guilty" of any crime, blasphemy or otherwise, and dismissed the case. What would I do as spokesman of the jury? I stated that I would fully abide by the law and accept the decision of the jury and declare him, "not guilty." That was no joke, as well as being the last word of the program . . . but not many bothered to watch it to the bitter end.[103]

It was very difficult to see a way out of this entrenchment in the midst of a political battlefield of gun smoke and belligerence, which is what I believe smogged the atmosphere between the West (mainly, the US and Britain) and Iran back in the late eighties; both sides saw each other as representatives of evil incarnate – while the real Satan and his minions probably stood cheering and hooting with laughter in the front row of the deplorable theatre of war.

How I wish things could have been different, but that's something only experience, further education and a healthy helping of grey hairs were to bring. Alas, I was not knowledgeable or eloquent enough to explain my stance on the matter as clearly at the time. I was in a conundrum. I needed to state the truth, which was to abide and stick to the law (old and new), which was always my firm position. Hey! But that didn't imply any support for the fatwah, even though to Mr. Joe Public it sounded as if it did. Stating the historically sound opinion of Islamic law, while at the same time dismissing the validity of the ayatollah's fatwah, was the only thing I could do: a classic oxymoron.[104] This was way too confusing for the average *Daily Mail* reader to get their head around. Far easier to believe, "Cat wants Rushdie dead!"

If I knew then what I know now, it might have turned into a more fruitful debate. Wiser proponents of Islamic law could have looked a bit deeper for a solution to this modern-day dilemma. In fact, when Rushdie publicly re-embraced Islam and issued an apology (even if he wasn't sincere, as he confessed later), it could have been a turning point – but that was not to be.[105]

Free speech is not a new issue by any means, and certainly not just connected to *The Satanic Verses* and fatwahs. It was central to the development of Western "enlightenment." According to John Milton (author of *Paradise Lost*), freedom to print "unlicensed" books is necessary "in order that the truth should emerge." That certainly throws a different light on the subject, a moral imperative we should all be able to embrace. I am also a personal fan of Hegel's saying, "When liberty is mentioned, we must always be careful to observe whether it is not really the assertion of private interests which is thereby being designated."

This is a critical debate, which not only Islamic scholars but also lawmakers in liberal democracies in the sweeping age of AI and social media increasingly have to face: the tussle between true and false, freedom of speech vs. public order, and the rights of conscience and human integrity.

Hate speech has been recognised as a crime in many countries. The principle is designed to restrict the ability of people to cause offense and harm to others, particularly large groups or communities. There are restrictions against using the "N" word against people of colour, even sensitivities about observing traditional gender identification; the denial of the Holocaust is considered a crime by certain governments, antisemitic speeches or literature have been outlawed.

Yet the ability of the so-called "free press" and governments to shout out and magnify certain issues, while totally shutting down others, raises uncomfortable home truths. Just look at the violent prosecution of Edward Snowden and imprisonment of Julian Assange after the WikiLeaks releases, clampdowns on the press at times of military conflict (such as that implemented by the US during the First Gulf War), and the limited space given by the Western press to the Palestinian *Naqba* – "The Catastrophe," or the killing and displacement of the Palestinian people reaching back to 1948 – as well as an ever-expanding range of privacy and personal identity issues. All this demonstrates that we have not quite reached the idyllic Disney space station called Tomorrowland yet.

*

The violent attack on Rushdie in 2022, thirty-three years after the issuance of the fatwah, by an assailant during an open lecture near New York, was shocking and gruesome. I was able to express my sympathy for Salman, because it was precisely the kind of action that I believe shouldn't happen in a civilised world, where laws – Islamic or otherwise – are meant to safeguard people from self-appointed judges and vigilantism. Sadly, there is no express peace train that can carry us to that world yet, and it certainly was not in service at that time either.

How all these issues that I have raised will be viewed and treated in the future, I do not know. But, personally speaking, one thing is for sure: the role some journalists took in shadow banning me, and limiting my ability to help people perceive and appreciate the true and spiritually invigorating heart of Islam's message, may have served an unexpected purpose – which they will probably come to regret. The whole distasteful experience simply provoked me into studying Islamic jurisprudence in much greater depth, especially the subject of music and the status of fatwahs – also picking up an unexpected honorary doctorate of law from the University of Exeter, as well as my guitar.

My present attitude to the subject of law and music took time to evolve. But I believe that true Islam – when freed from intransigence and prejudice – allows for significant flexibility where the harmony of coexistence, peace, and saving of lives is concerned. Seeking the greatest benefit for the majority may be more valuable than the pursuit and punishment of individual crimes. The Prophet himself, in many recorded instances, did not react to abuse hurled by his opponents, but continued with a higher purpose patiently to invite people to the message of peace, and the elevation of humanity's consciousness to the divine presence.

> *Cat's in the yard, fancy free*
> *Dog barges round, says,*
> *"You can't catch me! No siree."*
> *There was a time, when I was younger*
> *I'd chase the tail of any danger*
> *About to learn, about to learn*[106]

CAT ON THE ROAD TO FINDOUT

Paradise Beneath Her Feet[107]
1990

How can I tell you that I love you,
I love you, but I can't think of right words to say . . .[108]

MUM WAS NOT feeling well and was becoming forgetful; she finally agreed to be checked by a specialist. It wasn't long before we learned that she had developed a dangerous form of brain cancer. Our hearts sank. My brother, sister, and I proceeded to arrange specialist treatment. Following an emergency operation, she went through chemotherapy at Hampstead's Royal Free for a couple of months and then returned home to Reading.

Anita and Alec were only two doors away, and they cooked and looked after her as much as they could; Anita stayed over some nights to keep especially close. But there was no running away from the fact that our mum's personality had changed.

She would sit in the garden for long periods just staring at the scene, watching the swans glide gently upon the Thames, lacking motivation, with nothing much to say. Strangely, she seemed more at peace than I'd ever seen her before.

The prognosis was not good. I began to plan her return to London and got the builders to prepare a room in our new house in Queen's Park for her, if or when a critical time came.

Unlike other animals (as far as we know), we are creatures that have to live with the knowledge of our own mortality, but nothing is as hard to face up to as the inevitable prospect of losing the most important love of your life. My mother's beauty and character continued to shine out, even during those dark and cloud-filled days. She still kept her smile, gracefully balancing between acceptance and hope. Mum was never any good at concealing the truth or telling "white lies"; it was so easy to see through her, blushing uncontrollably whenever she tried. Her eyes were almost transparent in their open, untainted honesty. "A thousand hours I've looked at her eyes, but I still don't know what colour they are."[109] It was Mum I wrote those lyrics about.

She taught me to love.

Death is not something that we can put off; everyone should prepare for it – believer or non-believer. While Mum still had her mental faculties, I gently suggested that she prepare a will and testament, which she did. It began "In the name of Allah . . ." She requested that her burial be carried out according to Muslim tradition and divided her inheritance and possessions among her children very carefully. Mum was not much of a hoarder – I'm pretty sure she'd already handed the drawings of mine she'd stacked away to Anita for safekeeping, anyway.

As a family, regardless of what the doctors said, we managed to hold on to a miraculous hope, praying that things might get better for Mum.

The wheel of life continued to turn, and now Fawziah was expecting our sixth child. My hands were overwhelmingly full, what with my mother's condition getting increasingly bad. I still had to run the charities; battle a government that was continually laying roadblocks in the way of justice and equality for Muslim schools; deal with the press and fatwahs; and try to tackle disunity and disputes between Muslim communities and the mosque. The challenges were ongoing and relentless.

It was getting critically close to the time when Fawziah was expected to give birth. Mum's health was worsening: her mind was not able to focus, and her memory was fading; a simple conversation with her was not possible anymore, and she needed twenty-four-hour care. Anita and David agreed that we should move her into my house, where she could be surrounded by family and enjoy private nursing. The kids knew that Grandma was very ill, but they talked to her as if she was still all there, accepting her silence as a sign of her approval of whatever they said or did.

Mum was unaware of the commotion happening when the big day came and Fawziah went into labour. The contractions were growing more intense and coming faster. We rushed into the car and drove her to the Wellington Hospital, near the Central Mosque off Finchley Road. Time dragged on, and it was becoming unbearably painful and dangerous, so finally she agreed to a Caesarean section.

The baby was born, and the doctors immediately told us that our newborn boy had some serious problems. After a thorough examination, they gave us the news: he had Edwards's syndrome. It was a colossal shock. Our son's heart had no walls or cavities, so his chances of survival were basically nil. Most babies with this disease die in the womb; the minority of sufferers who survive generally die in the first three months. If they have no serious physical complications, they might live a year or more. That was not the case with our baby.

We decided to name him Abd Al-Ahad: servant of the Unique. He was transferred to the Royal Brompton Hospital, which specializes in heart diseases. We consulted other specialists; the prognosis was the same. The doctors offered to operate, but it was clear that "home" for most of his short, painful life would be a hospital, as an object of medical experimentation on the operating table. Considering the total absence of normal cardiac partitions, we ultimately felt the reconstruction and endless scalpel incisions on his tender heart and body, living with total reliance on an incubator and tubes, was too horrendous a prospect for our angelically pure, sinless baby.

At one point, the nurse took a piece of paper and drew a diagram to explain the internal structure of Abd Al-Ahad's heart. I was totally stunned: the shape she sketched perfectly resembled the name of God – Allah – in Arabic! This was a clear sign to remind me that the beginning and the end of our existence are with Him alone. The Prophet, peace be upon him, also said, "There lies within the body a piece of flesh. If it is sound, the whole body is healthy; and if it is unsound, the whole body is diseased. Verily this piece is the heart."[111]

Fawziah and I both knew that everything was ultimately in God's hands; all we could do was provide our little baby with however much time He would allow us to have, until taking him back. We were able to give him a few drops of Fawziah's breast milk and a small taste of honey, enough to taste the best of this transitory world before his departure.

The inevitable hour came when our baby's breaths ran out. The fifteenth night of his short life became one of the longest nights for us; it was 6 June, 1990. The family had gathered together to be close to him in the hospital. I was holding him in my arms and reading "Surah Ya Sin," the thirty-sixth chapter of the Qur'an. Just as I finished the last verse, Abd Al-Ahad breathed his last. The night had passed, and dawn had arrived.

> **All it takes, when He wills something to be,**
> **is simply to say to it: "Be!" And it is!**
> **So glory be to the One in Whose Hands**
> **is the authority over all things, and to**
> **Whom alone you will all be returned.**[112]

The Prophet had three sons, all of whom died in infancy. This gave me a new sense of closeness to the Prophet Muhammad's own sorrowful experience. The hope is that the next meeting with my child will be in the endlessly flowering meadows and blossoms of God's eternal abode of wishes, where all sadnesses are removed, under the shade of intensely green trees, hanging with fragrant fruits, within open palaces of divine light, reunited again, in the beautiful company of winged, heavenly souls.

We buried our baby in a grave in the green pastures of Hendon cemetery, with a small wooden sign: "Abd Al-Ahad Ahmad bin Yusuf Islam, born 27 Shawwal 1410 H. Died 12 Dhul Qi'dah 1410 H." Two empty grave spaces were also purchased next to him.

> *Oh very young*
> *What will you leave us this time?*
> *You're only dancing on this Earth for a short while* [113]

Back home, the signs were not looking that positive for Mum, and her condition was deteriorating. She seemed to have lost the alertness in her eyes and would often look straight ahead or quite blankly at you. She now had around-the-clock care, with nurses coming to give us a break, mainly during the night. The surgeon who had operated on her had told us that she possibly had less than a year to live following the procedure; there was no guarantee they had been able to remove all the cancerous growth in her brain. We had to prepare ourselves for the worst.

It was now July 1990, approaching the month of Hajj, and my secretary received yet another invitation from the Palestinians to attend a special 'Eid Festival celebration organised to take place in the Negev desert in the Holy Land.[114] This would be my fourth visit. I wanted to revisit the region and see how things on the ground had changed. I gratefully accepted the invitation and took my five-year-old son, Muhammad, along with me for the experience.

After getting off the plane at Ben Gurion Airport, little did I know what was in store as we walked over to the immigration desk. The female officer examining my passport immediately led us to a room where officials in army uniform and policemen detained me and my son for three hours, ripping open and searching everything in our bags. I could just hear some of them whispering, "It's him, Cat Stevens."

Finally we were told, "You're going back to London."

"What? Why is this happening?" I asked an official. No answer was given, and that's the way it was left. My poor little lad, Muhammad. Up to this point he probably thought that having a famous daddy was a generally useful thing – this trip would broaden his education.

On returning to London with my son, I immediately complained bitterly to the Foreign Office and sought legal advice. The result was a stonewall: there was no legitimate avenue to challenge the Israeli decision. It appeared the impact of my public visits to Palestine inevitably was seen as unhelpful to Israeli policy. Before too long, reports were leaked to the press that accused me of supporting a "terrorist" organisation: Hamas! It was a heinous lie.

The whole distasteful slur was obviously meant to damage my reputation even further (if it wasn't already permanently misshaped through my mismanagement of the *Satanic Verses* saga). The tactics used to disparage the Palestinian cause were now being used against me, to divert any possible sympathy for the real victims of the occupation, many of

29 | *Paradise Beneath Her Feet*

whom were the impoverished, women, children, and invalids whom I had met first-hand during my visits. Fortunately, they will all be my witnesses on the Day of Judgment.

After that experience, following Abd Al-Ahad's death and with the continued strain of Mum's illness, Fawziah and I were sapped to the bone. An opportunity arrived for us to fly over to Egypt for a week's break. The Organisation of the Islamic Conference (OIC) was meeting in Cairo, and I was invited as part of a delegation representing British Muslims. Anita, who also helped out and stayed close to Mum, suggested that the week off would do us and the kids good, and Mum seemed stable enough, so we prepared for the journey.

The plane touched down in stiflingly hot Cairo on the evening of 30 July. All the children were with us, five excited young faces enjoying the new strange smells and ancient surroundings, as well as the special attention we received from the conference's protocol officers. They sped us rapidly through VIP channels and piled us into waiting cars. Soon we were charging along the highway, escorted by police motorbikes, sirens blaring, past the famous City of the Dead, eyes affixed beyond the dark-tinted windows, trying to glimpse the pyramids. Through the batty traffic we blazed at top speed till we reached the centre of town and arrived at our hotel, overlooking the Nile.

The next morning I was driven to the conference venue and took part in the flurry of the first morning's plenary session. There was a high security presence as President Hosni Mubarak and other heads of state strode in for the opening of the procedures. The day consisted of long stretches of police cordons, TV crews, flashing cameras, speeches, endless hand-shaking, hugging, and political posturing.

This nineteenth session of the conference had been called to finalise and launch the OIC's Cairo Declaration of Human Rights, probably an attempt to remind Europe and the West that Islam has a long-forgotten historical connection with the development of universal and religious freedoms, to be found one thousand and four hundred years ago in the original Constitution of Madinah. More advanced than the "Great Charter of Freedoms," commonly known as the Magna Carta, the constitution, instituted by the Prophet himself, upheld the sacred rights of diverse religious communities, while acknowledging theological differences, and provided a system of social welfare – regardless of race or colour – for all. Groundbreaking concepts at the time.[115] Sadly, a brief glance at the dire state of most Muslim countries made one soon realise – like the pyramids – how derelict such noble dictates had become.

By the end of the long, Arabic speech-filled session, the main dignitaries were spirited away in a long train of black Mercedes limousines, flags fluttering, surrounded by an army of security guards. I was shuttled through the late afternoon traffic heat, back to the hotel, unaware of what was in store.

I walked into the hotel room to see Fawziah packing our suitcases. Looking up with tears in her eyes, shaking with emotion, she told me, "Mum has just passed away. Anita just called to tell us."

My world had now changed forever. Cairo was the last

place on Earth I wanted to be. Accepting God's decree, but with our hearts heavy, we scrambled our belongings together and booked the next available flight back to London.

Fawziah's father and mother had made arrangements for the funeral to take place as soon as possible, following Islamic custom. The funeral prayer was fixed for the next day: Wednesday 1 August, the day we flew back. The date of Mum's burial happened to be 10 Muharram, a special day in the Islamic calendar, connected to the fast of Ashura, which is itself linked to Yom Kippur,[116] also the same fateful day the Prophet's grandson Hussain was martyred (a time of mourning for Shia Muslims).

On landing, Fawziah and I sped as fast as the taxi could take us, from the airport straight to the Central Mosque. The funeral (*janazah*) was scheduled to take place after the midday prayer, and we had less than an hour to get there. It was touch and go, but we made it with minutes to spare. Outside in the open courtyard, most of the family was standing beside the coffin, and the call to prayer began to sound through the muffled loudspeaker. The lid of the coffin was still open. I set eyes on my mother's still but beautiful face. It shone with a sort of peaceful radiance, and her body was shrouded by a light white cloth as she lay serenely in the pale wood casket. Anita was by her side, eyes red sore from weeping; she had taken part in the ritual washing of Mum's body along with my mother-in-law and other sisters from the family.

Gently, I kissed Mum's forehead and quietly whispered a farewell prayer over her before she was taken into the mosque hall. David and his children were all present, as were my childhood friend Andy and his family, also my cousin Lambros, and many others who knew and loved Mum deeply.

The black hearse and convoy of cars filed out of the driveway and travelled northward along Finchley Road towards Hendon cemetery. Passing the bustle of pedestrians, buses, market shops, and everyday commercial life, we slowly drove. Most people on the streets were apparently unperturbed, too oblivious and busy to consider the last stop that our shared mortality must one day lead us.

Grandmother and grandson: both had died within two months and were laid to rest within inches of each other. Mum had become Muslim, and that was the greatest inheritance she had left me, together with her imprint on my character: her fairness, love, open-heartedness and eternal optimism.

Peace be with you, Mum – forever and always.

> *You and your shiny golden hair*
> *You give me strength*
> *To bring the world*
> *To see that I'm not lying,*
> *You and your shiny golden hair*[117]

Not long after Mum's departure, I had a dream where I saw the roof of my home blown off. There was no parental shield over my head any longer. Mum and Dad were gone, and I was a child no more, in a world exposed to ever-more dangerous climactic perils, as each day blew by.

Peace Camp:
Between East and West
1991–9

SADDAM HUSSEIN HAD invaded Kuwait: one of the top-ten blunders in military history. Early in 1991, what he described as the "mother of all battles" gave birth to Operation Desert Storm and to Saddam's final overthrow. The operation was spectacularly successful from the vantage point of the so-called "alliance." But its reverberations and the dangerous ancient religious cracks it exposed in Iraq, and the whole volatile region, would give birth to a new breed of mutant "beasts." These would be difficult to subdue, causing further hostilities, imbalance, and untold deaths to last through to the next millennium and way, way beyond – only God knows where or when it will all end.

The job of making peace can sometimes be as dangerous as war itself. During the early stages of the Gulf conflict I became involved in trying to unify Muslim organisations in the UK and help broker an initiative to reduce tensions between the main antagonist Muslim countries: Saudi Arabia, Kuwait, and the Republic of Iraq. A small delegation of British Muslims, including myself and some other representatives from the Midlands and north of the UK, was formed to visit the region and meet with the Muslim rulers of the frontline combatants; our mission was to mediate and offer our services for the cause of peace and avoidance of war.

Jumping jets between Jordan, Saudi Arabia, and Iraq for the next two weeks – meeting princes, ministers, ambassadors, and high-level representatives from all sides – we pleaded with them to reduce the military build-up and to withdraw Iraqi troops from Kuwait, with commitment to no further hostility.

President Saddam Hussein had started a perverse policy of holding "human shields" at strategic locations, wilfully using the "guests" as insurance against an allied attack. Part of the delegation's mission was to secure the release of as many UK ex-pats as possible. We had not yet succeeded. So I agreed to stay on in Baghdad to accomplish this task, while the rest of the delegation returned to Britain.

While the president was receiving all kinds of representatives from various Western countries who requested the return of their nationals, he seemed to be deliberately avoiding me. Days and weeks passed by, and the situation was looking more and more ominous. Confined to the Al Rasheed hotel, I appeared to be on a waiting list that never seemed to get shorter. After a while, I had the eerie feeling that yours truly, Mr. Islam himself, might now be one of the "guests," reminding me of that famous hotel in California which the Eagles sang about, "You can check out anytime you like. But you can never leave."

For over two weeks I was more or less "imprisoned," with only the bare rations of hotel food available to me and many other fellow foreigners, among them journalists. Hard, brown bread and heavily diluted orange juice for breakfast with minimal choices for lunch were getting too much for all of us. The reporter John Simpson, whom I met there at the time, didn't look quite as needy as we did; God blessed the BBC's outpost with a little bit extra.

Finally, I received news that former prime minister Sir Edward Heath was jetting his way to Baghdad to arrange the release of the four hundred or so Brits still held. It was then I was told I'd soon be going home, with four British Muslims from Harrow – a meagre gesture of appreciation for my perseverance. Whatever, I was happy to have done my bit and couldn't wait to see my family again.

Back in London, we continued our efforts to work towards a peaceful resolution. One of the proposals we had put forward, during our meetings with Iraqi and Saudi officials, was a plan to establish a "peace camp" on the borders, between Saudi and Iraqi troops. Meetings were held in London to which most national peace movements and volunteer activists were invited. There were members of the Campaign for Nuclear Disarmament (CND), Greenpeace, the Medical Campaign Against Nuclear Weapons, and the Fellowship of Reconciliation, as well as members of Muslim community organisations. Our peace camp proposal seemed to catch on. It was unanimously agreed to use all our potential networks to make it happen and avert the growing noise of war. A policy statement was drafted: "We are an international, multicultural team working for peace and opposing any form of armed aggression, past, present, or future, by any party in the Gulf. We are going to the area with the aim of setting up one or more international peace camps between the opposing armed forces. Our object will be to withstand non-violently any armed aggression by any party to the present Gulf dispute."

The initial team set up the peace camp between the Saudi and Iraqi border, about 420 kilometres southwest of Baghdad; its spot was an old pilgrims' resting place at the Iraqi border post on the road to Makkah. At one point, the base included seventy-three people – forty-five men and twenty-eight women – from fifteen countries. The camp was entirely made up of good-hearted individuals with no political affiliations or external support; their message of humanity was courageous and peaceful.

Little could I have dreamed of the connection this unique initiative had with a long-lost Swedish relative of mine. What I was to discover years later pointed to a possible "genetic" link between the idea of the peace camp and my very own great-uncle from Sweden – on my mother's side of the family. Astonishingly, the Reverend Albert Wickman, a wildly passionate anti-war campaigner, also known as the "White General," had proposed a similar plan just before the eruption of the First World War! Impossible? No, this was a published fact, according to an archive piece in the *New York Times* dated 31 March 1914.

CAT ON THE ROAD TO FINDOUT

Well, my uncle never stopped that war, and sadly neither did we have an effect on ours. The Gulf Peace Team maintained their encampment from 24 December 1990 to 27 January 1991. But the drums of war were getting louder and louder. The campers were there to witness the planes zooming overhead to bomb Baghdad on the morning of 17 January. The Iraqi government arrived at the base and evacuated the peace campaigners, seeing them off safely to Jordan, ready to be transported back home to Britain and various other countries.

Stop the World – I Want to Get Off was the title of an Anthony Newley hit musical in London, 1961. I never saw the show, but thirty years later was rapidly getting to appreciate the relevance of the title. The world was spinning into a vortex of darkness, drifting deeper and deeper under massive shadows of ignorance. There was no room for uplifting spiritual engagement or nations of peace, only the ugly reconstruction of age-old prejudices, barricades of fear, and loathsome images of "the other."

Many of my fans were confused and traumatised, peeking through the spaces of frightening headlines and negative news reports built up daily by the media. All essential references to faith and divine knowledge were ignored in favour of those dealing with war and violence. Radical military dictators like Saddam or Colonel Gaddafi or angry young Muslim dissidents waving placards: these were presented as the true faces of Islam. The spiritual kings of the heart were overlooked or offered – if anything – brief comments on obscure, long-wave radio programs at some ungodly hour when most of the country would be sleeping. Men like Charles le Gai Eaton, a deeply thoughtful intellectual, former British diplomat, and editor who had written some of the most profoundly spiritual books on Islam, was one of those voices the world needed to hear. But little time was offered to such luminaries.

The wise words of Yusuf Ali, in the first commentary that I had come across during my initial reading of the Qur'an, sprang to mind: "In a reasonable world, the preaching of a reasonable faith like that of Islam would win universal acceptance. But the world is not altogether reasonable . . ."[118]

For so many years I had avoided looking at anything remotely linked to Islam because of my own comfortable occidental culture, with all its brightly polished, iconic personalities and glittering colonial history. Had it not been for the intervention of God, sending me the Qur'an through the hand of my brother, I would likely have joined the majority of critics and branded the religion as regressive, a rebel train jam-packed with a billion people belonging to an incomprehensible breed of humankind, steered by corrupt dictators, reversing at slow pace backward down a disappearing tunnel. Many Muslim nations hadn't yet clocked onto democracy! But now the mist had dissipated, and I was able to see the hypocrisy of that heavily tinted, one-sided Western view.

When Algerians crossed the much-publicised bridge of democracy in 1991 and voted en masse, the FIS (Islamic Salvation Front) party peacefully won the elections with a huge overall majority. There was, however, certainly no international welcome mat to greet them. The guardians of the "free" world unanimously booed the result, and the military moved in to violently overthrow the fairly elected government and send its active supporters to prison. It was called the "Black Decade." There was no outcry. Due to limited cell space in the city prisons, the captives were banished to concentrated compounds in the scorching regions of the Sahara Desert, with many allegedly killed or tortured.

It wasn't long before the exiled party members evolved into much more extreme underground movements and militant groups, the hardcore of which included ex-Afghan *mujahideen* fighters – who would eventually plant the seeds for a dangerous new breed of so-called Islamists seeking their brutalised version of an "Islamic State."

The next short-lived Muslim democratic victory to make the headlines was the Balkans. After the gradual break-up of the former Yugoslavia, an Islamic-inspired party had won the Bosnian elections, under the leadership of Alija Izetbegović, a former lawyer, author, and prolific thinker and politician. He had written a book called *Islam Between East and West*, which was a highly intelligent treatise on cultures and civilisation, explaining how many political philosophies failed to provide human beings with what they need.

After a successful referendum for total independence from Yugoslavia, it wasn't long before all hell broke loose. Serbian Orthodox Christians had begun fighting Croatian Catholics. Soon they both revealed their hatred and turned violently against the Bosniak Muslims, stuck somewhere uncomfortably in the middle.

I received a frantic call from a doctor working with one of

the Islamic aid agencies in Bosnia-Herzegovina. The brother pleaded with me over the phone, "Do something for the children who are being killed here! Organise an international concert, use your talent." It was very emotional. I was sick in bed with the flu at the time, but immediately felt inspired and began writing "Mother, Father, Sister, Brother." I had also half-finished a poem called "The Little Ones" (which I sang to a tune "lifted" from a traditional melody sung by the Dubliners, "The Captains and the Kings"):

> *Oh they've killed all the little ones*
> *With their eyes open wide*
> *There was nothing to help them*
> *On the day that they died.*
> *No bed to run under*
> *No cupboard to hide*
> *Oh they've killed all the little ones*
> *With their eyes open wide.*

The genocide in Bosnia at the end of the twentieth century was a defining moment. A terrifying anti-Muslim rhetoric paved the way for unimaginable crimes and massacres to be carried out. A new phrase entered the journalists' dictionary: "ethnic cleansing." I watched helplessly as European politicians met, discussed, dithered, and delayed – as usual. Children were being slaughtered, family homes and mosques burned and pillaged, women raped – oh God! How can the world let this go on?

As chairman of Muslim Aid, much of my effort was directed towards providing basic relief for the victims. The public responded. Tents, blankets, clothes, and food were delivered in long, extended convoys. In June 1992 I travelled with Dr. Darsh to Sarajevo and other areas to see the suffering and destruction first-hand. Destroyed, bullet-ridden homes, bombed roads and bridges and injured people were everywhere, with children and mothers crammed into ruined buildings in cattle-like conditions. It was sickening, but it helped us understand the scope of the barbaric onslaught and the unbearable losses borne by this fledgling, militarily aborted democracy.

The sudden exposure of a hitherto forgotten enclave of Islamic European culture and civilisation, which Bosnia represented, was a turning point for me. The TV pictures showed blond-haired, blue-eyed Muslims reciting verses of the Holy Qur'an amid plumes of smoke and fury from the ongoing war, then chanting traditional Islamic songs. Bosnian music is stirring and strongly reminded me of the tones I had grown up with as a child. For hundreds of years, the Balkans were a close-knit mix of demographically connected cultures. Greek, Turkish, Serbian, Bosnian, Bulgarian, Macedonian, and Croatian peoples shared food, music, and family structures. That was before.

At some point during the heat of the terrifying war, a small cassette of Bosnian songs fell into my hands. The melodies were hauntingly beautiful, bursting with love for the homeland, such as "Ja Sin Sam Tvoj" ("I Am a Son of Yours"). Though I still had some way to go – my uncertainty about whether to use musical instruments was still rather entrenched – I understood music's importance and the vital role played by inspiring motivational songs in keeping

30 | *Peace Camp: Between East and West*

Bosnian spirits high under such unimaginable conditions. It became the most adored and endlessly played musical cassette in our home; my children absolutely loved it and it had a powerful impact on my future attitude to making music.

Attacks against Islam and Muslims were on the increase everywhere through direct military aggression, political double standards, and the relentless barrage of agitated media reportage. It was clear that the root of the problem emanated from centuries of mistrust and hatred, based on the spread of racist misinformation and ignorance of what Islam spiritually meant and stood for in the evolution of God's religion.

Ignorance was not limited to non-Muslims. Sadly, professed Muslims – born within the confines of a few hundred years of demoralisation and vanquished history and heritage – were starved of sophisticated learning opportunities; they were easy to provoke. The growing frustration pumping through the veins of certain young Muslims and a new radical leadership – observing worldwide apathy at their suffering – fuelled a hardening of attitudes. Among those affected were a number of Algerian, Iraqi, Palestinian, and Syrian exiles, many of them displaced outcasts from successively harsh and oppressive regimes. The narrow understanding some Muslims had about the mission of the Messenger, peace be upon him, to humankind was in total contrast to the universalism and wisdom that characterised the Prophet's essential teachings.

Fifteen hundred years ago, the Prophet of Islam's unique,

non-divisive management of conflicts was made clear when, acting as peacemaker, he brought brotherhood and harmony to the Arabian Peninsula, which had for so long been a hotbed of war and hatred between battling Arabs as well as some Jewish tribes, endlessly fighting each other. Surrounded by ever-encroaching invasions and clashes between the Persian and Roman empires, the Prophet became one of the most historically successful architects of conflict resolution ever to appear in this most volatile region of the world.[119]

Knowing this from the insider's view, I began to feel an even heavier pressure of responsibility to convey the true historical legacy of the Prophet, so often distorted and mistold. Without overselling my credentials, it struck me that I could record a simplified audio version of the life of the Last Prophet, to offer a more accurate picture of him and of his truly unifying mission. The Muslim community had few spokespeople and even fewer international "stars" or well-known personalities to raise the profile of his incredible life and achievements.

I had a job to do!

The awful attacks on the Prophet of Islam's personality, spearheaded by *The Satanic Verses* and followed by the genocidal hatred unleashed in the Balkans – wreaking hell and destruction and bleeding the life out of innocent souls – made it unbearable to sit back and passively watch.

So I began writing a book, a short and simple biography of the Prophet's life. This became the focus of my creative work for the next two years. Along with my family duties and charity endeavours, I felt it was somewhat incumbent upon me to try to raise the curtain a bit higher on the human story of Islam; my aim was ultimately to produce a spoken-word album – my first official recording in more than fifteen years!

Being acutely aware of commercial demands and public taste, I wondered how my non-Muslim fans would react listening to their old "Cat" merely reading a book aloud. That led me to consider what I could possibly add into the recording to melodise it (within the limits of my extremely paranoiac approach towards musical instruments). One hugely popular song in my fragmentary collection of Arabic and Urdu cassettes stood out: the anthem sung by the women and children of Madinah to welcome the Prophet, after he had escaped the persecution of the Makkan tribal chiefs. It was called "Tala'al Badru 'Alayna." I went ahead and recorded the song in Arabic and English, using only vocals and percussion, the two instruments considered uncontroversial by even the strictest Muslim theological critics.

> O the white moon rose over us,
> from the valley of Wada'
> And we owe it to show gratefulness,
> where the call is to Allah.[120]

To avoid any compromises with the music business, I decided to launch my very own label, Mountain of Light. Its first major product was *The Life of the Last Prophet,* released in 1995 as an audiobook. The album was possibly seen by some as the return of Cat Stevens . . . but that was to be expected, I suppose.

There was a large crowd awaiting me in Harrods CD and record department. *The Life of the Last Prophet* was on show and playing quietly over the PA system. This was the special launch of my first album after seventeen years, on the fourth floor of the prestigious department store. Some fans were sympathetic, but confused. Not knowing what to expect after such a gap – and definitely not as elated as they would have been if it were another Cat Stevens record – a few dedicated souls were moved enough to buy the CD, and queued patiently for it to be autographed: "Peace, Yusuf."

Needless to say, *The Life of the Last Prophet* did not scratch the US or UK charts; however, it became a massive hit in countries like Turkey, where I was told it sold "over a million" copies. It was also a wake-up call for me to witness the impact my voice could make on mainstream levels again – a return to Catmania! The whole of Turkey seemed to wildly embrace me. Whatever the reason for the outpouring of love, I was deeply touched. The mournful tones and melodies of Anatolia were so moving, they brought me back to my own Byzantine-tempered musical background. The bouzouki was shared by both Greeks and Turks as a national instrument.

The signs were everywhere that music was still an important contributor to the vast-expanding range of the human experience in our common, God-given, creative, and inventive nature. Something unexpected was about to reawaken that feeling within me again.

The war in Bosnia was nearing its end, and I was invited to the Langham hotel, opposite the BBC's Broadcasting House, to meet the new Bosnian foreign minister, Dr. Irfan Ljubijankić. Dr. Ljubijankić was one of the unsung heroes of the war. For most of the forty-four-month siege of Sarajevo he had worked tirelessly as a doctor in the basements and corridors of bombshelled, makeshift hospitals. With no proper light or heat, he'd helped attend to thousands of injured patients, many of whom had suffered blown-off limbs and shrapnel wounds. I felt humbled.

During our meeting he unexpectedly played me a cassette; it was a song he had written and sung himself on piano, entitled "I Have No Cannons That Roar." It was extremely touching. "Please use it if you can for helping the cause," he said, and placed it in my hands.

Within a month of that poignant meeting, I heard the tragic news: Irfan had been martyred – his helicopter shot down in a missile attack above his homeland in Bihać. My heart was crushed. But his spirit still lived, and his final request spurred me on to do something with his song. My knowledge and attitude regarding the position of Islam and music had broadened considerably.

As a tribute, I decided to produce an album of the songs I had collected during the war. *I Have No Cannons That Roar* was recorded in London and Sarajevo by a host of Bosnian singers, including Dino Merlin. It was the first time I had relaxed my attitude to the use of instruments. Most of the Bosnian artists' recordings contained full arrangements. Still personally non-committed, I tagged along with my own a cappella song "The Little Ones."

When the war in Bosnia-Herzegovina was finally over, there was jubilation – although the Dayton Agreement for peace was still flawed with anomalies and long-term potential problems. An invitation from President Izetbegović arrived to receive the Golden Rose of Peace Award and sing at a celebratory concert in Sarajevo, and I accepted. This was to be my first official return to the stage in almost twenty years! It was a monumental moment and signalled the power of music to raise people's hopes and move on from the desolation of yesterday's simmering war.

> *I have no cannons that roar*
> *But I have faith in God and love*
> *And I'll surrender you to no one else*
> *My mother, Bosnia, my love* [121]

Apart from my new activities in the recording studio, charity work still remained high on my list of priorities, especially schools and Muslim children's education. Fortunately, some very good news was about to land on our doorstep, which would improve the mood and boost the status of Muslims in the UK.

A New Millennium
2000

WHILE PASSING THROUGH the transit area of Vienna airport after another brief visit to Sarajevo, I received a call on my brick-sized, crackly mobile phone; my secretary garbled something about our school and the government...

"What... what did you say?" It took me a while to understand. "What?! We've got government aid? Islamia school... what... we've won grant-maintained status?!"

I couldn't believe it. It was a historic moment: we were the first Muslim school in England to be recognised. After twelve long years of struggle, the massive election win in 1997 by New Labour under Tony Blair had brought a more inclusive approach to the Muslim presence in Britain. Labour boasted more Muslim councillors and MPs than any other party, and there was a greater sense of loyalty to the principles of socialism on the part of British Muslims, logically because the majority were from average working-class backgrounds.[122]

This offered a new glimmer of hope: the case to limit the number of "separate" faith schools could not be fairly made while the state accepted some religions and denied others – that geriatric doctrine could not be artificially oxygenated any longer. Fair play – a commendable trait nurtured within the historic core of the British cricketing disposition – had won the day.

Everybody waited for the clocks to go haywire and explode at the turn of the millennium – a ploy, some said, to get people to buy more gizmos, hard drives, and equipment to back up their personal records . . . but midnight came and went without a blip.

Great news arrived from the palace that Prince Charles had agreed to visit our little primary school on 10 May. Children and teachers were so excited, and the classrooms and halls all got a fresh coat of paint in preparation. The press rang us non-stop asking for security passes for the occasion. It was a historic, as well as symbolic, gesture by one of the key figureheads of British society, and was genuinely embraced by the community.

The prince was born the same year as myself, so I felt we had a lot in common (like . . . er, we were both famous at a very young age?). I had a great regard for his broad, tolerant wholesome-Earth philosophy. He showed genuine respect for and exceptional knowledge of Islamic civilisation and had, for some time, been interested in the close connection between Islam and the Abrahamic tradition (he privately admitted to being a bit of a Cat Stevens fan, too).

The Islamia schools were doing excellently. Our private

secondary girls school, which we had opened in 1989 (just in time for Hasanah's move), was topping the national league tables consistently – as if defying critics who claimed Islam was unfavourable for the education of girls. Now we had become the first government-aided Muslim school in Britain; good news all around.

The day came, and I was there to meet His Royal Highness at the primary school gates with our Canadian head teacher and convert, Abdullah Stephen Trevathan. The atmosphere was positively dreamy as we walked around inspecting children's desks and schoolwork. At one point my youngest daughter, Aminah, who had just started secondary school, was standing by the teachers in the staffroom and smiled broadly at him. Somebody whispered, "That's Yusuf Islam's daughter, Your Highness."

He shook her hand and smiled, saying something that I couldn't quite hear, but along the lines of, "Clever daddy you've got, little miss." She was so excited.

He ended the tour by giving a speech to everybody in the main hall and paid an immense compliment to the school and its struggle to maintain a sense of spirituality in a largely despiritualised world: "I'm one of those who happen to believe there is no incompatibility between community-based activity, like the education offered here in this school, and integration into the wider community. Indeed, somebody with a firm sense of his or her own cultural identity and history, I think, is much more likely to contribute to the society, as I am sure many of you will when you grow up and leave this school . . . You are ambassadors for a sometimes much misunderstood faith, and some of the adults here will

31 | *A New Millennium*

know that I believe that Islam has much to teach increasingly secular societies like ours in Britain."

There was loud applause before he was given some framed artwork lovingly prepared by the children. The whole visit was so indelible; it would be engraved in the hearts and minds of the parents and children for the rest of their lives – apart from exactly what he might have whispered to my daughter.

It was also during that eventful year that I agreed to take part in the filming of VH1's *Behind the Music* series. The director, George Moll, was a very friendly guy who promised not to pull any nasty punches. He had transparent blue eyes that seemed to hold no dark or sinister intentions. I trusted him. The US needed to hear my side of the story directly. For too long I had been portrayed as some screwball who had lost his compass, ditched the American dream, and given up everything for which most people work their socks off. I needed to recommunicate my unswerving dedication to the ideals I had sung so much about, and make clear my firm belief in universal peace, love, and the pursuit of happiness (minus commercials).

Many of my friends and family were brought forward and interviewed. It was definitely going to be a revealing, in-depth look into my life – ups and downs and sideways. While discussing the scope of the bio, I had convinced the producer, Bill Flanagan, that we should visit the Dome of the Rock and Masjid al-Aqsa in Jerusalem, to capture some of the spiritual atmosphere that I had breathed there while on my journey. They had positive calls with the authorities in Israel and assured me everything was fully arranged. The previous problems I'd experienced were all behind me – or so I thought.

Not quite.

When I finally arrived in Tel Aviv's Ben Gurion Airport on a late flight from Frankfurt on 12 July, the immigration officers were there, ready to march me to a small confined room where I was told to wait. It looked like a cell, six feet by six feet, with no water or any other facilities. My four roommates were three Gazans and one American who had come to attend a wedding. There were two double bunkbeds and hardly any space to twirl your toes.

Oh, not again!

Maybe it was not so much my old "Cat" persona but my new name, Joseph/Yusuf, that rattled them, reminding them of a previous undesirable guy called "Joe" whose ten intensely jealous brothers had tried to make him disappear. Just like him, here I was, caged for a crime that I never committed, patiently waiting for God and time to vindicate me. The best I could do was to repeat a chorus line Elvis once wrote, "Truth is like the sun. You can shut it out for a time, but it ain't goin' away."

The film crew paced back and forth on the other side of the airport hall, awaiting news; they were told that I was still in the "lounge" (a highly imaginative description for a crummy, non-air-conditioned immigration cell). Flanagan of VH1 had contacted Israeli officials in the US ahead of the visit and pleaded that he had clearly been given clearance. They were as bewildered as I was about the delay.

Such a pity. The basic objective of revisiting Jerusalem for VH1 was to underscore the great heavenly connection in

31 | *A New Millennium*

Jerusalem between Islam, Christianity, and Judaism, which had led to my acceptance of Islam: like the harmony of the sun, moon, and Earth – infinitely higher than the alligator-infested political swamp Palestinian and Israeli negotiators were now stuck in.

After several hours, officers finally opened the door, handed me back my luggage, and put me on the next flight back to London. That suited me absolutely fine. At last! I was not going to be roasted in that hot, poky room and could look forward to the prospect of sleeping under my own roof; a thousand times better than the lot of many other unfortunates in the Holy Land who were still sorrowfully displaced, stranded deep inside the well of despair – again, like the beloved son of Jacob – dreaming of their long-lost homes and olive gardens.

The VH1 crew stayed on and managed to get some stunningly picturesque shots of the golden Dome of the Rock and old cobbled streets of the sacred city, which were used in the documentary without any hint of the backroom story of my secret internment at the hands of the Israeli "intelligence" services.

The one-hour documentary was completed after extra filming in London, Konya in Turkey, Los Angeles, the Balkans, and New York. It was an epic enterprise, which was eagerly awaited by many, particularly in the US. *Behind the Music: Cat Stevens* by VH1 got the highest viewing ratings ever for that series and was nominated for an Emmy.

I was back in the spotlight. The Cat was back on TV . . . and in the charts! Universal had already put out the *Ultimate*

Collection of my music recordings and, for the first time in twenty-odd years, I agreed to be involved in its promotion; I needed to work harder to win back my alienated friends and allies who, for the past decade, had been forced to watch me duck and dive to survive the nasty cannonade of press snipers. I made sure, for instance, that the CD package advertised my latest Mountain of Light works, *The Life of the Last Prophet* and the follow-up albums, *I Have No Cannons that Roar* and *A is for Allah*. I wanted them to discover and have access to an uncensored presentation of my latest creative endeavours.

The three-story office HQ in Highbury was ablaze with activity, each of which demanded my time and a different hat. The ground floor – arguably the most hectic – housed the Mountain of Light office and packing area for delivering our CDs and merchandise. On the top floor, our tenants, Muslim Aid, had decided to remain, despite my resignation from the board. Their offices were always buzzing with staff and volunteers, running various campaigns for delivering aid to an ever-growing list of disaster zones. The middle floor was taken up by my recording studio, a control room, and a carpeted prayer area.

    A humble space was reserved on the ground floor for my secretary, Sarah Sherrif. She largely remained hidden behind thousands of letters piled onto her ever-groaning desk. The poor girl was permanently overloaded, dealing with endless calls and enquiries; invites and requests were flying in from all over the world, clamouring for my attention or presence at this or that Islamic event. Requests for loans, donations, marriage guidance, and all sorts of demands, including messages from Muslims for me to write more children's songs or to recite the whole Qur'an, steadily poured through the letterbox of the front door on a daily basis. Sarah also had to tediously transcribe and type my weekly talks for the Islamic Circle – I guess you can say she was pretty busy.

Countless letters came from ardent fans talking about my music, some pleading for me to return. I was becoming more aware of how my albums had a profound impact on many souls, all with different stories: some seeking, some lost, and some just full of thanks, somehow my songs had opened an intimate door into the home of their hearts. It made me think more seriously about revisiting my legacy. Through my records and musical journey I had explored life's meaning with the intention of hopefully discovering an ounce of extra happiness. Many were listening, essentially trying to understand what was going on inside themselves and how to make the world a kinder place for us all to live and love in.

A few of the messages we received were really harrowing. It seemed my songs had helped many people; some who had even been on the edge of suicide were able to reconsider and see another morning of life, illuminated again. Others had arrived at a more inclusive perception of God's presence and found a deeper connection with the divine. A few delved as far and wide as possible in their personal ambit and became stronger by re-exploring their own religious roots and commitment.

A rather testing moment for me as a "daddy" arrived. One day at my office in Highbury, Majid Hussain, a young man from Manchester with a fairly obvious northern accent, whom I had taken under my wing and employed at Mountain of Light, unexpectedly asked in a very sweet and humble way for the hand of my daughter. Hasanah had got to know him while working at the office, and both were impressed: he by my daughter – and she with him.

Majid clearly had a strong love of Islam and the Prophet, peace be upon him. What was I to do? While I was initially reticent and protective, like any father, I couldn't really fault him. Knowing him for some time and seeing him on a daily basis, I remembered the saying of the Prophet:

> *If there comes to you one whose*
> *religious commitment and character*
> *you are pleased with, then [accept your*
> *daughter's wish to] marry him.*[123]

And so, with Hasanah's happiness and consent, my wife and I both agreed.

I wasn't going to make it that easy. Having read something in the Qur'an about how Moses was offered the hand of the flock-herder Jethro's daughter to marry, I recalled the father adding a condition that Moses should work for him for eight years, after which he would be free to go his own way.[124] As Hasanah was our first precious daughter and it would be hard on Fawziah and me to lose her, I proposed that Majid should work for Mountain of Light for at least four years as a condition. He took it bravely on the chin and accepted.

The marriage took place in the Brondesbury Park Hotel, a "Muslim-friendly" hotel I had established and donated for the benefit of our charity trust. It was just a stone's throw from our school centre. All the family and close friends were there: men in one hall and ladies in another (a basic custom so the ladies could let down their hair and feel more comfortable and relaxed). Our imam from the school, Shaikh Babikir Ahmed Babikir from Sudan, conducted the wedding.

Right after the official ceremony came the moment I got to know my daughter's musical taste. With her mother's help, she had compiled a cassette of songs and lively Turkish bass-drum-thumping music, modern and traditional, which blasted over the PA system. Everybody had a great time, ladies and children especially, who danced with blissful abandon into the echoey hours of the night.

Hijacked
2001–2

UNIVERSAL RECORDS DECIDED it was a good time, following the great public response to the VH1 documentary and the *Ultimate Collection*, to release a box set of my music and a new greatest hits. They asked me to get involved in the compilation of tracks as well as its design.

They didn't need to strain too hard. I had always loved getting engrossed in the arty side of things. The job of putting together albums, from the texture of paper to images and illustrations, even down to the choice of CMYK palettes and fonts, was always a fun thing to do. The box set was going to be a panoramic venture that would span my whole musical career, so it had to be pretty downright perfect.

I met Ben Levenson, Universal's guy from New York. He was a musical encyclopedic genius who'd memorized most of the details you'd ever need to know about the seventies – and beyond! David Costa of Wherefore Art was artistic director, famed for his amazing work on album designs, from the Beatles to Elton, Queen, the Rolling Stones and back as far as George Harrison's *Concert for Bangladesh*; he was a true master. My old producer, Paul Samwell-Smith, was also expressed in from his sleepy château surrounded by vineyards in the south of France to remix some of the archived unreleased sessions. It was nice to work with him again; Paul's spindly fingers had not changed or got any shorter, and his approach was still extremely delicate, carefully restoring the magical ambiences and echoes, familiar to my fan tribe since the *Tea for the Tillerman* days.

The front image of the lavish box set, inspired by Japanese artist Tadanori Yokoo's original 1972 poster, included a ninety-six-page self-penned autobiographical booklet entitled "In Search of the Centre of the Universe." It was bound together in a box with photo collages, lyrics, and song-by-song commentaries from Paul, Alun Davies, and others, full of anecdotes from behind the studio glass about the history and making of the records. The four-CD set was divided into distinct stages of my musical journey – "The City," "'The Search," "The Hurt," and "The Last" – and chronologically they encompassed all of my hits and key tracks, as well as a treasure trove of hidden, never-heard-before demos.

Without wanting to get too carried away, banging my own drum and bowing to the usual convention of blitz-like PR campaigns, I agreed with Universal's marketing team to do some select promotional work for the launch. It was Tuesday, 11 September when I walked into BBC Broadcasting House in London for an in-depth radio interview with "Whispering" Bob Harris.

The discussion between us went on for almost two hours. Periodic BBC tea offerings were useful energisers, but I was empty and exhausted by the time the control room's red light finally went off. As we walked together out of the studio, a small TV monitor on the side desk played breaking news about the World Trade Centre in New York. We stopped and peered incredulously at the thick smoke pouring out of one of the soaring Twin Towers. Someone said that a light aircraft must have accidentally careered off its charted course and crashed. Bob and I looked at each other with disbelief at the sight. He then guided me past the surreal spectacle to stand in front of a BBC logo for the usual promo snapshot.

Bob thanked me, and we said goodbye.

By the time I had reached my office in Highbury, the news fully hit us: there had been a terrorist attack, and four planes had been hijacked by Muslim extremists on a suicide mission. Two had deliberately crashed into the upper floors of the Twin Towers, extinguishing the lives of thousands of innocent civilians; a third had nose-dived into the Pentagon; a fourth had crashed in Pennsylvania.

Hell's gates were opened.

One of the eeriest things for me was that some four months before the attack, I'd picked up some felt-tip colour pens and spent the morning doodling in my sketchbook. Among the pictures I illustrated was a memory of a strange dream. The image was of a towering skyscraper doubly reflected in a pair of sunglasses, with fire bursting out around the middle to top floors. I named it "Anita's Nightmare" at the time. I can't for the life of me remember why. Was it a premonition or what? I didn't make any connection until years later when going through my archives. I came across the small print of a photo I took of that sketchbook . . . then looked at the date on the printouts: 14 May, 2001!

I had been a Muslim for twenty-four years before the earth-shaking events of 9/11. This was truly the worst time I'd ever experienced; my efforts to communicate a heavenly narrative were now entirely wrecked by the aftershock created by this hideous terrorist attack. Islam had been commandeered by those delusory individuals who saw themselves as self-appointed liberators of the oppressed Muslims of the world. We didn't even know their faces.

What these deviants did was an even greater disservice to the truth. Their vicious, Armageddon-styled agenda enabled right-wing, neocon politicians – as well as antagonistically charged media institutions – to rise up and become even more offensive, branding entire Muslim populations as religious psychotics. Muslims were instantly demoted en masse in the eyes of the world to the level of anarchic human-beasts, bent on the destruction of Western civilisation, willing to sacrifice themselves as well as innocent bystanders for the cause.

Muslims in America and elsewhere came under attack from their neighbours, at work and at school. Innocent people were blamed for an atrocity committed by a violent cult. Now a storm of hate and vengeance was unleashed upon the community, and the Muslim faithful were roped together and judged guilty by religious association.

In certain cities, police had to control angry mobs as they waved the Stars and Stripes and headed towards mosques and Islamic centres, bent on venting their fury at the nearest symbol of Islam. News reports were overloaded with increasingly frightening stories: petrol bombs were thrown into Arab-American community centres; many Muslims were spat at and harassed. One man was arrested for trying to run down a Pakistani woman in a supermarket car park. Such responses were as irrational as the actions of the twisted ideological perpetrators of the original attacks.

The press scrambled for my opinion about the terrible event. I immediately wrote an article for the *Daily Mirror* quoting one of the clearest verses of the Qur'an, upon which every heinous act of homicide will be judged:

> **If anyone murders an [innocent] person it will be as if he has murdered the whole of humanity. And if anyone saves a person it will be as if he has saved the whole of humanity . . .**[125]

However, most people had already switched off, their minds made up: every Muslim was now to be treated with equal suspicion.

Plato is reported to have coined the adage, "Ignorance is the root of all evil." No matter the source, it's an accurate assessment of one of the worst ailments that bedevils humankind. The attack itself, as well as the aftermath, were testimony to the nature of that common disorder on a massive scale. Unfortunately, it seemed the prophecies by the Last Prophet, peace be upon him, about times to come were being witnessed all too clearly, in our very era. He said:

> *Religious ignorance will spread, knowledge will disappear, there will be much killing.*[126]

The attack on the World Trade Centre opened the doors to a cataclysm. The hunt was on; gross acts of vengeance increased, and mass killing ensued. Afghanistan became a prime target, as al-Qaeda's chief, Osama bin Laden, the mastermind identified as responsible for the attack, had taken shelter in its mountainous caves and unassailable hollows, and the residual goodwill of the Afghan warlords who ruled the region. No doubt he was benefitting from the payback earned for his active part in the war against the Soviets a decade or so earlier.

Nothing in the world would ever be quite the same. Airport security, particularly in the US, went through a massive overhaul, and every passenger had to suffer unparalleled inspection and frisking. Racial profiling hit an abysmal level of intrusive depth. Anyone with a Muslim name could be justifiably placed under surveillance and tracked. That left me with little place to hide, with a name like Yusuf Islam and my previous record of siding with Muslim causes like relief and Muslim schools.

It was time for me to wake up. I needed to be more publicly out front and even more proactive in reasserting shared values of peace and coexistence. I wanted people to know that Islam in no way dented or violated my altruistic sixties spirit and yearning for planetary happiness, or my long-held anti-war commitment and concern for the future of our world.

"The Concert for New York City," at Radio City Music Hall, was being organised for 20 October 2001, including

Paul McCartney, David Bowie, and Elton John, and I too was invited. Though I couldn't make it on stage, I managed to record a satellite appearance at TV-am studios in Camden, which was broadcast Stateside, live from London.

For the first time in over twenty years, I revived "Peace Train." The message was powerful and warmly embraced by the New York audience, even though it was sung without any instruments. Something awakened that had been hidden for many years – like Rip Van Winkle, emerging from the Catskill Mountains – it was my musical voice! Alive and well.

Upon the release of my box set in the same month, I donated half the proceeds to the victims of 9/11 and the other half to orphans in war-ravaged countries, including Afghanistan. It was a charitable gesture on behalf of the Muslim community to demonstrate our human bond, without favouritism towards one particular side or nationality. It is good to remember that a number of the victims in the bombing were Muslims, too, as were some of the firefighters who bravely risked and even lost their lives on that fateful day.

During the next few months, I joined along with other voices and accepted as many press interviews as possible, trying to calm the nerves of those who had been alienated. But no matter how much I or other spokespeople tried to explain that the aberrational and criminal behaviour by a small cell of Muslim extremists was, in fact, a blatant rejection of true Islamic values, the damage had been done. The torrent of hatred generally against Muslims and Islam was becoming more ferocious.

In Pristina, Kosovo, the offices of our Small Kindness charity, which we established in 1999 and which had been running an "Orphan & Family" project for mothers and children, were suddenly raided by NATO forces. Helicopters landed, and troops broke in without warning. All the computers were snatched, and the poor unsuspecting staff – mostly local women – were traumatised and confined to a single, unheated room for hours until the search was over.

The raid happened during winter in Ramadan while the staff were fasting. Obviously, there was nothing untoward or sinister to uncover and NATO returned everything intact. Thanks a lot! But it gave us little comfort. Any organisation or charity with an Islamic name was under investigation, and we were no exception. The flow of vital funds for our work with the poor and displaced victims of natural tragedies and aggressions slowed down to a trickle, mostly due to new, stringent banking procedures and the strangulation it caused in the minds and hearts of donors.

If the 9/11 attack itself was madness, the policies that followed in response were no evidence of any serious effort to restore sanity. Finding it hard to nail the actual culprits behind the atrocity as bin Laden continued to elude capture, President George W. Bush and his close military-industrial consorts decided to vent their frustration and hit out at something – indeed, anything! It became the caricature of an enraged man rushing to kill a fly with a machine gun.

Not satisfied with slow progress in Afghanistan, the US administration looked elsewhere for its scapegoat. Saddam Hussein, who had absolutely nothing to do with 9/11 (also a previous "golden boy," supported and trained by the US and Saudi Arabia when confronting Iran), was now fiercely accused of holding "weapons of mass destruction." The world's media bombarded the public with fearful propaganda, rehearsing us all for the possibility of annihilation with well-crafted "intelligence" reports. The theatrical props were hurriedly built and set on stage for Saddam's last stand.

It was a scam but discovered too late. Iraq was already in the gunsights of President Bush and his secretary of defence, Donald Rumsfeld. The overthrow of Saddam, dismantling of Iraq, and ongoing "war on terror," and its effect on the whole Middle East region, created insecurity on an unprecedented scale. The signs of doomsday accelerated. We had entered the new millennium with a God Almighty bang!

> *The evil that's been done*
> *Still is carrying on*
> *And on this night*
> *There'll be no peace*[127]

As the pressure on Muslims in the West was becoming chokingly unbearable, I looked for a breath of respite. The United Arab Emirates was less involved in war and seemed interested in more positive things – like business. Dubai, in particular, was a very broad and progressive-looking Arab nation state of the UAE where I discovered new roads of opportunity: Dubai Internet City had just opened, and it was inviting companies to set up and develop a new dynamic media hub.

To me this was a truly God-gifted opportunity to start something fresh, away from the depressingly dark shadows that had enveloped us, to a more welcoming, sun-kissed environment. I knew it got pretty hot over in the Gulf, but A/Cs were in good supply to manage that problem, and winters were even better than your average British summer! So I flew to Dubai and rented a space for Mountain of Light in a brand-new office block, which had a view to the sea. Then I recruited a managing director from Malaysia to prepare a business plan for mainly English- and Arabic-speaking Muslim countries.

The more time I spent in the emirate, the more I loved it. There was an impressive, multicultural mix of people from Europe, as well as from India and the Middle and Far East. Many European ex-pats and Asian entrepreneurs were beginning to gravitate towards Dubai. The city was being built ultra-fast to an amazingly high-spec standard; deadlines were met with more speed and efficiency than I'd seen in any other country. There were lots of lovely palm trees, large white sand beaches, sunshine, clean, air-conditioned mosques, and impressive shopping malls with an endless variety of halal food and restaurants. Pretty irresistible, really.

Having written and collected some tuneful little songs, I started work on a children's album. "I Look, I See" and "Your Mother" needed some fresh, young voices. My close friend and *nasheed*-singing artist from South Africa, Zain Bhikha, had already worked with me on "A is for Allah," and he helped to arrange for the recordings in a studio near Joburg called Yellobrick. Zain brought his son Rashid, who sang really well, along with some young school friends who could also hold a note.

South Africa was literally a goldmine; it beamed with natural musical talent. I used to say you could place three South Africans in a room and a few seconds later they'd be clapping and singing a three-part harmony, in perfect pitch. The country thrived on the power of song; the apartheid system could never have been gumbooted out without it. Music helped drive the spirit of the anti-apartheid movement and was a core element in Nelson Mandela's long walk to freedom. He once said, "It is music and dancing which makes me at peace with the world, and at peace with myself."

South Africa was the homeland of *King Kong*, the all-black stage musical I fell in love with as a street kid. In some way my own musical heartbeat was reborn in Joburg. While the recording process was going on, I brought in a small Zulu chorus group to work on a few of my old classics like "Peace Train" and "Wild World," adding a selection of drum samples and loops – minus instruments in order to comply with the broadest Islamic view (Saudi ears in particular). Luckily, I hadn't lost my touch. The singers were well blown away by the songs and arrangements.

We were unknowingly creating history by producing the first really catchy album of Islamic songs in English for Muslim kids living in the West, who up to then had been starved of their own cultural soundtrack. The children's album took its title from the song "I Look, I See."

It would be impossible to overstate how much music lit up and affected the early years of my life. It was my hope that this project would help Muslim youngsters feel good about themselves and Islam, supporting the spiritual values of their background, free from religious negativism that many were suffering post-9/11. I wanted to help restore their faith and joy in their own cultural belonging.

The photo used on the CD cover was taken by my daughter Maymanah. We gathered a group of bright-faced pupils from Islamia primary school, crammed them together, looking out of the window of our cute, whitewashed house in Hampstead Garden Suburb, necks outstretched, gazing up at colourful hot-air balloons floating across the sky (courtesy of Photoshop). The cover was bright and chirpy; the songs zappy and catchy – kids just loved it!

> *I look, I look, I look, I see*
> *I see a world of beauty*
> *I touch, I touch, I touch, I feel*
> *I feel a world around so real*
> *And everything I do*
> *I dedicate to You*
> *Cause you made me, I am for You*

A Guitar Comes Home
2002–3

AFTER SPENDING MORE time in the United Arab Emirates, I finally rented a spacious three-bedroom villa in the scenic area of Jumeirah, close to the sand beach and rippling sea. The city was fast becoming a choice place for me to retreat to and concentrate on my writing and creative work.

During the winter holidays of 2002, my wife and children came to stay for a break. Among their bags and possessions was a rather unexpected item. Muhammad, who was taking media studies in Richmond College at the time, had bought himself a black Yamaha guitar, which he brought with him from London. This was the first time an instrument like that had been in our house since I had auctioned my collection off for charity in 1981 – over twenty years earlier!

I didn't get mad with him, which I might have done during the more puritanical phase of my Muslim life. The fact that I had studied and practised Islam for almost a quarter of a century by that time meant I could breathe deep and take a few steps back.

One of the major things that helped me during my long-evolved spiritual search was the ability to expose myself to new prospects; that's what got my foot in the door of Islam in the first place. My understanding of the subject of music had increased through the study of the historical development of law and reasoning (*fiqh*); it enabled me to view the whole issue more broadly. I'd come a long way. Like Ingrid Bergman said, "Getting old is like climbing a mountain: you get a little out of breath, but the view is much better!" What I had learned enabled me to understand the following advice of the Prophet, peace be upon him:

> *Consult your heart. Righteousness is that about which the soul feels at ease and the heart feels tranquil. And wrongdoing is that which wavers in the soul and causes uneasiness in the breast, even though people have repeatedly given their legal opinion [i.e. fatwah].*[128]

It was time to be more assertive, grounded in my firmer knowledge of Islam. I was not going to be overly concerned about backchat or criticism. To go against my growing inner certainty would mean to accept being a slave to other people's opinions and ignore the light of discernment God had provided me.

Though it was true that the majority of scholars had sided with music's disallowance, I realised that a "majority" is not the same as a consensus, which carries legal imperative. As long as its prohibition was not stated clearly in the Qur'an, and as long as the hadith related to the banning of music were not unquestionable, and mostly classified as "weak," it meant that there was room for a broader view.

There are numerous authenticated sayings and recorded events that clearly showed the Prophet's allowance for song and certain expressions of music on occasions. This meant the subject was still wide open for discussion.[129] The issue of music was not as black and white as it was boldly pointed out to be by certain objectors just after I had entered through the doors of Islam. My doubts could not just be swept under the carpet anymore; there was not enough undisputed evidence to support the exclusion of music from human life and activity. The Qur'an emphasises this:

> **Ask, O Prophet, "Who has forbidden the adornments and lawful provisions God has brought forth for His servants?" Say, "They are for the enjoyment of the believers in this worldly life, but they will be exclusively theirs on the Day of Judgment. This is how We make Our revelations clear for people of knowledge."**[130]

Without placing myself on any high academic pedestal, I certainly had experienced life and knew enough to recognise the fact that music is ever present in this universe. Nature has its own magnificent songs in praise of the Creator, and everything works in perfect harmony together, whether in jungles, oceans, or deserts; birds sing, creatures howl, seas

33 | *A Guitar Comes Home*

crash, and winds whistle; stars and planets hum and hearts beat – it is all music of one kind or another.

There is no verse in the Qur'an specifically mentioning or accurately defining the word "music" (there is no such generic word in classical Arabic), and there is not a single chapter in *Sahih al Bukhari*,[131] recognised as the most authentic collection of the Prophet's sayings, that specifically deals with the subject of music (though there are chapters about so many other issues like "Eclipses," "Gifts," "Drinks," and even "Lost and Found Things"). This spoke volumes to me. Although there were some cautionary prophetic sayings about musical instruments in other collections (remembering those I fell upon earlier in the pages of that frightening red-vermillion booklet from South Africa), the absence of any clear Qur'anic prohibition obviously forced scholars to issue fatwahs – both for and against.

I was now coming round to accepting the more assertive view about music, supported by a list of historic eminent scholars. Surprisingly, this included Ibn Hazm, a formidable scholar of hadith and leading proponent of the strict Zahiri (literalist)[132] school of thought from Al-Andalus. He was known more for his religiously rigid interpretation of Islamic sharia and its strict application. It was Ibn Hazm who boldly rejected the validity of "all" sayings outlawing musical instruments.

The more I dug around, the more I uncovered.[133] For long periods of the Islamic Caliphate, down through the centuries, music and singing were present, always within certain moral limits. Early on in the history of Islamic civilisation, in the eighth century, the Abbasid caliph of the Muslim world,

Harun Al Rashid, came to power. He was a great patron of the arts, music, and literature, and his intellectual centre in Baghdad, "The House of Wisdom," boasted the largest library in the world. It was during Al Rashid's reign that *One Thousand and One Nights* was written and compiled, one of the most imaginative and influential novels ever published – and still exploited to this day by our friends in the Disney corporation.

In Al Rashid's court there was an extraordinary Muslim called Ziryab, a courtier, poet, musician, singer, astronomer, chemist, geographer, and strategist. He was sent from Baghdad to Cordoba in Spain, where he is credited as having introduced and refined Al'Oud (the lute – the father of guitars) by adding a fifth string, and had a great influence on Spanish music as well as the Andalusian music traditions of North Africa. The lute finally made its way into Europe, and the rest is history. In conclusion, the blues and rock 'n' roll probably owe Ziryab a few back royalties.[134]

All these considerations added to my growing conviction.[135] It was the Prophet's well-known saying, "Leave that which makes you doubt for that which does not make you doubt," which finally enabled me to move more towards music. I now had *more* doubt about its prohibition than its permissiveness. And God knows best.

This was a watershed moment for me. After all these years of travelling, I had reached the crossroads again. My own son had unwittingly reminded his father that it was time for him to change. Hey! Wasn't that the motif of a song I once wrote? Sons definitely have the unnerving ability to make their

33 | *A Guitar Comes Home*

fathers take another look at themselves; my own words were turning around and facing me, head-on! I also remembered what happened playing those Arabic music cassettes of Umm Kalthoum to my own ailing father, how they awakened in him the spiritual ambience of his younger days in Egypt and softened his heart towards Islam.

One quiet morning, after dawn prayers, when everyone else in the Dubai villa had gone back to their beds to grab a bit more sleep, I saw the guitar lying on the sofa. We suspiciously eyed each other for a little while . . . then I slowly approached . . . picked it up . . . and began to play. By the time I remembered where F and B7 were, it gave birth to a new song.

> I've travelled the wind East and West
> And I know I'll never, never rest
> Till I've found that happiness
> In your good company [136]

It seemed the far-sighted advice of my wise imam, Dr. Darsh, all those years ago, was now hitting its target.

But I was certainly in no rush to dash out and publicly bang my tin pan in the alley . . . not just yet. Only my close family knew what was happening; they were just starting to enjoy the sound of me playing guitar and actually singing those old "Cat" songs, lounging about in the kitchen.

I Look, I See was finally released and received with much joy and adulation. It became one of the most popular Muslim children's albums in the English-speaking world. Parents at last had a CD that they could play in their cars while their children learned the basics of faith, kindness, and a sugar-coated dose of good manners. "Your Mother" was a favourite song on the album and talks about the mercy and devotion children owe to their mothers, a fundamental teaching so often repeated by the Prophet.

One main aim of music, as I see it, is to make the world a happier, more harmonious place for us to live in together. The Beatles did it for me; I wanted to be able to do the same for others. The only other thing required to go along with a good song, however, is a better lesson plan to follow it up with. In that respect, putting poetic theory into practice is always easier said than done. The Beatles had once sung, "All You Need Is Love." Agreed. But when the group broke up, it didn't seem like they had learned those words by heart.

Looking back at my life as a singer-songwriter, no matter how great my music and albums were, there was a hunk-load of work to be done on the personal and ethical side. The truth is: my songs were better than me!

The main problem in my search for perfection was finding a lofty model to follow: Beethoven? Einstein? Brando? Lennon? It was mentioned to me once that the wise old "Tambourine Man" himself, Dylan, upon hearing that I'd become Muslim, proverbially commented, "He's finally stopped trying to be the prophet and begun to follow the Prophet."

Absolutely true, sir.

I was awoken to my own impotence as far as constructing my own private road to heaven. We may dream, but we dream alone. It takes an external *force majeure* to truly wake us up and shake off the human tendency to imagine things will get better on their own simply by keeping our eyes shut; eloquently encapsulated in a saying by Lawrence of Arabia: "All men dream: but not equally. Those who dream by night in the dusty recesses of their minds wake up in the day to find it was vanity, but the dreamers of the day are dangerous men, for they may act their dreams with open eyes, to make it possible."[137]

Writing songs for kids was a labour of love. I felt that it was something of a calling to colour their lives, and boost their natural curiosity about the world; I wanted to move them towards greater things – and what could be greater than God?

Strangely, I remember somewhere back in the blue sky days of my own childhood, I had a curious daydream that was still lingering in the back store of my mind: a picture of a smiling, white-haired old man sitting on a log in a forest, surrounded by children as he read from a storybook. The elderly man looked a lot like the Tillerman, comfortably seated on the cover of one of my most recognizable albums; or could it have been his relative, that white-bearded old Russian I once illustrated for my short children's story "Dixie"? Or perhaps it was a peculiar peek into the future – a glimpse of me?

While my CDs were lining up on the shelves of the Muslim children's market, there remained a large gap between myself and my original group of fans, those in the Western half of the world who were left alone and abandoned after my inexplicable pop-vanishing act. How could I bridge the divide? Should I record a new album of music? I simply hadn't written enough songs at that point, so that idea was quickly buried.

Then, it struck me. Having gone through the emotive process of making the VH1 documentary, I remembered how well the songs delineated my life story. I began to flirt with the idea of writing a musical again. There was no need to compose too many new songs for it; my much-cherished catalogue was tailor-made. But one irritating question kept scratching at the door: Would a pop-star-turned-pilgrim story like mine satisfy the theatrical critics? A jukebox musical was not enough for me; it needed to be on another level.

I set to work writing a synopsis. It was necessary to do something different, but many producers I spoke with had a pre-fixed, two-dimensional concept of what a "Cat" musical should look like and how best to crank it up and stuff it full of hits. From my perspective, I wanted a more spiritual experience; the audience would have to leave the theatre feeling broader, not quite the *Mamma Mia!* runaway hit most producers wanted! I was certainly not in the mood for selling my hard-earned lessons for the sake of a West End hit.

One of the benefits of this creative exercise, and many scrappy beginnings, was that it became a catalyst for me to write a whole new batch of songs. I was inspired again.

> *I dream of an open world*
> *Borderless and wide*
> *Where the people move from place to place*

> *And nobody's taking sides*
> *Maybe there's a world that I'm still to find*
> *Maybe there's a world that I'm still to find*
> *Open up O world and let me in . . .*[138]

While work on the musical was slowly inching forward, my head lost among the scrims of numerous drafts and scenarios, something really bad happened in London. It turned out to be a tipping point for me and my family. The incident was a direct result of the stigmatization that had affected many after 9/11. Since that fateful day, innocent Muslims – myself and family included – had been placed in the dock and judged guilty due to the actions of a crazed, dislocated group, to whom we bore no similarity and with whom we had no connection whatsoever.

My eldest daughter, Hasanah, was now vice-president of my organisations and was running Mountain of Light with her husband, Majid, in London. One unsuspecting day, they strolled into Lloyds Bank around the corner from our offices in Highbury. Wearing her usual modest headscarf, she deposited a three-thousand-pound cheque and requested a withdrawal of seven hundred pounds. She'd been going there on a regular basis doing company business for a couple of years, but apparently the bank teller was a temporary staff member due to an absence that day. She saw Hasanah's passport, looked at her headscarf, then noticed a tiny crease on a page in the document but said nothing about it. The lady apologized and asked them to wait one moment, then went behind the counter and made a call.

After about half an hour, police marched, heavy-booted,

into the bank, and Hasanah and Majid were physically apprehended. Majid was handcuffed, and they were both whisked away to a nearby police station and locked up in concrete, windowless cells.

My poor sweet baby Hasanah was weeping and shaking uncontrollably – nothing like this had ever happened. Her soft heart sank into depression. The world she knew, just a corner's walk away, had changed for ever.

After almost three hours in confinement, they were both released. It was all a simple "mistake." As they walked out of the station some of the officers started whistling "Moonshadow." They had obviously now discovered the connection after checking Hasanah's identity and thought it was quite a joke.

I was in Dubai at the time. Hearing over the phone about what had happened pumped me full of righteous anger. The wave of toxic prejudice that had consumed the UK's media and political clergy had resulted in a frenzy that was now percolating throughout the public streets and workplaces, spreading out of control, even to my very own front door.

Hasanah was so distraught she began to have panic attacks. I quickly arranged for the couple to fly over to Dubai. They needed to escape the horror of what they had been through and breathe the air of Muslim-friendly surroundings to recover their sanity and get back to normality. It was approaching summer, and the heat was increasing, but it was still a welcome change compared to the icy-cold, hate-filled climate that had descended upon the UK and much of Europe.

33 | A Guitar Comes Home

Unfortunately, the dark episode had a long-term effect on my daughter's psychological state. She could never be in a small, confined space from that day on.

The family's feelings were summed up by her statement to the press at the time, "My husband and I were born and raised in Britain, but it doesn't feel like home anymore."

On Stage Again
2003–4

THE FIRST THING one should learn in the music business is never to believe your own publicity. In my case, that lesson was even more needful. I thought long and hard about returning to front of stage, and the obvious dangers it would bring in terms of baroque applause and adoration. But if I didn't, the alternative would have been to allow others of less good intent to fill that blank space with untrue characterisations of me. Continual attempts to damage my reputation have been devised, again and again, from simple snide remarks to libellous headlines. It was no longer about the desire to satisfy my ego; there was a serious and important job to do in conveying a deeper understanding about the central heart of Islam's message. And I was probably best placed, in my still privileged position, to try to do that.

*

One of the things that helped distract Hasanah and Majid from the bank incident was the up-and-coming anniversary of Islamia primary school. It had been twenty years since we opened the door to the first class of thirteen children. Little ponytailed Hasanah and her bubbly sister, Asmaa, had been in that inaugural team of brave three- and four-year-old cadets who entered the large Victorian mansion's doors in Brondesbury Park.

The school had fought and won a tough battle with the British government, placing it on equal footing with Christian and Jewish schools – and by doing that, making history. We proved that Muslim schools were able expertly to deliver the British curriculum as well as providing a family-friendly environment where Islam was appreciated and valued. Our teachers were bringing up moderate young British Muslims who loved their faith and culture, without diminishing their root-sense of belonging to their country of birth.

We decided it was time to celebrate and put on a show. The famous Royal Albert Hall in South Kensington was booked for the big occasion. It would be called "The Night of Remembrance."

Many moons before, I had stood in that claustrophobic bowl, wagging my head in wild abandon, eyes tightly closed, trying to ignore the thousands of eyes penetrating the hollow abyss of that monumental, red-velveted, royal chamber of horrors. That was how much I had once loathed being on stage, especially in the round, in old "Albert." The fear of making a musical mistake haunted both me and my band – they knew the hell I'd let loose if they bummed.

Times had certainly changed. I was spiritually confident;

it was even possible for me to open my mouth and casually chat as well as sing. One problem remained: I was still a perfectionist. So old bossy-boots of "Majikat" days would probably test everybody to examine the limits of their competence again.

While Hasanah and Majid were busy preparing for the big event, designing posters and leaflets, organising rehearsals and finalising the list of artists and scholars, I had been selected to receive the World Social Award in recognition of my Small Kindness relief work with children and victims of war-torn countries. Previous winners included Pope John Paul II, Steven Spielberg, Sir Paul McCartney, and Luciano Pavarotti. Naturally, I was pretty floored to be counted among such esteemed company – particularly alongside a Beatle.

The ceremony took place in Hamburg's Musikhalle in July 2003. I arrived with Fawziah and our tall, handsome son, Muhammad, who walked beside me down the regal red carpet.

It was a star-studded night, with Morgan Freeman, Lech Wałęsa, Michael Douglas, Robin Gibb, and Christopher Reeve (former star of *Superman*), now confined to a wheelchair, all sharing the stage. Also on the podium was a young, paraplegic, Iraqi boy who had lost both of his lower limbs in the war and who bravely strode on using his newly donated artificial legs to receive a special award. The presentation was made by Mikhail Gorbachev.

One of the most moving moments of the evening took place in the green room just before the show started. I saw Christopher Reeve in his wheelchair and went over to introduce myself, hesitatingly: "Cat Stevens, remember?" He smiled broadly. As he could not move easily or respond much, I leaned down close to the level of his ear and sang a couple of verses of "Moonshadow." Christopher's spirit was to pass away one year later.

Not long after, I discovered that Christopher was an ardent follower of Paul Brunton, the man whose book *The Secret Path* changed my life during my internment, when I was physically wrecked and immobilised in hospital back in 1969.

> *Oh, if I ever lose my legs*
> *I won't moan and I won't beg*
> *Yes, if I ever lose my legs,*
> *Oh if . . .*
> *I won't have to walk –*
> *No more*[139]

It looked like the musical waves I had been making were rippling across the pond. An interesting call came in from Steve Buckingham, a producer who ran a renowned label called Vanguard and Sugar Hill, Dolly Parton's label, in Nashville. He had heard my recent children's recordings and was extremely eager to link up with me. After a few transatlantic telephone calls we arranged to meet in London.

He and his boss, Lawrence Welk Jr., flew in on a private jet and arrived at the steps of our humble north London hotel in perfectly uncreased shirts, cowboy boots, gold signet rings and snazzy, chiseled haircuts: the Nashville "sheen" was all over them. I can't recall if Steve and Lawrence actually parked two diamond-saddled chestnut stallions outside the lobby – but that was the sort of southwest, Arizonan aristocracy they seemed to belong to.

Steve knew I was very slowly returning to making music and made one heck of a plea for me to fly to Nashville and make a record with him. I was showing interest. As they had come so far I treated them to an earful of newly recorded versions of "Peace Train" and "Wild World," which I'd produced in Joburg. The pulsating world music, soundscape of African percussion, and Zulu singers made them even more excited. I told Steve I'd be in touch if I decided to get serious about making another mainstream album.

"The Night of Remembrance" gig took place on 20 October 2003, on Hasanah and Majid's wedding anniversary. The excitement was building as the crowds entered the high-domed splendour of the hall, with its gilded velvet seats and deluxe royal boxes: truly a model jewel of Victorian swank. Many Muslims had never stepped into a music venue before. This would be a very new experience for us all. The stage set was draped gracefully by six long, banner-like projector screens backed with an enormous curtain of twinkle-star lights, as dreamy as the soft vocal praises of God that echoed around the five-thousand-seat amphitheatre.

The lights dimmed, and the audience fell to a hush. Out of the darkness a young girl in a spotless white scarf and school uniform was spotlighted on stage and spoke eloquently:

A long time ago, way before my time,
Some babies were born into this world.

Their parents looked at them and said,
"Now, which school are we going to send you to?"
The babies didn't really know what to say . . .
But somewhere, someone had an idea:
And so Islamia School was born.

What followed was a divinely breathtaking evening, unlike anything ever seen by the community before. There were short talks from two charismatic, thought-provoking young Muslim intellectuals – Shaikh Hamza Yusuf (previously, Mark Hanson) and Dr. Tim Winter (both converts, from San Francisco and Cambridge, England, respectively). A variety of international artists took over the bulk of the program, including a Muslim rap group called Native Deen from the US, Indonesia's vocal harmony group Qatrunada, Khalid Belhrouzi from Morocco, and my South African protégé Zain Bhikha, backed by a Zulu choral group. They gave powerful performances of world music that inspired and enthralled the awestruck audience.

This was my first professional performance on stage since the historic Sarajevo concert, and it inevitably brought back the butterfly feelings from the old days. This time I had full cognisance of my role as an arts ambassador of Islam in the West. The last time I actually stood on the stage of the Albert Hall was back in 1974, on the "Bamboozle" tour, with my band and a nineteen-piece orchestra, conducted by Del Newman. Thirty years on, my only backing was some discreet playback and a live solo percussionist named Ged Lynch, kindly loaned by my good old friend and world-music lover Peter Gabriel. During my performance I sang "I Look, I See,"

"God Is the Light," "Peace Train," and "Tala'al Badru 'Alayna." Throughout the rest of the show, I acted as host and introduced the artists.

My gradual re-entry and descent into the mainstream of music and live appearances were now becoming quite evident. It was through Peter Gabriel's office that another invitation came, to attend Nelson Mandela's 46664 AIDS benefit concert in Cape Town, South Africa, on 29 November 2003. This would be quite a cyclopean step. I had not yet made the transition to playing my guitar on stage. "What shall I sing?" I gulped. Then the idea flashed: the recordings I had done in Joburg with the Zulu chorus could be perfect. "Wild World" – with extra words in Zulu – was already written.

Peter arranged for me to rehearse in his Real World studios in Box, not far from Salisbury's historic Stonehenge. The plan was to use his own band's percussion and drums, with Peter doing a duet with me. It sounded great. He suggested we use additional vocal support from the famous South African Soweto Gospel Choir. Sorted!

The historic benefit concert was a hair-raising affair for me. Forty thousand people in the audience going absolutely bonkers at the Green Point Stadium, Cape Town, with a star-studded list of performers: Robert Plant, Queen, Baaba Maal, Youssou N'Dour, Bono and the Edge from U2, Johnny Clegg, Jimmy Cliff, Anastacia, Beyoncé, Dave Stewart, and many others. Most importantly, the whole event was presided over by its iconic host, Nelson Mandela himself, with the help of old Father Christmas's friend Bob Geldof.

The stadium was absolutely colossal. As soon as I entered, I really thought I'd made a big mistake and just wanted to hide away in one of the little hospitality tents backstage until it was all over. But the cause was so good, so important: the HIV/AIDS problem had hit South Africa harder than any other country, and there needed to be more awareness. And what better person to honour than Nelson Mandela, a master of peace-making and reconciliation? So there was much to help propel me.

The moment came when Peter announced my name: "Cat Stevens . . . Yusuf!" That boomed over the massive PA stacks, followed by a volcanic eruption of deafening applause. The roof – had there been one – would certainly have been blown off and might have landed on Table Mountain! As a symbol of my ascension from the deep well of my long musical *in absentia*, the reception was utterly ecstatic. Slowly, I walked on, wireless mic in hand and began to sing, "la, la, la, la, la, la, la . . ." When the crowd realised it was "Wild World," they went even more ballistic. I sang some of the words in Zulu, instead of "Oh, baby, baby" they became "Oh, bana, bana" ("Oh, child, child"). The closing words of the song – "Take good care" – were given a new, chilling meaning by the theme of HIV/AIDS.

Universal Records, now fully animated and actively working my catalogue, had finally released a deluxe *Very Best of . . .* compilation album that included a bonus DVD of concert footage from 1971. We were flying high in the charts again. Concurrently, Sheryl Crow was also having a big hit with a cover of my song "The First Cut Is the Deepest," slightly more "countryfied" and following on from the already-successful 1977 cover version by Rod Stewart.

All this was highly gratifying, but I was thinking about other things – a stage musical, for instance. A Swedish second cousin of mine, Sissela Kyle, a popular actress and comedienne in her own right, linked me up with Anders Albien, a successful director in Stockholm. We talked about ideas and recruited dramatist and TV writer Stephen Plaice, from south London. Spending long, drawn-out, tea-and-coffee-filled days in the secluded lounge of the Brondesbury Park Hotel, glancing occasionally at the graceful leaves blowing on the trees outside the window, we bounced off each other's ideas and play-acted the scenes until, finally, an initial draft was complete.

Anders booked the Jerwood Space rehearsal rooms, not far from Shakespeare's Globe Theatre by the Thames, and we handpicked a cast to workshop the show. The lead part – me – was played by Ramin Karimloo, then the main understudy for *The Phantom of the Opera*. A small audience, invited to witness the first production run-through, loved it and applauded vigorously. Unfortunately, I didn't. The story had dramatically altered from the original subject, the inner exploration of a restless soul (like Siddhartha, imitating Cat Stevens) searching for the blissful state beyond the veil of illusions, assisted by his telepathic alter-ego, Moonshadow. It had gradually morphed into a shallow tale of a confused pop singer, bulldozing through an unlikely crop of characters and psychics, as he struggles with his ego and a near-death experience, before "seeing the light" and returning to his childhood sweetheart and parents' waiting arms.

Not too pleased with the result, I decided to put the musical idea to bed and say, "Nighty-night," until I came up with something better.

> *When a door is closed,*
> *Somewhere, there's a door that's opening*
> *When a light goes out*
> *Somewhere, there's a light that's shining*
> *God made everything just right* [140]

Prrr...Grrr
2004

NOT TO GET too swept away by all the chirpy noise surrounding my music revival, I decided to refocus on Small Kindness charity work. The war in Iraq was creating unprecedented numbers of fatherless families and had wrecked the whole country's social infrastructure. There were more orphans than ever relying on handouts and external support. We urgently needed to expand the donation base. Many Muslim friends in the States wanted to help, so we prepared to open a new zonal office in Los Angeles.

I had met a friendly young American, Mohammed Khan, at an Islamic Society of North America conference, who had excellent connections among NGOs in New York and Washington. In the late spring, Mohammed arranged an introductory meeting for Small Kindness in the UN building, where I gave a short talk to UN reps and a bunch of other nice, rose-faced people affiliated with a host of different charities.

We then flew to Washington to meet the head of USAID (United States Agency for International Development), Andrew S. Natsios (a fellow Greek), one of the top guys in charge of a multi-billion budget for US foreign aid and development. We explained our work in the Balkans, and he seemed genuinely willing to help.

While on the rounds in the capital, I visited the White House office of President Bush's Faith-Based & Community Initiatives project. David Caprara, the director, was a kind-natured Christian gentleman who seemed to foster a huge hope for bringing peacemakers of different faiths together.

We sat down and shared a welcome (but recognizably American) cup of tea, and a suggestion was made to arrange an audience with President Bush himself. I felt uncomfortable. The president, with the key support of Tony Blair, had initiated the bombing of Iraq, despite worldwide protests. The ever-increasing list of fatalities didn't look like it would end prettily, nor anytime soon. My conscience was extremely uneasy. So I apologized as politely as possible, explaining my moral dilemma, and asked to be excused.

David grimaced visibly as those words fell out of my mouth. He probably knew much better than I did what the consequences might be of my undiplomatically bold-faced rebuff. I didn't quite comprehend its impact at the time, but that decision seemed to have rather ominous repercussions that would surface later that year.

Back home in London, I started writing new songs. I now had my very own warm-woody Spanish guitar that I'd picked up on Denmark Street, along with a great-sounding German

AER acoustic amp. My brother David had left his cheap domestic Yamaha organ at our house, and it had all sorts of ridiculously unrealistic-sounding instruments and rhythms on it. I loved it! Obviously, I had missed out on the synth boom of the eighties, so I had a bit of a party trying out all those one-press sounds and string-and-rhythm combinations – even a barking effect, a legacy from the "Was Dog a Doughnut?" days.

I was messing about on it one day when I fell upon a catchy, Latin-based chord sequence sounding like a brassy, street band Mexican fiesta-like ruckus. The lyrics practically wrote themselves, proving to me that I could still summon up words that carried a good message without any cringing "preachy" overtones.

> *I like to take a walk out in the midday*
> *Checking life out in the park*
> *I like to take a walk out in the midday*
> *But avoid city after dark* [141]

Now that I had a wider selection of song material, I picked up the phone to Steve Buckingham in Nashville. I wished to take up his offer to work on an album. Steve was jubilant. He told me he'd pull everything together: a couple of weeks with the top session guys in the best studio in town.

The date was fixed: 21 September 2004. Little did I know the deep symbolism of that particular date, the dreaded autumn equinox, when the north prepares for the long evenings of darkness that winter brings, as nights get longer and days shorter. To the ancient Greeks, the September equinox marks the return of their mythical goddess Persephone back to the darkness of the underworld, where she is reunited with her husband, Hades.

The metaphor of light turning to darkness was more than coincidental. What happened to me and my daughter on our way to Nashville was one day and night to remember . . . actually, to forget.

I had decided to bring twenty-one-year-old Maymanah with me, as not only would she enjoy the trip but she was also pretty nifty with a Nikon camera. After quite a few tiring hours on the Boeing 747, we at last approached the East Coast. As we did so, the captain unexpectedly announced something about "heavy traffic." We were being diverted to make an emergency stop in Bangor, Maine. The plane veered off course and soon touched down in a rather eerie-looking airport, with a large scattering of grey-painted military planes parked conspicuously on the tarmac. Almost immediately, the door opened and seven tall, blue-uniformed FBI officers boarded and surrounded my daughter and me.

"Is your name Yusuf Islam?"

"Yes." I hesitantly affirmed.

"Do you mind coming with us and answering a few questions?"

Was there a choice? My heart began jumping, and Maymanah's face turned aspirin-white. This was to be the beginning of my "nightmare in Bangor."

We have all seen badly produced films; fortunately, most of them are quickly forgotten. The drama we found ourselves in was like some lousy Hollywood thriller movie. And yet in this particular one, I was the star! Nobody ever let me in on the plot, let alone the script. Wait a minute! I thought to myself, *Am I supposed to be the baddie?*

Three agents escorted me, separating me from my daughter, marching past the corridors and immigration offices of the airport, across a shiny, speckled cement floor (the only nice thing I can remember) into a private room. They began interrogating me. It seemed like a terrible mistake. My ticket said "Washington, D.C."!

The FBI men kept asking me to spell my name. "Y-U-S-U-F," I patiently repeated. They looked puzzled. "Are you sure that's the only way you spell it?"

The officers treated me respectfully enough, but one impenetrable question – like some uncontrollable monkey – was somersaulting around in my mind: Why? Nobody was willing or able to answer that question.

"What's this all about?" I asked.

They knew who they were dealing with and what their orders were – which was more than I had to go on. They asked me to take an oath and answer more general questions, which I did. They printed the statement and asked me to sign it . . . which I did. Then the officer said, "Sorry, sir. You are inadmissible."

I felt sick. At least in the past I could recognise my own Moonshadow. Could there be a ghostly "double" hiding within their database system? Was it a mix-up of names? I didn't understand. They were not under any kind of obligation to give me a reason; the green visa waiver form I had so neatly filled in had effectively denied me any right of appeal or to receive answers. It was only after the inspector of immigration read a long-winded legal reference number that he

35 | *Prrr . . . Grrr*

mentioned some implication of "terrorism." No further details necessary.

Good God! Was this the same planet I'd taken off from? I was devastated. A couple of months earlier I had been having meetings in the heart of Washington with top officials from the Faith-Based & Community Initiative, talking positively about support for my charity. Had I changed? No.

What had changed was the newly introduced, highly controversial "No Fly List" profile. I was one of the earliest victims of this new "Big Brother" character-rating system, hastily imposed. Even Senator Edward Kennedy was on it!

The most upsetting thing, naturally, was being parted from my daughter for the following thirty-three hours, not knowing how she was or when or where we might see each other again. My phone was confiscated; I couldn't contact my family either.

Cut to Nashville.

Dolly Parton, Steve Buckingham, and the studio musicians were waiting (probably with a yellow ribbon tied around a Gibson guitar neck), totally clueless about the situation, all ready to welcome me, blissfully unaware of my ordeal. This was beginning to look like a VH1 replay.

Meanwhile, I was led outside into a waiting SUV, uncomfortably squeezed between two heavy-duty FBI officers for a two-hundred-mile drive to Boston. We changed vehicles three times during the grueling five-hour ride. When we arrived at an airport hotel, I was escorted and confined to a suite where all internal doors had been removed. I was permitted to order room service and was shown the bed where I was expected to sleep – which was nigh on impossible

CAT ON THE ROAD TO FINDOUT

with four armed officers in sight, playing cards and chatting in the adjoining room. But I was so wrecked and exasperated, somehow I did.

The next morning, I cautiously opened my eyes. Was it all just a terrible dream? I switched on the TV in my confined hotel room at Boston Logan airport: gross! I was frontline news on every channel. Film of me in a beige "spy-looking" raincoat, being escorted down the stairs of the plane by FBI agents, was repeatedly shown throughout the morning. The word had spread like a plume cloud from a mighty atom bomb: everybody was aware of my ill-fated journey. Uh-oh! It was meant to be a low-profile trip, due to my fear that it might raise too much hype about my return to the studio. Media attention was the last thing I wanted. It seemed God wanted otherwise.

Finally, the reel of the B-movie spun to an end and the lights came up. I was relieved of my anguish, put on a plane, and neatly packaged off back home to Britain. Mercifully, my daughter was scheduled to arrive the same day, on a separate flight.

One of the most unexpectedly endearing memories of that whole unfathomable drama happened as we landed at Heathrow. The two US agents assigned by Homeland Security to accompany me were getting ready to say goodbye as I got down my cabin luggage. They couldn't quite believe it when – as per protocol – a Scotland Yard officer boarded the plane to escort me off and through immigration – a Pakistani officer wearing a perfectly wound white turban and long black beard!

"As-salamu 'alaykum," he said in a warm brotherly tone.

"Wa 'alaykum as-salam," I replied.[142]

35 | Prrr . . . Grrr

A manic mob of press were waiting past security, waving their hands frantically to attract my attention so they could stick a mic up my nose and photograph me.

"What do you have to say about this, Mr. Islam?"

"Half of me wants to smile; half of me wants to growl," was my reply. I tried to repress my anger, suggesting, "It must be a case of mistaken identity . . . a mix-up of names." After all, the FBI officials asked me to spell my name enough times (I failed to mention how many autographs I'd signed for the adoring immigration officers at Bangor airport).

The explanation given by the US authorities to the media, however, was less than generous and offered masses of room for speculation and doubt. The insinuations linking me to alleged support for terrorist groups must have been leaked (courtesy of an Israeli database, I would imagine) and inevitably were included in the flurry of questions and the speculative articles to follow.

"It's said that you were refused on grounds of national security. What do you have to say about that?" bawled one journalist.

"It's crazy," I replied. "Everybody knows me from my charitable work and now there have to be explanations. But I'm glad I'm home."

Another correspondent pressed me further to elaborate, "What do you mean?"

"People make mistakes," I continued, "and I hope that that's what this will turn out to be – a big mistake."

The sentiment was mirrored not long after by Jack Straw, the foreign secretary, then in New York, meeting with US secretary of state Colin Powell. The discussion was filmed as part of a fly-on-the-wall news item. As they walked on the White House lawn, Mr. Straw turned to Mr. Powell and said the action "shouldn't have happened."

True, Mr. Powell later confirmed, "We have no charges against him. We have nothing that would be actionable in courts, or in the courts of the UK, I'm sure. But it is the procedure that we have been using to know who is coming into the country, know their backgrounds and interests, and see if we believe it is appropriate for them to come in."[143]

Really, Colin? How could you get something like this so wrong?

All forms of terrorism and injustice, including 9/11, are as inimical to my faith as a Muslim as was the bombing of innocents in Vietnam or Iraq. They had just sent home the man who had received the World Social Award for humanitarian relief work helping children, as well as having just been nominated for the Man of Peace Award by Nobel laureates. What kind of mixed message was this?

Then the penny dropped. I suddenly remembered the invitation to meet President Bush, which I had politely declined ... Could that have been the reason for my deportation? A vendetta? *No! Don't be silly, Yusuf.* But as Mikhail Gorbachev quite rightly said while handing me the Man of Peace award, "Every person who takes a critical stance to make the world a better place has a difficult life."

I was just so happy to return home, as were my family to receive me. They had been worried silly, watching the non-stop barrage of news over the previous thirty hours. The only negative aspect of being back in London was having to

35 | *Prrr . . . Grrr*

scramble through the journalists and photographers hanging around our front door twenty-four/seven.

Thankfully, some commentators and TV personalities took a lighter view of it. Jon Stewart, on his *Daily Show*, quipped: "It's a real success story in the war on terror. You know, we finally got the guy that wrote 'Peace Train.'" David Letterman on the *Late Show* chimed in as well: "Yes, Martha Stewart is going to jail and Cat Stevens is being deported. Man, I feel so much safer now."

Sometime later, Jack Straw said that he'd heard from the US chargé d'affaires's office in London and the advice was that I should apply for a "visa" and arrange an interview at which point any issues could be hopefully cleared up. In the meantime, he claimed he'd continue to pursue my case energetically.

Not to miss a beat, my solicitors engaged a US legal firm to investigate and, if necessary, prepare to sue the US government for this irrational and embarrassing act. However, their advice was that Homeland Security would invoke the defence of sovereign immunity. According to the Federal Tort Claims Act,[144] the US government is not liable when any one of its agents commits the torts of assault, battery, false imprisonment, false arrest, malicious prosecution, abusive process, libel, slander, misrepresentation, etc., etc.

Oh! I see. Me thinkest . . . better just get a visa.

Sometime later, I decided to write and record my version of the whole no-fly drama in a song, recorded with the help of Paul McCartney, Dolly Parton, Alison Krauss, Holly Williams (granddaughter of Hank), and the Royal Opera House singers. The song was called "Boots and Sand," a take-off of those spaghetti western movies we all loved. Jesse Dylan directed the video, which we filmed in the Californian desert – I was kindly permitted into the US, because by then, of course, I had my very own B1 multiple visa.

> *I was travelling boots and sand,*
> *High bound for miracle-land*
> *Met a man called Buckingham*
> *He said, "Jo! Won't you join our band?"*
> *Nickel jangled in the jukebox,*
> *Bird o' Nashville sang!*
>
> *So I carried on the long, long road*
> *To a place, where we'd been told*
> *All your records turn to gold*
> *Birthland of rock 'n' roll*
> *As we reached the border*
> *Seven sheriffs arrive*
> *Me 'n' my gal,*
> *Saddled outside!*
>
> *Sheriffs: "Is your name this?"*
> *Me: "I guess it is."*
> *Sheriffs: "You're on our 'no song' list."*
> *Me: "O no sir, no! This can't be so!"*[145]

An Other Cup
2006

THE FLIGHT FROM Heathrow to Dubai took about seven hours. I was beginning to travel between the two bases regularly on Emirates, which was fast becoming the choicest "halal" airline (not to mention being sponsors of my local Highbury football team, Arsenal!).

The Gulf was beginning to feel more like a second home to me; it was a place where the family could enjoy a relaxing time away from the stifling pressures of Islamophobia in the UK. Hasanah and Majid had been so shaken by the obscene bank fiasco they were now contemplating leaving. So I offered them the villa in Jumeirah, for them to live and stay as long as they wanted. It would be a welcome relief: clear skies and daily sunshine, no double-takes at women wearing a scarf in shops or banks (in fact, there were separate lines in banks reserved for ladies who preferred to be more discreet). Lots of Qur'anic radio stations – and even halal McDonald's burgers! It was a spiritually scrumptious new world.

The US no-fly episode still felt something like an irritable pebble in my shoe, but it had plus sides; it had raised my profile considerably. Reenergised, I returned to the idea of recording a new album with more determination. Picking up the guitar after so many years made me feel just like I did when I first began to learn chords back in the sixties; I was like an amateur with no fear and nothing to lose, enjoying writing songs again. A powerful gush of new musical ideas poured out of me – more than enough for an album.

It was time to go into the studio. But I needed help. A guy called Rick Nowels contacted me, a well-experienced, Grammy-award-winning songwriter and producer from the US, who'd worked with Madonna, Dido, John Legend, and many others. We arranged to meet in London. I liked Rick's gentle nature, and he seemed to be a fan of sorts; his blond hair and almost McCartney-ish round face were instantly trustable – he made me feel comfortable. Rick was a lover of melody, and that was certainly my passion too. I needed that in my new recordings, as many music "patrol guards" would be on watch, scrutinising whether or not I still had it.

We decided to try a test. A studio was booked in Wembley, London, and I dusted down an old, unreleased demo of a song written and recorded back in 1968, called "Greenfields, Golden Sands." Laying down an electric piano first onto a looped percussion click-track, I then added a vocal. It was warm, crystal-clean, and translucent; Rick brought to the fore my softer vocal approach and gave a beautiful dewy freshness to the lyrics.

One day we'll all realise,
I'm not the only one
Just raise your eyes up
And you'll be gone

Those words contained another mysterious ripple of John Lennon's tranquilizing dream. We were both yearners in search of a more peaceful world, staring skyward and singing, "I'm not the only one," in unison from different corners of space at different altitudes and times. When I heard those exact words repeated in his famous anthem "Imagine" three years after I wrote the song, it seemed quite spooky.

I was looking forward to working with Rick. There was no doubt we'd make some good music together. Having been out of circulation for so long, I left it up to him to choose the musicians and the studio, as I had with Paul Samwell-Smith all those years ago. The recording process had certainly gone through changes since then; digital computer technology had transformed the experience beyond analogue recognition. I needed to cross over the old drawbridge and understand how to enter this new, fragmented, digital environment. You can imagine how cheering it was for me to be informed by one of the pioneering tech geniuses, some years later, that the very first song Apple converted to MP3 was "Father and Son"! Apparently, Steve Jobs was a huge Cat fan.[146]

Rick booked a few weeks of sessions in Mayfair Studios near scenic Primrose Hill and introduced me to Pete Adams (on keyboards), Ian Thomas (on drums), John Themis (on bass and guitars), and Luís Jardim (on percussion). It was like being acquainted with a new family; instant relationships formed. I made sure Alun Davies came along too, knowing he'd bring that special, cozy Welsh ambience. And it soon felt like home.

Rick and the guys loved my slightly erratic, paintbrush approach, intrigued by how intricately my studio skills and arrangement ideas slowly shaped the musical vision, bit by bit, and decorated each song until everything was all mixed and framed together.

The songs were mostly new, but I also re-dusted some old favourites: "I Think I See the Light" was picked out of the dustbin of *Mona Bone Jakon*; we gave it a Ramsey Lewis R & B feel, more bluesy with a cool, Delta-sounding brass part. "The Beloved" was the newest, probably the most spiritually themed song on the album, to which Youssou N'Dour added a wildly inspirational, ad-libbed chant in Senegalese. Alun's gentle picking complemented me on my guitar for "Maybe There's a World," very seventies, like many of my "eyes-closed" lyrics, dreamily yearning for a would-be world without borders – a song I'd written for the musical that never happened.

As we moved into the depths of recording, a surprise invite came in from Paul McCartney's office to perform at a mini-concert in Düsseldorf for Paul's Adopt-A-Minefield charity. Whoa! In heaven's name. How could I dream of refusing a Beatle? Rick was aching to come along. I asked him to play that familiar-looking Hofner bass; Alun accompanied me on acoustic.

The invitation-only gig was held by the side of the flowing Rhine River at the Sheraton hotel ballroom before a crowd of suited, wealthy German businesspeople and their plus ones. During rehearsal we ran through "Where Do the Children Play?" and tried out some of our recently recorded songs. That's when we discovered that "Maybe There's a World" dovetailed perfectly into "All You Need Is Love."

People were sitting around large circular tables, covered by sparklingly white tablecloths and chintzy cutlery, their faces glowing by candlelight. As we played through our set list, Paul's face suddenly lit up as we began to sing "All You Need Is Love." He was not expecting that! We called him on stage to join in, which he did, to the audience's mug-swinging, Germanic delight. We ended the night with "Let It Be." It was a phenomenal event for me; I got to feel a little like John must have, shoulder to shoulder on one mic with Paul doing close harmonies. What a blast.

While many long-term fans were ecstatic about my return, I needed to do some serious explaining to the Muslim world about my reasoning for picking up the guitar and making a record again. The music industry was linked with carnal excess and widely shunned as "un-Islamic," so the impact of my decision to make music would be difficult for traditionalists to understand without any commentary.

My job was twofold: first, to win back my musical followers and confirm who I really was beneath all the piled-up trash that the media had lobbed over me; second, to remove the suspicions in some Muslim minds that I had somehow left Islam by writing and singing again.

One particular song I recorded on the new album seemed a perfect response to both. "Don't Let Me Be Misunderstood" was a cover of a song by one of my all-time favourite artists, Nina Simone, who had definitely influenced me. She was undoubtedly the greatest female jazz, blues, and protest singer of those turbulent years, a powerful voice in the Black civil rights movement of America and a musical genius. The song stated my innocence and purity of intention; ultimately, it was a prayer to the Lord of the universe, asking for help.

Finding a name for the album took some time. Finally, I fell upon the symbol of a "cup," which, of course, had a direct connection with *Tea for the Tillerman*. But even in its own right, the ontology of the cup was intriguing. Through my research into the place and history of music in Islamic civilisation, I discovered that the popular worldwide habit of saying, "Let's go grab a cuppa," appeared to have kicked off in Yemen in the fifteenth century, where the trend was said to have begun by Muslim devotees who wanted to keep awake and remember God in the dark, sleepy hours. From there, coffee allegedly spread to Makkah, then Cairo, and then the whole Muslim world before reaching the city of Vienna, from which most of Europe picked up the craze.

The final title of the album became *An Other Cup*. I detached "other" from "another" because of the alienation I'd received after embracing Islam. Controversies that had been circulated about me and my inner choices would obviously make some people think twice about buying the new CD – did it contain the same "Cat" they used to cuddle up to and love, or some "other"?

Universal was one of the first companies to reach out to grab the new album and offer an attractive deal. The megacorporation had already gobbled up my previous labels, Decca, Island, and A&M. They seemed hungry for more. In the end, I settled on a split-level home for . . . *Cup*, and signed deals with both Universal's Polydor label (UK) and Atlantic (US). The agreements required me to do a number of interviews and appearances. It was my first mainstream album for almost thirty years, so here was a chance to explain the reason for my unprecedentedly long sabbatical of musical exile. The BBC was evidently interested in doing a special in-concert jointly with a documentary. This was a good opportunity to set things straight.

Alan Yentob was the interviewer of the episode of *Imagine*, a one-hour, in-depth look at my life. He was extremely sharp but amiable and never seemed too bothered to shave for the camera. Alan made me feel quite relaxed in front of the lens and had obviously done a lot of homework. It was a relatively painless experience; his questions were not too uncomfortable and went some yards in restoring my faith in the media.

The concert special was filmed in the Porchester Hall in London. My wish was to create a homey "café" environment, reproducing the early, Moulin Rouge shop background. Producers loved the idea, but then went on ornamenting the vision further with their own "Eastern" touches of palm leaves, Moroccan brass lamps, and Persian samovars. Not quite the café I grew up in, but still.

The audience was made up of about two hundred family and friends sitting at tables, being served a five-course meal of musical nourishment by a distinguished, grey, more sedate, wiser "Cat" – looking more like the legendary Jedi master from *Star Wars*, Obi-Wan Kenobi, than the two-time star pin-up the world once knew.

An Other Cup was released in November 2006. I deliberately chose to only use my first name, "Yusuf," on the cover to demonstrate that I was not proselytizing or selling "Islam." Strict Muslims could also not point a finger and say I was degrading the religion through involvement in the "corrupt" business of music, as the Malaysians had done previously with *Back to Earth* . . . anyway, "Yusuf" looked and felt much more personal and friendly.

The album was received with open-hearted appreciation by the fans and media at large. Everybody warmed up to the *Cup*; the sound was sonically clean, the songs melodious and my vocal cords were still intact. People wondered where the dickens those twenty-eight years had gone.

Promotion was going to be an uphill grind, however. I was not in any mood to do the touring rounds and market myself like some new up-and-coming artist – and yet, strangely, I suppose that's what I was. So I decided to swallow my inhibitions and just get on with it. I did a minimum amount of interviews and photoshoots, though I know Universal were expecting a whole lot more.

Across the pond, the hungry Atlantic record company reps recognised that we needed to brew up something like London's "Yusuf's Café" concert experience for the US. But what about that no-fly-list issue? Time was running out, and we had to get it sorted. My solicitor arranged an appointment with the American embassy to obtain a visa for the States, remembering Jack Straw's original advice. That meant I needed to go through an interview process.

Arriving at the embassy in Grosvenor Square as scheduled, leaving my beloved mobile and car keys at the security desk, I was led by a polite guard through the main hall and into the office of a smart-suited lady who appeared quite unemotional, bordering on serious. We shook hands and sat down.

The interview that followed was probing, with many questions aimed at my role in Muslim Aid, especially the charity I had given in the Holy Land back in 1988. It seemed that this was the biggest cryptogram for her to solve. I repeated that my visit with the delegation had been purely humanitarian, to see first-hand the situation of the Palestinians and the conditions they were living under, give some immediate charity, and report back. I told her that the Israelis attempted to smear the mission by suggesting that we were supporting a group called "Hamas," whereas their name was not even born until August 1988, five months after the visit. I explained that everything was done in the full glare of the press and with the knowledge of the UK Foreign Office. The discussions didn't go much further. She posed a few more, basic questions and the meeting was at an end.

By now, US promotion deadlines were getting perilously close. We waited for a couple of weeks without indication about the status of my application. Flights needed to be booked. Through some friends and contacts, Senator Hillary Clinton's office was contacted. Very soon after that, we received the news: visa approved.

This was a turning point, nowhere near as dramatic or high-profile as the original deportation, but substantial in its implication. The good news meant that I could fulfil some desperately needed public appearances in the US to help Atlantic push the new album's release.

It was a bit scary to hear the pilot announce the plane's descent into New York's Kennedy airport. I reached for my passport and, not for the first time, checked my visa – it was still there. As the plane descended onto the tarmac, I peered out of the window to check for any signs of military vehicles. All clear. The aircraft finally heaved and halted at the gate. After the seven-hour flight, as I stepped off the gangway, an officer with gun and holster met me as soon as I exited the aircraft, and said, "As-salamu 'alaykum."

Phew! I knew from that moment that things were going to be different. The cop guided me through immigration, baggage, and customs in a zip-flash and, after only thirty minutes or so, I was in a limo speeding my way to old Manhattan. My new business manager, Marc Marot, and the Atlantic crowd must've taken a deep breath and now let out a sigh of relief. Everybody was smiling, eager to hear me play and sing in the Big Apple again.

The launch for *An Other Cup* took place at Lincoln Centre, overlooking Columbus Circle. White wintry flurries of snow gently fell outside the giant wall-to-wall window on Central Park South as two hundred or so people sat down. It was an audience of elite movers, shakers, and friends within the music world. The format for the evening would involve a relaxed interview on an antique leather couch with Nic

Harcourt, blended with a forty-minute mini-concert, which was recorded and broadcast by KCRW-FM live. People were just so excited to have me on their soil again, sounding much as I used to but with a bunch of new songs. It began:

> NIC: *You finally made it?*
> YUSUF: *Yeah. Well, this is one small step for man, and a giant step for common sense! (laughter)*

The happiness of the evening was unfortunately dampened with some melancholia, as Ahmet Ertegun, the founder of Atlantic Records, had died only three days earlier. He was one of the pioneering innovators in music history; the fact that he was originally Turkish – and a Muslim – didn't stop him from making his historic mark and promoting soul music to the whiter world. He discovered Ray Charles, Aretha Franklin, Otis Redding, Led Zeppelin, and so many talented artists. Ahmet also wrote a lot of classic R & B songs. The evening was dedicated to him.

The US didn't quite know how to respond to me. Their love for and attachment to Cat Stevens was not immediately translated into hugging and kissing Yusuf. Critics were naturally going to compare the new album with my previous work. Responding to a question about that at the time, I made it clear that I had embraced my past while keeping my feet firmly in the now: "The cup is there to be filled . . . with whatever you want to fill it with. For those people looking for Cat Stevens, they'll probably find him in this record. If you want to find Yusuf, go a bit deeper, you'll find him."

Judging by the rave reviews, it appeared that people's

bottom-line expectations were surpassed. Though sales of the album were quite decent, it wasn't a massive *Billboard* hit chart-wise, except in Germany; but it signalled a historic musical return: "the musician remains as masterfully adept at blurring distinctions between spiritual and romantic ecstasies as he is at evoking his trademark idealism in the lilting harmonies of 'Maybe There's a World.' Fans of his vintage catalogue will find intriguing riches outside the more spiritually focused works here, too."[147]

After people heard a few of my new tracks, they began to recognise I sounded pretty much like the same fella they all knew – just elevated a few floors up in the spiritual department. Unashamedly grown-up, flaunting a slightly longer and peppery-grey beard, I was less high-strung and not as tyrannical as I had been when I was last in the business. Many who now worked and toured with me must have thanked God for that.

Shamsia
2006–9

GREAT NEWS! HASANAH gave birth to a little daughter, Ariana, early in 2006. Over six years, nothing had happened for the young married couple – until Dubai. This changed everything. I had my first grandchild: a babe without nappy duties! Ah, it was fantastic and a whole new side of poo-free life and love opened up.

As our family was expanding and on the rise, so, too, was Dubai. Majid and Hasanah were now fully running the Mountain of Light operation from the offices in Media City. Our roots were beginning to settle in what was once a dry, barren, sandy landscape. Dubai was fast becoming one of the safest, most technologically advanced, dashing, and comfortable cities in the world. As well as swish air-conditioned malls and glittering new glass skyscrapers, dream villa projects were springing up all over the place.

I realised we should stop renting and buy our own piece of this Muslim-friendly desert vision.

There were lots of exquisite designs to choose from: a massively ambitious Palm Island project stretching out into the sea (big enough to view from space!), modern, arabesque villa designs, beautiful mosques with surrounding springs and meadows, even a new elite Emirates Hills section – aiming to mirror Beverly Hills in terms of value. Nice, but my taste had always been much less flashy. We put down a deposit for something more cozy.

Spending more time in Dubai opened up many opportunities; one of the great benefits was the increased space and freedom I had to think and write. I returned again to my dream of creating that elusive musical.

Late one warm, star-sprinkled night, I trawled the internet looking for inspiration. After scrolling through some old children's stories, my cursor came to rest upon an old Inuit fable. It was a short story about a crow who lived in the endless darkness of the Nordic lands. The bird flew here and there, until it discovered a dazzling land with flowers, trees, and carpet hills, bursting with gorgeous colours and hues, all happily basking in daylight under a sunny sky. On his return, after hearing the news about this miraculous, light-filled world, the local people excitedly sent the crow on a special mission to bring some of that glow back to them. As he was returning with a sample, the people started shouting enthusiastically. This startled the crow. The ball of light accidentally dropped from his beak and exploded on impact, filling the dark lands with glorious light. Alas, the crow warned them that it would only last for six months; he would have to keep returning every year. So the Inuit learned to live half the year in light and half the year in darkness.

I had found my big idea!

Working on the synopsis, I headed towards a new metaphorical adventure: a journey out of this world. The story began on a faraway night planet called Alaylia (from *layla*, the Arabic for night). A dark and devious princess (Zeena) ruled over shadowy forces (the Zalims) that had taken over the world; they bred fear and division among people, keeping them mercilessly enslaved. There were no days and only moonlight shone out of the permanently black sky.

Our young hero, Stormy, dreams of a happier place, Shamsia, the mythical world of the lost sun. After an unexpected encounter with his alter-self, a mysterious Moonshadow, Stormy discovers his purpose: to find that perfect world of light and perpetual happiness. He sets off, leaving behind his unattainable, childhood love and his hard-working parents (à la Moulin Rouge). The odd duo journey deep into an uncharted, metaphysical world where they meet a host of bizarre characters dwelling in the darkness on their quest to reach the supernatural light, in the hope of bringing it back to their family and the poor, oppressed people of the planet.

Doubtless, the plot sounded a bit post-apocalyptic, but the way our world was headed – considering the ever-increasing number of souls living and dying in poverty while battling to survive – made the underlying message totally relevant to our time:

In this world of darkness
Evil rules by night
But somewhere in the shadows, someone's seeking light!
No one loves their neighbours here, nobody has the time
No one cares for anyone else
In a world where the sun don't shine [148]

I had unwittingly stumbled into Plato's Cave,[149] one of the most profound stories ever told. The allegory is based on the Greek philosopher's thesis that most human beings are like prisoners chained inside a cave: all they see are shadows of objects on the wall in front of them, cast by puppeteers behind their heads (whom they never see). One courageous man decides to leave the cave. Not much time passes before he finds himself standing in open grounds, basking in sunlight. He can barely open his eyes due to the strength of the glare. As his eyes adjust to the light, he sees the beautiful colours of a gloriously sunny day, a strikingly blue sky, tall trees, and flowing rivers, followed by the sunset and a spectacular night, full of sparkling stars that surround a beautiful, white, glowing moon.

Rushing back to the dark shadows of the cave excitedly, he informs the dwellers about this incredible experience. Sadly, they presume that the man's dangerous walkabout must have damaged his mental reasoning; they conclude that anyone who tries to drag them from the safety of the cave should be considered an enemy and even killed. And they return to watching shadows on the wall.

Plato's allegory was retold by Hazrat Inayat Khan, one of the early spiritual pioneers in America and founder of a Sufi order. He used different words, but the meaning was similar: "pleasure is only an illusion, a shadow of happiness; and in this delusion man may pass his whole life, seeking after pleasure and never finding satisfaction."[150]

Fawziah and I made up our minds to prepare for leaving the UK and establish a new home base. After all those years of struggle, doing our best to educate and raise our children, we felt we'd managed fairly well and were now able to move on. Our second-eldest daughter, Asmaa, prepared to take over the running of the schools and charity foundation. She was extremely bright and was trained as a lawyer; we knew she was highly capable of dealing with the challenge and would run things well.

Our son Muhammad was also talented; he'd written a bunch of really interesting songs and was busy in Kensaltown Studios with producer Martin Terefe. I only got involved when he asked me, adding a little harmony or playing an organ part here or there. Soon Muhammad had finished a whole album and was looking for a stage name. He finally chose "Yoriyos." It was the Anglicized spelling of the old family surname, Georgiou.

The album was called *Bury My Heart at Wounded Knee*; it was the title of a book I had about the history of Native Americans in the late nineteenth century. Wounded Knee was the site of the last great battle with the US army. Chief Crazy Horse's heart was buried there by his parents.[151]

I was really impressed with the theme of the album, especially the conscientious nature of the songs he wrote. My son could not just write – he could sing too! The album was released by Universal Records. Whoever heard it loved his fresh frontier-country style, but the problem was that critics would inevitably want to compare him with his dad.

My sentimental love of London had not disappeared, but the place had seriously changed from the chummy old city I once knew and scrambled around, knobbly-kneed in schoolboy shorts. Now it had been invaded by an army of grey-helmeted parking meters, unsmiling policemen with guns, disastrous foreign policies, CCTV on every corner, suspicious bank clerks, official "brown" envelopes dropping in your letterbox incessantly, not to mention the cold, rainy summers. The reality that George Harrison was no longer on this planet contributed to the dismal mood too.

We had gone through all the options. A permanent move back to my father's homeland of Cyprus was possible, as we had a flat there. But Cyprus had no great understanding of Islam and in that respect bore too many similarities with the UK.[152] The island would always be there for us, but at the time, after everything we'd endured, Dubai's year-round warmth and clear skies were the preferred choice – at least for the time being.

Perhaps the move to the Arabian Peninsula – as Inayat Khan had cautioned – was just chasing an illusion, but at the time it seemed as if I had found my "Shamsia." We knew that the UAE had a strong, economically driven impetus and we would have to learn to live with a new set of irritating "norms," like obtaining residence visas on a rotating basis, blistering summers exceeding 100°F, and not being able to walk through breezy parks of autumn leaves. But the pluses outweighed the minuses as far as stress levels were concerned. Dubai's clean, family-friendly, and fairly tax-free environment made it pretty irresistible.

My creative songwriting had reached a new peak due to the work on *Moonshadow*, the musical. With endless riffs and ideas exploding out of me, I decided the simplest thing would be to record a new album. I wanted to get busy on a follow-up to *An Other Cup*, as my fans seemed ready for a refill. Many had communicated their yearning for a return to my soft, intimate acoustic guitar sound again – that seemed like a good idea to me, too.

   I began to re-immerse myself in late sixties music and started listening to artists such as Joni Mitchell, Tim Hardin, Paul Simon, James Taylor, and Carole King, as well as a few folk groups like the Dubliners. Nourished by that hugely delectable bowlful of talent, I became inspired to write a new range of songs. This was a very different approach to my previous style of writing; in the past I would naturally isolate myself from other musicians' work, to avoid being influenced. This time it was quite enjoyable to open the doors and invite them in.

   And so, the next album was acoustic and folk-oriented. Self-produced with a group of great musicians recruited by my old US friend and ex-radio-hit-picker David Spero, I made sure most of it was recorded live with few overdubs, giving the album an organic feel. We recorded at the House of Blues Studios in Los Angeles. The album's title track, "Roadsinger," was in fact a first take!

   The lyrics of that song bore a double meaning: on the face

of it, the narrative told the story of an unshaven and dustily rugged Clint Eastwood character who, on his return after a long period away, is treated as an outcast by the conventional, starchy old townsfolk. They turn their backs and slam their doors in his face as he walks down the empty main street. But once he starts to sing, an innocent child's face peeps out from behind a misty, grocery-store window, smiles, and lovingly draws the shape of a heart on the glass.

The message was pretty clear. It was a dramatization of my own story, borrowed from the vaults of those horse-whipped, grit-filled Wild West films. It enacted my return into the music industry (the old boom town), walking past a Wanted poster nailed on an oak tree, displaying the notorious baddie (me, courtesy of *Teaser and the Firecat*'s pin-up cover) in my new status as a no-fly-list outlaw.

> *Roadsinger came to town*
> *Long cape and hat*
> *People stood and stared*
> *Then closed their doors as he passed*
> *He strolled the empty street*
> *Kids banged on tin cans*
> *Then the panting dogs began to bark*
> *As the Roadsinger sang*

Universal decided to release "Roadsinger" as a double A-side single, coupled with my other western-tinged biopic song, "Boots and Sand," supported by a Beatle, Paul McCartney, and Dolly Parton, as a teaser for the new album.

*

Roadsinger was released in May 2009, back on Island. Without my realising it, the album was a hint of what lay ahead . . . yes, back on the road again. My first promotional show was in the US at the El Rey Theatre in Los Angeles. An exclusive venue with a very limited capacity made it the "gig-to-be-seen-at." Packed with industry faces and a smattering of film stars as an invitation-only showcase, it was my first West Coast performance in over thirty years. The backdrop was an enlarged image of my VW peace van, and the excitement of the night was reminiscent of my first shows at the Troubadour. There was a warmth flowing from the audience I hadn't felt for a long time. I began the cozy set with "Welcome Home," a befitting song from my new album:

> *Saw a sign on the path: "All Seekers this way"*
> *A fairy sat and laughed, and threw a petal my way*
> *As I neared the bridge, two soldiers stood and stared*
> *"No one passes by us but, hey! You're welcome here."*

In London, later that same year, I was asked to perform at Island Records' Fiftieth Birthday Party at the Shepherd's Bush Empire. Again, it was very much an industry occasion; my old record company guru Chris Blackwell was there, as was Paul Samwell-Smith. The Basing Street family was reunited in celebration of the "pink label" that had launched some of the most interesting, non-homogenous artists and groups of the seventies. My son was also on the bill with his rock fusion band, Noxshi. Here we were, father and son, playing on the same stage – who would have thunk it? Bono and the Edge made a special appearance, Bono introducing me with a list of one-line epithets: "A seeker. A troubadour. A pilgrim. A poet. A guitar picker. A natty dresser. A singer and writer of some of the best songs ever written. A serious Cat."

The floor shook with excitement. As I came on there was an incredible roar. Wow! It was such an emotionally packed night, it almost made me think twice about leaving London. Everybody melted when I sang "Father and Son," with people commenting that they couldn't believe how much I sounded like . . . er, myself.

Before leaving the UK and strolling off into the sunrise, I decided to widen the range of my audience; I felt I'd done enough small-circle industry gigs. This time I would do a limited tour in a few handpicked cities for the public. Though it would be my official farewell to old Blighty tour – and thirty years since my last show at Wembley – it was more realistically like saying "Hello" again to my loyal fans.

The four-city tour was rightly called "Guess I'll Take My Time . . ." After Dublin, Liverpool, and Birmingham, all the glitches had been worked out and we had a superb, emotionally charged show. The Royal Albert Hall was the final grandstand. Walking off stage at the end of the final encore, I felt I had physically and psychologically said my goodbyes to London.

Boxing up all our possessions for the UAE was a tedious task but helped me to rediscover long-lost tapes and keepsakes that had been hidden, forgotten or just buried deep within the dark recesses of my disorganised drawers; it was a bit like being handed back some lost memory cells. Fawziah even recovered a metal trunk full of clothes her mother had given her when we got married – still ironed.

Moving house (and country) gave me a renewed lease of life and energy. The fact that I had now reached what most people consider the age of retirement (being sixty-two at that point) was purely coincidental. I knew it was time to free myself from the chores of running the trusts and schools and hand it over to the next generation. As well as my daughter Asmaa, who had now married, Muhammad and Aminah, our two youngest, would remain in the UK, and became trustees. Aminah had one more year until she finished her university studies, then she planned to come out and join us.

Hasanah and Majid had prepared a big welcome for us at the villa. Oh, what a relief it was to finally step through the door into our new, toy-filled home and hug our two excited little granddaughters, Ariana and Liyana (the latest cutie). The expanding Islam family was, in some way, following the tradition of the Prophet, peace be upon him, and migrating to a friendly and welcoming city to settle and freely practise our beliefs.

> **As for those who emigrated in the cause of God after being persecuted, We will surely bless them with a good home in this world. But the reward of the Hereafter is far better, if only they knew.**[153]

In the Arabian Gulf, my thoughts and view of life moved to higher planes. Ignoring the rapidly constructed and slightly overcrowded city skyline, what struck me was the endlessly clear sky, displaying the blurred, patriarchal sun and crisp motherly moon, daily and nightly majestically dominating the ever-shifting dunes of the desert; their constant presence seemed to clear up my cluttered mind. Maybe that is one of the reasons so many of God's messengers came from this starkly lit, dust-carpeted home, a place infused with permanent light, where the divine wind of inspiration blows through the open hearts of those who sustain humankind's living connection with God.

All Aboard!
2010–15

WHEN PAUL DAINTY, a pal and former promoter from Australia, pleaded for me to return and do a tour there, he must have almost fallen off his chair because, this time, I accepted. It was a coup. The triumphant success I had enjoyed down under during the early seventies was unparalleled – apart from a scream-filled tour of the Beatles before me in 1964, perhaps. One in four Australian homes had one of my albums, and Festival Records couldn't produce gold discs fast enough.

What would they expect of me this time? My visit in March 1984 – ostensibly as a Muslim preacher – was at the invitation of the Australian Federation of Islamic Councils. At that time, I was dressed in a turban and a long robe and was in my undeniably zealous, straight-faced phase. Not quite the old "Cat" the Aussies once loved, flocking in droves to see.

This time, on my return to Australia and New Zealand, I brought my Gibson guitar and was fully ready to reconnect. It was 2010, and the world had drastically altered. What hadn't altered, regretfully, was revealed during pre-tour interviews. The Australian press (like the American, UK, and German press, and every other mainstream news outlet desirous of maintaining their "critical" credibility) felt it was their journalistic mission and moral duty to question me again, and again, about my position vis-à-vis *The Satanic Verses*. Over the years, the myth had reached the status of "fact"; my true stand (repeated again and again), never having once mouthed my direct support for the infamous fatwah, seemed destined to remain "classified information."

"Yusuf and the Roadsters" landed in early June. My entrance back on stage in the land of Oz – after thirty-six years – was designed to be an understatement. As the lights dimmed, I played the first chords of "Lilywhite," walking out casually in my long "Roadsinger" brown travelling coat, into the spotlight.

> *Back upon the mended road – I pause,*
> *Taking time to check the dial . . .*

The audiences in Australia were positively over the moon. I'd finally made it back. For them to hear me sing those songs live again was miraculous; none of us believed I'd ever be standing up on stage playing them again. The love was just overwhelming.

My set list ensured that nobody had to wait too long to hear their old favourites: "The Wind," "Where Do the Children

Play?," "I Love My Dog," "Here Comes My Baby," "First Cut . . ." New songs like "Midday," "All Kinds of Roses," and "Boots and Sand" also got some recognition. The excitement and intensity of the show increased with the gradual addition of musicians, bolstering the group's size and dynamics on stage.

After half an hour of the show, I casually strolled stage-left and sat on an old wooden crate. As the applause died down, the massive backdrop projected a small solitary planet, suspended in the midst of an endlessly dark and empty sky. Here, I took up the role of the "storyteller": "Some say there are only two kinds of stories: ones about leaving home, and those about coming back . . ."

A preview of my musical script for *Moonshadow* was integrated into the show. In this section of the concert, I played the part of some kind of Shakespearean actor, narrating the plot while plonking my guitar. On the screen behind, the fantastic world of Alaylia was panoramically projected: dreamlike illustrations I'd had created by a talented Turkish artist called Dogan. The reception the mini-musical received was highly enthusiastic, enough to make me think seriously about Australia as the place to stage it.

Indeed, I actually returned to open the show in Melbourne at the Princess Theatre some years later. But without going into it too much, suffice to say it ran for fewer than one hundred days. Reason? Oh, there were lots of them, but one particular mistake was not checking the competition we were up against at the time. Just down the road was a rebooted, classy production of *Annie*! That cheeky little orphan girl and her lovable dog. We were doomed. A valuable, age-old piece of theatrical wisdom was painfully learned overnight – never, ever pit yourself on stage against a kid or a dog! After that major dent in my theatrical ambitions, my next hope would be to revisit *Moonshadow* as a children's storybook or animated film sometime in the future.

God's generosity increased, and the subtle goodies of old age were beginning to slowly introduce themselves: upon my return to Dubai following the *Roadsinger* tour, another incredible gift was presented to me and Fawziah, a baby grandson. He was born to Hasanah on my very own birthday, 21 July. What a gift! They named him Muhammad Sulaiman.

Once I had written a song called "I've Got a Thing about Seeing My Grandson Grow Old," but the prospect had not been quite so set in stone at that time. As more of the new, wide-eyed generation moved in, playfully pulling on Granddaddy's beard, life on this planet was looking less limitless. More time and effort needed to go into "prioritizing."

A bunch of offers were coming through my agents, WME, inviting me to continue rolling my tour out to elsewhere on the globe. I found nothing particularly objectionable about that possibility; I was feeling quite warmed up. Among the requests was a special invite to attend a rather daring "Rally to Restore Sanity and/or Fear," to be held in front of the White House on the National Mall in Washington, on 20 October 2010. It was organised by satirical comedians and TV hosts Stephen Colbert and Jon Stewart, who were raising the stakes as the US midterm elections approached, and Barack Obama was seeking a second term in office.

"Fear" was still a major factor used vigorously by opposing political sides in trying to convince voters to plump for them. The threat of the "other" was revived to make people forget the economic hardships and everyday domestic imperatives that had dented the boastful confidence of the American Dream. On the face of it, I realised the rally was essentially to help keep the Democrat light burning in the Capitol. I accepted.

Backstage, I met Steve and Jon, who introduced me to their wacky idea of doing a duelling duet with Ozzy Osbourne: I'd sing "Peace Train" and then he'd charge on and interrupt me with a blazing version of "Crazy Train." It was a bit of a farcical spoof, but I was up for it. The Roots were the backing band.

The sun shone over the iconic White House lawn against a stark blue sky. I mingled and met Tony Bennett, Mavis Staples, Kareem Abdul-Jabbar, and Sheryl Crow while waiting for my name to be announced. When it was, the crowd went wild; they couldn't believe this was actually happening (possibly thinking I was still handcuffed due to the no-fly list). Many desperately called out for me to finish the whole song; some booed Ozzy semi-jokingly, but he blasted on. The gag definitely worked.

Far away from public parades of US democracy on lush green lawns and the echoes of "Peace Train," a rowdy return to the protest of the sixties erupted, but this time in parts of the world largely lacking in electoral opportunities or political rallies. Marches, demonstrations, and spontaneous street-level uprisings spread rapidly in response to the death of a young vegetable seller from Tunisia, who had set himself on fire in protest against the merciless injustice of his government. The young man's fury towards the "system" had ignited the hearts of millions. Inspired, I lent my voice to the chorus calling for change, and wrote and recorded a song in support:

> *My People!*
> *When you gonna leave my People?*
> *Give them room to breathe – my People!*
> *Stop oppressing – my People!*
> *All they want is bread and clothes,*
> *Space to rest and left alone.*
> *My People!*

The orchestrated downfall of Saddam in Iraq – assisted by the hasty support of many Western countries – kicked off a domino of dictatorship downfalls, in what became known as the Arab Spring. It seemed the feuds and divisions that had bedevilled the Arab lands all those centuries ago had returned with a vengeance, only to go even deeper, leaving crevices for more radical elements like IS (Islamic State)/Daesh to cause injury to the already fractured and bleeding body of the Muslim world.

These things were not going to deter me from doing my best to continue promoting the clear message of Islam, as I understood it. "Life is what happens while you are busy making other plans," John Lennon rightly sang. And so it reached my ears that I was finally to be inducted into the Rock & Roll Hall of Fame. This was a welcome sign that my efforts in restoring bridges had been noticed and that my contribution to unrolling the red carpet of music history had somehow struck a lasting chord.

By this time, Islam had become my every breath and heartbeat, so I could now ease up and accept being known as Cat Stevens again, as well as Yusuf. It was important for my fans to understand that the songs I wrote were a true and vital part of what made me who I was. I'd simply emerged out of the shadows, like Joseph, returning to a family he was forced to leave behind; I needed to mend the broken relationship with those I'd become distant from. The US, in its role as a global, latter-day empire, was still having a hard time understanding Islam, and I felt it was my destiny to help make it more familiar. I never lost hope in the good nature of everyday Americans, striving together in the pursuit of worldly happiness; but maybe it was necessary to probe a little bit further, beyond the limits of comfy, earthly borders, to a place slightly more foreign: a place we are all in fact headed, called Eternity.

The great Hall of Fame event would be in New York's Barclays Centre, Brooklyn. It was pretty hair-raising; I hadn't played a large gig like this in the Big Apple or its vicinity for decades. Art Garfunkel agreed to do the introduction for me. I loved Art, and we had some history together, all the way back to my folk-clubbing days in London, though we never rubbed shoulders at the time. During the recording of the *Numbers* album, we grew closer. He represented the soft, folky, highly legitimate rock royalty of the seventies. I was honoured.

On 10 April 2014, I walked out on stage and the crowd just

let go of all those years of doubts and misgivings and cheered at the top of their voices. It was as good as it gets. A lot of the music and entertainment business aristocracy were there, including Steven Spielberg, Bill Murray, Jackson Browne, Sting, and a host of other sparkling and well-dressed attendees, together with my co-inductees Peter Gabriel, Kiss, Bruce Springsteen (introducing the E Street Band), and Dave Grohl and Krist Novoselic for Nirvana.

The joy was momentous, especially for my fans, many of whom had thought they'd never see me again. It was time to thank them and all those who helped propel me forward: my mother and father, my brother David, Mike Hurst, Chris Blackwell, Paul Samwell-Smith, Barry Krost, my longtime friend and guitarist Alun Davies, and, of course, my "hard-headed woman," Fawziah. The speech had been roughly worked out, and I had some notes, but most of it rolled off from memory. Thankfully, my sense of humour seemed to be on form that evening, and those in the crowd, who never imagined I had one, were kinda taken by surprise.

Following my talk, I grabbed my guitar and took to the stage to sing three of my most well-known classics: "Father and Son," "Wild World," and "Peace Train," with a large, Black, twenty-piece choir. The audience stood up; they were understandably blown away, particularly as my voice still sounded like the original records. The reception was rapturous.

There were a lot of tears that night. After the performance, I met with Stevie Nicks (she was there with Sheryl Crow and Bonnie Raitt to sing a tribute to Linda Ronstadt, who was not able to appear). Stevie told me how impossible it was to even

CAT ON THE ROAD TO FINDOUT

watch me, as she had to perform herself and might've broken down under the emotional weight of it all. Unknown to me, she and Lindsey Buckingham had always been huge fans.

Coming back in contact with my long-lost utopian seekers and friends in the US was important; it cut out the grunting, anti-Islamic trolls for a blissful moment and enabled many to reconnect with my message of respectful coexistence. The chatter created by those who insisted on misreading my actions and intentions was silenced – for a little while – as we embraced at the gates of heaven again.

I was now facing a rather difficult problem: how to explain my musical endeavours to the Muslim community. Having found my inspiration and justification to sing and record for the wider public again, I was severely criticised – as expected – by elements within certain Islamic quarters and was deeply hurt by rumours casting doubt on my commitment to Islam. It occurred to me that I should write a short book to clarify my position for the Muslim community, making clear to everyone my intentions, and providing justification from the Qur'an and hadith. I needed to spell out the reasons why I chose to pick up the guitar again and address the oft-repeated view concerning music. So I devoted myself to the task of writing the book and broadening people's understanding about the subject, bearing the simple title, *Why I Still Carry a Guitar*.

Some thought that I had left music because I believed it was *haram*, whereas the actual reason was because there were doubts about it. It was not 100 percent one way or the other. As there were varied opinions on the issue, early on I chose the safest position available – and I also had other priorities at the time.

My promise back there in the Pacific Ocean was to God. When I walked away, it was obvious to me that my body could not be in that world while my heart was in another. I needed to commit myself mind, body, and spirit, to complete my surrender to the Almighty, and whatever that meant in terms of sacrifice – my food, my drink, my clothes, my fame, and anything that was doubtful – I had been given something infinitely more valuable. Learning to bow my head on the ground five times a day was better than all the things I'd acquired, put together. No record sales, gold, or applause could ever match a fraction of the bliss I felt, every day the sun rose and set, directly connecting with my maker.

After the passage of time, having gone through a fair share of trials as a new Muslim, I was wiser and confident enough to make my mind up about the matter. With my feet solidly on the path of Islam, I could now revisit some of the pastures of my musical past without necessarily plunging headlong back into those old, ego-infested potholes again, knowing that God was the final judge. The motivation to pick up my songwriting talent again was supported by the saying, "Speak to people according to the level they understand. Do you want God and His messenger to be rejected?"[154]

As Cat Stevens, more so as Yusuf Islam, I had a significant role to fulfill. I was uniquely positioned to become a glass portal through which the West could see Islam, and Muslims could see the West. Having passed through the exhaustingly complex maze of everyday Western life and culture, and then been granted invaluable insight into the often-veiled "otherness" of the Qur'anic view of the universe, I naturally wanted to share it. That didn't make me a teacher, but more of a potential specimen for those who are searching for and pursuing happiness on all sides of the divide. Believe me, folks, it's out there!

The calls for me to do a full US tour were now deafening, and I was finding it harder and harder to resist. Our agent came up with a list of dates, which would start in London, then briefly pass through a few cities in Europe before heading out to the US, commencing on the East Coast and ending up on the West – I agreed. Within a few hours of the tickets going on sale, our North American tour was already sold out.
 The new tour was called "Peace Train . . . Late Again!"
 Always loving any creative process, I designed an old, rickety train station platform as a stage set to accompany us. When we finally started production rehearsals, everybody instantly fell in love with the station and wished they could take it home.
 It was soon time to head out west, and so off we chugged.
 The first "Peace Train" show in North America was in Toronto, at Massey Hall, one of my all-time favourite venues, where I had first experienced the phenomenon of people holding lit candles and Zippo lighters to express the spirit of love and togetherness, turning the auditorium into a galaxy of sparkling stars. The set list included some heavy, R & B-rooted songs from my new album, *Tell 'Em I'm Gone*, which were about as rock 'n' roll as I would ever get. The tour proved the sparkle had not gone away – except now, lighters were replaced by mobiles. My ability to chat between songs

had vastly improved, as I was far less concerned with looking cool and I was more relaxed in my identity. It was much easier for me to open up in front of my audience. Many of the words of my songs could be understood from a new perspective. A lot of them had somehow come true or were being confirmed: ecological doomsday was fast approaching, the world had proved itself to be incurably wild . . . and the sleepy-headed Peace Train was still taking its time.

> *Ooh-aah-eeh-aah-ooh-aah . . .*
> *Come on, come on, come on!*[155]

Unfortunately, we received official confirmation that we still had some miles to go before disembarking in the land of peace, love, and cotton candy. It came by means of persistent refusals from the US embassy to allow my wife to travel with me on my trips to the States. We discovered that Fawziah's ESTA (Electronic System for Travel Authorization) had been unceremoniously withdrawn, meaning she now needed to get a special permit to travel to the US. After we did the necessary things and filled out the official application forms, homeland algorithms still refused to provide one. It seems that whatever allusions were still circulating, due to my unjustified inclusion on the no-fly list, they were still creating repercussions. Somewhere inside the dark sinews of the cyberworld's infested system, a nasty bug was still lurking. It was pretty obvious that the source of the problem was my "profile," not Fawziah's. Same thing happened to my daughter Asmaa: she had actually bought a ticket to visit a friend in the US, but couldn't use it.

Though I was granted a special O-1 visa,[156] my problems didn't end there. At the airport, my boarding card for the US was always stamped with a red "SSSS"; that meant every time I checked in for a flight, I had to be taken to the side and body-searched, full-on, while my possessions were emptied out, X-rayed, and minutely examined!

Will this ever end, I wonder? I just hope it won't be like the words in "The Wind," "No, never, never, never . . ."[157]

When the Prophet, peace be upon him, was directly asked, "Which Islam is best?" he replied, "To feed [the poor and the needy] and to greet with the message of peace those whom you know and those you do not know."[158] Well, if that does not reveal his love-wish for the wellbeing and peacefulness of humanity, I have no idea what more on Earth could.

Being inspired by such sayings, Peace Train was the name given to a charitable project I began to focus on; its main object is to deliver food and relief to the poor, those stuck in dire circumstances, impoverished townships and refugee camps around the world – and its motto is another of the Prophet's sayings:

> *Oh People! Spread peace, feed others,*
> *uphold the ties of kinship, and pray during*
> *the night when people are sleeping, and you*
> *will enter Paradise with Salam [peace].*[159]

The fact that starvation is still a daily reality for hundreds of millions of families is an indictment of utter political failure in our highly overestimated "modern world."

Road to Findout
2020 and beyond

THERE ARE TIMES when one must take a jump into that which looks scary. For some, a change in the pattern of life appears to be a departure from the relative safety and security of what feels solid and familiar. But thresholds of indescribable beauty and progress would never be experienced if we simply remained stuck in one safe and comfortable spot. Life has thrown a lot of surprises at me, forcing me to open my mind, move, change tracks, and do things differently. As T. S. Eliot wrote:

> *We will not cease our exploration*
> *And the end of all our exploring*
> *Will be to arrive where we started*
> *And know the place for the first time.*[160]

It was coming up to the fiftieth anniversary of *Tea for the Tillerman*, and the record company was asking what we might do to mark the occasion. My son, Muhammad, who had been speaking to them, came up with a naive suggestion, "Why don't you re-record it?" There was a brief moment of silent disbelief.

"What a stupid idea!" I said. "Let's do it!"

The world had certainly moved on since *Tillerman* was first released in 1970, but the probing and commentary of our humanity in those songs have certainly stood the test of time. Modern life's new atmosphere was reflected quite accurately on the cover: Tillerman the Second had landed back on Earth from outer space, only to discover the world had become decidedly darker and more dangerous. The two mischievous kids were still playing next to him – but this time, Timmy, the blond-haired boy sitting up on the tree branch, is streaming the latest groovy-tastic music, while his chum Grady below him is gleefully ray-gunning multitudes of "the-ugly-enemies" into bloody blobs on his game-infested mobile phone. The Tillerman himself wore a spacesuit and helmet – probably in readiness for COVID.

The purity of the physical world was not the only thing that had suffered a downturn; the spirit within most human beings was seriously in relapse. To revive the sentiments of the soul-seeking sixties and seventies was a moment of "calling." Yes, it was the right time for the Tillerman's message again. My songs seemed to have grown larger and even more in tune with the passage of years. Like the earth, I suppose, when you leave it fallow for long enough, it supernaturally replenishes itself (probably why the Tillerman needed to sit down and take a fifty-year tea break).

The seconds tick the time out.[161]

That lyric from "On the Road to Findout" becomes more and more meaningful as the hourglass trickles. The question we must ask ourselves is how to make the best of our time before we turn into a motionless heap of sand.

The need to find out and make sense of this world and how to fit in were the most important driving forces in my life. Mishaps, like almost falling off a rooftop in the West End, landing up in hospital, half-dead from exceeding the dose of pleasures as a pop star and almost losing grip on life in the waves of the Pacific Ocean, all pushed me urgently to seek to understand both the "here" and the "beyond": from the moment my conscience awoke and I rubbed my eyes, misfortunes and discomforting situations forced me into overdrive, demanding action on account of my upgraded awareness.

Aristotle once said, "All men by nature desire to know."[162] For humans, as thinking beings, life is a process of learning, yet we know that there is a limit to our time here on Earth; one day we will not be here. This is where questions of the afterlife become vital: what lies behind this physical realm is an issue we should all be concerned with. This is where faith takes us to a higher level of human perception. It is not enough to be alive: there must be a purpose, and our intelligence demands to know what it is. The gift of knowledge is from God, and He is the knower of all things.

> **With Him are the keys of the unseen – no one knows them except Him. And He knows what is in the land and sea. Not even a leaf falls without His knowledge, nor a grain in the darkness of the earth or anything – green or dry – but is written in a perfect Record.**[163]

As I continue to travel the road to findout, I am open to the fact that, over each hill and horizon, there is so much left to probe... and mindful of the fact that those angels who began their duties at St. Joseph's are still busy recording every move.

My early encounter with religious education laid the groundwork and helped establish the direction in which I am bound – I am truly grateful for it. Because it seems quite obvious to me that today's discordant imbalance within the broad human ethos has stunted and suppressed the spiritual growth of much of humanity's total life-and-death, experiential reality and created deformities in our behavioural, social, and habitual patterns. This has made naturally divinely conscious, devotional beings bow down like slaves at the modern altar of a newly manufactured saint – "the modern secular man" – while he magnanimously hands out his sacramental catechism of spiritual impossibilities and doubts.

Trying to avoid being enlisted to this post-modern, materialistic creed does not mean we have to become monks or nuns either. We do not need to suppress or fight our natural love of nice, healthy, worldly things or separate the spirit from our daily physical requirements and endeavours. The Prophet, peace be upon him, repeatedly prayed,

> **Our Lord! Grant us the good of this world and the Hereafter, and protect us from the torment of the Fire.**[164]

Moderation, therefore, is a vital part of remaining upright and balanced. We occupy a unique position between the spiritual world and the physical one: between the world of unseen angels and the world of earthly creatures and beasts. But tightroping between the two is not easy. Like most physical creatures, we need to hunt for food and shelter, but we are also in desperate need of wisdom and moral guidance. "Man does not live by bread alone," Jesus said.

For many centuries, man has been boasting of progress because, through the means of scientific conveniences, foolishly, "he has mistaken comfort for civilisation," as Benjamin Disraeli said. The result is that we have barricaded ourselves into darkness by habitually accumulating more than our souls have space for, while continually hankering for yet more. Too much emphasis on corporeal satisfaction (as Mick Jagger suggestively taught us) has driven human beings down to new sub-levels of existence.

> *Where's it leading to, freedom at what cost?*
> *People needing more and more and it's all getting lost*
> *I want back – I want back,*
> *Back to the time when the Earth was green*
> *And there was no high walls, and the sea was clean*[165]

Strange that "lifelessness" is something that, before birth, every human being has already passed through. Even stranger

39 | *Road to Findout*

is the fact that after spending an apparent eternity in non-existence, once we wake up in this world, we tend to brush that limitless pre-period under the carpet like an inconsequential speck of dust and then get caught up in the business of living in the "now." But then that's quite logical because, before consciousness, there isn't that much to think or talk about, I suppose.

Looking to the future is quite a different matter. Anyone who hasn't contemplated the end of life's path, and what may lie beyond it, can justifiably blame themselves, once they reach that point, for not having sought more information beforehand – if it is not quite what they had envisaged.

The meaning of being alive – and conscious of it – must surely account for more than basic survival as we compete in the great race to the grave, nonsensically dancing around blindfolded on this earthly ball, suspended in the midst of an infinitely dark and mysterious universe. Fine, I am here now, but what will it be like when I am not?

The powerful urge to have answers for the gaping mysteries that face us, as we stare through the soul's window at our own astonishing existence in this boundless universe, is precisely what has driven inquisitive pilgrims (and the occasional pop star) throughout the ages to leave the coziness of their homes and firesides to try and find out. I wrote this book to encourage those contemplating what may exist beyond their front doorstep. Important questions are still knocking. For those who take the trouble to get up and answer the call, the reward – like the clear, gushing rivers from a mountain eternally nourished by sweet heavenly snow and melted by divine light – promises to be endless.

CAT ON THE ROAD TO FINDOUT

Some people think that such descriptions of paradise are based on wishful fairy tales in order to keep humankind from realising its lack of purpose and ultimate destination – originating from nothing and then thrown back into the great empty dustbin of time. Of course, it's entirely up to the individual if they want to believe that, but – consciously or unconsciously – they would be denying the likes of Jesus, Abraham, Moses, Muhammad, and all the greatest bodies and souls who have ever strolled this Earth. They will have labelled them as misguided, delusional, or simply liars – in my opinion, a seriously dangerous error of human judgment.

Had I not discovered Islam before I encountered Muslims, I too might have dismissed the religion as backward and hostile with nothing to offer in terms of advancing the human condition of happiness and peace. As George Bernard Shaw once said, "Islam is the best religion, and Muslims are the worst followers." How regretfully right I would have been about many well-publicised, badly behaved Muslims and dubious self-serving governments – how wrong I would have been about true Islam.

Having studied a good sampling of world religions, I sincerely believe that the religion of the Last Prophet has a significant part to play in the final establishment of world peace. Unbeknown to most, Islam actually includes a mechanism for the institutionalisation of peace on a global scale: the Qur'an requires human beings (certainly those of the three major Abrahamic faith communities) to observe four sacred months each year, during which fighting and war are forbidden![166] This fact has been brazenly overlooked and disregarded throughout the centuries by endless Muslim governments, rulers, and footloose militants – a potential game-changer even the UN hasn't yet clocked on to. These peaceful months were primarily meant for tribes and people to answer the call of Abraham, travel to Makkah, and worship in safety, without fear of attack (remember, this was even before the formation of Judaism, Buddhism, Christianity, and Islam).

The imperative for peace to reign on the planet in accord with the yearly congress of pilgrimage is a God-send. Why shouldn't this invaluable mandate be recognised and implemented internationally? Just imagine if all the nations of the modern world adopted this formula and people were allowed to breathe the air of peace, go about their business, and return to their families again without fear of bombs or bullets for one whole third of the year; would that not make them think twice about muddying their faces, grabbing their guns, and diving back into the trenches?

For every nano atom or cell in this universe, be it under our feet or one hundred billion light years away, there is a law that governs its functions and existence. It is imbecilic to imagine that human beings have been left out of this. An essential part of human law is connected to consciousness of good and bad; the gift of freedom to choose between them has been granted to every conscious soul by the Creator; the primary rule is to live a good life in a manner that causes no undue harm to others. Surely that is the great middle way for every race, religion, government, or nation?

"Law is the sum of the conditions under which the wishes

of one person can be united with the wishes of another in accordance with a universal law of freedom." That maxim was perfectly stated by Immanuel Kant, one of the shapers of modern secularism, three centuries ago. Funny, but that's not far off from the religious paradigm, is it? Jesus himself prophetically taught the same principle twenty centuries ago when he said, "Treat people the same way you want them to treat you, for this is the Law of the Prophets."[167] A directive, again harmonised by the Last Prophet: "None of you have faith until you love for your fellow brother what you love for yourself."[168]

The principle of the multi-religious and multi-ethnic society is mentioned in the following verses of the Qur'an:

> **So let the people of the Gospel judge by what God has revealed in it. And those who do not judge by what God has revealed are truly the rebellious. We have revealed to you O Prophet this Book with the truth, as a confirmation of previous Scriptures and a supreme authority on them. So judge between them by what God has revealed, and do not follow their desires over the truth that has come to you. To each of you We have ordained a code of law and a way of life. If God had willed, He would have made you one community, but His Will is to test you with what He has given each of you. So compete with one another in doing good. To God you will all return, then He will inform you of the truth regarding your differences.**[169]

He made you into peoples and tribes so that you may get to know one another. Surely the most noble of you in the sight of God is the most righteous among you.[170]

I still believe in the Peace Train. But I also know that not everybody's ready to jump up on it – but that's life. Not everybody is a Yusuf/Cat Stevens fan, either. Regardless, the philosophy of the Peace Train is quite simple: no devotee of a particular faith will be excluded, and there will be no room for Americans if there's no room for Russians or Chinese; no room for Saudis if there's no room for Iranians; no room for Israelis if there's no room for Palestinians; no room for Turks if there's no room for Armenians or Kurds. The ticket to board is obtained by accepting and following a few essential rules: keep your space clean, don't take what doesn't belong to you, make room for others, and treat people as you would wish to be treated . . . and so it happily chugs away.

I've been on an amazing journey, which began in the narrow streets of London, and led me through the most iconic cities, to perform upon the great stage of Western culture, ascending the dizzying heights of wealth, recognition, and artistic pinnacles; freely exploring vast ranges of religions and philosophies, wandering through churches, temples, all the way to the Holy abode in Jerusalem – ignoring myths and warnings – and crossing the foreboded desert heartlands, to arrive at the House of One God in Abrahamic Arabia. What finally elevated my perspective was a luminous Book which perfectly alchemised my thoughts, beliefs, and human nature, opening my eyes to Oneness, as well as to my place and purpose within the universe:

> *Oh I've been smiling lately, dreaming about the world as one,*
> *And I believe it could be, some day it's going to come . . .*[171]

It is humbling to learn how much my songs mean to many of my musical followers. At one time art and music were all I had to present, but that was before I was given a book that helped me change from within and experience that inner peace I sang about. Even while the signs of Armageddon are ominously around us, I still have hope. Standing and just waiting for the end to arrive is the epitome of fatalism, whereas the Last Prophet said,

> *If the Hour [of Resurrection] is about to be established and one of you was holding a palm shoot, let him take advantage of even one second before the Hour is established to plant it.*[172]

No matter what separates us in belief, philosophy or even musical taste, these differences need not lead to wars. Diversity does not have to obstruct harmonious coexistence: unity is nature's holy ground out of which grows the earthly plurality we all can enjoy. Look again at a beautiful garden of palm trees, pine trees, and oaks; they don't squabble or argue about who's best, who might be tallest or deserves priority and more claim to the soil. We should all be content to soak up the glorious sunshine and drink the pure water God sends down for all from the sky.

39 | *Road to Findout*

So, like the Tillerman, I will continue to work to plough and plant more seeds. My longing for peace between all branches of the great tree of humanity remains a work-in-progress; whatever happens beyond that? That's up to God.

> **Those who believe and do good will be admitted into Gardens, under which rivers flow – to stay there forever by the Will of their Lord – where they will be greeted with "Peace!" Do you not see how God compares a good word to a good tree? Its root is firm and its branches reach the sky, Always yielding its fruit in every season by the Will of its Lord. This is how God sets forth parables for the people, so perhaps they will be mindful.[173]**

An Unspoken Poem

When I was a little foetus, Angels used to meet me
In my little womb, just beneath my mother's heart
Their wings of colour lit up the dark
Oh Lord, I loved hearing them sing
Praises to the King and Creator of everyone,
And everything!

When I got a little bigger, I exercised.
Mummy had to suffer with my little dance
'Fore I knew it I was ready up for my entrance
My birthday came and time was right
Now my long night was almost over
Wow! It's bright!

Then the gift of seeing my Mother,
Smiling eyes of love looking down to me
I was very tiny then, you see
Now I've drunk a river of milk
From a source like silken glass, but soft
Thank you, God, for everything!
I can't wait till I see you again . . .

Yusuf Islam

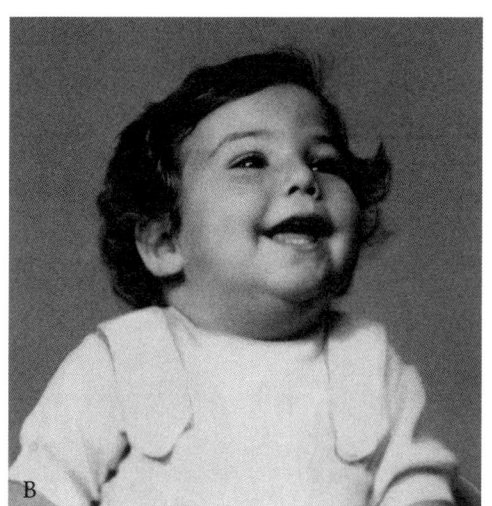

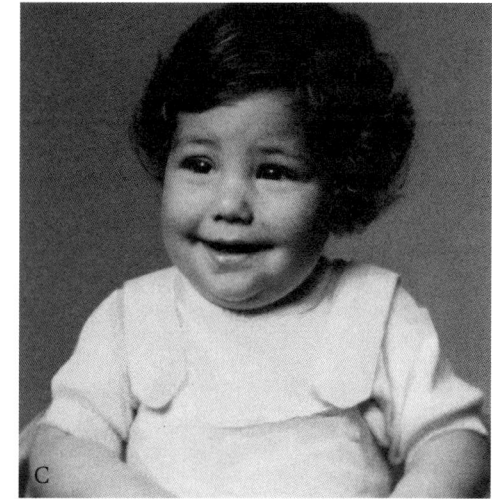

A Dad, Mum, Anita, David and Baby Steven, at his Greek Orthodox christening
B Baby Steven (laughing)   C Baby Steven (unsure)

A Dad during the First World War B Stavros Georgiou Adams
C Dad during the Second World War D Mum on a boat to England E Ingrid Elizabeth Wickman

F Mum and Dad at the Moulin Rouge's tea and coffee machine
G Moulin Rouge, 245 Shaftesbury Avenue, London, WC2

A Dad and his "sonny boy" B Steve and his sister, Anita
C & D Steve and his best friend, Andy Koritsas

E Steve and Mum at the baby grand F Steve in the basement kitchen
G The JAS Trime H Dave, Cat's brother and manager I Cat on The Walker Brothers' 1967 UK tour

A Jimi Hendrix, Cat, Gary Leeds, and Engelbert Humperdinck on The Walker Brothers' tour
B Cat recuperating in the London Clinic hospital   C Cat strolling a London mews

D & E Cat in his Redroom above the Moulin Rouge
F Clive McLean, Cat, and Barry and Paul Ryan
G Redroom studio set-up H Brother David and Patti D'Arbanville in the living room

A Portobello Road fire escape B 1970 Plumpton Jazz and Folk Festival with Alun Davies
C TV appearance D Publicity photo E *Tillerman* photo session, Hampstead, London

F Revisiting Foyles bookshop, London G Two brothers in Curzon Street, London
H Cat and Jimmy Cliff I Cat and band in New York J Cat testing the water of the Pacific

A Prince Rupert Loewenstein, Abe Summer, Barry Krost, Cat, and Jerry Moss
B Dynamic Studios, Kingston, Jamaica C Painting in Walham Grove, London
D Cat and Roland Young in the art department of A&M E *Foreigner* photo session

F, G & H Cat practicing his yoga and meditation exercises

A Steven D. Georgiou passport photo, 1974   B Visiting a feeding hut in Addis Ababa, Ethiopia
C, D & E Meeting the kids as UNICEF ambassador in Ethiopia and Kenya, 1974

F & G Writing *Numbers* and relaxing in Rio de Janeiro H Alun and Cat in Davos, Switzerland
I Mountain view in Davos J Exploring the Ethiopian landscape

A Le Studio, Morin Heights, Canada B Recording "Old Schoolyard" in Le Studio
C Photo session with Muslim cap D Cat with his faithful Amberthwiddle
E Majikat Earth Tour, 1976

F Dad and the two Georgiou boys G Cat lost on a donkey somewhere in southern Cyprus
H Mum, Dad, and Cat, with cousin Lambros working in the background, Stavros Restaurant

A Return to Le Studio with Paul Samwell-Smith for *Back to Earth*
B Road-strolling between sessions C In-flight and beardless Cat
D Cat with his road manager, Carlos Braganza Jones

E UNICEF visit to an orphanage in Cairo F With a tour guide in Luxor
G, H & I The journey continues to villages and camps in Chittagong, Bangladesh

A Dad's last visit to Paphos
B & C London Central Mosque and marriage to Fawziah Mubarak Ali, 1979
D Reading the Qur'an in Curzon Street
E First lecture given at the Mind Body Spirit Festival, Olympia, London
F Final "Cat" concert at Year of the Child, Wembley, London

G Islamia Primary School, Brondesbury Park, London H Yusuf in a robe made by Fawziah
I Mum with Yusuf and his three eldest children, Asmaa, Hasanah, and Maymanah (carried)
J Mum on the steps of the Dome of the Rock, Jerusalem

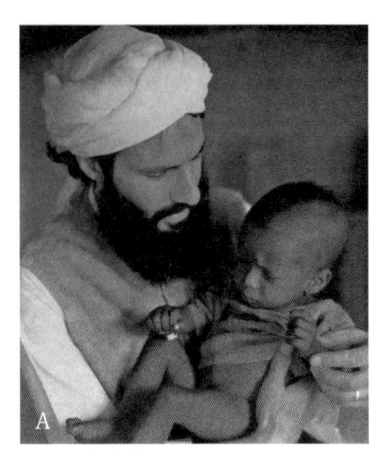

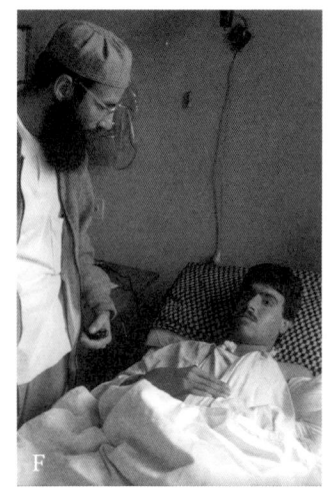

A Visit to Sudan during the drought of 1984   B Launch of Muslim Aid in London
C British Muslim delegation to Palestine, 1988   D Press conference in Jerusalem
E Visit to a shelter in Sarajevo, Bosnia and Herzegovina   F Visit to a hospital in Jerusalem

G Prince Charles visiting the Islamia Primary School
H Yusuf and nephew Daniel in the studio I Launch of *The Life of the Last Prophet* in Harrods
J Meeting Bosnian president Alija Izetbegović in a London hotel K Peace concert in Sarajevo

A Receiving the World Social Award from Mikhail Gorbachev, Hamburg, 2003
B Back on stage at Nelson Mandela's 46664 AIDS benefit concert, Cape Town, 2003
C Meeting with Mandela and Annie Lennox at the 46664 book launch in London, 2004
D Father and son, Yusuf and Muhammad   E With Sir Paul McCartney for "Boots and Sand"

F With Professor Ekmeleddin İhsanoğlu, upon receiving an honorary Doctor of Laws degree from the University of Exeter, 2007 G Performing at Glastonbury in the "legends" slot, 2023
H Rally to Restore Sanity and/or Fear, Washington, D.C., 2010
I & J Induction to the Rock & Roll Hall of Fame, New York, 2014

A Working holiday with grandkids at La Fabrique Studios in the south of France
B Yusuf and the Peace Train Chugger at the AKM Cultural Centre, Istanbul
C Yusuf and Fawziah at a safari park, Sharjah, UAE

Notes

THE ROOF

1 "But I Might Die Tonight," *Tea for the Tillerman*, 1970.

THE OLD SCHOOLYARD

2 "(Remember the Days of the) Old Schoolyard," *Izitso*, 1977.

JESUS VS. SUPERMAN

3 You can still find my big moment of fame if you ever come across that DVD hidden away among the old black-and-white British films of the fifties.
4 My father had taken Adams (Adamos), his own grandfather's name, as a surname a long time before that.

THE SCENE

5 Early demo song, Cat Stevens, published by Cat Music Ltd.

THE DECCA DAZE

6 Fortunately, the US has subsequently passed a law allowing the songwriters to get back their rights after a certain number of years.

7 "The View from the Top," *New Masters*, 1967.

I GOT EXPERIENCED

8 Maurice was formerly married to Eve Taylor, manager of Sandie Shaw, Val Doonican, and Adam Faith.

I THINK I SEE

9 Boris Karloff died on 2 February 1969, in King Edward VII Hospital, Midhurst, West Sussex.

10 "I Think I See the Light," *Mona Bone Jakon*, 1970.

11 "Sitting," *Catch Bull at Four*, 1972.

THE REDROOM

12 "Miles from Nowhere," *Tea for the Tillerman*, 1970.

13 "Pop Star," *Mona Bone Jakon*, 1970.

AS CLOUDS PARTED

14 "I Wish, I Wish," *Mona Bone Jakon*, 1970.

TILLERMAN GOES TO THE USA

15 "On the Road to Findout," *Tea for the Tillerman*, 1970.

THE BODHI TREE

16 Timothy Leary, *Turn On, Tune In, Drop Out*, 1966.

17 "Into White," *Tea for the Tillerman*, 1970.

18 *New York Times*, 24 October 1971.

BULL AND THE POLAR BEAR

19 Ibid.
20 *Circus*, 23 October 1973.
21 "The Hurt," *Foreigner*, 1973.

EXILE

22 Jalal al-Din Rumi, "The Song of the Reed," from *Rûmî: Poet and Mystic (1207–1273): Selections from His Writings*, trans. R. A. Nicholson (London: George Allen and Unwin, 1950).
23 The Saihō-ji Temple in Kyoto
24 Robert M. Pirsig, *Zen and the Art of Motorcycle Maintenance* (New York: William Morrow, 1974).

WAVE

25 "Blackness of the Night," *New Masters*, 1968.
26 "Music," *Buddha and the Chocolate Box*, 1974.

THE GIFT

27 Muhammad Asad, *Islam at the Crossroads* (Arafat, 1934).
28 "On the Road to Findout," *Tea for the Tillerman*, 1970.
29 The Qur'an, The Opening, 1:1–7, trans. Dr. Mustafa Khattab.
30 Ibid., The Blood Clot, 96:1–5.
31 Ibid., Sincerity, 112:1–4.
32 "The Wind," "Music," and "Katmandu."
33 The Qur'an, Time, 103:1–3, trans. Dr. Mustafa Khattab.
34 The Bible, Matthew, 22:37.
35 The Qur'an, Women, 4:48.

JOSEPH'S STORY

36 "I Never Wanted to Be a Star," *Izitso*, 1977.
37 "Child for a Day" was originally written by my brother for his musical *Alpha Omega*.

Notes

38 The Qur'an, Joseph, 12:77.
39 "Father and Son," *Tea for the Tillerman*, 1970.
40 The Qur'an, Joseph, 12:101, trans. Dr. Mustafa Khattab.

THE GOLDEN DOME

41 Jalal al-Din Rumi, *The Masnawi*, verse 2620, trans. R. A. Nicholson, http://www.masnavi.net/1/10/eng/4/2613/.
42 "It is not for the sun to catch up with the moon, nor does the night outrun the day. Each is travelling in an orbit of their own," the Qur'an, Ya Sin, 36:40.
43 Ibid., The Prophets, 21:32.
44 Ibid., The Inevitable, 56:75–6, trans. Dr. Mustafa Khattab.
45 Ibid., The Prophets, 21:30.
46 Ibid., The Believers, 23:13–14. Before the invention of such instruments, scientists and thinkers, like Leonardo da Vinci as late as the fifteenth century, had depicted the human as a tiny, dwarf-like child already fully shaped and curled up within the walls of the sperm.
47 Ibid., Family of Imran, 3:190, trans. Dr. Mustafa Khattab.

SHAHADAH

48 "Daytime," *Back to Earth*, 1978.
49 *Melody Maker*, 25 November 1978.
50 US Declaration of Independence: "We hold these truths to be self-evident, that all men are created equal, that they are endowed by their creator with certain unalienable rights, that among these are life, liberty, and the pursuit of happiness."

BACK TO EARTH

51 "Is not the key to paradise the declaration that there is no God but Allah?," *Sahih al Bukhari*.
52 The Qur'an, The Heifer, 2:156, trans. Dr. Mustafa Khattab.
53 "Father," *Back to Earth*, 1978.

NEW CULTURAL HOME

54 Frederick Gibberd also designed the Liverpool Metropolitan Cathedral as well as the terminals at London's Heathrow Airport.
55 Matilda Battersby, *Independent*, 28 December 2014.
56 "Too Much Heaven," The Bee Gees.
57 1. Shahadah – to believe and declare that there is no God but Allah and that Muhammad is His servant and messenger; 2. Salat – praying five times daily; 3. Zakat – giving to charity; 4. Siyam – fasting in the month of Ramadan; and 5. Hajj – the pilgrimage to Makkah, at least once in a lifetime if a person is able.
58 It can be the offering of a goat or any cattle-like creature in place of a ram.
59 The Qur'an, Luqman 31:6 and The Congregation, 62:11.
60 *Sahih* is Arabic for "authentic."
61 Historically, during the conquest of Arabia, the shaikh asserted an austere brand of Islamic, monotheistic puritanism, based on the actions and words of pious predecessors – referred to as the *Salafiyyoon*. Mainly due to this, the kingdom of Saudi Arabia had gained respect and was widely recognised as a stronghold of conservatism; being the home of the two holy shrines of Islam it abounded with a sense of status and religious credence.
62 *Maliki, Shafi'i, Hanafi* and *Hanbali*.
63 Similar to the way in which I perceived the Talmud, being the collections of writings and judgments based on the original Torah.
64 The Qur'an, The Prophets, 21:92, trans. Dr. Mustafa Khattab.

LAST LOVE SONG

65 "Last Love Song," *Back to Earth*, 1978.
66 The Qur'an, The Criterion, 25:74, trans. Dr. Mustafa Khattab.
67 The Islamic calendar is based on the twelve-month lunar calendar. Because of this, the length of the Islamic year is 354

Notes

days, eleven shorter than the 365-day solar calendar. Therefore, Ramadan moves gradually from winter to summer every sixteen years or so.
68 Eagan Margery, *Boston Herald*, 18 May 2006; see https://en.wikipedia.org/wiki/Louise_Wightman.
69 *Sahih Muslim*.

YEAR OF THE CHILD

70 "Daytime," *Back to Earth*, 1978.
71 The Qur'an, Family of Imran, 3:191, trans. Dr. Mustafa Khattab.
72 Ibid., The Sovereignty, 67:1–2.
73 The Bible, Proverbs 9:10.
74 Prophet Muhammad prophesied that Jesus would descend towards the end of time and destroy the antichrist, and set things right on this tormented, war-ridden Earth – something all three monotheistic faiths amazingly seem to agree on.
75 The Bible, Matthew 22:38–40.
76 Malcolm X, *The Autobiography of Malcolm X* (New York: Grove Press, 1965).

WHERE DO THE CHILDREN PRAY?

77 *Sahih al Bukhari* and *Sahih Muslim*.
78 This was before the national curriculum was initiated in 1988.
79 *Sahih al Bukhari*.
80 Fifteenth day of the first month, Muharram, in the Islamic calendar, 1404 AH.

TROUBLE

81 The original meaning of the Arabic word *salafa* is "that which is passed," or "come to an end."
82 "Entering the Marketplace (Stage 10), Riding the Ox Home."
83 Muhammad Bukhari, *Al-Adab al-Mufrad*.
84 *Sahih al Bukhari* and *Sahih Muslim*.

CALL TO ALMS

85 Jesus Christ, the Bible, Luke 12:12.
86 "Whoever raises two girls until they reach adulthood – he and I will be together on the Day of Resurrection – and he interlaced his fingers [meaning in Paradise]." *Sahih Muslim*.
87 "In the End," *An Other Cup*, 2006.

HAMPSTEAD TO THE HOLY

88 The Qur'an, The Heifer, 2:136, trans. Dr. Mustafa Khattab.
89 Ibid., The Table Spread, 5:21, and Bani Israel, 17:1–7 and 104.
90 Ibid., The Heifer, 2:83.
91 "Ruins," *Catch Bull at Four*, 1972.

SATANIC FORCES

92 Ishaan Tharoor, "How Israel helped create Hamas," *Washington Post*, 30 July 2014.
93 "Wild World," *Tea for the Tillerman*, 1970.
94 The Qur'an, The Spider, 29:2, trans. Dr. Mustafa Khattab.
95 "I wish to express my deepest outrage at the insensitivity of Penguin Books in publishing Salman Rushdie's book, *The Satanic Verses*. This book is clearly blasphemous in nature and deeply offensive to the Muslim community . . . I urge you to give the contents of this letter your most urgent attention and take a responsible decision."
96 The Qur'an, Family of Imran, 3:103.
97 Ibid., Repentance, 9:61.
98 *Fard Al-'Ayn* in Islamic law refers to legal obligations that must be performed by each individual Muslim, including prayer, charity, fasting, and pilgrimage.
99 Retrospectively, you could say that my public stance on the question was more or less similar to my position on music: I was absolutely petrified about doing or saying something wrong, so I went with the herd, and sided with the conservative view in the interest of safety – fearing the wrath of God if I did otherwise.

Notes

100 "He stayed in our attic a few times in Islington," *Newsnight*, 11 February 2019.
101 Molly Ivins, quoted in the *Washington Post*, 9 January 2015.
102 "Editing Floor Blues," *Tell 'Em I'm Gone*, 2014.
103 Interestingly, the actual history and institution of a "jury" appears to have originated between the eighth and eleventh centuries in the Islamic world. The Islamic *lafif* was a body of twelve members drawn from a neighbourhood and sworn to tell the truth and bound to give a unanimous verdict about matters which they had personally seen or heard, binding on the judge, to settle the truth concerning facts in a case, between ordinary people and obtained as of right by the plaintiff.
104 If there are a number of options, how can you believe in an "only option"?
105 "My bid to embrace Islam was pretence: Rushdie," rediff.com, April 2008.
106 "Cat & the Dog Trap," *Tell 'Em I'm Gone*, 2014.

PARADISE BENEATH HER FEET

107 "Once a man approached the Prophet, desiring to travel on an important expedition with him. He (peace be upon him) asked, 'Do you have a mother?' He said, 'Yes.' He (Allah bless him and give him peace) said, 'Stay with her because paradise lies beneath her feet.'" *The Sunan of Ibn Majah and Nasa'i*.
108 "How Can I Tell You," *Teaser and the Firecat*, 1971.
109 "Sun/C79," *Buddha and the Chocolate Box*, 1974.
110 The Qur'an, The Heifer, 2:278–9.
111 *Sahih al Bukhari* and *Sahih Muslim*.
112 The Qur'an, Ya Sin, 36:82–3, trans. Dr. Mustafa Khattab.
113 "Oh Very Young," *Buddha and the Chocolate Box*, 1974.
114 'Eid Al Adha, the festival celebrating the end of the pilgrimage season.
115 Cairo Declaration of Human Rights, 1990.
116 The fast of Moses: commemorating the day God delivered the Children of Israel from their enemy, the Pharaoh.

CAT ON THE ROAD TO FINDOUT

117 "Shiny Golden Hair": one of my very first songs written in 1965, in dedication to my mother.

PEACE CAMP: BETWEEN EAST AND WEST

118 Yusuf A. Ali, *Meaning of the Holy Qur'an*, commentary 2331.
119 Juan Cole, *Muhammad: Prophet of Peace Amid the Clash of Empires* (New York: Bold Type Books, 2018).
120 "Tala'al Badru 'Alayna," *The Life of the Last Prophet*, 1995.
121 "I Have No Cannons That Roar," *I Have No Cannons That Roar*, 1997.

A NEW MILLENNIUM

122 The tendency of Muslims to attach themselves to socialist ideals can be observed from much of the Arab world embracing Marxism following the Second World War, as well as the fact that it was another victorious Labour government that accepted and oversaw the creation of Pakistan back in 1947.
123 Al-Tirmidhi and Ibn Majah.
124 The Qur'an, The Stories, 28:23–8, and the Bible, Exodus, 2:16–21.

HIJACKED

125 *Daily Mirror*, 14 September 2001; the Qur'an, The Table Spread, 5:32.
126 *Sahih al Bukhari*.
127 "100 I Dream," *Foreigner*, 1973.

A GUITAR COMES HOME

128 Ahmad Ibn Hanbal and Darimi, as reported in *Forty Hadith of Imam an-Nawawi*.
129 An example of an event that happened at the time of the Prophet made it clear to me his attitude to music when it had no harmful connections or effects. "Aisha [the wife of the Prophet] said that her father actually walked into the house of the

Prophet while he was resting and she was listening to two small local girls singing a famous battle song about two tribes. Her father was shocked and protested, 'Musical instruments of Satan in the house of Allah's messenger!' But the Prophet said, 'O Abu Bakr! There is an 'Eid [festive enjoyment] for every nation and this is our 'Eid.'" *Sahih al Bukhari*, vol. 2, book 13, chapter 3, Hadith 952.

130 The Qur'an, The Heights, 7:32, trans. Dr. Mustafa Khattab.

131 Though there is no specific chapter on the subject of music, there is a hadith that mentions forbidden things like alcohol, and fornication linked to music, in the chapter of "Drinks." However, the hadith has been pointed out to be weak on account of a break in the narrative, as well as other anomalies, which do not meet the strict requirements of validation normally practised by Imam Bukhari.

132 Born at the end of the first millennium in Andalusia, Ibn Hazm followed a plain and literal interpretation of the Qur'an and hadith, as opposed to the use of analytical reasoning.

133 Imam Malik, the renowned founder of the Maliki school of thought, as a young man had even contemplated becoming a singer in the City of the Prophet, Al Madinah. This would have been unthinkable as a profession if music was so clearly prohibited, as this was less than eighty years (only two to three generations) after the passing of the Prophet, peace be upon him.

134 Salim T. S. Al-Hassani, *1001 Inventions* (Washington, D.C.: National Geographic, 2012).

135 *Al-qawāʿid al-fiqhīyah*, or legal maxims of Islamic law, are understood to number five: 1. Matters are determined according to intentions; 2. Certainty is not overruled by doubt; 3. Hardship begets ease; 4. Harm must be removed; and 5. Common custom is a basis for judgment.

136 "The Wind East and West," 2002.

137 T. E. Lawrence, *The Seven Pillars of Wisdom* (London: Jonathan Cape, 1935).

138 "Maybe There's a World," *An Other Cup*, 2006.

ON STAGE AGAIN

139 "Moonshadow," *Teaser and the Firecat*, 1971.
140 "Doors," *Tell 'Em I'm Gone*, 2014.

PRRR...GRRR

141 "Midday (Avoid City After Dark)," *An Other Cup*, 2006.
142 "Peace be with you," "And upon you be peace."
143 *Sydney Morning Herald*, 25 September 2004.
144 28 USCS 2680(h).
145 "Boots and Sand," *Roadsinger* (bonus track), 2009.

AN OTHER CUP

146 After Steve Jobs passed away in 2011, it was discovered that three of my songs were in the top ten on his iPhone.
147 Jerry McCulley, Amazon.com.

SHAMSIA

148 "World o' Darkness," *Moonshadow the Musical* and *Roadsinger*, 2009.
149 Christopher Booker, *The Seven Basic Plots* (London: Continuum, 2004).
150 Hazrat Inayat Khan, *The Alchemy of Happiness* (Farnham: Servire, 1978).
151 Dee Brown, *Bury My Heart at Wounded Knee* (New York: Holt, Rinehart & Winston, 1970).
152 To be honest, the UK has since developed admirably in its blending of cultures within the British ethos. I never could have guessed that London would one day evolve sufficiently to elect a Muslim mayor in Labour's Sadiq Khan, who came to power in 2016 and won further terms in 2021 and 2024.
153 The Qur'an, The Bee, 16:41, trans. Dr. Mustafa Khattab.

ALL ABOARD!

154 Ali Ibn Abi Talib, *Sahih al Bukhari*.
155 "Peace Train," *Teaser and the Firecat*, 1971.

Notes

156 An O-1 non-immigrant visa is for an individual who possesses extraordinary ability in the sciences, arts, education, business, or athletics.
157 "The Wind," *Teaser and the Firecat*, 1971.
158 *Sahih al Bukhari*.
159 *Sunan Ibn Majah*.

ROAD TO FINDOUT

160 T. S. Eliot, "Little Gidding" (*Four Quartets*) (London: Faber & Faber, 1942).
161 "On the Road to Findout," *Tea for the Tillerman*, 1970.
162 Aristotle, *Metaphysics* (350 BCE), Book 1, Part 1.
163 The Qur'an, The Cattle, 6:59, trans. Dr. Mustafa Khattab.
164 Ibid., The Heifer, 2:201.
165 "Ruins," *Catch Bull at Four*, 1972.
166 The Qur'an, Repentance, 9:36. The months are the eleventh, twelfth, first, and seventh of the lunar calendar.
167 The Bible, Matthew, 7:12.
168 *Sahih al Bukhari*.
169 The Qur'an, The Table Spread, 5:47–8, trans. Dr. Mustafa Khattab.
170 Ibid., The Dwellings, 49:13.
171 "Peace Train," *Teaser and the Firecat*, 1971.
172 Muhammad Bukhari, *Al-Adab al-Mufrad*.
173 The Qur'an, Abraham, 14:23–5, trans. Dr. Mustafa Khattab.

Credits

All reasonable effort has been made to identify and contact the copyright holders of the photographs and text extracts in this publication. Any omissions are inadvertent.

PHOTOGRAPHS

All photographs are from the archive of Yusuf Islam, except for those listed below.

Page 5 (plate section), photograph F: Copyright © IMAGO/ZUMA Press Wire
Page 6, A: Copyright © Barry Peake/Shutterstock
Page 7, D & E: Copyright © Gered Mankowitz
Page 8, A: Copyright © Michael Putland/Getty Images
Page 8, C: Copyright © TopFoto
Page 8, E: Copyright © Barrie Wentzell
Page 9, I: Copyright © Arthur Usherson
Page 9, J: Copyright © Jim McCrary/Redferns/Getty Images
Page 10, C: Copyright © Brian Aris
Page 11, F, G & H: Copyright © Dick Polak
Page 14, C: Copyright © Didi Zill
Page 14, E: Copyright © Penni Gladstone/UCLA Library Special Collections
Page 16, C: Copyright © IMAGO/ZUMA/Keystone
Page 18, C: Copyright © Mike Hollist/Associated Newspapers
Page 21, G: Copyright © Jamie Wiseman/Shutterstock
Page 22, A: Copyright © DPA Picture Alliance/Alamy Stock Photo
Page 22, B: Copyright © Dave Hogan/Getty Images
Page 23, I: Copyright © Kevin Kane/Getty Images

TEXT EXTRACTS

Page 105: From *The Secret Path: A Technique of Spiritual Self-discovery for the Modern World* by Paul Brunton (1955). www.paulbrunton.org

Page 158: From *Turn On, Tune In, Drop Out* by Timothy Leary. Copyright © 1966. Reprinted by permission of Ronin Publishing, Inc.

Page 202: From *Zen and the Art of Motorcycle Maintenance* by Robert Pirsig, published by Vintage. Copyright © Robert M. Pirsig 1974, 1999. Reprinted by permission of The Random House Group Limited.

Page 296: From "Too Much Heaven." Words and Music by Barry Gibb, Robin Gibb, and Maurice Gibb © 1978 UNICEF MUSIC (FOX). All rights administered by Unichappell Music Inc.

Page 333: From *The Autobiography of Malcolm X* by Malcolm X (Grove Press, 1965).

Page 396: From *A Man for All Seasons* by Robert Bolt (1960). Reprinted by permission of the Bolt estate.

Page 417: From "Hotel California." Words and Music by Glenn Lewis Frey, Donald Hugh Henley, and Don Felder. Published by UNIVERSAL/MCA Music Ltd. ON BEHALF OF CASS COUNTY MUSIC AND RED CLOUD MUSIC. © 1976 Fingers Music (ASCAP). All rights on behalf of Fingers Music administered by WARNER CHAPPELL NORTH AMERICA LTD.

Page 525: From "Little Gidding," from *Four Quartets* by T. S. Eliot. Copyright © 1940, 1941, 1942 by T. S. Eliot, renewed 1968, 1969, 1970 by Esme Valerie Eliot. Used by permission of Faber and Faber Ltd.

Acknowledgments

My deepest gratitude to Dr. Shabbir Akhtar, Alex Zolas, Asmaa Georgiou, and Domenica Alioto, for helping me during the writing as well as editing process. Many thanks also to Dogan Ur, Muhammad Adamos, Dan Franklin, Andreas Campomar, James Hodgson, Andrew Tennant, Fatih Kondu, Nour Dekhili, Barry Krost, Majid M. Hussain, David Fairservice, Noelandro De La Pena, Ian Whiteman (Abdul Latif), Zafar Ashraf, and Qutaiba Almahawli.

So Much Left to Know...